International Joint Ventures

International Joint Ventures
SOVIET AND WESTERN PERSPECTIVES

A Project of the Center for Foreign Policy Development
(CFPD) at Brown University, the Institute for World
Economy and International Relations (IMEMO) of the USSR
Academy of Sciences, and the
All-Union Research Institute for Foreign Economic
Relations, of the State Foreign Economics
Commission, of the USSR Council
of Ministers

EDITED BY

Alan B. Sherr
Associate Director, CFPD

Ivan S. Korolev
Deputy Director, IMEMO

Igor P. Faminsky
Director, All-Union Research Institute

Tatyana M. Artemova
Leading Research Fellow, All-Union Research Institute

Evgeniya L. Yakovleva
Senior Research Fellow, IMEMO

Q

QUORUM BOOKS
New York • Westport, Connecticut • London

Library of Congress Cataloging-in-Publication Data

International joint ventures : Soviet and Western perspectives /
  edited by Alan B. Sherr ... [et al.].
     p.   cm.
  "A project of the Center for Foreign Policy Development at Brown
University, the Institute for World Economy and International
Relations of the USSR Academy of Sciences, and the All-Union
Research Institute for Foreign Economic Relations, State Foreign
Economics Commission, of the USSR Council of Ministers."
  Includes bibliographical references and index.
  ISBN 0–89930–606–3 (alk. paper)
  1. Joint ventures—Soviet Union. 2. Soviet Union—Foreign
economic relations. I. Sherr, Alan B. II. Brown University.
Center for Foreign Policy Development. III. Institut mirovoĭ
ėkonomiki i mezhdunarodnykh otnosheniĭ (Akademiia nauk SSSR)
IV. USSR Council of Ministers. All-Union Research Institute for
Foreign Economic Relations.
HF1557.I57 1991
338.7'0947—dc20   91–16

British Library Cataloguing in Publication Data is available.

Library of Congress Catalog Card Number: 91–16
ISBN: 0–89930–606–3

First published in 1991

Quorum Books, 88 Post Road West, Westport, CT 06881
An imprint of Greenwood Publishing Group, Inc.

Printed in the United States of America

The paper used in this book complies with the
Permanent Paper Standard issued by the National
Information Standards Organization (Z39.48–1984).

10 9 8 7 6 5 4 3 2 1

Contents

Tables

Preface

Perhaps the most important foreign policy question of the 1990s is how the West and the Soviet Union can work together to strengthen the process of economic restructuring in the Soviet Union. While economists and policy-makers continue to sift through the many possible approaches to this issue, business people on both sides have pushed ahead to explore the limits of present legal and economic structures in the Soviet Union. As a result, increasing attention is being given to a uniquely challenging and potentially rewarding mechanism for international economic cooperation—the joint commercial venture.

Under Soviet legislation enacted in January 1987, and subsequently amended, a foreign firm is allowed to join a Soviet entity in operating a business enterprise on Soviet territory in almost any sphere of economic activity. The most difficult and important questions of East-West economic cooperation, and of the ability of the Soviet economic system to perform to world-class standards, are brought into sharp focus by the joint venture mechanism. Can key elements of a free-market economic system—competition, private property, and wage incentives, for example—effectively be incorporated into the Soviet economic system? What changes in current Soviet domestic law, both in theory and in practice, are necessary in order to encourage the establishment and smooth operation of East-West joint ventures? In what ways do Western and Soviet economic priorities conflict, and how can these differences be resolved? In what days do joint ventures affect, and how are they affected by, Soviet reforms?

Work on *International Joint Ventures* began in 1987 in response to the perceived need for a comprehensive study of these questions and the principal issues surrounding the negotiation and operation of joint ventures in the Soviet Union. This book is not intended to be a "how-to" course for business people; rather, its aim is to combine a strong theoretical base with practical analysis of the problems that Soviet and Western business people have encountered in the Soviet economic environment. The book maintains a historical perspective, but places primary emphasis on presenting realistic visions of present and future policy directions. Its intended readership includes Soviet enterprise managers and joint venture general directors, Western business executives, Western and Soviet policymakers, scholars and students. It is being published in both English- and Russian-language editions.

This book is unique in that it develops in parallel both Western and Soviet viewpoints on key issues. In general, alternating chapters are written separately by Soviet and Western authors. The reason for such a division of labor is to avoid the least-common-denominator effect, by which differing views are reconciled through negotiation or persuasion until both sides are about equally happy (or unhappy) with the result. Indeed, the book is structured to allow for, and even encourage, expression of all points of view. In many cases, chapters written by Soviet authors were subject to comments and criticisms in chapters written by Western authors, and vice versa, in order to elicit the most thorough and complete analysis possible.

International Joint Ventures is a joint effort of several U.S. and Soviet research institutes. On the U.S. side, the Center for Foreign Policy Development (CFPD) at Brown University is dedicated to the study of Western policy toward the Soviet Union, with a special emphasis on the role of the public (in this context, the business community) in developing and implementing that policy. The book is an integral part of the Center's Project on Soviet Foreign Economic Policy and International Security, which since 1987 has specialized in the study of Western investment in the Soviet Union. The Institute for World Economy and International Relations (IMEMO) of the USSR Academy of Sciences is the leading Soviet academic research institute devoted to the understanding and development of the international aspects of Soviet economic policy. The All-Union Research Institute for Foreign Economic Relations of the State Foreign Economics Commission (SFEC) is an arm of the Soviet government, responsible to the USSR Council of Ministers. The Institute provides both theoretical and practical analyses to the SFEC relevant to its responsibility to advise the Soviet government on policy options for Soviet foreign economic development.

The book begins with overviews of basic issues, proceeds with assessments of how joint ventures presently fit into the Soviet economy and process of perestroika, and concludes with views on how governments and business people can help shape the future of Western-Soviet economic cooperation.

Specifically, the three chapters in Part I focus on motivations for Western business people to invest in the Soviet Union, and steps that Soviet officials and business people can take to help satisfy and strengthen those motivations. Another way to approach the question of motivations is to face head-on the balance between risk and return as viewed by the prospective Western

business partner. Taking a long, hard look both at the immediate perils of
entering the Soviet market and the long term potentials, what factors ought
to be put in the balance and how should they be weighed? It is hoped that
the thorough airing of these issues at the outset will help Western and Soviet
policymakers and business people appreciate the practical boundaries of
joint ventures in the Soviet Union.

A particularly interesting problem that is soon raised when considering
motivations for joint ventures revolves around the potential for technology
transfer. Obtaining the latest in technologies and management know-how
is certainly an important incentive for Soviet officials and managers, and in
many cases is consistent with the interest of the Western partner in developing a reliable operation in the Soviet Union. However, such transfers are
more suited to some areas of commerce than to others, both with respect
to Western motivations for supplying new technologies and Soviet capabilities for absorbing them. This area is given special prominence in Part I.

The stage setting continues in Part II, as Soviet and Western authors
survey the experiences gained in joint ventures in other countries with centrally planned economies. The situation in the Soviet Union is sufficiently
unique to preclude any hard and fast comparisons, but even rough analogies
to the hard-won experiences of Eastern Europe and China can be instructive
if the essential points of divergence are appreciated.

In Part III Soviet and Western authors turn to the painful process of
economic reform in the Soviet Union and its implications for Western trade
and investment. Perspectives are given from both sides on how the Soviet
economic reform process affects prospects for Western business, and vice
versa. Specific attention is given to the legal framework according to which
Western firms would do business in the Soviet Union. Rather than stopping
with statements of lofty ideals for cooperation and mutual benefit, the
authors look hard at whether the other side is being realistic in its expectations. Where deficiencies are found, suggestions are forthcoming on how
hopes and reality can be brought together.

Part IV comes closest to a how-to approach. An examination of the
practical problems encountered by joint ventures in the Soviet Union gives
the reader concrete reference points for the analyses of the previous chapters,
for example, specifically how the transition from central supply allocation
to a wholesale market affects the climate for international business, how
the process of democratization in the workplace shapes labor-management
relations in joint ventures, and so on.

One of the principal obstacles to understanding the nature of these problems, and even to reliably identifying them, is the lack of even the most
fundamental information about how joint ventures have fared in the Soviet
Union. Only in late 1990 did the Soviet central government begin to collect
data on such key issues as the amount of goods and services being produced
by joint ventures, the number of employees working in joint ventures, the

number of joint ventures operating, and the amount of capital invested. In addition to providing and analyzing the latest such information, the editors devised their own questionnaire and administered it to a sample of joint venture managers. The results of this questionnaire are reported to supplement easily misunderstood data, such as the more-or-less steadily growing number of joint ventures registered by government authorities. Plots of such data can give only a one-dimensional impression of the impact of Western investment. Not surprisingly, a close look at the responses to the questionnaire reveals a much more complex picture.

One of the areas of complexity involves the availability of financial support for Soviet joint ventures. Soviet and Western experts give their views on the obviously critical question of how the development of financial resources should be addressed—not in the abstract, but with an eye to the realities of the Soviet economy and the competition for such resources that joint ventures face from other areas of the economy.

Although all of the chapters maintain an eye on the future—how today's policies can be changed to improve tomorrow's prospects—the two concluding chapters in Part V adopt this perspective as their central theme. This emphasis is the only appropriate response to the often frenetic developments of the present. New political parties are being established, parliamentary debate is surfacing, and union and autonomous republics are trying to find a new political and economic place for themselves in the forthcoming union in order to gain more rights to foreign economic contacts. Considerable changes are appearing in the laws that regulate national and foreign investments in the Soviet Union. Presidential decrees in recent months have added substantially to the possibilities for foreign investments in the country. Pending legislation, which aims to provide better protection for foreign investors, will cancel the bulk of the numerous existing regulations on joint ventures.

The concluding chapters also address specific, fundamental questions, such as the nature of Western interests in a stronger Soviet economy and the prospects for firmer commercial links to the Soviet Union. Debate has significantly shifted away from *whether* Western governments should encourage economic cooperation with the USSR to *how* they can effectively do so. But even a well-intentioned effort to improve economic cooperation can falter if there is not a thorough understanding of the basic motivations on both sides, as well as the difficulties and reversals that are likely to be encountered. The authors of the concluding chapters provide some recommendations on how Western and Soviet governments, as well as the business communities on both sides, can structure their approaches to optimize the chances for success.

The editors extend their thanks and appreciation to the authors who contributed to this book, some of whom were asked to revise their manuscripts several times in order to keep pace with new developments in the

Soviet Union. They did so with great professionalism and, in most cases, good humor.

The U.S. editor and the CFPD also gratefully acknowledge the financial assistance provided by the Ford Foundation, which made possible the design and successful completion of the book from the Western perspective.

Sincere thanks are also due on the U.S. side to Lorraine Walsh, CFPD publications editor, for her work in preparing the manuscript for publication. This was an especially difficult job with respect to this book because of the need to edit English-language translations of chapters originally written in Russian. Dr. Heidi Kroll, a CFPD research associate, contributed generously of her time and talent in reviewing drafts and making suggestions to authors. Her knowledge of Soviet economics was crucial to the development of the Western chapters and critiques of the Soviet chapters. A great deal of credit must also be given to John Stavis and Mark Hayes, assistants to the associate director at CFPD, who deftly handled a myriad of organizational tasks in relation to this book. Particularly demanding was administration of the questionnaire and coordination of manuscript review between the U.S. and Soviet editors. In addition to contributing his own chapter, CFPD senior adviser Jan Kalicki helped at the initial stages to shape the design of the book. CFPD director Mark Garrison gave unflagging encouragement to this ambitious project, and the Center provided a firm institutional base for carrying out research and writing.

The editors also gratefully acknowledge the heroic efforts, on the Soviet side, of I. S. Pilman of the All-Union Research Institute and the students of the Moscow State University. V. R. Yevstignieyev and other research workers of IMEMO's Department of International Economic Relations played a significant part in the preparatory work and in translating the manuscript from English to Russian.

Part I

Creating Favorable Conditions for
Western-Soviet Economic Cooperation

Chapter 1

Risk and Return in U.S.-Soviet Joint Ventures

Eric A. Stubbs

CONCEPTS OF RETURN AND RISK IN THE SOVIET UNION AND THE WEST

While the Western understanding of return is relatively straightforward, the concept of business risk is especially elusive and open to a multitude of interpretations. Even in Western literature enormous divergences are apparent between the academic understanding of risk, based on the notion of variance in rates of return, and business applications of the concept.[1] Nonetheless, there is a broad homogeneity to Western understanding both of the concepts as they relate to business and of the methods available for their assessment.[2] This chapter examines the risk and return issues involved in U.S.-Soviet business from the perspective of Western management both as theoretical questions and, to the extent that the sparse data will permit, by analyzing the experiences of Western participants in Soviet joint ventures and Soviet enterprises.

Meaningful concepts of business risk and return in the West derive from a manager's experience in the business environment. It is not surprising, therefore, that Soviet notions, informed by a very different economic and political system, can contrast sharply with Western ideas of risk and the relevant ingredients of competent risk assessment.

The fundamental operating principle of the Soviet economy, unlike the major Western economies, is predominantly administrative and bureaucratic in the broadest sense. Consequently, the importance of political and social factors is hugely magnified at the expense of pure cost considerations and, in turn, business risk and return are generally understood as much more politically dependent variables. Among the important implications of this contrast is the extremely heavy dependence of returns on political and bureaucratic factors. This can appear in direct forms—through centralized control of input and output prices, input acquisition, output distribution, and disposition of revenues in the case of traditional Soviet enterprises. More subtle channels are built on such issues as the determination of which Soviet organization has jurisdiction, or can influence a decision or facilitate input procurement most effectively. In general, the costs of inputs are not likely to be the determining factor in their availability to the enterprise.

The Soviet understanding of the concepts of risk and return is also far more heterogeneous, reflecting its environmental and institutional dependence. The enterprise director's notion of risk and its most important sources normally would be far different from that of the cooperative owner's or the government official's. This issue will be addressed in detail below, when Soviet concepts of risk are examined.

A third important result of the bureaucratization of the Soviet economy is the fragmentation of the targets presented to the Soviet enterprise in the plan. While there are six major target areas relating to production, labor productivity, profitability, capital construction, input, use, and innovation and technological progress, a plethora of divergent and often inconsistent objectives may develop.

On a philosophical level, the splintering of objectives and the relative downgrading of the importance of profitability that it implies can be understood as the product of the unique position that state-owned enterprises hold. The only really compelling rationalization for the nationalization of industry and property rights is that private profit maximization alone is not regarded by the society as a sufficient objective for industry. The decision to establish state-owned enterprises can be considered symmetric with the decision to look beyond profit maximization for industry goals.[3]

This raises a troubling ambiguity for the state enterprise with regard to the role of its profit targets: are profits a measure of enterprise effectiveness in the sense of value added, an instrument of government policy directed at one aspect of the larger social good, an indirect mechanism for monitoring conformity with "real" aspects of the plan, or a tool of governmental and ministerial political goals? Prior to the inception of reform efforts, profits in the Soviet industrial enterprise sector found their greatest use as a monitoring device to measure compliance with the plan and as a tool of government-pricing and investment policies. In recent years, efforts to promote efficiency and self-financing have made the role of profits still more ambiguous. The likelihood that most of Soviet industry will remain nationalized, regardless of the future course of the reform program, suggests that confusion over the intended role of profits will continue to haunt both enterprises and the political leadership for some time.

Recent Soviet moves to change the forms of financing available to enterprises might exacerbate these ambiguities if they continue to evolve to their logical conclusions. Soviet enterprises are now allowed to issue stocks to their employees and to other enterprises to help finance capital investment and community expenditures. These instruments, similar to Western consols, generally carry a fixed nominal interest rate with an indefinite term. In their current form they do not represent ownership claims or voting power in the conventional Western sense. These stocks could, however, presage a broader Soviet investments market that would eventually include the distribution of ownership interests and active trading. In this case, an even larger conceptual and operational wedge will be driven between the Soviet enterprise's role as a public trustee and its responsibilities concerning the private interests of its owners.

GENERATION AND ROLE OF PROFITS IN SOVIET ENTERPRISES

An important element to understanding the differences between Western and Soviet notions of return and risk is the determination of return in Soviet enterprises. Two issues emerge here: How is profit defined and determined? In what ways and to what extent does profit-seeking motivate the actions of firms and the behavior of managers?

It is difficult from a Western perspective to appreciate the very different and complex role that profitability plays in traditional Soviet enterprises. A popular misconception in the West is that profits are either nonexistent by design or unimportant in Soviet industry. This perception is reinforced by recent Soviet revelations that 12 to 14 percent of Soviet enterprises do not make a profit and are, in fact, subsidized to the tune of over 10 billion rubles per year. Another 40 percent of Soviet enterprises show a profit only by ignoring Soviet accounting standards that require charging physical capital depreciation against earnings.[4]

Since the Law on State Enterprises (LSE) was ratified, the Soviet government has attempted a series of economic reforms apparently intended to boost the priority of profitability and to harden the "soft" budget constraint of enterprises that, in the past, has allowed them to count on government compensation for their losses.[5] Specifically, khozraschet, or economic accountability, imposes upon enterprises the requirement that they cover their own expenses and generate a profit from their sales revenues. Although an enterprise that violates payment discipline is now liable to be declared bankrupt, the threat lacks credibility because enforcement of these provisions has been extremely rare despite the staggering industry loss rates.

Although aggregate statistics on loss rates and bankruptcies testify that enterprise profitability is not crucial to the survival of an enterprise, they do not address the more central issue of the relevance of profits to the microeconomic operations of a single enterprise. According to Western conceptions, a firm's profits are a residual reward that represents a return to capital and managerial talent and compensation for risks. Although firms may generate expectations for what a given project will yield in profits, actual profitability is rarely within the direct control of a firm, nor is it the subject of public policy.

In contrast, Soviet profits represent a category of financial accounts that are planned in advance with the expectation that if the enterprise executes its assignment properly, a given rate will prevail. Deviations from the realization of that rate may signal a departure from the plan.

Planned profit margins are derived in advance as the product of a government-set profit norm, and the value of enterprise capital costs as a fraction of total production costs. The planned margin is applied to planned average production costs to calculate planned ruble prices and profits. According to this technique, the profit margin would rise with greater capital use by the enterprise. Although this mimics, in a limited way, the Western notion that profits are a return to capital, it reverses the order of Western reasoning. In the West, the incentive to minimize total costs impels an enterprise to reduce capital use per unit of output along with other expenses. Where labor costs are high, the logic leads to greater capital intensity along with higher total profits, but less profit per unit of capital. The Soviet formula, in contrast, rewards capital use itself, irrespective of the trade-offs between capital costs and other expenses.[6]

Profit norms (now averaging 15 percent) vary across industries according to government policy. For example, it is 37.8 percent in light industry and 18.9 percent in food processing. The profit margin is added to average Soviet product costs to derive a wholesale goods price. Therefore, a low profit margin assignment may be part of a government policy to reduce the prices of goods produced by a given sector (e.g., agrotechnical equipment) and to subsidize their users (agricultural production).

In Soviet practice, under normal circumstances of plan fulfillment, profits can be regarded as an accounting convenience. It is out of profits that the enterprise pays charges to the state for capital use as well as profits "taxes," amounting to a fairly stable 55 percent of gross profit earnings throughout the early 1980s, averaged across the Soviet industrial sector.[7] The remaining 45 percent of profits are retained by the enterprise for allocation to its incentive funds (17 percent) and for payment of loans, debts, and interest (20 percent). Prior to 1977, a significant portion of profit retentions (11 to 13 percent) was also utilized for capital investments while loan principal and interest payments were correspondingly lower. However, the fraction of profits allocated to decentralized capital investments declined to 4 percent in 1980 and remained there through 1985. The share of decentralized capital investment funding may be on the rise again. Preliminary reports indicate that in 1988, decentralized funds accounted for 39 percent of enterprise investment funding.[8] An obvious implication of this variability in the fraction of profits devoted to decentralized finance of enterprise investment, combined with the fact that control over its disposition remains with the central authorities, is that satisfaction of investment requirements themselves provides almost no inducement for profit generation on the part of Soviet enterprises.

At the level of the individual enterprise manager, the persuasiveness of profits in motivating behavior depends first on the extent to which managers benefit from increases in profitability (or conversely, the coercive importance of failing to satisfy the profits plan) and, second, on the actual correlation between profits-based inducements and profits themselves.

In principle, both enterprise benefits and direct management rewards are designed to depend heavily on profitability. The law should create considerable incentive to generate profits by providing for the allocation of a fraction of total profits to the enterprise's material incentives, and to socio-cultural and housing funds. The fraction depends on the extent of fulfillment or overfulfillment of the enterprise profit plan. These funds are the source of worker bonuses and local social amenities construction funds. Moreover, the Material Incentives Fund (MIF) constitutes the sole source of management bonuses, comprising between 45 percent and 65 percent of most managers' incomes in 1974.[9] The determination of the value of the MIF depends, in turn, on the enterprise's success in fulfilling or overfulfilling the annual production plan with a coefficient based on the actual profits of the year, and the level of growth of labor productivity and the percent of higher quality goods produced by the enterprise. It does not depend directly on the total value of output or sales, however, although these are likely to be reflected in actual profits.

The mechanism by which the MIF and wages are related to profitability underwent some modification with the passing of the LSE. The LSE gave enterprises a choice (with the approval of higher authorities) between two accounting schemes for the determination of income or profits, hence wages and MIF, under cost accounting. The first forms a residual profit from total profits after direct costs including wages, minus credit charges and settlement with the government. Subject to some rules, the residual profit may then be allocated to the various enterprise funds, much as before. The second scheme is based on a definition of income less credit charges and payments to the government. A single pay fund is then formed from the remaining income minus allocations for the funds for social development, the development of production, science, and technology, and similar funds. Unlike the first scheme, there is no guaranteed wage fund here, and worker compensation is more closely tied to the actual economic fortunes of the enterprise. Not surprisingly, by the end of 1988—eighteen months after the LSE had come into force—only 943 enterprises had adopted the second scheme.

To argue that profits have a significant impact on enterprise behavior through the MIF, it should follow that the size of the material incentives fund is directly related to enterprise profitability. What little evidence there is on this issue does not, however, support that notion. Three Soviet studies in the past fifteen years have attempted to explore this relationship by regressing planned and actual values of MIF on the factors that ostensibly determine its value, including actual output, gross profits, labor productivity, and sales growth for annual data on various samples of Soviet enterprises between 1966 and 1975.[10] In every case, the value of MIF was at best only weakly related to the variables that theoretically underlie it.

These studies suggest that there is little to induce management concern with enterprise profit levels from the standpoint of personal rewards. In fact, many of the most attractive rewards to Soviet managers are nonpecuniary, taking the form of a car and driver and social recognition. This, coupled with evidence that internal funds are not significant in investment financing, suggests that, on the whole, profit seeking is not important to managers or enterprises in the Soviet Union.

RISK IN SOVIET ENTERPRISES

The multiplicity of performance criteria—numbering as many as three hundred across six categories for a Soviet industrial enterprise—and the fundamental bureaucratization of the Soviet economy combine to explain many features of Soviet attitudes toward risk in enterprises as well. Not surprisingly, Soviet attitudes toward what constitutes risks are colored to a great degree by the environment in which agents operate. Moreover, because of their differing bureaucratic vantage points, perceptions of risk are also likely to vary among Soviet economic actors, including enterprise managers, government officials, and cooperative owners.

In Western business practice, risk can either inhibit "risky" investment or motivate further investment to avoid losses to rivals. The organization of the Soviet economy with its monopoly producers, guaranteed markets, and low risk of insolvency eliminates most of the latter form of risk. As a consequence, downside risk associated with change and innovation dominates, resulting in industrial inertia. Responsibility for decisions is shared through the administrative structure and does not end with the enterprise director's office, but extends through the director into the political and governmental apparatus, insulating him or her to some extent from responsibility for shortcomings in this regard. Given the monopoly orientation of Soviet industry, the threat of competition does not carry the same coercive potency in motivating economic behavior as it is thought to have in the West.

Soviet risk and return concepts, from the perspective of the local government official contemplating a joint venture within his or her jurisdiction, are likely to revolve around the venture's impact both on the official's relationship with higher authorities and objectives for the development of the local economy. Given the greater centralization of Soviet government administration, the framing of both of these considerations is heavily influenced by regional and superior policymaking bodies.

The endorsement of higher authorities would incline local governments toward receptivity to joint ventures in most circumstances, but the potential for divergent interests among levels of government could complicate the equation. At the all-Union level, government policy clearly favors an export orientation and importation of advanced manufacturing technologies and skills in joint venture proposals. Local governments might, in contrast, be more sensitive to the immediate interests of the local populations and could prefer production directed at domestic markets.

To the extent that the joint venture is a priority to higher officials, local officials are likely to concern themselves with the success of joint ventures within their jurisdiction as a reflection of their own competence. That concern may translate into a concern with joint venture viability as understood by the foreign partner. From the civil official's viewpoint, risk in this context is likely to be associated with predominantly nonpecuniary issues such as impacts on local employment opportunities and satisfaction of local consumer needs, as well as acquisition of hard currency for the local government treasury.

Because supply procurement is a political and bureaucratic problem in the Soviet Union and not an economic issue as it usually is in the West, the local official might consider input supply availability to be no more than a marginal risk for joint ventures with official approval. Instead, when considering the risk factors that relate to a joint venture's success, the civic officer is more likely to focus on risks related to the generation of sufficient hard currency to allow foreign repatriation of profits.

While superficially similar to what is commonly an important foreign concern, this Soviet focus can result in an underestimate of the significance of other important factors, such as supply disruption, and does not distinguish between controllable and uncontrollable risks. The Soviet perceptions are, however, an understandable concession to the realities of doing business in a goods-starved, administrative economy: it is often true that business can sell nearly anything in the Soviet Union, and that supply procurement, even for foreign joint ventures, is likely to remain more a political than economic issue for some time to come. Moreover, the bureaucratic nature of the economy does muddy the distinction between controllable and uncontrollable risks in many cases.

The opportunity to earn hard currency remains one of the major attractions to Soviet enterprises contemplating collaboration through a joint venture. Recent Soviet rule changes, which permit enterprise retentions of a larger fraction of hard currency earnings from export trade and joint ventures, have enhanced incentives.[11] This presents a striking and ironic contrast to the relative lack of interest one might encounter toward increasing enterprise ruble profits and highlights the domestic demonetization that afflicts the Soviet economy with increasing severity.

As long as the Soviet government continues to subsidize loss-making enterprises—a practice that would be difficult and dangerous to halt abruptly given its present pervasiveness—pecuniary gain at the expense of increased risk is not likely to be a priority concern of the Soviet partner. Instead, considerations relating to difficulties in their ability to deliver quality inputs on schedule, implications of diverting talented workers from the primary enterprise, the potential to generate hard currency, the enterprise's capability to absorb new technology, and dangers of output shortfalls in the short run are likely to take precedence in their assessment of risk and return potential.

Producer cooperatives are in many respects the closest Soviet analog to a Western business entity in their similarity to a conventional business partnership. Like Western businesses, they face firm budget constraints, must purchase most of their inputs by negotiated contracts, and sell in a relatively open market. As a result, the definition of profits for cooperatives as net income is also more similar to Western conceptions. On the other hand, the economic, social, and political terrains that cooperatives traverse are both much more ambiguous than those of any Western counterparts, and their long-term form and survival remains uncertain. Their productivity level is good, however, compared to Soviet norms. Probably as a result of both greater worker efficiency and the more straightforward incentives structure of cooperatives, labor productivity levels in Soviet cooperatives appear to be at least 50 percent higher than at state enterprises.[12]

The precarious social standing of cooperatives stems in part from their unique flexibility and consequent ability to exploit rapidly and effectively the shortcomings and frictions endemic to the Soviet economy. The enormous wealth that some cooperative members have amassed through speculation and service-oriented activity has attracted the attention of criminals and the bitter resentment of other workers. Although, in part, the cooperatives' exploitation of bottlenecks might be considered unconscionable, it is an inevitable product of an economic organization with substantial impediments both to the efficient flow of official commerce and to cooperative use of underutilized industrial capacity. Cooperatives have been disappointing as vehicles for the promotion of competitive efficiency and innovation for a variety of reasons, including government restrictions on cooperative activity in some fields where state enterprises currently operate, and enterprise resistance to engaging in direct competition with them. This failure has sharpened popular images of cooperatives as exploiters with no redeeming social value, thereby adding to uncertainty over their long-term political prospects.

Joint venture partnerships with Soviet cooperatives, as the best embodiments of entrepreneurial energy in the Soviet Union, may appear to be an attractive option to Western firms. However, four potential vulnerabilities exist in this strategy. First, the political issue of the future of cooperatives has not been resolved, and a sudden reversal in Soviet policy is possible, leaving the Western partner in an uncertain position.[13] Second, the access to inputs enjoyed by cooperatives, and hence the joint venture, is limited and heavily dependent upon official support, so input contracts could evaporate along with government forbearance. Third, the restrictions imposed in December 1988 on cooperative involvement in currency and goods transactions with foreigners create an ambiguity regarding the legality of cooperative involvement in joint ventures. Finally, in the minds of many Soviet nationals, cooperatives are associated with corruption, exploitation, and ethnic frictions, and guilt by association could become a significant risk for the foreign partner if nationalist or economic unrest escalates.

THE WESTERN PERSPECTIVE: UNCONTROLLABLE RISKS

From the perspective of a Western partner, uncontrollable risk factors are those that are not amenable to alleviation by the joint venture's own strategic choices, although the firm's policies may guard against or limit damage from some forms of risk. Their analysis is all the more difficult because they involve not only the direct partners to the joint venture—the Western firm and its Soviet partner—but also the Soviet government, Western government, and other international firms.

Member nations of the Council for Mutual Economic Assistance (CMEA) have traditionally received high marks as business risks for several reasons:

- They have been characterized by strong internal political structures, enhancing stability and permitting economic adjustment when required.
- Central planning has been thought to simplify the redirection of internal resources.
- The economies have been stable, if sluggish.
- The umbrella theory of risk pooling postulated that CMEA would bail out any individual member caught in an economic crisis, effectively sharing the risk internationally.

The events of the last decade have compelled a reassessment of all of these propositions. The abrupt rise in ethnic clashes and expressions of nationalist sentiments provide graphic evidence of the erosion of the traditionally stable, if repressive, Soviet regime. Strikes in the Soviet Union and Poland, as well as disputes over reform strategy in the nation's highest leadership circles and in the Congress of People's Deputies, demonstrate the difficulties that current efforts at economic adjustment confront. While the government of the Soviet Union has retained a firmly entrenched directive planning mechanism, the difficulties that they have faced with worsening shortages of food and consumer goods, in redirecting resources out of military investment, and in promoting growth amply demonstrate that equating central planning with easy resource reallocation is overly simplistic. The Soviet economy has also deteriorated in the past five years to the point where economic growth is at a standstill. Finally, the Polish debt crisis of the early 1980s provided ample evidence that the prospects for risk sharing across CMEA neighbors had been overestimated. The Soviet Union's current fiscal troubles combined with its retreat from the Brezhnev doctrine diminishes the chance of future risk sharing still further.

An important component in risk assessment is the evaluation of a variety of economic factors. Soviet trade strategy is important among these for its implications for foreign exchange generation and because it points to specific opportunities, risks, and strategies with respect to which foreign firms should be sensitive. Trade strategy is an integral part of overall development strategy, making its assessment an important part of an overall prediction of Soviet economic prospects in the long term.

Stalinist autarkic trade policy was a classic case of spurring domestic industrialization through import substitution and subsidizing heavy industry at the expense of agriculture and consumer industries. Import substitution is usually associated with an overvalued exchange rate, which minimizes the relative book value of imported inputs and discourages exports. Export performance usually suffers as a consequence.

During the 1980s, the Soviet Union moved away from its autarkic tradition, doubling the level of hard currency trade in GNP between 1976 and 1985 (although even at the latter date, total hard currency exports were a mere 4 percent of GNP). However, the Soviet government appears to be vacillating on the application of this policy to joint ventures by softening its initial insistence that joint ventures generate hard currency through exports to permit internal hard currency generation through import substitution or direct hard currency sales.

This is probably a concession in part to the formidable obstacles facing a policy shift toward export promotion. Because industries that develop under the protection of an import substitution program tend to be uncompetitive, a shift to export promotion can cause wages and profits to plummet, resulting in bankruptcies and unemployment. Moreover, the degree of intrusion into investment and pricing decisions exercised by the Soviet government is likely to be incompatible with the flexibility required for export promotion. Additionally, the combination of short-term industry losses, devaluation that raises the prices of imports, and the need to relax government controls makes it very difficult to assemble a political constituency that would favor a transition to export promotion on the basis of its own interests.

Internal investment priorities and infrastructure development are other factors relevant to how foreign business interests assess risk. A preference for large, prestigious projects over basic infrastructure, or a tendency to spread investment resources across projects too thinly, are two warning signs of potential problems. Where projects rely heavily on imported capital and materials or subsidized inputs, these warnings should be considered more serious still.

The Soviet Union has not generally been guilty of the latter policies, although their gas pipeline consumed large quantities of imported materials from Western Europe. Their preference for "giantism" in projects goes back many decades, however.[14]

The Soviet economy as a whole is severely undercapitalized, with approximately 1.1 trillion rubles worth of productive capital, or only 1.25 times annual GNP, in place.[15] The Soviets' poor record for project completion and tendency to spread resources too thinly across them, slowing progress on all, exacerbates the problems.[16] In part, resources are spread thinly due to the "camel's nose" phenomenon: industrial ministries pressure for new projects rather than complete ones already begun in an attempt to expand their budgets and commitments to future growth.[17] Once the camel's nose is under the tent, the ministries feel that future financing to finish the project will likely become available. Unless this problem is corrected, Soviet opportunities for significant productivity improvements are likely to be lost.

One key to maintaining a stable and hospitable business environment is sound macroeconomic management and, particularly, fiscal policy management. A nation that is vulnerable to poor fiscal management may be a poorer risk from the foreign partner's viewpoint for several reasons: First, it increases the chances of recession or lengthy economic stagnation. Second, inflation risks are higher and inflation may be more severe. This, in turn, upsets cost forecasts and, if exchange rates are fixed, could impair export profitability.

The magnitude of the government's budget deficit relative to its GNP is a primary risk indicator for the strength of a nation's fiscal management. At 100 to 120 billion rubles or 11 to 13 percent of GNP in 1988, the Soviet Union's deficit represents an unambiguous signal of risk in this regard.

One indirect product of the deficit has been the alarming increase in the Soviet money supply. The first public release of Soviet money supply statistics occurred in August 1989, in an interview with the newly appointed minister of finance, V. S. Pavlov.[18] In the first half of 1989, the Soviet money stock rose by 9 billion rubles to a total of over 100 billion rubles. Since 1973, circulating currency stocks increased by a factor of 3.1.[19] Over the same period, production of consumer goods—the primary market where cash is utilized—doubled according to Soviet figures.[20] The most recent Soviet estimates put average inflation over the last twenty years at 3.4 percent per annum. Although credible, not enough information on fiscal linkage among the sectors of the Soviet economy and on the velocity of money is currently available for the proper assessment of this figure.

The rapid growth of money supply during 1989, and indications that wage inflation is far outstripping production increases, suggest much higher inflation rates in the near future. Unofficial estimates of Soviet inflation rates for 1988 are on the order of 7 to 8.5 percent.[21] However, wage rate increases in the first half of 1989 have averaged 24 percent at annual rates,[22] which, along with the increased money supply, could lead to an inflation rate as high as 20 percent in 1990 as the sum of its actual, hidden, and repressed forms.[23]

The emergence of new, and so far uncontrolled, forms of fiscal transactions underlines the importance of careful and sophisticated fiscal and monetary policy development to future Soviet economic health. Recent Soviet moves to consider endorsement of the broader use of checks and debit cards by consumers, and enterprise cooperative transactions that involve payments by enterprises from their noncash accounts to cooperatives, thereby transforming these accounting balances into circulating currency, could complicate the task of monetary management still further. By increasing the velocity of money, inflationary pressures may rise while governmental control of the money stock diminishes.

The Soviet Union appears to be vulnerable to poor fiscal management for a number of reasons. Although precise figures on the size of Soviet military expenditures are not available, there is no doubt that they absorb a substantial fraction of the Soviet Union's best resources.[24] The Soviet Union appears to be exerting effort to control military spending. However, the impact of this policy, even if successful, is not likely to be reflected in the civilian economy or government budget for at least five years. Second, Soviet fiscal administration continues to be weak due to its subordination to material planning. This problem is aggravated by the magnitude of Soviet subsidies to industry and agricultural support and foodstuffs imports, together totaling some 130 billion rubles per year, or nearly 25 percent of the state budget. A third, and related, factor is the disconnection between savings and investment on the macroeconomic level. This has two effects in that it complicates the reconciliation of aggregate supply and demand and makes it nearly impossible to achieve a socially optimal trade-off between consumption and investment. Finally, political pressures in the midst of the Soviet economy's poor performance have increased, and may have prevented a scaling back of subsidies and other government support for industries and consumption.

The secondary role that financial management has traditionally played has produced other obstacles to strong fiscal control. There is a nearly automatic (though not proportional) link between government deficits and the money supply, leading to inflationary pressure whenever expenditures significantly exceed receipts. Because reserve requirements do not exist for bank lending, and because retail sale of government bonds to consumers has been discredited through abusive past practices, Soviet options for withdrawal of excess liquidity are extremely limited. The dearth of alternative financial instruments, on both the retail and commercial sides of banking,

compound these problems by reducing the adaptability of the Soviet financial system as a whole.

International business competition is another facet of uncontrollable risk that impinges on the decisions of the foreign partner. In recent years, the idea that international competitive forces will compel Western firms to enter the Soviet market due to its potential as a low-cost manufacturing base, its untapped domestic demand, and its impact on worldwide economies of scale in production and acquisition of manufacturing experience has become common.[25] It is asserted that these factors should motivate American firms to consider pre-emptive entry into the Soviet market to avoid being locked out by Japanese and European competitors in the future.

While these arguments are compelling, broader international participation in the Soviet economy can provide benefits to the Western firm. As the concentration of foreign business within an area increases, so does the likelihood that a critical mass of suppliers will emerge to create a self-sustaining enclave of foreign-partnered businesses in the Soviet Union that overcome some of the shortcomings of the Soviet Union's supply network.[26]

However, pre-emptive entry by other Western nations carries the risk that by persuading the Soviets to adopt their technical standards for equipment and products, other nations will acquire an advantage over U.S. manufacturers. A competitive advantage accrues to the export business interests of a country that succeeds in persuading another to adopt its norms in two ways. The exporter nation may enjoy significant lead time over other exporters in penetrating the market of the client country before other exporters can retool to produce in conformity with the same set of standards, and economies of scale may accrue from being able to apply the same standards to domestic and export production.

Germany appears to have acquired such an advantage through the Soviet Union's recently announced plans to adopt DIN (German Industrial Norms) standards for two-thirds of its technical norms by 1993.[27] To the extent that other European nations are interested in the Soviet market, Germany may gain doubly if this announcement disposes the European Community (EC) as a whole toward greater receptivity to DIN standards.

West German firms figured in roughly one-seventh of the Soviet Union's joint ventures as of June 1990, while U.S. partners were involved in fewer than 10 percent. The relative success of West German firms demonstrates the importance of two risk characteristics that exert a strong positive influence on the prospects for German–Soviet partnerships: duration of corporate relationships, and the degree to which government policy is sympathetic to commerce with the Soviet Union.

Even small- to medium-sized German firms commonly have a record of fifteen to twenty years of trading relationships with the Soviet Union prior to establishing a joint venture.[28] Larger firms may enjoy relationships that are the products of more than a century of interactions. Long relationships breed familiarity with Soviet business practices and permit an institutional memory to develop so that a joint venture may appear to be a logical extension of previous business efforts rather than a novel undertaking.

Under these circumstances, the joint venture itself may become a vehicle for managing some controllable forms of risk. German companies have established joint ventures for a variety of reasons. In some cases it has been a response to concerns over their global competitiveness or even impending bankruptcy. While German manufacturing wages are among the highest in the world, and, as a consequence, corporations risk being undercut in the world marketplace, Soviet wages have remained extremely low. A manufacturing base in the Soviet Union may be able to compete more effectively in price-sensitive export markets as a result.

Joint ventures may also facilitate German business efforts to cope with the rapidly shifting administrative landscape of the Soviet Union. Changes in Soviet trade policy, the organization of Soviet trade relations, and the composition of top management can throw a Western firm's commercial efforts into complete disarray. Trade policy changes can alter Soviet import priorities, while important professional relationships are vulnerable to personnel changes. In the uncertain climate of Soviet trade, a joint venture can provide a flexible alternative for Western firms interested in maintaining a presence in the Soviet domestic market. This may become a particularly significant competitive advantage if the Soviet Union succeeds in decentralizing wholesale trade for enterprise input purchases, and if the importance of long-term ministerial-level relationships built by some Western firms recedes.

Western government policy is, of course, crucial to joint venture risk assessment, since any transaction or partnership is potentially vulnerable to government embargoes or trade restrictions. Restrictions placed on the Ford Motor Company's transactions with the Kama River Complex following the Soviet invasion of Afghanistan, and the broader restrictions triggered by the Polish Solidarity crisis in the early 1980s demonstrate the volatility of East-West relations.

On a more general level, business inevitably relies on government for signals regarding both the anticipated trend in Western-Soviet relations for the next few years and the attitude of the domestic government toward business involvement in the East. Consensus within the Western domestic political arena regarding the status of Soviet-Western relations can be another indicator of the future risks and prospects for East-West commerce.[29]

Aside from setting the tenor of the relationship, Western government policy can have an important impact both on the absolute risks associated with joint ventures, and on the relative competitiveness of one Western nation's business initiatives versus another's. Recent German actions provide a useful example.

Although official statements of German policy tend to hold closely to the positive but restrained stance of its major allies, German government practice has in some instances been more aggressive in setting the stage for the safe conduct of joint ventures and other business with the Soviet Union. The most notable recent example is the signing of a West German-Soviet treaty for reciprocal capital investment protection and the negotiation of a similar U.S.–Soviet trade agreement in spring 1990.[30] Among its provisions, the treaty guarantees that German investments in the Soviet Union shall be treated no less favorably than investments from any other nation. Although nationalization is not precluded, prompt compensation in hard currency is mandated, with appeal to international arbitration in the event of disputes over the amount. The treaty also grants German firms the right to repatriate all Soviet profits in hard currency at the prevailing official exchange rate.[31]

Other international influences on Western nations' competitive position in the Soviet Union include the efforts in some nations, such as Germany and France, to deepen their business contacts in the Soviet Union by launching training programs designed to introduce influential Soviet managers and officials to practical aspects of business and finance in the host nation. The German government has allocated 2.8 million DM to the program for 1989, and 6 million DM for each of the following two years, after which it is intended to be self-supporting. Although the direct cost is minimal, this program may provide enormous leverage through the opportunities it presents for influential business leaders on both sides to establish personal contacts.[32]

A common complaint within the U.S. banking community is that European and Japanese banks appear to consistently offer trade financing terms to the Soviet Union that their American competitors cannot match. This is generally regarded to be a strategy to build a relationship with Soviet banks by offering attractive initial deals or to retain the European parties to the trade transaction as clients. However, where large fractions of banking equity are government owned, as in several Western European nations, the political content of commercial policy becomes harder to avoid. Of course, the issue of commercial loan extension to the Soviet Union has itself engendered a highly political debate on both sides of the Atlantic, merging commercial considerations with disputes over Western national interests. More recently, European banking ties with the Soviet Union have expanded to include plans to establish a joint stock bank to be called the "International Bank of Moscow," which will be 60 percent West European owned.[33] Reportedly, the bank is expected to serve both joint ventures and Soviet enterprises involved in foreign trade; however, given the present structure of rules under which a private bank may operate in the Soviet Union, Soviet enterprise and cooperative finance is not likely to be an attractive option to foreign investors.

Soviet domestic political and economic conditions form another set of risk factors that complement the international political considerations outlined above.[34] It is impossible to do justice in a few paragraphs or pages to the complex dynamics and interplay of forces and challenges that shape the fluid world of Soviet domestic politics today. Instead, only a cursory mention will be made of the major risks faced by joint ventures operating within the Soviet Union. The premier characteristic of the Soviet political arena is the splintering of the superficial unity that had existed for decades. This fragmentation has developed along ethnic lines, as in the Nagorno-Karabakh crisis, along national lines, as in the Baltic and elsewhere, and along special interest lines, ranging from environmental lobbies to coal miner strikes.

Apart from the general violence that may be triggered by an escalation of tensions surrounding any of these, each form of fragmentation carries its own specific risks. A rise in nationalist sentiments could lead to pressure to expropriate foreign interests within a region or in the Union as a whole. While capital protection treaties might mitigate losses in some circumstances, it would be difficult to put much faith in treaties should the situation become that polarized. The push for greater economic autonomy for republics also presents distinct risks for the Western partner. Access to supply lines that cross republic borders could be compromised, possibly with little advance warning. Autonomy that distributes authority over enterprises among republic- and Union-level ministries may be an obstacle to trade and development even within a republic.[35]

Another type of risk that might become relevant with the growth of the joint ventures movement concerns the vague Soviet administrative hostility toward competition that is evidenced in both enterprise relations with cooperatives and in the rare instances where a joint venture might have infringed on an enterprise's export business. Even in the comparatively liberal setting of Hungarian business, a pharmaceuticals joint venture faced a delay of one year in receiving an export license due to the intense lobbying efforts of a domestic Hungarian firm with which the joint venture would be competing.[36]

A peculiarity of Soviet industrialization has been the extremely low priority of environmental concerns despite the promotion of socialism as a vehicle for reconciling industrial objectives with social welfare. The Chernobyl nuclear disaster, concerns about the ecosystems surrounding Lake Baikal and the Aral Sea, opposition to the diversion of large river systems for irrigation projects, and concerns over open-pit mining have ignited popular sentiments in the last decade.[37] In recent years, the expression of concern over these problems that was initiated by informal and semiofficial "Green"[38] groups has entered the political mainstream.[39] Even in the sphere of national defense, where the prerogative of the Soviet government is rarely challenged, environmental groups have succeeded in closing a chemical weapons disposal plant and prevented the environmentally hazardous demolition of surplus missiles.

Prospects for increased Soviet government and popular activity in the

environmental field raises several risk and return issues for the Western business partner. First, a number of cases of local government action, fueled by popular pressure, to close plants due to alleged environmental hazards have already occurred. The Soviet federal government has also authorized the closing of major polluters in extreme cases, as with a paper production plant on the Aral Sea.[40] Concerns over the integrity of urban water supplies and potential hazards to juvenile health have also motivated a re-examination of industrial priorities and processes in many locations. Building delays and possible abandonment of a planned petrochemical complex in Bash Kiriya provides yet another instance where environmental concerns have taken precedence in ad hoc policymaking, thereby imperiling joint ventures in a particular field.[41] The accumulation of these events suggests that local industry supply lines could be disrupted by similar actions in the future.[42] In the longer run, greater official and local scrutiny of the potential environmental ramifications of projects should be expected—possibly leading to increased expenses and project delays.

A serious Soviet environmental cleanup would be expensive.[43] Efforts to support a cleanup could include levies, taxes, and fines on industry, with a possible impact on the bottom lines of any joint ventures affected. The impact on business is difficult to predict, however, in the face of uncertainty over environmental standards as they affect new operations, pollution abatement and waste disposal, and the cleanup of pre-existing sites.

SOVIET BUSINESS ENVIRONMENT: A LOOK TO THE FUTURE

One of the unfortunate ironies facing Soviet reform efforts is that it is vastly more difficult to modify a modern, industrialized economy than it would be to build a new economic system from scratch. In part, this is because of the multitude of special interests invested in the current political and economic structures. A more important consideration, however, is the degree of clockworklike interdependence that has evolved in the Soviet system of economic relationships over its seventy-year life. This interdependence makes the task of designing and implementing a reform strategy that is effective without unduly upsetting the integrity of the economy a true dilemma of reform.

The irrational price structure and Soviet directive planning mechanism are popular targets for reform prescriptions from both Soviet and foreign analysts. But, in a nation where competition is stymied by high levels of industrial concentration compounded by huge geographic separation among markets and absence of free entry, an abrupt change would risk runaway inflation, shortages, and serious unrest. Moreover, a too rapid change to the planning structure would strike at the center of a powerful superstructure. Dismantling this pivotal element of the Soviet economy without constructing an alternative infrastructure risks widespread disorganization and confusion in the marketplace.

While it would be difficult to imagine two more crucial reforms from the perspective of foreign business interests than rational pricing and market-driven production and supply, neither of these is likely to be realized in the short term. Concerns of international business that are more easily address-able in the near term are likely to revolve around creating, and providing access to, a robust supply infrastructure, and building confidence in the Soviet government's control of the economy. Addressing these two issues in the near term is likely to yield extra dividends in the long term by setting the groundwork for still more ambitious marketization efforts.[44]

A number of impediments stand in the way of a successful integration of Soviet and Western business. Not the least of these are the striking contrasts in the definitions and roles of profits and risks under the two systems. In some respects, the Soviet political-economic structure appears to be con-verging to a Western market-Socialist model. Yet there is a danger to ex-aggerating that movement. While the Soviet government bureaucracy has demonstrated a willingness to tolerate the imposition of concepts of private industrial ownership from abroad, its evidence discomfort with cooperative ownership and residual reward, and the association of ownership privileges with enterprise bonds ("stocks") belies the notion that ownership will be easily or universally accepted. This discomfort is nowhere better illustrated than by the curious irony that a foreigner may now own private capital property in the Soviet Union, but a Soviet national may not. Moreover, this reluctance to trade in the old thinking for the Western commercial paradigm reflects something far more fundamental than simple blind conservativism. State ownership, with all that attends to it, is deeply ingrained in the foun-dations of the Soviet social contract and state legitimacy.

Can Western capitalism coexist within the Soviet Union's borders with the modified socialist system evolving there to their mutual benefit? Assum-ing that some structural adjustments occur in the Soviet Union and that internal political pressures do not explode, the answer would appear to be affirmative.

The Soviet economy has been brought down by the crushing weight of its own complexity. The attention to detail that material control as a vehicle for social policy demands has exceeded the combined capabilities of the economic behemoth represented by Gosplan, Goskomtsen, Gossnab, and the ministries. Ideology aside, a primary reason for the West's preference for fiscal, monetary, and tax levers to effect social and economic policy is their flexibility and simplicity. The Soviets appear to be coming to recognize these virtues, if for no other reason than that the logistics of control may soon force this shift. However, it also requires the adoption of a considerably more sophisticated appreciation of the potential of financial instruments to shape real behavior.

Monetization and fiscalization of an advanced economy is an extraordinarily difficult project. Its prerequisites include both the creation of an unambiguous connection between performance and monetary rewards, and commodity convertibility—an association between possession of money and rights to resources at the bearer's discretion. These, in turn, require decentralized control over pricing to permit the equilibration of markets. However, there is nothing inherent to these concepts that precludes either state ownership or the active promotion of a social agenda (by fiscal means).

Should the Soviet Union confront these challenges and develop a practical strategy for meeting them, prospects for increased Soviet-Western economic relations should be improved.

NOTES

1. J. March and Z. Shapira, "Managerial Perspectives on Risk and Risk Taking," *Management Sciences* 33 (11) (November 1987): 1404–18.

2. John Calverley, *Country Risk Analysis* (London: Butterworths, 1985) provides a useful outline of risk assessment methodology.

3. The complex social role of enterprises is amply illustrated by the varied references within the *Law on the State Enterprise* (henceforth, LSE): *Vedomosti verkhovnogo soveta SSSR 1987* 26, item 385, English translation in *Current Digest of the Soviet Press* 39 (30–31) (1987): "At the state enterprise, the worker collective, using public property as its proprietor, creates and augments the people's wealth and ensures the combination of interests of society, the collective, and each worker." [Art. 1/2].

4. Filomena Jaseviciene, chief of the Economics Department of the Lithuanian Council of Ministers, "Lost Millions: Let's Decrease Losses by Enterprises," *Tiesa* (23 November 1988): 1. Report by Deputy B. I. Gostev, USSR Minister of Finance, "On the USSR State Budget for 1989 and the Implementation of the USSR State Budget for 1987," *Pravda* (28 October 1988): 4–5 [for translation, see Foreign Broadcast Information Service, *Daily Report, Soviet Union* (hereafter *FBIS-SOV*) (28 October 1988): 52–62].

5. Hungarian economist Janos Kornai coined the expression "soft budget constraint" to refer to budget constraints that exert no disciplinary power over enterprise expenditures or efficiency due to government guarantees that shortfalls will be subsidized.

6. In fact, where capital use in production is expensive and labor is cheap—hence a smaller part of total costs—the formula rewards capital even more, defying the logic that an enterprise should use more of a cheap input. Other targets, such as NNP (Net Normed Product), introduced in January 1982 might, however, mildly discourage the use of expensive resources.

7. Tsentral'noe statisticheskoe upravlenie SSSR, *Narodnoe khoziastvo SSSR 1985* (Moscow: *Finansy i Statistika*, 1986), 548–49.

8. Vladimir Popov, "Perestroika and the Demand for Capital in the Soviet Economy" (mimeograph September 1989), presented at the Geonomics Institute of Middlebury College, Vermont, October 1989.

9. Cited in Jan Adams, "The Present Soviet Incentive System," *Soviet Studies* 32 (July 1980): 360.

10. I. D. Drize and Zh. I. Sidrova, *Obrazavanie pooshchritel'nykh fondov na predpriyatiyakh* (Moscow, 1975), 1–63. V. I. Kletskii, *Material'noe stimulirovanie proizvodstvennikh kollectivov vpromyshlenosty* (Minsk, 1976), 211–21. N. A. Vasil'eva "Fond mateelial'nogo pooshchreniya i fondoovrazuyushchie pokazeteli," *Izvestiya sibirskogo otdeleniya ANSSSR* (Seria obshchestvennykh nauk) 11 (1977), 137–43. Referred to in A. Freris, *The Soviet Industrial Enterprise* (London: Croom Helm, 1984), 163–54.

11. M. Tretyakov, "Losses or Income," *Pravda* (31 July 1989): 5 [*FBIS-SOV* (14 August 1989): 117–19] reports that control over up to 45 percent of hard currency export earnings may now be retained by Soviet enterprises.

12. Eric Stubbs, "Soviet Domestic Economic Reforms and the International Business Environment," Briefing Paper #2 (Providence, R.I.: Center for Foreign Policy Development, Brown University, June 1989), 35.

13. It is worth recalling that although the private sector accounted for over 70 percent of Soviet trade at the height of New Economic Policy (NEP), by 1932 it had been almost entirely eliminated.

14. Barbara G. Katz, "Giantism as an Unbalanced Growth Strategy," *Soviet Union* 4 (2) (1977): 205–22. This traditional preference does not seem to have abated under perestroika: the new McDonald's restaurant built in Moscow as part of a joint venture is the largest McDonald's in the world.

15. Report by Nikolai Ryzhkov to Congress of People's Deputies, Moscow TV Service (7 June 1989): 1212 GMT [*FBIS-SOV* (8 June 1989): 15–30].

16. Of 714 capital projects scheduled for completion in 1988, only 14 percent were actually finished: "Scarcities: What Are the Sources of This Phenomenon and How is it to be Overcome?" *Pravda* (20 December 1988): 1 [*FBIS-SOV* (22 December 1988): 64–65].

17. In 1985, a mere twelve workers on average were employed at the Soviet Union's 350,000 construction sites. While it is difficult to interpret this figure without more information, it does suggest that personnel are spread thinly. Yu. Rytov, "The Traditional Overrun Construction Schedule," *Izvestiya* (4 February 1989): 1 (*FBIS-SOV* (10 February 1989): 86–87].

18. V. Golovachev, "Everyone Needs Money," *Trud* (8 August 1989): 1–2 [*FBIS-SOV* (16 August 1989): 95–99].

19. Soltan Dzarasov, "Stopping the Printing Press," *Sotsialisticheskaya industriya* (12 November 1988): 3 [*FBIS-SOV* (18 November 1989): 82–84].

20. Dzarasov, "Stopping the Printing Press," 82–84.

21. Nikolai Shmelev, interviewed by Ezio Mauro, *La Republica* (4 February 1989): 4 [*FBIS-SOV* (14 February 1989): 76–77].

22. Nikolai Ryzhkov, Moscow International Service (5 August 1989): 1700 GMT [*FBIS-SOV* (7 August 1989): 59–60].

23. Some moderation of wage inflation should be expected as a consequence of a new Soviet decree that took effect 1 October 1989, imposing taxes on enterprise supplements to the wage fund beyond 3 percent per year. The taxes are graduated from a one ruble per ruble addition to the wage fund up to a three rubles per ruble addition. Unless this decree is supplemented by measures to reduce the deficit and provide more consumer products, it will merely attack the symptoms of inflation

and not the cause, reducing real wages in the enterprise sector and increasing worker dissatisfaction and migration to cooperative employment.

24. Indications that the Soviet Union spends 77.3 billion rubles, or about 9 percent of GNP, on defense may be accurate but not very illuminating. Without some comparison of defense input prices relative to civilian prices, it is impossible to judge actual resource use from these figures. Figures from Ryzhkov, Moscow International Service: 1212 GMT [FBIS-SOV (8 June 1989): 15–30].

25. James Hecht, "Joint Ventures, U.S. Economic Development, International Relations and National Security," paper presented at Conference on Superpower Commerce: Economic Relations with the USSR and U.S. National Interests, Center for Foreign Policy Development, Brown University, Providence, R.I., 2 December 1988.

26. Reportedly, one European automobile manufacturer has taken this approach seriously enough to offer free consulting services to any of their suppliers who are interested in exploring the possibilities of establishing joint ventures in the Soviet Union.

27. "Soviet Union Adjusts Technical Norms," Suddeutsche Zeitung (23 June 1989): 29 [FBIS-SOV (6 July 1989): 78].

28. Unless otherwise noted, references below to German experience are derived from a series of interviews of trade and government officials, business people, and academics conducted by Alan Sherr and the author in Germany in May 1989.

29. In the German case, there is broad agreement among politicians of all stripes that commerce with the Soviet Union is in Germany's interests. The more liberal groups believe that greater integration into the world economy can moderate Soviet international behavior and may lead to positive demestic reform as well. The more conservative groups support it on economic grounds. Much of their political support stems from the heavily industrialized regions of Germany, which stand to benefit from trade growth.

30. I am grateful to Dr. John Hardt of the U.S. Library of Congress for providing a translation of the treaty. France, too, has recently signed a capital protection treaty with the Soviet Union, along with an agreement to launch a cooperative program in the sphere of training cadres for economic activity: "Soviet-French Talks," Pravda (6 July 1989): 1, 3 [FBIS-SOV (7 July 1989): 47–49].

31. The last provision is especially surprising because it appears to refer to profits earned in rubles as well as hard currency, which could deplete Soviet hard currency balances in the future. Moreover, the conversion at official exchange rates vastly overvalues ruble profits and provides an incentive for joint ventures to eschew more difficult hard currency sales in favor of Soviet ruble sales, undercutting one of the major initial purposes of Soviet joint ventures.

32. U.S. firms have also provided seminars for Soviet business interests, although on a more limited scale and without U.S. government participation.: T. Galyuk, Report on 3-M seminar in Moscow, Sotsialisticheskaya industriya (7 May 1989): 3 [FBIS-SOV (15 May 1989): 23].

33. TASS Report, "Joint Bank Set Up," Izvestiya (24 May 1989): 2 [FBIS-SOV (6 June 1989): 51]. There are currently several banks operating in the West that are wholly or partly Soviet owned.

34. Many of the domestic political issues are analyzed in Alan Sherr, "Socialist-Capitalist Joint Ventures in the USSR: Law and Practice," Briefing Paper #1 (Prov-

idence, R.I.: Center for Foreign Policy Development, Brown University, May 1988).
The economic issues are outlined in Stubbs, "Soviet Domestic Economic Reform."

35. K. Prunskene, "Republican Economic Accountability: How to Make It a
Reality," *Sovetskaya litva* (26 April 1989): 2 [*FBIS-SOV* (10 May 1989): 63–66].

36. This instance was reported in interviews conducted in West Germany, May
1989.

37. A. Sheehy and S. Voronitsyn, "Ecological Protests in the USSR, 1986–88,"
Radio Liberty Research Bulletin (11 May 1988): 191/88 reports many of the recent
demonstrations, meetings, and protests.

38. For example, a group known as the "Ecological Fund" was established in
1988 by the Philosophy Department of the USSR Academy of Sciences and the Soviet
Philosophical Society to bring together people interested in fighting pollution: "New
Organization for Environmental Protection Set Up," *Radio Liberty Research Bulletin*
(9 December 1988): 538/88.

39. For example, K. S. Salykov, the chair of the committee of the USSR Supreme
Soviet for questions of ecology and the efficient utilization of natural resources, has
asserted that 20 percent of the Soviet populace lives in a "zone of ecological disaster":
interview by Ye. Manucharova, *Izvestiya* (14 June 1989): 3 [*FBIS-SOV* (22 June
1989): 71–73].

40. That the Soviet Union suffers a relative shortage of paper and ranks only
forty-seventh in the world in its production makes the closing of a large, new plant
particularly notable.

41. TASS Report on the confirmation hearings of Vladimir Gusev, for the position
of deputy prime minister and chair of the Council of Ministers' Bureau for the
Chemical-Timber Complex (29 June 1989): 1236 GMT [*FBIS-SOV* (30 June 1989):
31–36]. It appears that the petrochemical facility may be built despite vocal popular
opposition.

42. Some events do, however, point in other directions: a number of waste treatment and water treatment installations planned for Lake Baikal were removed from
the plan without local or republic opposition. Y. Manko, "A Hand in Someone
Else's Pocket," *Pravda* (15 August 1989): 3 [*FBIS-SOV* (23 August 1989): 94–96].

43. Soviet estimates are in the order of 50 to 60 billion rubles annually. V. I.
Akovetskiy in Manko, "A Hand in Someone Else's Pocket." U.S. Environmental
Protection Agency officials who have toured the Soviet Union estimate that this
value would hardly cover cleanup costs in the Baltic republics alone.

44. The word *marketization* is not meant to suggest that the Soviet Union must
necessarily move to a system of Western-style markets, where prices predominantly
reflect private valuations and tradeoffs. It would be unrealistic to suppose that the
Soviet government will abdicate its role in determining and implementing relative
social values for goods and production. Instead, marketization refers to a Soviet
evolution away from the imposition of social values through the blunt and rigid
tools of real planning toward the more flexible and sophisticated approaches of
price, tax, and fiscal levers. The argument here is that the Soviet government need
not abandon its directive social role, only that it reconceive the means of achieving
its ends.

Chapter 2

Conditions for Creating a Favorable Investment Climate in the Soviet Union

Vladimir V. Ranenko and Evgeniya L. Yakovleva

The experience of 1988 in forming and operating joint ventures made it possible to identify some of the positive and negative features of joint venture legislation. On the one hand, the number of such enterprises increased rather steadily, and the number of investor countries participating in the process expanded. Some large joint ventures (those with a charter fund of more than 10 million rubles) were established in such areas as machine building (the Soviet-German Khomatek, and the Soviet-Italian Sovitalprodmash), computer technology (the U.S.-Soviet Dialog), pharmaceuticals (the Soviet-Bulgarian Usol'efarm), and the food industry (the Soviet-Japanese Plienga-gode). A number of joint ventures were also set up and began operating in the sphere of business (i.e., engineering, consulting and training of management personnel).

On the other hand, an analysis of operating joint ventures also revealed some negative aspects, such as:

- the complexity of procedures for conducting negotiations and making decisions concerning the creation of joint ventures, particularly the inconvertibility of the ruble and resulting problems of hard currency self-sufficiency;
- problems caused by the limited share of foreign investors in the charter fund and the obligatory nomination of only Soviet citizens to the top two positions (in the case of joint ventures with partners from non-socialist countries);
- the appearance of a considerable number of joint ventures engaging in intermediary and trade operations and receiving large profits because of the shortage of many commodities on the Soviet market and imperfect price formation in the Soviet Union.

These negative features called for appropriate action and were addressed in the 2 December 1988 Decree of the USSR Council of Ministers 1405 entitled, "On the Further Development of the Foreign Economic Relations of State, Cooperative and Other Social Enterprises, Associations and Organizations." This decree gave all state enterprises, associations, organizations, and production cooperatives the right to create joint ventures.

The decision to establish a joint venture must be approved by a higher administrative body: for cooperatives, this means by the Council of Ministers of a Union republic where there are no oblasts (territories), by a kray (regional) executive committee, oblast executive committee, the Moscow City Executive Committee, Leningrad City Executive Committee, or by the ministry in charge of the enterprise where the cooperative has been formed. The procedure for preparing proposals on forming joint ventures was thereby further simplified. The decree also rescinded the mandatory Soviet majority share in the charter funds of joint ventures and allowed representatives of Western partners to assume the positions of chair of the board or general director of an enterprise.

Joint enterprises were granted the right to make decisions on loans, to discharge employees and to pay their employees in rubles, to decide questions of risk insurance, to revise financial-economic activity, and to transfer shares within the enterprise.

Furthermore, the decree introduced new privileges for joint ventures and their foreign partners:

- the opportunity to reduce or eliminate customs duties on the import into the Soviet Union of the commodities that are necessary for production;
- a reduction in the profit tax to 10 percent for joint ventures operating in the Far East economic region, with a "tax holiday" lasting at least three years;
- the opportunity to reduce or eliminate the tax on a foreign partner's profits, primarily in the case of joint ventures producing consumer goods, medical equipment and medicines, and high-tech products (also applies to joint ventures located in the Far East economic region);
- the allotment of housing and other services to foreign employees of joint ventures, with payment in rubles, as well as the granting of customs privileges.

In addition, Decree 1405 set regulations for an entire series of issues relating to foreign economic activities, in accordance with the principles of Soviet reforms. It is important to note that all of the country's enterprises, associations, production cooperatives, and other organizations have had the right to directly engage in foreign trade since 1 April 1989. Under its own command, each enterprise retains a certain portion of their hard currency earnings from the export of products and services, and they may use part of these earnings to acquire consumer goods and medical equipment and medicine, and to improve the material-technical base in the social and cultural spheres. This situation makes it much easier to solve the complicated problem of hard currency self-sufficiency for joint ventures, since it greatly expands the opportunity for the sale of their products on the Soviet market with payment in foreign currency. Naturally, the great expansion in the number of participants in foreign economic ties in the Soviet Union required the introduction of a formal system of government control to regulate their work.

Decree 203 of the USSR Council of Ministers, dated 7 March 1989, is entitled, "On Measures of State Regulation of Foreign Economic Activities." According to this decree, joint ventures must register as participants in foreign economic relations, and they have the right freely to export their own products (and services) and import commodities for their needs. Any intermediary activity they engage in must have the approval of the USSR Ministry of Foreign Economic Relations.

However, Soviet legislation in this area is still incomplete; it would be more correct to call it a compilation of juridical and normative acts regulating the procedures for forming and operating joint ventures in the Soviet Union. In fact, one of these documents has been officially ratified by the USSR Supreme Soviet—the decree of the USSR Supreme Soviet Presidium dated 13 January 1987, "On Questions Related to the Formation and Operations on Soviet Territory of Joint Ventures, International Associations and Organizations with the Participation of Soviet and Foreign Organizations, Firms and Management Bodies." The provisions that regulate the particular procedures for establishing and operating joint ventures, setting norms and rules for various aspects of their production and financial activity, are delineated in a series of government decisions. The decisions are legal documents, which are mandatory for cooperative and social organizations throughout the Soviet Union. The particular applications of specific provisions are clarified by a series of departmental normative acts, such as the instructions on procedures for registering and taxing joint ventures from the USSR Ministry of Finance, on material-technical supply from the USSR State Committee on Supply, on credit from the USSR State Bank, on assessing the worth of natural resources, buildings, and equipment when they are added to charter funds from the USSR State Committee on Prices, and on insurance from the state insurance agency, Ingosstrakh.

A number of practical matters are still not regulated, such as the legitimate use of profits received by Soviet partners, reinvestment or other uses for profits earned by foreign partners (including ruble profits), responsibility and contract guarantees for joint ventures in their relations with Soviet commodity producers and management bodies, and guarantees to the foreign partner.

INCONSISTENCIES IN LEGISLATION

A change from initially restrictive to more liberal legislation would, it seems to us, be comprehensible and favorable to foreign investors. In the case of the Soviet Union, however, the situation is different. Soviet legislation cannot be called harsh, even with reference to the first decrees and resolutions on joint ventures in 1987. Subsequent decrees have removed many restrictions on the activities of joint ventures, while introducing some new ones. Specifically, this applies to restrictions introduced by Decree 203 on intermediary activity. Under present conditions, joint ventures must receive permission from the Ministry of Foreign Economic Relations to carry out such activities. The joint ventures must be registered as a participant in foreign economic relations, while initially such registration was not required. In the past, joint ventures acquired such rights automatically.

Only the formulation and adoption of a single law on foreign investments, a law on joint ventures, or a systematic consideration of problems that have emerged within the framework of a law on foreign trade and other types of foreign economic activity—which is being prepared at the present time—will provide a complex solution to these problems. The present body of legislation concerning foreign investments in the Soviet Union is still inferior to analogous legislation in the developed capitalist and newly industrialized states, as well as to that in China and in East European countries such as Hungary and Yugoslavia.

In some cases, there are difficulties in the practical application of this legislation. As noted earlier, a large number of various departments have issued instructions supplementing state decrees and resolutions that affect joint ventures and other forms of foreign economic relations. These instructions frequently restrict the opportunities of joint ventures more than resolutions passed by the Council of Ministers.

Relations between departments and joint ventures are generally developing in a contradictory way at the present time. On the one hand, departments often complicate and restrict the process of forming and operating joint ventures. The process of making decisions and registering joint ventures is still lengthy and complicated, although what is required formally is simply agreement in the high-ranking administrative body. Internal instructions of various kinds, such as those relating to the use of duplicating equipment, complicate the work of joint ventures. Difficulties arise in their contacts with sanitation departments, fire departments, customs, and other services, and in the process of testing their products. Unfortunately, bribery has also become widespread in joint venture relations.

The persistence of the Soviet Union's extremely bureaucratic system and the lack of a full-fledged system that allows various departments and economic organizations to participate in international economic relations are the main reasons why the process of establishing joint ventures is so slow and arduous. Perestroika in the foreign economic sphere has eliminated a number of old organizations (e.g., the USSR State Committee for Foreign Economic Relations and the USSR Ministry of Foreign Trade) and created new ones (e.g., USSR Ministry of Foreign Economic Relations and the USSR

State Foreign Economics Commission). However, the process of defining their spheres of influence and responsibility has not yet been completed.

Practice has shown that under these conditions it is especially difficult to create and facilitate the work of multibranch joint ventures—those with activities that fall into the sphere of influence of several ministries and departments. However, there are the beginnings of a system to regulate relations between central administrative bodies and the Soviet enterprises, institutions, and cooperatives that play a part in the world arena by registering them as participants in foreign economic relations, by giving them licenses to export and import various commodities, and by introducing quotas. A system of contract relations among Soviet economic organizations themselves has not yet taken shape.

To some extent, state agencies must interfere in the work of joint ventures in those cases where all enterprises should be regulated within a unified framework for purposes such as security and environmental preservation. This applies to fire departments, sanitation and epidemiological services, and vehicle inspection. Every developed nation obviously needs to exercise such management with respect to all enterprises, both joint and national.

Interference by state agencies in the work of joint ventures is also dictated by the distinctive quality of their economic relations. In a formal sense, joint ventures are completely independent of departments. In reality, under conditions of a transitional economy, joint ventures cannot exist without the help of departments. Ministries often appropriate hard currency to Soviet enterprises to help them establish joint ventures and to help with deliveries. But where there is in fact economic dependence, conditions exist for the ministries to take a more authoritative approach in organizational and economic matters.

The experience of the Soviet-German enterprise Lenvest is a graphic example of such relations. Lenvest was required to supply a large part of the footwear it produced to Lentorg, the state trade organization. The latter, pursuing its departmental interests, insisted on selling the footwear at a price one and a half times that proposed by the joint venture. As a result, a compromise was reached between the two proposals that not only hurt consumers' pocketbooks, but also did not stimulate the joint venture to improve the quality of its products.

The departmental system should gradually lose ground as the process of economic perestroika continues. The face of the departmental system will evidently also change, possibly more than once. Proposals call for a sharp curb in the influence of industrial ministries and an increase in the role of regional and territorial administrative bodies. The possibility that departmental reshuffling will occur in the foreign economic sphere exists as well.

In their desire to overcome existing departmental impediments and facilitate the existence of joint ventures, some Soviet specialists propose that all work related to joint ventures be concentrated in one place by the creation of a new institution, like the Main Committee for Concessions that existed in the 1920s. It seems that the creation of such a "superdepartment" would truly simplify the life of joint ventures in certain matters, and help to carry out a uniform state policy. However, it would in actuality be another monopoly, and hence, would not lend flexibility to the process and could make any decision absolute, even an incorrect one.

Regardless of the title or extent of competency of future departments, their role with respect to joint ventures should amount to: working out strategic goals and methods for attracting foreign capital, generalizing and disseminating information regarding the experience of joint ventures, coordinating the work of joint ventures, and participating in the most important projects with their funds.

The degree of infrastructural development plays an important role in the creation of joint ventures. The Soviet Union is a country with a relatively poorly developed production infrastructure. In this respect, matters related to housing, transportation, communications, and information are sore spots for joint ventures.

Much has been done in the Soviet Union in recent years, however, to solve these problems through government channels. For example, well-known Soviet publications like *Vneshnyaya torgovlya (Foreign Trade)*, *Izvestiya*, and *Pravda* disseminate information needed by joint ventures. New magazines are constantly appearing, such as *Merkurly* and *Pryamyye svyazi (Direct Ties)*. Handbooks are also being published about business opportunities in the Soviet Union. The Ministry of Finance and the Ministry of Foreign Economic Relations gather information about joint ventures as they register them. Starting in 1991, the registration of joint ventures will be carried out by Union republics, not by the Ministry of Finance. As a result, the question is already being asked as to which organization can best collect information about joint ventures and publish it in centralized form.

Cooperatives and joint ventures themselves actively participate in solving infrastructural problems. Joint enterprises are being formed to rent automobiles, repair and rent property premises, and engage in publishing. For example, the joint Soviet-German enterprise Khomatek is building a technological and commercial center in Moscow. The center will house representatives of small- and medium-size companies from Germany, providing apartments, offices, garages, educational institutions, printing plants, and a computer center. Despite definite progress, the information shortage and several other shortages are still far from ending; therefore, this is an area ripe for the activities of joint ventures.

A complete network of organizations is now operating in the Soviet Union to assist in establishing and operating joint ventures. Assistance in finding partners and signing agreements may today be found through various channels, primarily through a number of state institutions. The State Foreign

Economics Commission, operating under the Council of Ministers and the Ministry of Foreign Economic Relations, is concerned with developing new forms of cooperation. A special consulting firm under the USSR Chamber of Commerce has also been set up to deal with these matters. Soviet trade representatives abroad, whose functions have grown in recent years, can provide help choosing a partner and an area for cooperation. A number of scientific research institutions are also engaged in such services. For example, the USSR Academy of Sciences has an agreement with the Academy of Sciences of Finland to assist in selecting partners for joint ventures. The All-Union Scientific Research Institute for Foreign Economic Relations, working under the State Foreign Economics Commission, is developing methodological materials to help in the creation of joint ventures and to provide advice to partners. The Institute of World Economy and International Relations of the USSR Academy of Sciences has set up a special commercial section to arrange meetings and seminars for interested parties. The USSR Foreign Trade Bank has concluded a number of agreements in cooperation with banks from Italy, France, and Germany, by which it will assist firms in these countries in consulting and searching for partners for joint ventures.

Cooperatives and their associations, such as the multipurpose cooperative association Sovinterkontakt-Agroservis in Moscow, Servis-Informatika in Leningrad, the Inter-regional Cooperative Federation in Naberzhyye Chelny and the Rossiya Association of Cooperatives, have taken an active role in the organization of joint ventures. In addition, branches of foreign companies located in the Soviet Union are helping to organize joint ventures. A legal branch of the U.S. company Coudert Brothers, the Petergof Consulting-Intermediary Company, and others are working in Moscow. International public organizations, such as the U.S.-Soviet Trade and Economic Council and the Association for Cooperation with Foreign Countries, are participating in organization of joint ventures. Individuals not aligned with these groups also provide consultation to partners. As a rule, these individuals are employees of state organizations or scientific research institutes. Finally, joint ventures themselves help to create new joint ventures. For example, the Soviet-Finnish joint venture Vneshkon'sult provides an extensive set of services to potential partners. The U.S.-Soviet Sovinter-Invest is an intermediary investment company with a broad profile. A whole series of such joint ventures have already been established.

An association has been created in order to facilitate the creation and functioning of joint ventures. Approximately two hundred joint ventures have joined it. The association provides members with information, legal and other assistance, and participates in the composition of legal documents to regulate the activities of joint ventures. It also submits proposals to the government concerning the creation of favorable conditions for joint ventures.

The first joint bank in the Soviet Union has also been formed. Its task is to further the development of mutual economic relations, including joint ventures.

Despite the large number of such organizations, the demand for information-consulting services has not yet been met. Moreover, the need for these services is growing as Soviet enterprises embark on greater international cooperation, and as small- and medium-sized Soviet and Western companies assume a greater role. The need to expand the variety and improve the quality of such services presents a problem. Joint ventures undoubtedly have an advantage in this area over other organizations; a Western partner can contribute intermediary consulting experience, while the Soviet side can contribute knowledge of branch or region, the Soviet economy, administration, and communications.

Development in other areas of production and the social infrastructure of the Soviet Union also lag behind the needs of the economy and population. At the same time, some generalized data indicate substantial possibilities in individual areas of the infrastructure. For example, the Soviet Union has an extensive network of roads and of oil and product lines, as well as thousands of populated points connected by air routes. The effective utilization of this potential, as well as its growth, are hindered by several factors: the monopoly of transportation departments, the fact that transportation workers do not bear the responsibility for the quality of their services, and by shortcomings in the technology and organization of transportation services. Modern forms of communications, such as the telephone, are obviously underdeveloped. Telex and telefax communications are in limited use. Some weak points in the production infrastructure are storage and outdated technology and organization for preserving agricultural products and raw and other materials.

The scale of housing construction has grown in recent years in the Soviet Union. Capital investments in housing construction have grown, but the average availability of housing to the Soviet citizen remains on a low level: 14.3 square meters in the cities, and 16.1 square meters in rural areas. Yet the government has set for itself the difficult task of giving every family a separate apartment or individual home by the year 2000. The development of hotels, and the services they provide, is clearly inadequate. Towns in the Soviet Union are poorly suppled with cultural, athletic, and medical facilities.

These areas are greatly in need of attracting foreign capital, experience, and knowledge. Although a relatively large number of joint ventures have been established in these areas, they are not able to make up the deficiency. It is worth mentioning that, in view of the great deficiency in these areas, joint ventures will evidently be able to offer their services for hard currency for a long time to come, both to foreign citizens and organizations and to Soviet enterprises and institutions.

At present, there is obviously a severe shortage of qualified personnel in the Soviet Union to work in foreign economic relations, though the availability of such personnel is a prerequisite for a fertile investment climate. In recent years a great deal has been done to expand the training of such personnel. Joint ventures have participated in this training. In a number of cases, for example, Soviet specialists are being trained at the enterprises of their foreign partners. The first joint ventures specifically for training personnel are also being established in the Soviet Union. It seems to us that this offers great prospects for joint ventures for several reasons: Soviet higher educational institutions have not developed course programs, there are too few qualified teachers, the quality of instruction is not high, few foreign specialists are hired to teach, there are no specialized textbooks, and language creates a barrier.

The experiences of the first joint ventures, both positive and negative, will serve as an important component in the investment climate of the future. Other Soviet enterprises are turning to them for advice; the ways they have solved particular difficulties are being applied to solving others, and changes are being prepared in the legislation on joint ventures. For example, the need to attract qualified personnel to joint ventures and to interest them in the results of their work has given rise to the first deviations from the accepted Soviet method of setting wages. The 2 December 1988 decree of the Council of Ministers strengthened this practice, confirming that joint ventures themselves may make decisions regarding the hiring and firing of personnel, the types and amounts of wages, and incentives for Soviet citizens in rubles.

CURRENT INVESTMENT CLIMATE

We would like to note some characteristic features of the current investment climate in the Soviet Union. First, it is influenced by both positive and negative factors, operating in opposite directions. Positive factors are abundant resources, strong intellectual potential, a large domestic market, the ongoing improvement of legislation on joint ventures, and improved political relations with the outside world. Among the features that make the Soviet Union inferior to many investment-receiving countries are the tendency to preserve the severity and centralization of domestic economic relations, ruble inconvertibility, the inadequate development of the production and social infrastructure, and the declining economic and political situation. For example, other East European countries have advanced further along the road to economic reform, have more developed investment legislation, and grant greater and more differentiated privileges. Special economic zones already exist within their boundaries.

Second, the investment climate is at present not always identical for national and joint ventures. Many Western businesses, including U.S. firms, see this as a kind of limitation on the rights of joint ventures, but that is not quite the case. For example, joint ventures currently enjoy much greater privileges in the area of taxation and have greater freedom in other areas (i.e., supply and sales) than other Soviet enterprises. It is unlikely that joint ventures would prefer to conform to national standards in these matters.

At the same time, a situation has arisen in which some joint ventures experience great difficulties in their normal operations because they are not included in the system of centralized planning and material-technical supply and sales. In a number of cases, joint ventures have expressed a willingness to adopt the national standard in these matters. This seems to us to be quite possible, if both sides agree to such a solution. But not all foreign companies choose to solve their problems in this manner.

It seems that, in the future, it would indeed be more sensible to introduce a unified system for national and joint ventures. During the present transitional period, conditions for this do not exist.

Third, the investment climate differs even for various Soviet enterprises. Soviet partners in joint ventures are not just state enterprises and associations, but cooperative and local executive bodies as well. For example, a number of joint ventures have been created with the participation of the city executive committees of Naberzhyye Chelny and Yalta. Different Soviet partners fill differing legal capacities in economic activities, including those relating to joint ventures.

In conclusion, we will attempt to describe the present investment climate in the Soviet Union as a whole. What have been the results of creating joint ventures? By 1989, more than 3 billion rubles in capital investments, part of which (approximately 1.3 billion) came from abroad, were attracted in the course of three years. The products of joint ventures yielded 0.5 billion rubles in products, and they earned 200 million rubles in exports.

Is that a lot or a little? How should we judge the success of the Soviet Union in attracting foreign capital? It seems that such results are not at all bad for a beginning. We reach this conclusion not only because in creating joint ventures the Soviet Union has surpassed Yugoslavia and Hungary—two countries that began creating joint ventures long ago and have been the most successful in this field of all the East European countries. (One should remember that these are small countries that do not have the enormous Soviet economy, with its rich potential and large market, which is undoubtedly the main attraction of the present investment climate in the Soviet Union.) Rather, even compared with China, if you take into consideration the length of time in which joint ventures have existed, these results look good.

At the same time, the prospect for creating joint ventures in the Soviet Union is not cloudless. For example, only a small number of the foreign companies that have wanted to create joint ventures have been able to do so. In 1988, only two of a total of one hundred U.S. companies were successful. Moreover, only a small number of the joint ventures that have been registered have actually begun operating—according to estimates, in 1989 a few more than three hundred of almost fifteen hundred that were registered.

Most joint ventures are rather small in size. Almost two-thirds of them (59.3 percent) have a charter fund of less than 1 million rubles. About one-third (26.8 percent) have a charter fund of between 1 and 5 million rubles. Only 5.9 percent are in the framework of 5 to 10 million rubles, with 6.9 percent having more than 10 million rubles.

Capitalist companies have contributed 33.8 percent of the charter funds, companies from developing countries only 1.4 percent, and other Eastern countries 6.0 percent. In other words, the foreign contribution is less than half the total of charter funds, although Soviet legislation does not now limit the foreign share.

The actual deposit of capital into the charter funds of joint ventures is a problem. In a number of cases, funds exist mainly on paper, and in others the share of borrowed funds is disproportionate. The latter often come from Soviet banks, which means a greater risk for the Soviet side. Investments are generally made in the nonproductive sphere. Only one-third of all joint ventures are created in order to produce goods.

Other East European countries, Yugoslavia, China, and Asian socialist countries take little part in joint ventures in the Soviet Union. Joint ventures are very concentrated geographically. Most of them (913) are located in the Russian Republic. Of these, many are located in Moscow (620) and in Leningrad (94). Joint ventures are also developing briskly in Estonia and in the Ukraine, where there are eighty-four and seventy-four joint ventures respectively.

As can be seen from the above, the total picture is rather contradictory. Though there are good results quantitatively, the qualitative side looks far worse. As we tried to demonstrate earlier, this is largely the result of the positive and negative features of the Soviet investment climate.

The present investment climate in the Soviet Union can be described as moderate at best. Furthermore, this moderate investment climate is deteriorating under the influence of a growing crisis in the economy and increasing instability in the country's economic, political, and social spheres. As a result, trends in mixed entrepreneurship are developing, which are not the most desirable from the Soviet point of view.

Under such conditions, it is extremely important that the Soviet Union make a greater effort to improve the investment climate. This is necessary not only for joint ventures but primarily for Soviet enterprises. Much has already been done: basic laws for entrepreneurship have been enacted—such as the Law on Property or the Law on Land, both of March 1990, and others—and various forms of property are developing. Further progress along the path of economic reform will make it possible for Soviet and joint ventures to "straighten their shoulders" and will create a fundamentally different and more favorable investment climate. If foreign investors support these efforts, positive advances in cooperation will proceed even faster.

Chapter 3

Soviet Technology and the Potential of Joint Ventures

Julian Cooper

It is generally acknowledged that the Soviet economy lacks the technological dynamism characteristic of the leading capitalist economies, and that it possesses an industrial structure in urgent need of modernization. This chapter first reviews the current state of the technology in the Soviet Union in order to point out the priority areas for technology transfer via joint ventures. It then explores the potential of joint ventures with Western firms for raising the technological level and promoting improved innovative performance.

STRUCTURAL DETERMINANTS OF SOVIET TECHNOLOGY

The present-day state of technology in the Soviet Union can be regarded as the outcome of the functioning over several decades of what has come to be known as the "administrative system." Essential features of this system have been state ownership of almost all means of production, a centralized system of directive planning securing the nonmarket allocation of material resources, and a hierarchical structure of state economic administration tightly enmeshed with the institutions of political power. At least during its early years, this system secured rapid economic growth in accordance with the priorities of the party leadership. In the course of time growth rates declined: extensive growth through the rapacious mobilization—but inefficient use—of resources could not be sustained, while institutional inertia frustrated efforts to adapt to new circumstances. When real change came on the agenda in 1985, the new leadership inherited an economic structure and technological capability profoundly marked by this past experience.

With high-quality resources of all types in extremely short supply, the central authorities have sought consistently to concentrate them in those economic activities judged to be of the higher national priority. For equipment and materials this has been achieved through the nonmarket, administrative system of resource allocation; and for human resources, through the wages system and differential access to goods and services, notably housing and welfare provision. This applies not only to current production, but also to the spheres of investment and research and development. Once well established, priorities among major sectors of the economy—such as high priority for heavy industry (and within that, defense) or low priority for consumer-related activities—became institutionalized and difficult to alter. In practice, this structuralization of the economy by priority has been influenced also by the sometimes perverse impact of the mechanism of economic planning and management, which has tended consistently to promote quantity at the expense of quality. This set of factors influencing the structure of the economy and patterns of technological development has not been without contradictions.

The impact of these factors over time has led to the formation of a pyramidic, qualitatively stratified, economic structure. At the upper levels are those high-priority activities that have enjoyed privileged resource provision, not simply in terms of quantity, but above all in terms of quality. These sectors tend to have the best technology and also, in relative terms, the strongest research and development (R&D) capabilities. As one descends the economic pyramid, the quality of resources typically available at each level declines, and resort is made to quantitative compensation, with low-priority activities being undertaken with the mass use of resources of inferior quality. In these circumstances it is not surprising that Soviet technology exhibits such wide variation, with the coexistence of peaks of genuine achievement and troughs of quite extraordinary backwardness.

Before examining from the above perspective the current state of technology in the Soviet Union, a further factor must be considered: the nature of the process of innovation. In market economies, while resort is made to government intervention, in a general sense innovation can be regarded as organic to the economic system, undertaken by firms on their own initiative in pursuit of market opportunities and profits. It is precisely this organic quality that is absent in the traditional Soviet-type economy: innovation takes place not on the initiative of the enterprise itself in response to perceived actual, or potential, customer demand, but through external pressure exercised by agencies superior in the organizational hierarchy. This pressure, primarily of an administrative character, is supplemented by special economic arrangements intended to override the noninnovative (or, rather, anti-innovative) character of the basic economic mechanism. This can be termed "induced" innovation in contrast to the "organic" innovation of a market economy. In the shortage economy, to draw on Hungarian economist Janos Kornai's insightful analysis, customer power is weak or nonexistent.[1] In these circumstances it is not surprising that the defense sector has the best record of innovative success: not only does it possess an effective, priority-reinforced, inducement mechanism, but in the Ministry of Defense it has a powerful single customer subject to external competitive pressure of a kind not met in the rest of the economy.

The question of external competition brings us to a final important determinant of Soviet technological performance: for much of the Soviet Union's history the level of participation in world scientific, technological, and economic relations has been lower than might have been expected given the country's economic strength and world power status. This relative isolation means that in many sectors the level of technology has been shaped overwhelmingly by domestic factors. This is not to deny that in certain high-tech fields access to foreign scientific and technical achievements has been restricted by deliberate Western denial policies.

A COMPARATIVE PERSPECTIVE OF TECHNOLOGY IN THE SOVIET ECONOMY

It is not surprising that the economic relations that have prevailed in the Soviet Union essentially unchanged for more than fifty years have left their mark on the country's technology. The pattern of achievement is uneven, but this unevenness exists as much within sectors of the economy as between them. Some activities have enjoyed priority over long periods and exhibit genuine strengths in technology. But for much of the economy the inter-relatedness of the various sectors, and the commonalty of the economic conditions they have faced, have produced a leveling down of technology to a lowest common denominator. Over time some vicious circles of backwardness have evolved, now presenting formidable obstacles to the successful realization of a modernization strategy.

An indication of the comparative level of technology is provided by Table 3.1. Taking the year 1987 (at the time of writing the most recent for which comprehensive comparative data are available), this sets out a variety of indicators giving a snapshot view of the position vis-à-vis the United States, Japan, Germany, Great Britain, and France. The inadequacies of the indicators are frankly acknowledged: international comparisons of this kind are frustrated by a lack of suitable data, not only for the Soviet Union, but also for major Western countries. The available information tends to be of a highly aggregated nature, concealing important qualitative distinctions. However, this limited range of indicators serves to bring out some of the characteristic features of Soviet technology and to illustrate the magnitude of the current task of modernization.

Energy

The Soviet Union's per capita output of electricity is comparable with that of other major industrial powers, but a higher proportion is consumed

Table 3.1

The Level of Technology in the Soviet Union: Comparative Indicators (1987)

Indicator	USSR	U.S.	Japan	FRG	UK	France
Energy						
Electrical output (kWh)*	5881.0	11313.0	5564.0	6891.0	5274.0	6833.0
Electricity consumed per industrial worker (kWh)	25095.0	32978.0	25106.0	18743.0	15537.0	21105.0
Nuclear output (bn.kWh)	187.0	482.6	187.8	130.5	55.2	266.4
% of total	11.2	17.7	26.1	31.2	18.3	70.4
Materials						
Steel output (kg)*	572.0	335.0	806.0	613.0	302.0	219.0
% oxygen steel	33.5	62.3	70.2	82.5	70.5	74.8
% electric steel	13.4	37.7	29.8	17.5	29.5	25.2
% continuously cast steel	16.1	59.3	93.3	88.0	77.5	93.1
Plastics output (kg)*	16.0	105.0	82.0	140.0	34.0	70.0
% thermoplasts	56.0	74.0	82.0	65.0	71.0	85.0
Chemical fiber output (kg)*	5.0	17.0	14.0	16.0	7.0	4.0
% synthetic	59.6	91.2[a]	77.7[a]	82.4[a]	75.1[b]	90.0[b]
Cement output (kg)*	485.0	335.0	586.0	462.0	237.0	424.0
% dry technology	16.0	58.0	78.0	90.0	n.	n.
Paper output (kg)*	22.0	138.0	105.0	131.0	60.0	95.0
% by sulphate process	49.0[a]	86.0[a]	91.0[a]	n.	n.	75.0[a]

Sources: **ENERGY** Per capita output of electricity: *Narodnoe khozyaistvo SSSR v 1987g* (Moscow, 1988), 646-47 (hereafter *Narkhoz 1987*); Electric power consumed per worker in industry: USSR, calculated from *Narkhoz 1987*, 59 and 364; other countries, calculated from OECD, *Energy Statistics, 1986/87* and ILO, *Yearbook of Labour Statistics, 1988*; Output of nuclear power and nuclear power as percent of total electricity output: USSR, *Promyshlennost' SSSR* (Moscow, 1988), 134; other countries, UN ECE, *Annual Bulletin of Energy Statistics for Europe, 1987* and OECD, *Energy Statistics 1986/87*. **MATERIALS** Per capita output of steel: *Narkhoz 1987*, 646-47; Percent of total steel output produced by oxygen converter, electric arc furnace, and continuous casting technologies: USSR, *Promyshlennost' SSSR* (Moscow, 1988), 159; other countries, calculated from UN ECE, *The Steel Market in 1987*; Per capita output of plastics and percent of output taking form of thermoplasts: *Narkhoz 1987*, 646-47; *Narkhoz 1988*, 684; Per capita output of chemical fibers: *Narkhoz 1987*, 646-47; Percent of chemical fiber output taking form of synthetic fibers: USSR, *Narkhoz 1987*, 140; other countries, calculated from UN, *Industrial Statistics Yearbook 1985* and *1986*; Per capita output of cement and share of cement output derived from dry process technologies: *Narkhoz 1987*, 646-47 and 657; Per capita output of paper: *Narkhoz 1987*, 646-47; Share of output of woodpulp by sulphate process: calculated from UN, *Industrial Statistics Yearbook 1986* (excluding mechanical process).

* Per capita   a 1986   b 1985   c 1984   d 1983   e 1982

f 1986 (apparently refers to stock of machine tools in civilian industry only)

Table 3.1 (continued)

Indicator	USSR	U.S.	Japan	FRG	UK	France
Machine building						
Total stock of machine tools						
(mt) in economy (000 units)	6889.0[d]	2193.0[d]	601.0	1120.0[b]	768.0	618.0[c]
% numerically controlled (NC)	1.8[f]	4.7	11.3	5.7	7.1	5.0
Metal-cutting mt output (000u)	156.0	95.0[a]	110.0	100.0	19.0	n.
Including NC mt	21.0	4.6[a]	35.3	17.7	2.7	1.9
% NC	13.5	4.8	32.1	17.7	14.2	n.
Industrial robot output (u)	14700.0	4273.0	26580.0	n.	n.	n.
Computers						
Personal computer output (000u)	51.0	8668.0	n.	n.	n.	n.
Consumer goods						
Passenger car output						
(units per 1000 population)	5.0	29.0	65.0	74.0	20.0	55.0
Television output						
(units per 1000 population)	32.0	93.0	132.0	60.0	53.0	36.0
% color TVs	51.2	84.9	88.3	100.0	97.1	97.5
Video recorder output (000u)	45.0	12304.0	30544.0	2995.0	805.0	2.0
Communications						
Telephones						
(units per 100 population)	12	76[e]	56[b]	64[a]	52[c]	61[b]

Sources: **MACHINE BUILDING** Machine tool stock in economy and percent numerically controlled machine tools in total stock (various years): USSR, *Material'no-tekhnicheskoe obespechenie narodnogo khozyaistvo SSSR* (Moscow, 1988), 220 and 224; other countries, Machine Tool Trades Association (UK), *Machine Tool Statistics 1988*, 24; Output of metal-cutting machine tools and output of numerically controlled (NC) machine tools: *Narkhoz 1987*, 642-43 and 656-57 and *Narkhoz 1988*, 675 and 685; Output of industrial robots: USSR, *Narkhoz 1987*, 24; U.S., *Statistical Abstract of the United States* (1989), 742; Japan, *Referativnyi sbornik, Ekonomika promyshlennost'* (1989), item 5V243. **COMPUTERS** Output of personal computers: USSR, *Narkhoz 1987*, 24; U.S., *Statistical Abstract of the United States* (1989), 743 (refers to PCs of unit cost less than $10,000). **CONSUMER GOODS** Output of passenger cars: USSR, *Narkhoz 1987*, 153; other countries, Economist Intelligence Unit, *International Motor Business* (April 1989), 91-108 and *Referativnyi sbornik, Ekonomika promyshlennost'* (1989), item 5V248; Output of television sets and percent color: USSR, *Narkhoz 1987*, 152; other countries, *Yearbook of World Electronics Data* 1 and 2 (1989) (Elsevier); *Statistical Abstract of the United States* (1989), 748; *Annuaire Statistique de la France* (1988), 608; Output of video-recorders: USSR, *Narkhoz 1987*, 153; other countries, as television sets, above. **COMMUNICATIONS** Telephones in use: USSR, *Narkhoz 1987*, 338; other countries, UN, *Statistical Yearbook 1984* and *1985/86*.

* Per capita   a 1986   b 1985   c 1984   d 1983   e 1982

f 1986 (apparently refers to stock of machine tools in civilian industry only) in industry. Geographical factors have promoted a concentration on large-capacity generating plant and high-voltage transmission technologies, in both of which there have been respectable achievements. The pioneer of commercial nuclear power, the Soviet Union has been relatively slow to diffuse the technology. Following the Chernobyl accident several projects have been abandoned, shortcomings in control systems are being rectified, and the effort to create a new generation of safer reactors intensified, with increased emphasis on international cooperation.

The oil and gas industries are notable more for the scale and rapidity of their development than for the high level of their technologies, although this is not to deny specific strengths and innovations, in, for example, the welding of large-diameter pipelines. In the 1970s the coal mining ministry took over the development and production of new equipment, previously a responsibility of the machine-building industry. The reorganization has not proved successful: mining technologies have not kept pace with modern developments. The oil, gas, and coal industries illustrate a characteristic problem of the Soviet economy. The production of equipment takes place, as a rule, in a different ministry from the basic activity. Interministerial bureaucratic obstacles complicate customer-supplier relations already difficult because of the weakness of customer power. On the other hand, if equipment manufacture is transferred to the customer ministry, the enterprises and the R&D organizations concerned become isolated from the rest of the engineering industry and their capability is gradually eroded. It is this kind of problem that leads many economists to argue for the abolition or radical transformation of the powerful, hierarchically structured industrial ministries that dominate Soviet industry.

In one respect there has been striking failure in the energy field. A relative abundance of energy until recent years, low domestic energy prices, and the operation of the economic mechanism have combined to produce a profligate energy system. Energy-saving and conservation technologies have been neglected and resources extracted often with little regard to environmental consequences. This is a field that could well offer scope for joint ventures, especially after the price reform that must be implemented soon as an essential condition for successful economic reform. It is inevitable that energy prices will rise substantially, forcing users for the first time to take energy saving seriously. Whereas Western economies have more than fifteen years of experience in adapting to the shock of higher energy prices and have developed appropriate new technologies for enhanced energy efficiency, the pricing practices of the Soviet economy have served to isolate the country's technical specialists and managers from this experience. The joint venture could offer an effective means of reducing this gap within a relatively brief period of time.

Materials

The Soviet economy is material-intensive or, more accurately, is characterized by relatively wasteful use of traditional materials. This can be illustrated by the ferrous metals and chemical industries. The steel industry exemplifies many of the problems of Soviet technology. While the output of steel has fallen steadily in recent years in other major industrial countries, in the Soviet Union its growth continues. Elsewhere the old open-hearth technology has almost disappeared; in the Soviet Union it still accounts for half of total output. The oxygen steel-making process was first employed in the Soviet Union at about the same time as in the West, but its subsequent rate of diffusion was chronically slow. Now a similar diffusion lag is opening up in the use of the electric-arc process, vital for the smelting of high-quality steels. But worst of all is the record with continuous casting: this was a Soviet technological breakthrough, but in its country of origin barely one-fifth of all steel is produced with its use, compared with 90 percent or more in other countries. The very rapid diffusion of continuous casting in Japan was achieved in part through the purchase of a Soviet license for the technology. The sluggish diffusion rates characteristic of the Soviet steel industry can be explained by technological conservatism, shortcomings in the investment process, and the weakness of customer power.

The bulk of the inflated output of the Soviet steel industry is a product of low quality, its inadequate standards of hardness forcing users to build metal-intensive, overweight machines in order to compensate for its inherent lack of strength. It has been estimated that, on average, Soviet civilian machinery products are 15 to 20 percent heavier than their foreign equivalents.[2] In the face of a powerful, near-monopoly supplier, customers lack the power to enforce higher standards and have to accept what they can obtain. Quality steels are produced, but in limited volume to meet the requirements of certain high-priority customers—above all the defense industry. To make matters worse, the defense sector has its own steel-making capacity, enabling it to meet much of its own high-quality demand, and this self-supply weakens customer pressure on the bulk producer, the specialized steel ministry.

The chemical industry exhibits similar features. Here we also find the bulk production of traditional products and limited-volume output of more modern, quality products. The underdevelopment of the plastics industry is exemplary. In terms of per capita output the Soviet Union is in a different league from the other major industrial powers, and the share of thermoplasts is also much smaller. The chemical fibers industry is also relatively backward, with a much lower proportion of synthetic fiber in total output. Whereas in other industrial countries, plastics, new composite materials, and ceramics are progressively displacing steel as the major material of the engineering industry, in the Soviet Union this process has hardly begun. In 1990 it is planned that civilian machine building will use only 18,000 tons of ceramic components and 82,000 tons of composite materials of all types.[3] Within the defense sector, however, the position is more favorable, and it is notable that in the current effort to declassify and transfer technologies from military and space programs to the civilian economy, composite and other new materials occupy a prominent place.[4] This process is opening up opportunities for joint ventures, an early example being an Italian-Soviet agreement involving the space missile industry's principal research center for composite materials.[5]

Similar patterns can be found in other materials-producing industries. In both the cement and paper industries, one finds a bias toward the volume production of relatively low-grade products using traditional technologies to the neglect of high-quality products and modern processes. In general, the materials sector of Soviet industry requires modernization on a substantial scale. Organization of the specialized production of modern, high-grade materials could offer substantial scope for joint venture.

Machine Building

As already noted, the machine-building industry is not well supplied with high-quality material inputs. Compared with the engineering industries of leading Western countries, greater reliance is placed on traditional metal-cutting technologies, and this bias, coupled with a severe underdevelopment of specialized subcontracting and the impact of an economic mechanism that has provided little incentive to the removal and replacement of old equipment, has led to a hypertrophied growth of the machine tool stock. As can be seen from Table 3.1, the total stock is now larger than the combined stocks of the five leading Western countries. The overall technological level is not up to Western standards: again we find the familiar pattern of the mass use of inferior resources. The Soviet machine tool industry is capable of producing modern machine tools up to world standards, but the volume of output of such machines is limited, and the highest priority sectors are the main beneficiaries. Again, the defense sector has resorted to self-supply, manufacturing some of the best Soviet production equipment at its own enterprises. Numerically controlled (NC) machine tools and industrial robots are manufactured in substantial quantity, as shown in the table. However, in these cases volume of output is an inadequate indicator. The NC machines are generally of a lower technological level than their Western counterparts, and the robots are predominantly simple manipulators. Both suffer from the poor quality and reliability of their domestically produced control systems.

Striving to minimize dependence on outside suppliers, Soviet machine-building enterprises produce for themselves many components and assemblies of a type that in the West are normally supplied by specialized manufacturers. This weakness of subcontracting relations raises costs and often leads to inferior quality. The overall technological level and quality of Soviet machines is frequently let down by the lack of vital precision components, such as hydraulic units, small electric motors, and sensors. This is an area in which there is extensive scope for highly specialized joint ventures, filling gaps and niches in the Soviet industrial structure.

While the Soviet engineering industry has real strengths in the manufacture of traditional products, it has not had striking success in meeting the challenge of the new information technologies. The fusion of microelectronic and mechanical technologies has presented Soviet industry with severe problems, partly arising from difficulties within the electronics industry itself but also from the problems of interministerial cooperation that are such a characteristic feature of the Soviet economy. As the recent displays of Soviet aircraft in the West have confirmed, even the high-priority aerospace industry is not immune to this interface problem: the basic aircraft are impressive, but their electronic systems lag behind their Western equivalents.[6]

Electronics and Computing

Of all the areas of technology, the one that has most frustrated Soviet efforts to keep up with world trends has been electronics and computing. Here the role of the Coordinating Committee on Multilateral Export Control (COCOM) cannot be ignored: there is little doubt it has effectively restricted access to the latest technology. The Soviet industry has responded by efforts to build up its own domestic capability, aided by the cooperation of members of the Council on Mutual Economic Assistance (CMEA) and their attempts to evade Western controls. In these circumstances it is not surprising that the development and production effort has focused on the top-priority sectors, above all defense, depriving much of the civilian economy of high-grade electronic equipment. Space precludes a detailed review, but there is general agreement that the lag behind Western achievements (and increasingly also those of the newly industrialized countries) is substantial, with little evidence of progress in narrowing the gap.[7] The problems of organizing the mass production of personal computers illustrate the general situation: in 1989 output reached a mere 120,000 units, the models built being predominantly poor-quality versions of the simplest Western eight- and sixteen-bit types. Printers, floppy disks, and software are in short supply. The vast unsatisfied demand must be met increasingly by resort to imports.

Now, under Gorbachev, microelectronics and computing are being granted much higher priority than in the past, with evidence of a serious effort to strengthen the basic research and development capability. Again, this is a field with rich potential for joint ventures, although in this case there is some evidence that the ministries concerned, habituated to a lack of legitimate business links with Western partners, may be ill prepared to take advantage of the new opportunities. It is indicative that, in this field, it is the new cooperatives, unencumbered by conservative bureaucratic structures, that have been at the forefront in making contact with foreign partners. In the West the rapid development of computing and electronics has been promoted by flexible, dynamic, organizational arrangements, and by transfers of knowledge and experience through direct interpersonal contact and a high degree of mobility of innovative personnel. For these reasons the joint venture, permitting ongoing, direct contact between Soviet and Western specialists, may be especially appropriate as a vehicle for helping the Soviet Union to overcome its relative isolation from the rich world culture of modern information technology. As some of the joint enterprises already created illustrate, they offer the potential of a phased acclimatization to this culture, beginning with the assembly of equipment from imported components, with later progression to full domestic manufacture that meets contemporary Western standards.

Associated with the lag in electronics is the backwardness of the Soviet telephone system. As can be seen in Table 3.1, the diffusion of telephones in the population remains at a chronically low level, equivalent to that attained in the United States by the late 1930s! Moreover, the use of modern digital exchange technology and fiber optics has hardly begun. There must be a danger that the shortcomings of the communications systems will hinder the wide application of computers and other modern information technologies. A major modernization drive is urgently required, with plenty of scope for foreign involvement.

Consumer Goods

Until the recent period, which has seen a sharp policy turn in favor of consumption and welfare, most consumer-related sectors have been located near the base of the pyramidic economy. This applies to the light and food industries and the manufacture of a wide range of household goods. The overall technological level is low and the quality of many consumer goods leaves much to be desired. Household electrical and electronic goods at times exhibit quite remarkable backwardness. Most washing machines now in production are of a type dating from the 1950s, almost half the television output consists of black and white models of notoriously poor reliability, and to date there has been no manufacture of dishwashing machines.

Recent measures have transferred responsibility for a substantial proportion of consumer-related technologies to the ministries of the defense sector, which have been charged with securing a rapid modernization and expansion of production. In effect, many enterprises are being pulled up from the base of the economic pyramid to its apex. More generally, defense industry involvement in the modernization of the economy is being enhanced through the partial conversion of enterprises from military to civilian production and the engagement of military-related research organizations in civil tasks.

As noted above, this brief review of the state of Soviet technology presents a far from complete picture but serves to illustrate characteristic patterns and trends. From it emerges an incontestable general conclusion: the Soviet industrial structure requires fundamental reshaping and modernization with an urgent need for the wide application of modern technologies, not all of which the domestic economy will be able to supply within the short and medium term.

TECHNOLOGY TRANSFER AND JOINT VENTURES

In terms of the usual quantitative indicators, the Soviet Union possesses a substantial research and development capability. By international standards the share of GNP devoted to R&D—approximately 4 percent—is high. Military research represents at least 40 percent of total expenditures and almost three-quarters of state-budget-funded R&D. However, the effectiveness of this research base, its ability to translate human and material inputs into new knowledge, products, and processes is not as high as it should be. Many problems have accumulated over recent years, and even the high-prestige institutes of the USSR Academy of Sciences have not escaped forces eroding their research creativity, leading to much concern at the current state of Soviet fundamental research. This is not to deny the existence of research programs of an impressive standard, in some cases at the forefront of world development.[8]

The inadequacies of the Soviet R&D system and the noninnovative nature of the economic mechanism have become acutely evident at a time of rapid change associated with new information technologies putting a premium on flexibility and adaptability. The state sector of Soviet industry is highly concentrated, dominated by large production and research establishments with little scope for the rapid creation of new, small-scale facilities to exploit promising discoveries and inventions. It lacks scope for spontaneity: moves to create new organizations, however small, face countless bureaucratic obstacles as decisions are referred up the administrative hierarchy. It is also rigid in another important respect: mobility of personnel among organizations is limited, providing little scope for "on the hoof" innovation of a type familiar in Western economies. If we add to these negative features the weakness of the reward system for successful innovation, then it can be seen that the circumstances are not favorable to the emergence of entrepreneurial activity. Finally, from this Schumpeterian perspective, it is worth noting that the traditional Soviet economic system lacks mechanisms for the removal of the old and obsolete.[9] In this extraordinarily retentive system, the new does not replace the old in a "gale of creative destruction," but accumulates alongside it, the novel always at risk of subjection to the tenacious grip of the past.

In the light of these unpropitious circumstances the East-West joint venture would appear to have much to offer. It is a flexible organizational form, well suited to the rapid exploitation of new technological possibilities and to insertion into niches in the administrative structures of the Soviet economy. The joint venture offers the potential not only of quickly introducing modern technologies absent, or only weakly present, in the domestic economy, but also of exploiting Soviet technological strengths that are undeveloped at present because of the rigidities and counterinnovative qualities of the economic system. By introducing an external standard of technology and quality directly into the Soviet economy, the joint venture by-passes the problem of translating Western market requirements into Soviet practice, offering the prospect of more rapid entry into the world market on a competitive basis.

Leaving to one side Soviet participation in the CMEA, it is worth considering the joint venture in the context of the range of modes of Western technology acquisition open to the Soviet Union. Useful here is the distinction between passive and active modes of technology transfer. Soviet practice has shown a distinct bias toward the former, above all in the import of machinery and equipment embodying modern technologies. At various times this import policy has been rendered more active by acquisition of technical expertise involving the active participation of Western personnel in the establishment of new production facilities. However, the normal pattern has been for such active involvement to cease on completion of the project. Transfer has also been realized through the purchase of licenses and know-how, by the collection and analysis of Western scientific and technical information, the copying and "reverse engineering" of products and processes, and, in the face of COCOM bans, illegal or regulation-bending acquisition of items of advanced technology. All these modes are of a relatively passive nature, usually involving little direct human contact for the exchange of knowledge, ideas, and experience. They also have the major weakness that, as a rule, they do not provide access to the very latest technology at the research frontier of world development. The technology acquired has usually passed through the processes of development and commercialization, so that the Soviet Union finds itself in a permanent follow-up situation involving a built-in time lag. As a rule, passive modes of technology transfer do not permit the elimination of technological gaps, although they may secure their narrowing, albeit with no guarantee against resumed future widening.

More active modes of transfer have been employed but have played a secondary role. They include study visits abroad by Soviet scientists and engineers, consultancy agreements, and joint research projects. However, until recently the Soviet Union has not been able to take advantage of some active forms of considerable importance in the West—in particular, transfers of technology among the affiliates of multinational corporations. The joint venture is of considerable potential importance precisely because it offers the possibility of technology transfer of a genuinely active nature, one that offers the possibility of reducing or even eliminating the time lag associated with passive forms of acquisition. And whereas most existing modes of active transfer involve a temporary relationship between Western and Soviet partners, the framework of the joint venture offers permanence, facilitating long-term cooperation and a fruitful build-up of experience and trust. Given these advantages, the important question is whether the Soviet economy will be able to reap the potential benefits.

THE HOST ENVIRONMENT AND CONDITIONS FOR SUCCESS

As related above, the traditional Soviet economic system provides an inhospitable environment, and it is questionable whether much could be expected from the insertion into it of an alien form, such as the Soviet-Western joint venture. But the situation is now changing in directions that offer much better prospects of success. The process of economic reform, while still in its early stages, is beginning to modify the traditional system in ways that should facilitate the organization and functioning of joint ventures created to enhance Soviet technological capabilities. The general thrust of reform runs counter to the obstacles, rigidities, and disincentives that hinder successful technological innovation, although it is true that at present these very same negative features are complicating the introduction of the reform itself.

Space precludes a detailed discussion of economic reform, but the following points are of direct relevance to the conditions of success for joint ventures. The first important change is the emergence of new, more flexible, forms of ownership alongside, and within, the traditional state sector. The development of cooperatives, leasing arrangements, temporary research collectives, extraministerial associations, and other new forms is helping to break down the rigid, hierarchical ministerial system. It should be easier for joint ventures to thrive within this diversified environment than in the hitherto monolithic economic structure. A second important development is the transition, admittedly hesitant, to market relations, displacing the dominance of administrative methods of economic management. This process should become more meaningful as progress is made in switching from the traditional system of industrial supply to wholesale trade. In turn this will require a far-reaching reform of the industrial price system. If joint ventures can be sure of obtaining the inputs they require through normal

trade relations with other enterprises, the prospects of success will be enhanced to a considerable degree.

Joint ventures operating to strict commercial criteria are more likely to
have an impact if the other organizations of the host environment are also
working to similar principles. A third aspect of the reform is thus highly
relevant, namely the transition to self-financing. Under the new arrangements enterprises have a genuine interest in profitable operation, although
at present the shortcomings of the old price system undoubtedly introduce
serious distortions. It is envisaged that in time a more competitive economic
system will emerge, offering much greater scope for entrepreneurial activity.
While there is little evidence that innovative performance has been improved
by the reform measures so far adopted—and indeed it may have deteriorated
as enterprises have sought easier and quicker means of raising profits—this
should change as the reform deepens.

Taking these and other reform measures together, it can be seen that the
host environment should become friendlier to joint ventures, providing better conditions for their success. For joint ventures to have significant impact
on the technological level of the Soviet economy, it is not sufficient that
each example should function satisfactorily in isolation. A number of self-
contained islands of advanced technology inserted into the existing economic
structure could provide some benefit if chosen with care to meet identified
vital needs. But if under the impact of competition, take-overs and mergers,
movement of personnel, or other means the advanced experience is diffused
more widely and taken up by existing Soviet organizations, the contribution
to technological modernization could be much more substantial. Joint ventures could serve as poles of modern technology and best practice, exercising
not only a direct impact, but promoting diverse secondary effects; and it is
precisely the provisions of the economic reform that should, in principle,
facilitate the achievement of such an outcome.

ACCESS TO TECHNOLOGY

One problem that could frustrate the use of joint ventures to enhance the
technological level of the Soviet economy is the existence of Western technology denial policies, in particular the COCOM system. If controls were
applied only to a relatively narrow range of technologies of manifest, direct,
military significance, few problems would arise. But the scope of the existing
controls is much broader, covering a wide range of advanced production
and information technologies, and other technologies judged to be of potential dual, miliatry and civilian use. Western companies will not be prepared to enter into high-tech joint ventures if they run the risk of running
afoul of COCOM rules, and in some fields Soviet partners may find that
the ventures offered by potential Western partners do not envisage the
transfer of the very latest technology. This is a large issue beyond the scope

of the present chapter. Leaving important general issues to one side, here a few observations must suffice.[10]

Given the centrality of the new information technologies to Soviet technological modernization, it is particularly unfortunate for the Soviet Union that it is precisely this field that is at present most vigorously policed. However, the situation is dynamic, not only because technological change is rapid, but also because an improving international climate offers real possibilities of easing the present restrictions. There would appear to be scope in the near future for a meaningful reduction of the range of controlled items in relation to such technologies as computers, control systems, robotics, machine tools, communication systems, and production equipment for the electronics industry and other sectors.

More relaxed East-West relations and a new openness in economic and military affairs in the Soviet Union offer possibilities for modifying control policies. A range of currently embargoed high-tech, dual-use items could be derestricted but monitored through agreed on-site verification procedures. A joint venture with permanent Western participation could provide an appropriate framework for an initial transition to such a scheme. An additional consideration is the new Soviet policy of partial declassification of hitherto secret military and space-related technologies, including, as noted above, some novel materials developed for the Soviet space shuttle.[11] Not only are new joint venture possibilities emerging, but the move should provide a more informed and complete appreciation of Soviet technological capabilities, which in turn may lead to the removal of some items from the control lists.

A final consideration is Soviet behavior in relation to Western technology denial policies. It cannot be disputed that, in the past, strenuous efforts have been made to obtain embargoed technologies, with resort to covert means and dubious trade diversion practices. In the new climate, when there are widening possibilities for legitimate access to Western science and technology, continuation of such behavior could prove extremely counterproductive. It is surely now in the interests of the highest Soviet authorities to halt the program of illegal technology acquisition. But there is an additional aspect of behavior that could also inhibit the formation of beneficial joint ventures. Soviet organizations in COCOM-embargoed fields appear to have become habituated to the belief that close, stable contacts with Western organizations are not possible. One detects a "go it alone" psychology, according to which the very existence of COCOM has become a pretext for not seeking business opportunities with Western partners, even in fields where such opportunites are now perfectly feasible, albeit not at the very forefront of the technology concerned.[12]

CONCLUSION

The Soviet Union is now faced with the formidable task of raising its level of technology to the latest Western standards. The stratified, pyramidic structure of the economy must be transformed, reducing the technological gulf between its base and apex. Technological modernization cannot be regarded as a once and for all process. What is required is the creation of economic conditions conducive to technological change at a more rapid pace than achieved hitherto by the traditional Soviet economic system. In the process of technological renewal and revitalization, the East-West joint venture has much to offer.

It would be wrong, however, to overstate the role of joint ventures. Many of those created to date are encountering considerable difficulties as they attempt to operate within an only partially reformed host environment. Assuming that these transitional problems can be overcome, joint ventures should facilitate the process of renewal, providing poles of advanced practice and filling vital technological niches. But they can be no substitute for the creation of a genuinely innovative, domestic, technological capability. Essential for this is fundamental economic reform. But economic reform is also a vital condition for the success of joint ventures. The excitement and challenge of the present is that conditions are now favorable for this benign dialectic to unfold.

NOTES

1. See Janos Kornai, *The Economics of Shortage* (New York: North Holland Publishing Co., 1980).

2. G. Stroganov, "Novye materialy i resursosberezhie," *Planovoe khozyaistvo* (1989): 5–9.

3. Stroganov, "Novye materialy," 5–9.

4. See, for example, D. Pipko, "Vse chem schedr 'Buran,'" *Sotsialisticheskaya industriya* (26 August 1989), on the transfer of materials developed for the "Buran" space shuttle program.

5. A joint enterprise is to be created for the production of composite containers and tubing for use in the food, chemicala and construction industries, "Sovetskaya sovetsko-italyanskaya deklaratisiya," *Pravda* (1 December 1989): 1–2.

6. See Alan Poslethwaite, "Russian Revolution," *Flight International* (9 September 1989): 26.

7. For an excellent survey, see Richard W. Judy and Virginia L. Clough, *The Information Age and Soviet Society* (Indianapolis, Ind.: Hudson Institute, 1989).

8. See Harley D. Balzer, *Soviet Science on the Edge of Reform* (Boulder, Colo.: Westview Press, 1989) for a comprehensive review of the current state of Soviet science.

9. For an analysis of Soviet and Western innovative performance drawing on some of the insights of the Austrian economist Joseph Schumpeter, see Philip Hanson and Keith Pavitt, *The Comparative Economics of Research and Development in East and West: A Survey* (London: Harwood Academic Publishers, 1987).

10. On the wider issues, see Julian Cooper, "Western Technology and the Soviet Defense Industry," in Bruce Parrott, ed., *Trade Technology, and Soviet-American Relations* (Bloomington, Ind.: Indiana University Press, 1985), 169–202.

11. See "Oborona b mirnom nastuplenii," *Pravitel'stvennyi vestnik* 17 (1989): 7 and B. Konovalov, "Programma konversiya," *Izvestiya* (28 February 1990): 2. As part of the State Program for Conversion to 1995, some four hundred scientific and technical achievements of the military-space industry are to be applied in the civilian economy.

12. This autarkic mode of thought surfaced during the Supreme Soviet confirmation hearings for the minister of the electronics industry. See BBC, *Summary of World Broadcasts*, SU/0506 C/1 (12 July 1989).

Part II

Joint Ventures in East-West Relations

Chapter 4

Capitalist Investment in Socialist Countries

Lyudmila A. Rodina

JOINT VENTURES: OBJECTIVES, DEVELOPMENTS, RESULTS

The legislative acts regulating the establishment of joint ventures in the socialist countries were introduced as early as the beginning of the 1970s, but this form of cooperation became widely accepted and practiced only since the mid–1980s.[1] The main reason for this delay was the unreadiness of the economies of the socialist countries for this kind of activity. The necessary legal foundation and adequate economic and organizational conditions were absent.

Additionally, foreign partners did not have a clear understanding of the potential and prospects of cooperation and conditions of work. All this gave rise to a feeling of insecurity among Western investors and caused great concern and skepticism about the prospects of a fast return of their investments and future profit margins. They had doubts about the ability to recover capital in case of the liquidation of the joint venture or other extraordinary events. And because of their lack of expertise in such cooperative projects, local partners experienced certain feelings of insecurity and ambiguity about joint ventures as well.

In keeping with world standards, and in order to create more attractive conditions for foreign capital, the original laws and legislative acts regulating joint ventures were amended and revised in almost all socialist countries. The majority of the countries abandoned their 49 percent limit on the share of participation by foreign capital. The restrictions on the spheres of activity of joint ventures were lifted as well. Taxation was reduced from 50 to 60 percent to 20 to 40 percent, and some special rates were introduced (i.e., some new joint ventures are tax-exempt in the first few years until they become profitable). In addition, joint ventures were provided with bank guarantees on the return of their investment and repatriation of profits, and the procedures for registration of new joint ventures were greatly simplified. On the intergovernmental level, agreements were signed to protect foreign investment and to avoid double taxation.

In conjunction with economic reforms taking place in the member countries of the Council for Mutual Economic Assistance (CMEA), these measures created a more favorable atmosphere for investments in joint ventures. By the beginning of 1990, the number of joint ventures in European CMEA countries reached 1,100 (without the Soviet Union). Compared to 1988, in 1990 the distribution of joint ventures by country was as follows: in Hungary, the number of joint ventures rose from 220 to 600; in Bulgaria, from 19 to 35; in Poland, from 23 to 400; and in Czechoslovakia, from 10 to 50.[2] In Romania the number of joint ventures remained constant at 8. In contrast to Romania, the number of registered joint ventures in Yugoslavia almost doubled, from 368 to 670, including 60 ventures that are completely owned by foreign investors.[3]

More than half of the joint ventures set up in the European CMEA countries are involved in industries that determine technical progress: electronic, electrotechnical, chemical, automotive, and others. About one-third of the joint ventures are involved in the service sector of the economy, including consulting in the areas of management and production, technical services, computer programming, and more (see Tables 4.1 and 4.2). This demonstrates the diverse and progressive role of the joint ventures operating in the territory of CMEA countries.

At the present time the total amount of capital invested in joint ventures is insignificant. According to the estimates of the European Economic Commission of the UN, the total value of investments in joint ventures in 1987 was approximately $400 to $500 million, or less than 0.1–0.2 percent of the total production funds of the European CMEA members. By the end of 1989, the amount of capital invested in joint ventures in European CMEA countries increased to $1.5 billion. In general, Western capital is being invested into small enterprises (up to 10 million dollars) mainly in the manufacturing of simple products, and in industries that can provide a fast return on investments. Large-scale investments most often are directed into the service sector and tourism, where risks are lower and returns are quicker than in the manufacturing industry. This shows that not everything has been done to create conditions conducive for the development of joint ventures, and that the transition to the market economy that joint ventures are geared to is not fully complete.

Some of the original objectives in the development of joint ventures have not been reached, particularly the ones concerning an expansion in the exports of joint ventures and an increase in earnings of convertible currencies. Even in countries where joint ventures have been a success, such as Hungary and China, exports account for no more than one-third of joint

Table 4.1
Distribution by Industry of Joint Ventures in Hungary, Poland, Czechoslovakia, and the Soviet Union (October 1989)

Code	Industry	Hungary	Poland	Czech.	USSR
15	Food industry	10	23	--	42
17	Textiles	4	2	1	6
18	Clothing	7	15	--	24
19	Leather	2	--	--	14
20	Wool and wool products	7	11	2	20
21	Paper and paper products	3	2	--	7
22	Printing and publishing	6	2	--	34
23	Coke, refined oil, nuclear fuel	--	--	--	1
24	Chemical products	12	7	1	25
25	Rubber and plastic products	3	3	1	14
26	Non-metalic products	7	10	1	14
27	Pig-iron and steel products	2	--	--	3
28	Metal products	8	12	1	13
29	Machine-building and equipment	13	11	7	48
30	Office equipment and computers	3	2	1	70
31	Electro-technical products	4	--	--	7
32	Information/communication equipment	5	3	2	12
33	Instruments	3	2	--	29
34	Automobile	1	1	--	6
35	Other transportation equipment	1	3	--	4
36	Furniture	4	3	1	28
37	Others	3	6	--	15
	TOTAL	108	118	18	482

Sources: UN Conference on Trade and Development, Resolution 550, Addendum 1 (4 December 1989): 16, 31, 39, 41.

venture output. In Hungary the trade balance in convertible currency of joint ventures is constantly in deficit, and the export quota is lower than the average for the economy. China began receiving hard currency from the operation of joint ventures, including the ones located in the special economic zones, only in 1988. Until now, the amounts of currency have been small. This situation can be explained by the fact that these objectives—exports and currency flow—were chosen without consideration for the mutual interests of partners and without proper evaluation of the potential of such forms of cooperation as joint ventures. Mixed companies that are formed in developed capitalist and developing countries are much better suited to meet such objectives. Under these arrangements, the final stages of production are designed to satisfy the requirements of the local markets by taking into consideration their specific needs and characteristics.

Currently it seems that there is a more realistic and more sober approach to the issue of joint ventures. They are no longer considered to be a magic cure for all problems of the foreign trade and international economic relations. The main objectives of joint ventures now are to attract foreign expertise and know-how, particularly in work management and organization, and then, using this knowledge, to increase the productivity of labor and to increase the quality and technical sophistication of manufactured products. Another important objective is to obtain modern technology and machinery. According to the opinion of Hungarian specialists, the way to measure the effectiveness and expediency of joint ventures is to take into consideration all the results of joint ventures activities, including their influence on the quality and levels of productivity in the related industries as well as the changes that occur in the production methods in general.

LESSONS FROM THE EAST EUROPEAN EXPERIENCE

Even though the conditions for development and operations of joint ventures with the participation of foreign capital are similar in European CMEA countries (see Table 4.2), the end results of their activities drastically differ. The greatest success was achieved by the countries where the transformtion from centralized administrative methods of planning and management to marketlike economic levers had been more complete.

It is appropriate to single out Hungary among all East European countries as the greatest—perhaps only—success story in the area of joint ventures. Although the first acts of legislature concerning joint ventures appeared in Hungary in 1972, by the early 1980s there were only a very modest number of Hungarian joint ventures—in fact, only three. Only with the further development of adequate legal, organizational, and, more importantly, economic and financial conditions conducive for the development of joint ventures did their numbers start to grow: 25 in 1983, 100 in 1985, 222 in 1988, and more than 600 in 1989. By 1989 the total amount of capital invested in Hungarian joint ventures reached 700 million dollars.

Since 1972 there have been more than one hundred legislative acts dealing with issues of joint ventures. Western partners are being guaranteed their share of participation (no longer limited to 49 percent), a reasonable taxation of 20 percent, and tax-exempt status for ventures in priority industries for the first five years. Joint ventures can be established not only in industry, sales, and tourism, but also in banking (there are already a number of banks with mixed capital). The policy of the Hungarian government is highly selective, with preference given to investments in excess of 4 million dollars.

On 1 January 1989, a new law about business enterprises affecting joint ventures came into operation. The opportunities for joint ventures have been broadened: with the permission of the Ministry of Finance and the Ministry of Trade it is now possible to form enterprises completely owned by foreign investors. Foreign participants in joint ventures can now be private individuals, not just legal entities.

Hungary is much further down the road of creating adequate economic conditions for the activities of joint ventures: there is a continuous increase in the degree of autonomy of Hungarian businesses. Between 1985 and 1987, 80 percent of the state-owned enterprises became self-governing and owners of their means of production. More and more businesses obtained rights to export their products. There is a single exchange rate between the forint and the dollar. In order to bring wholesale prices close to the world standards, the wholesale price reform took place. The state abandoned its subsidies to the industries. A wide network of commercial banks was created. All this allowed Hungary to increase the scale and diversification of the foreign investments inside the country.

The Soviet Union may be able to adopt Hungarian practice, particularly in the following areas: the diversity of legal forms in which joint ventures can be created, including enterprises formed on a contract basis without establishing new corporate structures (they are being widely used in Yugoslavia and China); establishing businesses wholly owned by foreign investors; choosing priority areas, from the state's point of view, for the development of joint ventures, supported by a regime of special financial and tax benefits; providing bank guarantees on the return of investment under special conditions; and the transfer of dividends abroad.

Hungarian experience shows that the development of joint ventures is impossible without the creation of a wholesale market in the country, price reforms, a transition to realistic exchange rates between internal and foreign currencies, the development of the banking system, the relinquishment of the monopoly of the state organizations on the control of internal and external trade, and a transfer of the real power over the means of production to enterprises and other producers, thus separating them from the ministries. Precisely because of the lack or insufficient development of such conditions, other East European countries are lagging behind Hungary in the area of joint ventures.

The Bulgarian legislative acts regulating joint ventures are similar to those in Hungary, providing for a large share of participation by foreign partners, fairly low tax rates, and broad spheres of activity. Nevertheless, this country does not seem to attract a lot of interest from foreign investors, mainly because of the difficulties in the development of the Bulgarian economy.

Since the initial formation of a number of Bulgarian-Japanese joint ven-

Table 4.2

Conditions of Development and Activities of Joint Ventures in European
Countries of the Council for Mutual Economic Assistance (CMEA)

	Bulgaria	Hungary	Poland	Czechoslovakia	USSR
1) Type of enterprise	Company with a limited responsibility; joint stock company; company fully owned by foreign partner	Same as Bulgaria + partnership, joint venture	Same as Bulgaria	Undefined by law; most JVs are joint stock companies. Some consortia	Undefined by law; in practice, companies with limited responsibilities, consortia, associations, trade houses, banks
2) Conditions and requirements for establishment of joint venture's (JV) formal permission	If 100% ownership of JV by foreign partner permission from Ministry of Economics and Planning and from Ministry of Foreign Economic Relations	In case of 100% foreign partner's ownership, permission from Ministry of Finance and Ministry of Trade	Permission of agency on foreign investment	Permission of authorities	Permission of higher authorities or permission of Soviet Ministers of the Republic
3) Limitations on the forms of activities	None. Anti-pollution requirements	None. Emphasis on the priority industries	None	None	None
4) Maximum time for examination of JV application	Undefined	90 days	2 months	3 months	Undefined
5) Organization responsible for JV registration		City Court in Budapest	Agency on foreign investments		Ministry of Finance

62

Investments and Property Rights

	Bulgaria	Hungary	Poland	Czech	Soviet
6) Limits on share of foreign partners	None	None	None	None	Up to 100%
7) Participants	Bulgarian legal persons, foreign legal and physical persons	Hungarian legal persons, economic associations without rights of a legal person, physical persons, but not in JVs and associations	Polish and foreign legal and physical persons	Czech legal persons, foreign legal and physical persons	Soviet and foreign legal persons
8) Minimum investments	None	None. If charter fund is more than 25 mln forints ($100K) and foreign contribution is 30%, then tax benefits	25 mln. zloty. If foreign contribution is greater than 20%, then possibility of tax benefits	None	None
9) Use of property	Can be leased	Can be purchased or leased	Can be purchased or leased	Can be leased	Can be leased
10) Protection of property	State guarantees on return of investments	Fully protected on conditions similar to Western	Guaranteed by the Ministry of Finance to be compensated in case of nationalization or expropriation	Compensation in case of expropriation	State guarantees based on intergovernmental agreements on investment protection

Table 4.2 (continued)

	Bulgaria	Hungary	Poland	Czechoslovakia	USSR
Financial Condition					
11) Definition of taxable profits	Sales - expenses - amortization = balance profits	Same as Bulgaria	Same as Bulgaria. 10% of profits can go to charity	Same as Bulgaria	Balance profits - payments to reserve funds - payments to development fund
12) Taxation of profits	30% if foreign investments are 40% (or more) or if they are greater than 1 mln levs in hard currency	35% if profits are less than 3 mln forints ($60K), 40% if greater. 20% in priority industries	40% minus 0.4% for each percent of exports (but no less than 10%)	40%, discounts for social needs and delays of payments of up to 2 years	30% with 2-year maximum delay of payments after declaration of profits. Can be lowered to 10% on Far East
13) Limitation on profit transfers and withdrawals	None	None	None	None	None
14) Additional taxes on profits transfer abroad	15%	None	30%	25%	20%, can be lowered or exempted
15) Other taxes	Taxes on additional costs, regional and local taxes. If foreign share is smaller, then income tax/salary tax	None	Local, communal and municipal taxes, turnover/sales tax	Income tax, possibility of turnover/sales tax	Income tax

64

Banking Operations

16) Permission for foreign currency transactions	Permission of authorities is required	Not allowed except JVs in customs zones	Special permission. 15% of hard currency from export operations must be sold to Polish Export Bank	Not required	Not required
17) Credit requirements in local and foreign currency	Credits obtained in Bulgarian bank or if permission for currency operations is granted in foreign banks	Credits obtained in Hungarian or joint banks. In special economic zones credits obtained in foreign banks with permission of State Bank	Credits obtained in Polish Bank (in hard currency and in zlotys) or in foreign banks with appropriate permission	Same as Poland, with appropriate permission Czech State Bank	Credits obtained in Vnesheconombank, bank specializing in foreign currency transactions, or in foreign banks with permission of Vnesheconombank
18) Fund types	Development funds. If 100% foreign participation, the company decides on issue of funds. Payment into funds after taxes	Independent decision. Payments are made after taxes	Reserve fund, 8% of profits after taxes	Reserve fund, social and cultural needs fund. Contributions into reserve fund can not be less than 5% of profits after taxes	Reserve fund until it reaches 25% of charter capital. Contributions of any size before taxes

Bookkeeping

19) Currency type for bookkeeping purposes	Lev	Forint, convertible currency in special economic zones	Zloty (most common)	Czech krone or other	Ruble (can be in other currency as auxiliary measure)

Table 4.2 (continued)

	Bulgaria	Hungary	Poland	Czechoslovakia	USSR
Relations with National Organizations					
20) Dependence on the state plan	State orders, cannot exceed 2/3 of total production if foreign share is less than 50%	Independent	Independent	Independent	Independent
21) Supplies from the local sources	Same conditions as for state organizations Contracts in levs or hard currency	Same conditions as for state organizations	Same conditions as for state organizations. Can be in hard currency	Based on agreements	Based on agreements, payable in rubles or hard currency
22) Distribution and sales inside the country	Levs or hard currency, market prices, except for products with prices regulated by the Soviet of Ministers	Participation in retail and wholesale activity. Mechanisms against unfair prices. State controls some products	Can be sold inside the country for zlotys or (if there is general permission) for foreign currency		Market prices, ruble and hard currency
23) Foreign trade	Permission is not required except when there are quotas on import-export	Permission is not required, except for licensed products	Permission is not required, except for licensed products	Required permission of State Ministry of Foreign Trade or through foreign trade organizations	Permission after registration with Ministry of Foreign Economic Relations or through import-export organizations
24) Customs fees	Foreign contributions, imports of materials and equipment for JV's production is duty free	Contribution of the foreign partner is tax free. No duties in special economic zones	Same as Bulgaria	No duties	Same as Bulgaria

Personnel

25) Employment of foreign nationals	Allowed	Allowed	Allowed	Allowed	Allowed
26) Wages	Local personnel in levs and hard currency	Local personnel in forints. Foreign workers can transfer up to 50% of their income abroad	Local personnel mostly in zlotys. Foreign worker partially in hard currency	Local partner in state currency	Local partner in rubles. Foreigners in rubles or in foreign currency or by agreement
27) Labor regulations	In accordance with Bulgarian laws	In accordance with the conditions of international labor organizations. Trade unions exist	In accordance with Polish laws	In accordance with Labor Kodex Labor Unions	Act independently, make their own decisions concerning labor. Creation of union of JV workers
28) Management limitations	None	None	None	None	One of two positions: chair of the board, or general manager, can be held by foreign partner

Source: *Executive Guide for East-West Joint Ventures* (Laxenburg, Austria: International Institute for Applied Systems Analysis, January 1990), with considerations for state legislation of CMEA countries.

tures in the early 1980s, there have not been any further developments in
this area. This is related in part to the absence of international agreements
between Bulgaria and other countries for the protection of investments and
avoidance of double taxation.

In the last years, a more accommodating environment for foreign
investors has been created, particularly for involvement in light and
chemical industry and machine building. In accordance with Decree 31
of the Council of Ministers of the People's Republic of Bulgaria (PRB)
on 25 May 1987, which regulated the activity of self-managing business
entities with the involvement of foreign capital, the right to make decisions concerning this activity was awarded to the businesses themselves.
Among other forms of joint ventures, creation of the joint consortia is
considered to have the greatest prospects and potentials. In 1987 five
consortia were formed in Bulgaria, involving German, Austrian, Swiss,
and Finnish firms and banks. Specifically, the ongoing activities within
the framework of consortia include modernization of three plants of the
cellulose and paper conglomerate, reconstruction of the electric equipment factory in Sophia, and automation of production lines in the textile and clothing industries. This form of cooperation is not limited to
involvement of foreign capital and equipment, but allows for the utilization of the marketing network of Western partners for the distribution
of ready-made products in other countries.

Imported machinery, equipment, and raw materials are duty-free if they
are a contribution of the foreign partner to the joint venture or if the
manufactured products are made for export. Joint ventures have the right
to conduct import-export operations. Payment for these activities can be
made in hard currency or in levs. There are no limitations imposed by the
tax system on the scale of operations or on the amount of profits. Total
annual profit of joint ventures is being taxed at the rate of 20 percent.

An important aspect of the aforementioned Decree 31 is the guarantee
to the foreign participant of transfer of profits abroad in hard currency.
Together with the agreement about protection of investments and avoidance
of double taxation, this creates a more attractive climate for foreign investors.

In January 1988, the Bulgarian Ministry of Trade was transformed into
the Ministry of Foreign Economic Relations, while the Ministry of Finance
(together with the State Planning Committee, State Committee on Research
and Technology, Price Committee, and Committee on Labor and Social
Work) was organized into the Ministry of Economy and Planning. These
two ministries are responsible for regulating activities of joint ventures.

In Poland, a decree of 1986 introduced significant changes in the area of
joint ventures. Until then, the only enterprises allowed to participate in joint
ventures belonged to the Polish government. Tax rates were linked to the
volumes of export and fluctuated between 10 and 50 percent. Fifteen to 25

percent of the hard currency generated by joint ventures had to be transferred into the state budget. There were severe limitations imposed on the freedom of management and operations of joint ventures (only a Polish citizen could be a general manager, the Polish share in the enterprise had to exceed 50 percent, and the activities of the enterprise had to be based on the state plan). Difficulties experienced by the Polish economy also played a negative role in the development of joint ventures.

In December 1988, Poland's Council of Ministers passed a new decree regulating the activities of joint ventures. In accordance with this decree, permission for joint venture investments is now granted by a new organ, the Administration of Foreign Investment. Among the areas of expertise and control of this new agency is the development of legal guidelines for joint venture activities, enforcing and promoting government policies, and creating better conditions for attracting foreign capital and other forms of cooperation. Foreign investors were allowed to be majority shareholders in joint ventures or to form companies fully owned by foreign investors, under the condition that the initial investment was at least $50 thousand. The maximum tax rate was lowered from 50 percent to 40 percent. The period of initial favorable tax treatment was extended from two to three years. If the joint venture was engaged in activities in one of the priority industries, such a tax regime could be extended up to six years. The upper limit of obligatory hard currency transfers to the government was lowered from 25 percent to 15 percent. In special cases, the Administration of Foreign Investment could make exceptions on the sums of hard currency that had to be sold to the state. The contribution of foreign investors could not be less than 20 percent of the total initial capitalization of the joint venture. From the Polish side, participants of joint ventures could be state enterprises, legal entities, and private individuals residing in Poland.

There are also changes in the legal act of 1982 regulating activities of "polonial" firms (firms that belong to foreign citizens of Polish descent). The maximum income tax was lowered from 75 to 65 percent. Required volumes of hard currency sales to the government were lowered from 50 to 30 percent. Until now, "polonial" firms played a role of minor importance in the Polish economy, accounting for only 1 percent of the amount of all Polish production. It is believed that greater involvement of foreign capital in the Polish economy will help to attract another $4 billion that is now, according to specialists, in the possession of Polish citizens.

The experience of Romania in the area of joint ventures is considered negative. Out of nine initial joint ventures, only five are operating (four with the involvement of Western capital, and one with a Libyan company). The main problems stem from the overcentralization of Romania and from the difficulties that the Romanian economy is experiencing.

Until now, Czechoslovakia did not have special legislation dealing with the issues of joint ventures. Instead, a combination of special norms and regulations was used. In 1986, the Czech Chamber of Commerce published a special collection of documents entitled "Joint Ventures in CzSSR" regulating the activities of joint ventures. In accordance with this document, the taxation at 40 percent was the lowest compared to the other East European countries. Joint ventures had to employ the mediation assistance of the Czech government export organizations not only for export contracts but also for activities within the country. This did not create positive stimuli for foreign investors, and the total number of joint ventures remained insignificant at only nine.

The analysis of the joint ventures performance in some of the East European countries and corresponding legislative changes demonstrate the active desire of these countries to attract foreign investments in the form of joint ventures. At the same time, this analysis shows that joint ventures represent a form of cooperation oriented toward the market economy. That is why their greatest successes were witnessed in countries where administrative command methods of economy management were more fully substituted by market and free-enterprise forms. Because this process of transformation of management methods is a lengthy and complicated one, it would be naive to expect instant returns and great successes from joint ventures in a short time.

All the same, this method of cooperation is being viewed by East European countries as one of the major ways to raise the technical and technological levels of production. It creates more favorable conditions for attracting investment capital, new technology, and modern methods of management, It promotes progressive changes in the economy and in the structure of production. It raises the technical and technological standards of products and thus causes a gradual increase in exports. However, joint ventures are still one of the most complicated forms of international cooperation. They require a good understanding of mutual capabilities, trust, and, as a rule, previous experience in cooperation. That is why all East European countries first went through a stage of simpler forms of cooperation. They started with the first acts of legislation on international cooperation, which were definitions of the concepts of cooperation and its forms and privileges. Unfortunately, the Soviet Union adopted laws on joint ventures without passing through such early stages of cooperation. That is why many profitable forms of cooperation (subcontracting or joint production with the division of labor or specialization) are not widely used. Soviet partners often reject profitable contracts if the form in which they are offered is not a joint venture. There are also fictitious joint ventures being created that do not really fit the definition of the term. This lowers the effectiveness of cooperation and often discredits the whole concept of the joint venture. In the author's view, the projects of the Soviet-American joint venture Tengizpolymer, and Tyumen' projects, are good examples.

SPECIAL ECONOMIC ZONES

In order to attract foreign investors, European CMEA members began creating special trade and tariff-free zones or declaring such zones in the locations of joint venture operations. Among European CMEA members, this practice of creating special economic zones is most widely used by Hungary. In accordance with Regulation 62 of 16 September 1982 of the Hungarian Ministry of Finance and Ministry of Foreign Trade, Hungary is allowed to establish joint ventures in duty-free zones and to declare the status of special economic zones in the location of joint ventures.[4]

The main objective for creating special economic zones is to increase the export of the products manufactured by joint ventures. Export and import activities of enterprises located in special economic zones are duty-free. In the case of Hungary, this is very important since, as a member of the General Agreement on Tariffs and Trade (GATT), Hungary cannot delay or annul the payment of tariffs under any other conditions.

Because imports into the zone are duty-free, it is cheaper to obtain foreign parts, equipment, and resources for the special zone than for ordinary joint ventures or for local Hungarian enterprises. If goods manufactured within the zone are being exported, then foreign-made components and parts are still duty-free. If these products are sold inside the country, outside of special zones, then foreign-made parts are taxed as ordinary imports with the burden of extra cost carried by the consumers. If costs of Hungarian raw resources, communications, labor, and services, low in comparison with the world market, are taken into consideration, it is clear that the total costs of manufacturing are low. This means that it is very profitable to produce in duty-free zones if the bulk of the production is export oriented.

Duty-free zones are being treated as foreign territories not only according to customs, but also in the way they relate to the rest of Hungary and to other countries. Enterprises located in the special zones are allowed to keep their funds in the amounts limited by their charter in Hungarian banks and financial institutions. They are free to deposit all the money in excess of charter capital in any Hungarian or foreign bank. They are free to manage their money and use it for any purposes, including import-export operations, without special government approval. Salaries of the foreign personnel employed by such companies can be fully transferred abroad (not just 50 percent, as in ordinary joint ventures). Pay scale is higher here than in the rest of the country and salaries are determined by way of agreement between an employer and employee.

Contributions of Hungarian and foreign partners can be made in hard currency only. Business deals and bookkeeping are done in a previously agreed-upon hard currency.[5] Enterprises located in the zones can apply for bank credits in Hungary or abroad. The transfer of goods between the zone and the rest of the country can be done only with the permission of appropriate agencies, and products that enter Hungary from the zones are subject to import duties.

Such zones are widely used by foreign companies for storage, safekeeping, repacking (for example, for obtaining tariff and other benefits for import into other neighboring countries), and such. Zones have to be surrounded by a fence of no less than three meters in height. It is prohibited to reside in the zones, and retail operations are prohibited as well.

Joint ventures operating in the duty-free zones can buy forints from Hungarian financial institutions. These funds in forints may then be stored in the financial institution and later used for payments of taxes, salaries, rents, services, appropriations, construction, repairs, and other work performed on the territory of the duty-free zone.

Joint ventures in duty-free zones are exempt from some of the regulations that control the activities of other Hungarian enterprises, specifically including regulations dealing with issues of profits, salaries, prices, investments, state control, procedures for funds formation, financial procedures, business trips, and the purchase and use of cars.

Regulations concerning workers' wages and compensations are different from the procedures in the rest of Hungary. There is no salary cap. It is legal to receive bonuses and additional pay resulting from the enterprise's greater savings and greater profitability. Such bonuses and additional pay are free from the taxes for retirement funds, social security, and other funds. In the case of foreign employees in a joint venture, their work conditions and salary have to be predetermined and agreed upon by the participants in the joint venture, otherwise, Hungarian labor laws are in effect.

Acting at the request of the foreign partner of a joint venture located in a duty-free zone, the Hungarian National Bank or Bank for Foreign Trade can guarantee a transfer abroad of its share of profits (after the required taxes and fees have been paid), and in case of a liquidation of the joint venture, a transfer of its share of capital and property.

In 1987 there were only three Hungarian joint ventures operating in duty-free zones: one joint venture with Denmark for the construction of portable homes, one with Canada for the production of automotive brake pads, and one with Germany for organizing shows and exhibits. The first joint venture, Hunflexbau, formed in January 1984 in conjunction with a Danish company, had folded because of the nonpayments of the Danish firm. The original plans stated that the beginning of the construction of portable wooden houses designed for export was supposed to start in the city of Sopron by the end of 1984. In 1987 there were five more joint ventures formed, and by 1989 their numbers surpassed forty.

There are plans under consideration for creating a Central European free economic zone in the area of the city of Sopron, with the adjacent border territory approximately equal in size (Austrian area) on the other side of the border. There are preliminary plans for the creation of special economic zones in the area around the cities of Zokhoni, Ozdah, and Mishkoltz.

The example of Hungary was closely followed by Bulgaria. Decree 2242 by the State Soviet of People's Republic of Bulgaria (PRB) on 14 July 1987, allows formation of free-trade (duty-free) zones on the territory of the country. Their main objectives are the development of production, services, trades, and other activities helpful for the diversification and facilitation of exports. Such activities can be conducted by foreign legal entities and private individuals independently or in cooperation with Bulgarian self-governing commercial organizations.

Under the umbrella of Decree 2242, rules of the Soviet of Ministers of the PRB dealing with the issues of creation and operation of free economic zones were developed and published. Such zones are created with the permission of the Soviet of Ministers at the request of state organizations, or at the request of interested self-governing commercial organizations. They submit a petition with a description of their purposes, areas of activity, and sources of income (in levs and in hard currency) needed for organizing the zone. This petition is accompanied by architectural and engineering plans for the future zone, its fencing and marking.

The Ministry of Foreign Relations determines the conditions and requirements of operation of the Bulgarian commercial organizations inside the zone. (This might include requirements and specifications on sorting, marking, packing, and storing of imported products destined for future export.)

A free-trade zone is an isolated part of a country's territory where economic activity is duty-free. This territory has to be properly fenced and marked. Products that were manufactured or processed in the zone or imported into the zone cannot be stored there for more than five years.

All payments related to activities in the zone, among the zones, and between the zone and the rest of the country are conducted in hard currency. The state is not responsible for payments or other obligations of zones, enterprises, and businesses.

Imports as well as exports from the zone that are the result of commercial activity within the zone are duty-free. The same rule applies to contacts and trade among the zones. Profits obtained as a result of trade, manufacturing, or other commercial activity inside the zone are tax-free.

Products and services of the free-trade zones sold inside the country are paid for in hard currency. Profits are taxed at the rate of 30 percent if they are transferred abroad and 20 percent if they are reinvested in Bulgaria.

It is legal to conduct all kinds of activities within the free-trade zones, such as production, manufacturing, loading, unloading, storage, and cargo treatment, and to perform operations in brokerage, banking, insurance, credits, and commerce. Activities not permitted within the zones are those harmful to the environment, hazardous to human health and hygiene, or forbidden by the Bulgarian legislature.

In accordance with the agreement on special zones, a special organization was created for zone establishment and management. All the national and state resources in the zone territory, such as land, water, forests, and buildings, are under the control of this organization. It is also responsible for developing zone infrastructure, such as roads, fencing, and piers, and for everyday social and cultural life in the zone.

This organization leases the land parcels, buildings, and other structures and provides electrical, water, telephone, telex, and other services. Its rates are closely related to the world prices on such services. After collecting rents or payments, this organization pays the appropriate Bulgarian agencies.

Activities of foreign legal entities and private individuals are regulated by agreement with the organization managing the zone. Agreements on the creation of joint ventures are subject to the general Bulgarian legislature that deals with these issues.

At the present time, in accordance with the decree of the Soviet of Ministers of 7 March 1980, free-trade zones have been created in the areas of Vidin and Ruse. The Bulgarian side is undertaking steps for establishing commercial activities in these two zones. There have been organizations established within the zone whose primary tasks are building the zone's infrastructure and supervising the zone. Such organizations are independent legal entities and are completely self-sufficient financially.

In the duty-free zone in the city of Ruse, one hundred hectares have already been developed of the total area of eight hundred hectares. A first business agreement involving the Austrian firm, Electrobrigita, has been signed. This firm will rent warehouses and storage facilities in the zone, and will provide different goods and services to the diplomatic personnel in Bulgaria and Romania. Projects exist on the creation of small (up to fifty employees) manufacturing facilities for assembling electronic and electrotechnical equipment. These projects involve Austrian and German firms. There was an agreement reached with the U.S. firm, Dow Chemical. According to this agreement, a Bulgarian-U.S. joint venture will be involved in the distribution of chemical products manufactured within the zone.

The duty-free zone in Vidin is still developing, with work being done on fencing, roads, and warehouses. Plans for the further development of such zones include the Black Sea coastal region near Varna and Burgasa, and areas on the Greek and Yugoslavian borders. The major limiting factor for development in these zones is the shortage of funds and construction capabilities.

Despite some very attractive features of special zones, such as low rent, cheap services, low labor costs ($500–$600 a month per person), opportunities for industrial activity, and advantageous geographic location, foreign companies are still very reserved in their approach to participation in the zones. Many of them share the opinion that the main deterrents in organizing free-trade zones are limitations of Bulgarian legislation (limits on profits, transfers, and ambiguities in relation to other legislative acts concerning import-export activities), poor forecasting on the future profits (there is no precise information on Bulgarian labor costs, resources, or rents), differences in economic organization, and methods of management.

The first Polish duty-free zone, closely resembling Bulgarian zones in its objectives and methods of operation, was established in November 1989. The creation of this zone became possible after auxiliary legal acts of 1986 and 1988 allowed Polish citizens to participate in joint ventures and a decree of the Polish Council of Ministers on duty-free zones in 1988 declared their formation. The city of Schetin was chosen as a location for the trade-free zone. The zone itself is being managed by the joint stock company Szczecin-Swinoujscie. Partners in this company are the port administration company, Polska Zeluga Morska, the import-export transportation company, Hartwig, and the city government of Szczecin.

Plans of the formation of the duty-free zone in the city of Schetin were rigorously discussed in 1983–84. The project was proposed by a number of "polonial" firms. In 1984, at the initiative of the Chamber of Export Trade, a referendum on the trade-free zone was conducted. The result of this referendum was a decision to establish a duty-free zone. However, because of the virtual economic blockade of Poland on the part of Western countries, this task could not be accomplished. In the last few years, the project of the duty-free zone in Schetin came into light again. A detailed plan for the establishment and development of the zone was carefully worked out. The experience of duty-free zones in China, Yugoslavia, Romania, and Bulgaria was extensively studied.

The first stage of zone development will incorporate such conventional warehouse and transport operation as loading, unloading, sorting, cleaning, servicing of ships, repairs, and social services. These activities do not require large-scale initial investments, since they will take place within the limits of the already operating seaport. For these purposes, the allocated land parcels in the Schetin port will house storage facilities where Polish and foreign businesses will be able to exhibit their wares and conduct trade and brokerage operations.

As the numbers of participating foreign and domestic companies grow, so will the technical capabilities of the zone increase. Numerous joint ventures will be formed to increase the zone's production and service potential. It is assumed that the duty-free zone will gradually transform itself into a zone of intensive economic activity, like the Chinese special economic zones.

Similar ideas form the foundation of the plans for a duty-free zone in Gdansk.

The transition to the second stage of economic reform in Poland, implying greater economic freedoms for Polish enterprises and local governments, gave rise to a new approach to the problem of special economic zones. The principles of free economic zones are to extend to portions of the townships and other territorial units. Thus, leadership of one of the Warsaw boroughs offered a project that would transform their borough Mokotov into a free economic zone. This project was accepted favorably by the city authorities. Declaring Mokotov a special economic zone will help to increase the rates of production in electronics, biotechnology, and other high-tech industries where the involvement of foreign capital and expertise is extensive.

A similar initiative came from the city government of Krakow, which plans to organize a duty-free zone in the vicinity of Valitze airport and a special industrial zone on the territory surrounding Lenin's metallurgical factory. On this land, leased from the state, the building of small modern manufacturing and service industries is proposed.

In Yugoslavia, as far back as 1953, it was decided to establish duty-free zones. However, a special legislature regulating their activities was developed only in 1963. By 1985 there were eight duty-free zones operating in the sea and river ports of Kopar, Pula, Rieka, Zadar, Kardelevo, Bar, Belgrad, and Zagreb. They were mainly used for international transit through the territory of the country and for storage. Their narrow specialization did not allow them to fully utilize the beneficial geographic location of the country.

At the end of 1985 two new laws were developed, one concerning the duty-free zones, the other the special conditions of the import-export financial activities in the duty-free zones. Now the development of such zones is closely linked to the attempts to stimulate export-oriented production and services. Export of goods manufactured within the zone is duty-free. Sales of the zone-manufactured products inside Yugoslavia are taxed as other exports.

An organization of cooperative labor with the rights of land lease on the site of the future zone can establish a zone. An agreement on the establishment of the zone defines all the rights and obligations of the zone's participants and founders in relation to its operation.

Zone formation is sanctioned by the Union on Executive Assembly. A zone-founding organization has to submit a project for future zone development, including justification for zone existence and technical, financial, and organizational plans for zone operation. With the development of the new laws and legislative acts concerning the duty-free zones, zone founders have to adjust their activities to comply with the new regulations within one year.

The diverse type of activities permitted in the Yugoslav zones are analogous to those that exist in Poland. To enhance exports and to improve operations of the zone's ventures, Yugoslavia enterprises are allowed to import into the zones, duty-free, a variety of parts, instruments, raw materials, and such. If these products are being used for other purposes, then the zone founding organization can be fined from 1 to 10 million dinars.

Involvement of foreign capital is of crucial importance for the development of export-oriented production within the zones. There are joint ventures with the involvement of Western investors (mainly American) who operate in the free zones on the Adriatic coast of Yugoslavia. However, in general, Western firms have expressed only limited interest in joint ventures. The main obstacles are the issues of ownership of the invested capital and the inequality of partners in the decision-making processes of the joint ventures. There is a scope of other problems and issues that, according to the opinion of Yugoslavian specialists, require resolution. That is why the existing legislative acts regulating zone activities will probably be further amended.

In Romania, the first duty-free zone was established in the port of Asulin in 1977. Its principals and regulations are similar to those in Yugoslavia. Because of severe difficulties in the Romanian economy, this zone is practically nonfunctional. There are plans for establishing a new economic zone with special privileges in the new Romanian port, Konstanza-South. The realization of such projects will depend on the condition of the Romanian economy.

All in all, special economic zones are viewed by the European countries of CMEA as a vehicle for attracting foreign capital, increasing effectiveness of foreign trade, and activating the countries' participation in the international division of labor.

It is reasonable to suggest that the above-mentioned types of trade-free zones could find application in the Soviet Union. At the end of 1988 a number of Soviet organizations were required to develop legislative acts in this field. Because of the sharp disagreements in approaches to objectives, requirements, and conditions for the creation of such zones, in September 1989 a compromise decision was reached to create, on an experimental basis, the first joint enterprise zones in the following areas: in Nakhodka (Far East), a zone for the processing of natural resources; in Viborg, on the border with Finland, a scientific-industrial zone; in Novgorod, a tourist-industrial zone. Each zone will have its own specialization. This will allow the best regime and the most optimal conditions for zone operation to develop, in accordance with the specific requirements and characteristics of the region.

The free-enterprise zone in Viborg will take the shape of a technopolis. The proximity of this zone to Finland and Leningrad's research centers and high standards of infrastructure will help to utilize the research capabilities of both sides, accelerate the application of the results in electronic research, and facilitate marketing of the new products. In accordance with earlier proposals of Finnish partners, joint development and production of personal computers will be a priority issue.

Another Finnish proposal certainly deserving attention is the project of creating a special industrial zone in the area of Imatra-Svetogorsk. This will help to better utilize the region's land and forest resources, industrial potential, and experience in joint ventures. This region can also be included in the Viborg zone or become its extension (maybe together with the area of Saimen Canal).

The first stage in the development of the Nakhodka zone will be oriented toward multistage processing of natural resources: lumber, medicinal herbs, and sea products. Among the advantages of Nakhodka are its three major ports, well-developed (by local standards) infrastructure, and experience in international cooperation. Here, conditions for the development of tourism and the construction of health and rehabilitation centers are present as well.

In addition to Nakhodka, there are other projected special zones, such as Grodskogo—a large railroad junction on the border with China, and the town of Posvet on the lake Hanko near the Chinese and Korean borders. In the future these areas might be suitable for establishing their own economic zones or become extensions of the Nakhodka zone.

As for Novgorod, proposals have been advanced to create a tourist-industrial zone based on local historical and cultural attractions, as well as enterprises for the manufacture of consumer video equipment, including enterprises undergoing conversion. Another advantage of Novgorod is its proximity to Leningrad, the Baltic republics, and Scandinavia. However, the people of the area have sharply rejected the idea of a special economic zone, partially because they were not informed or consulted about the future plans and projects of zone development.

In the course of this experiment, economic mechanisms of zone operation will be tested with appropriate changes and corrections. This experience will be reflected in the future legislation. Such an approach has its good and bad sides. On the one hand, it allows for flexibility in the solution of specific problems; on the other hand, it creates certain uncertainties and insecurities.

Some of the questions dealing with the zones' development and operation are still unanswered. It is still unclear who will manage the zones—local soviet or some special administrative body—and what will be the relations among them in dividing rights and responsibilities. Will the Soviet enterprises existing inside the zone be subordinate to the ministries, or will they be made independent through leasing and self-sufficiency? How will the problems of pricing and hard currency/ruble exchange be resolved? The need for special currency for servicing the zones ("hard" ruble) is clear. This currency will be used for business as well as for social needs. It is hard to imagine the development of market relations within the zones without such convertible currency. It is better to solve all these and other questions (tariffs, taxation, etc.) for the whole country, in the form of new legislation. This will open the way for initiative in all the republics who, using it as a model and foundation, will develop their own economic zones with the cooperation of the centralized government agencies.

At the present time, in many republics—such as Estonia, Lithuania, and the Ukraine—there are ready plans for establishing free economic zones (Tartu, Odessa, and Tallin). This demonstrates the diverse and far-reaching opportunities for this form of cooperation in the territory of the Soviet Union. However, for such plans to be carried out, a radical economic reform is needed. This reform will include price reform, conversion of the ruble (or establishment of a more realistic ratio between the ruble and other currencies), creation of a wholesale market, and development of market relations. The future of the joint venture will depend on how successful the Soviet Union will be on its road to progress in solving all these questions.

NOTES

1. Such acts were passed in Yugoslavia in 1971, Hungary in 1972, Poland in 1976, Bulgaria in 1980, and Czechoslovakia in 1985. Similar legislative acts have existed in Vietnam since 1977, China since 1979, Mongolia since 1980, Cuba since 1982, and North Korea since 1984.

2. The additional seven hundred joint ventures mentioned in the press are of a somewhat different nature. The majority of them are owned by polonial capital; in other words, they belong to foreigners of Polish descent and are geared mainly toward ending the deficit of consumer goods in Poland. For this reason, they are not included here.

3. UN Conference on Trade and Development, Resolution 550, Addendum 1 (4 December 1989): 3.

4. Territory can be declared a duty-free zone with the approval of the All-Hungarian Board of Tariffs and Finance, coordinated with the Ministry of Foreign Trade, Ministry of Internal Affairs, and Ministry of Transportation and Communications. For establishing a business or an enterprise on the territory of a duty-free zone, permission of the Ministry of Foreign Trade and of the Ministry of Finance is needed.

5. The Minister of Finance can require some paperwork to be done in forints.

Chapter 5

Internationalization of the Soviet and Other Socialist Economies: Lessons from the Chinese Experience

John Morton

Since the 1970s most socialist countries have adopted some law designed to encourage the formation of for-profit ventures between market-oriented Western business entities and their state-owned or privately owned counterparts in the East. While these joint ventures are looked upon with great favor, no socialist government has seriously suggested that the creation of East-West joint ventures will be a panacea for the host country's economic ills. Instead, joint ventures are intended to be a vehicle within which capital, foreign exchange, technology, and management expertise will be transferred into the host country in a way that may find more general application throughout the host country's economic system. At its peak, for example, foreign investment in the People's Republic of China was but a small fraction of that country's GNP. Accordingly, joint ventures will not, by themselves, solve the economic problems of the socialist economies. At best, they may provide a model for emerging market-oriented domestic industries and a nucleus for a local, entrepreneurial network of support industries that will provide sourcing and distribution products and services to the country's core manufacturing industries.

SETTING THE STAGE FOR THE CHINA EXPERIENCE

In early summer 1979, the Fifth National People's Congress of the People's Republic of China endorsed Chairman Deng Xiaoping's economic readjustment policy and ratified a series of criminal, organizational, and economic laws that both opened China's doors to outside investments and, to some extent, permitted local economic initiatives. In addition, the courts and legal system that had been effectively disbanded under Mao Zedong in 1957 were reinstituted, and on 1 July 1979, China adopted the Law of the

People's Republic of China on Joint Ventures Using Chinese and Foreign Investment.

After the enactment of this new joint venture law, there followed in very rapid succession a multitude of social, political, and legal reforms intended to stimulate China's sagging economy, update its technology, and infrastructure, enhance Deng's hold on power, and integrate the country more closely into the world economic system. Throughout the process, Chinese citizens were encouraged to act with greater independence in the economic sphere, even as they were subject to continued suppression in areas relating to politics and freedom of expression. More than 1 million party and government officials loyal to the old ways under Mao were forced to retire. As China's doors opened, many thousands of Chinese college graduates traveled to the West for advanced education, and small private enterprises were encouraged by the government. At one point, Deng Xiaoping announced that it was no longer inappropriate to be "rich and Chinese."

Development, investment, and change followed at a breathtaking pace. Westerners pumped several billion dollars into the Chinese economy during the 1980s, and a new and aggressive group of Chinese entrepreneurs emerged that took Deng's approval of wealthy Chinese seriously. What occurred has been described by some Westerners as a feeding frenzy of foreign and local investment that left in its wake an overheated and inflated economy along with widespread popular resentment toward the emerging wealthy class, the pervasive corruption among the ruling elite, and the intrusive constraints on personal liberties. Deng's reforms had clearly opened the door to more than just economic development, and it was not clear to Western observers in the late 1980s that the Chinese government could control the social and economic backlashes that Deng's economic reforms had unleashed.

Discontent on the part of Chinese intellectuals and students coupled with the frustration among workers in China as to mounting inflation, increasing corruption, and uneven distribution of wealth resulted in the now infamous student-led demonstrations in Tiananmen Square in spring 1989. The official reaction to the Tiananmen demonstrations appeared, initially, to be one of restraint and tolerance. This outward impression of forbearance, however, may have been caused more by invisible (and temporarily disabling) policy and power struggles within the government than by careful analysis and decisions by the Chinese leadership. In any event, on 4 June 1989, elements of the 27th People's Army moved into Tiananmen Square in force and brutally shut down the demonstrations—and, perhaps, the country. A large number of Western business people fled China (although most have since returned), and Western governments suspended millions of dollars worth of arms sales and direct assistance grants. In addition, the World Bank held up a 60 million dollar agricultural loan and put an additional 700 million dollars in other credits on hold. The Asian Development Bank shelved a proposed 25 million dollar loan to the People's Bank of China, and the Japanese government and Japanese banks withheld hundreds of millions of dollars of credits previously designated for joint Japanese-Chinese development projects. Perhaps most significantly, a multitude of East-West projects in various stages of planning, negotiations, or implementation were slowed down, postponed, or canceled, substantially impairing the economic development process in China.

THE CHINESE FOREIGN ECONOMIC LEGAL STRUCTURE

Since 1982 China has enacted many laws, rules, and regulations designed to encourage foreign trade and investment in and with the People's Republic of China. These laws have included the joint venture law previously mentioned, as well as laws relating to taxation, imports and exports, foreign exchange controls, special economic zones, resident representative offices, patents, trademarks, economic contracts and technology transfer, wholly owned foreign enterprises, dispute resolution, labor, insurance, and advertising. In April 1986, China adopted a new civil code that became effective on 1 January 1987, for the declared purpose of protecting the "legitimate rights and interests of citizens" and "juristic persons."[1] The new code included Chinese-foreign joint ventures within the definition of "Chinese juristic persons," thereby affording to such joint ventures the same civil rights and protections that are afforded to other Chinese citizens. The 1987 civil code affords protection to the property of a joint venture and provides mechanisms to resolve disputes and enforce contracts.

In addition to these laws, on 15 January 1986 the Chinese State Council announced provisions to balance foreign exchange receipts and expenditures within East-West joint ventures located within China and on 2 December 1986 promulgated a model bankruptcy law applicable only to state-owned enterprises effective in conjunction with the proposed State Enterprise Law. In April 1988, the first session of the Seventh National People's Congress adopted the relevant law pertaining to industrial enterprises, which became effective on 1 August 1988 and which, in Article 19, expressly provides that an enterprise may be terminated if, among other reasons, "it is declared bankrupt in accordance with the law."[2] The Chinese also promulgated in 1988 a law enabling the creation of Sino-foreign cooperative enterprises, which permits the establishment of cooperative enterprises between Chinese and Western business entities without much of the bureaucratic entanglements and delays that typically accompany the creation of East-West joint ventures in China.

Initially, the laws of the People's Republic of China pertaining to the structure, operation, governance, and termination of foreign enterprises operating within Chinese territory, whether as independent entities or as partners in East-West joint ventures, were few, brief, and extremely general.

With the passage of time, however, hundreds of pages of laws, regulations, rules, and provisions have been promulgated not only by the central government in Beijing, but also by the several Chinese provinces, many of the more significant municipalities, the port city zones, and the special economic zones. These laws are frequently published with very little prior notice and, taken together, create a morass that substantially increases both the risk and the complexity of doing business within the People's Republic of China.

Picking a path through the regulatory morass, however, is one of the easier problems related to doing business within the People's Republic of China. During the 1980s, foreigners attempting to establish economic beachheads in China had to overcome a seemingly endless stream of cultural, social, and infrastructural issues that directly affected their prospects for business success. Nevertheless, considerable business progress was made in China during this period.

From 1980 to 1989, billions of dollars poured into China from the West to finance a wide variety of transactions, including joint ventures, contract manufacturing arrangements, technology transfer agreements, barter arrangements, and East–West trading transactions. Most of this investment was focused, by Chinese design, in the fourteen port cities and in the special economic zones located along China's Pacific Rim. The combination of rapid growth and bureaucratic gate keeping resulted in substantial social and political turmoil as Chinese entrepreneurs and workers competed with each other to attract or take advantage of the many new opportunites within the developing regions, and as some corrupt government officials began to take advantage of opportunites afforded by the seamless web of required approvals and permits. Accordingly, as foreign investment in China grew, so also did corruption.

THE SOVIET EXPERIENCE: A CONTRAST

Against this backdrop, the Soviet Union began a modernization program of its own, with the adoption on 13 January 1987, by the Presidium of the USSR Supreme Soviet, of a decree permitting the establishment and operation within Soviet territory of certain joint enterprises involving Soviet and foreign organizations. This joint venture decree was part of Gorbachev's four-pronged reform movement, designed to reform the Soviet Union's policies with respect to foreign relations, economic and social attitudes, and political structures. In short, the Soviet Union declared its intention to begin the process of sweeping reforms on several fronts simultaneously, including not only legal reforms (inspired by those established in Hungary and China), but also economic, social, and political reforms designed to loosen the grip of the Communist party and increase individual liberties throughout the Soviet system.

The contrasts between the Soviet and Chinese approaches to reform are striking. The Chinese began their reform process in the countryside, permitting the establishment of "responsibility plots" for farm families to raise food for their own use or for sale at a profit in open and free markets. This reform created an immediate and significant increase in the domestic food supply and became a model for subsequently authorized urban entrepreneurial activities involving small businesses such as restaurants and retail shops. Throughout this process, China kept a tight reign on personal liberties and maintained the position of the Communist party as the exclusive source of power within China.

The Soviet Union, by contrast, began its economic reform movement among its intellectual, urban population and was very late in coming to the realization that increasing the food supply is a necessary cornerstone to any reform movement in Eastern Europe. As a result, the Soviet Union permitted private cooperative business ventures before it was able to provide essentials such as food, clothing, and shelter to substantial segments of its population. The Soviet Union did, however, recognize (as the Chinese did not, and still have not) that economic reform can not occur in the absence of social, cultural, and political change.

During my frequent visits both to the Soviet Union and to China, I have witnessed firsthand the consequences of the Chinese and Soviet approaches to reform. In my view, the predominant feeling among Soviet workers is one of frustration and discontent largely due to the pervasive shortages of virtually all consumer goods—from food to frisbees. Chinese workers, on the other hand, appear to be frustrated by their severe working conditions and by intrusive government political indoctrination campaigns. Soviet intellectuals (who manage to find and obtain sufficient, if not bountiful, supplies of food and consumer goods) seem to be primarily concerned about the fundamental stability of their social and economic systems during the transition from a centrally controlled, single-party system to a market-oriented, pluralistic system. Chinese intellectuals, on the other hand, are not only upset with the obvious and heavy-handed curbs on intellectual freedom, but also with the government's system of intimidation and sanctions to suppress dissent.

While the Chinese and the Soviets have many common problems, the Soviets seem to enjoy substantially greater intellectual freedom and substantially less material wealth than the Chinese. Perhaps the greater tolerance for the status quo in China relates in part to the general availability in China of ample (if not generous) supplies of food, clothing, housing, and consumer goods. I have no doubt, however, that the Chinese tolerance of intrusive restrictions on personal liberty is based, in part, on a palpable fear of chaos that is directly traceable to the almost total collapse of law and order during the Cultural Revolutions. In the Soviet Union, on the other hand, the fear of change is considerably offset by widespread shortages of food and consumer goods that provide urgent motivation for reform.

The Soviet and Chinese approach to reorganization started from very different perspectives but may have ended up in substantially the same place. In China, reform started with the agricultural sector and moved reluctantly to the cities. In the Soviet Union, the reform movement started in the cities and moved reluctantly into the countryside. More significantly, however, in the Soviet Union economic reform was accompanied by cultural and political reform, whereas in China, cultural and political reform were resisted, and economic reform was allowed to progress at a frenetic pace. In both systems, the consequences of reform have been social, political, and economic instability. The future is unclear for each government and each society. It is clear, however, that the next several years will be characterized by rapid change in both societies and by the prospect for severe political and social upheaval.

POPULAR RESISTANCE TO ECONOMIC REFORMS

The proliferation of East-West joint ventures and other for-profit activities in China and in the Soviet Union has been somewhat inhibited by the surprising degree of grass-roots resistance to East-West joint ventures and other for-profit activities that run afoul of popular notions of economic propriety ingrained over decades of internal social and political indoctrination.

In this regard, the cultural impact and popular acceptance of the current wave of economic reforms in the socialist countries of Asia and Eastern Europe has not been consistent. For example, countries with relatively recent experience with free-market systems, such as Hungary and Poland, have found it much easier to make the ideological leap. Countries without that experience, however, such as the Soviet Union, have found the transition much more complicated because of grass-roots resistance to those aspects of free-enterprise and market systems that appear to threaten the relatively risk-free existence experienced by most Soviet working people throughout their lifetimes. There is fundamental resistance to a reduction in the government-fabricated and -subsidized safety net, which has assured virtually all citizens a minimal but relatively secure standard of living. In China and the Soviet Union, there have been sporadic acts of violence by populations against local entrepreneurs who appear to have profited at the expense of their neighbors through their permitted private entrepreneurial ventures.

In both economies, the absence of a convertible currency and individual and institutional incentives to achieve efficient, market-oriented, quality-assured products have resulted in widespread shortages of consumer goods that government planners were hoping to supplement through the local production activities of native entrepreneurs. Because they are the first producers in their respective markets (monopolists), the local entrepreneurs who are able to produce desirable goods for local consumption can command premium prices for their goods and, in fact, can accumulate wealth at a significantly higher rate and level than their neighbors producing traditional goods.

Because of the sudden transition to a market-oriented economic system, there has been no time for working people to adjust to or even comprehend the complex concepts of supply and demand, competition, or sales and marketing—all of which energize and control market-based economies. As a result, the immediate and widespread popular reaction to many of the new individual initiatives and to the short-term monopolies enjoyed by these early entrepreneurs is one of suspicion, resentment, and sometimes violence.

A COMPARISON OF THE SOVIET AND CHINESE APPROACHES TO REFORM

Approximately eighteen months after the USSR Supreme Soviet adopted a decree permitting East-West joint ventures within Soviety territory, it promulgated a law on cooperatives that permitted private Soviet citizens to unite voluntarily to form an enterprise to conduct economic activities on a for-profit basis. During a recent visit to the Soviet Union, I met with five or six cooperatives that had been organized for purposes ranging from the development and sale of computer software to the development, construction, and operation of resort hotels. In more than one instance, these cooperatives had access to millions of Soviet rubles, and were well along in the process of establishing commercially viable business activities within the Soviet Union. In one case the cooperative with which I was working had actually entered into a joint venture with an Italian and a French company to provide educational and business consulting services within the Soviet Union and was involved in the process of negotiating to become the Soviet distributor for an American manufacturer of office equipment. By 1 January 1990 there were 193,400 cooperatives employing 4,851,500 people, and this figure was growing rapidly despite a number of obstacles to the development of cooperatives.[3]

In China, on the other hand, entrepreneurialism involving substantial capital investments and large enterprises is not as widespread as in the Soviet Union. While the Chinese appear to be more comfortable with notions of free enterprise and entrepreneurialism, their entrepreneurial activities, although widespread, have been limited in scope and scale. In contrast, some of the entrepreneurial cooperatives in the Sovet Union appear to have virtually unlimited resources (in rubles) and plans that range from the construction and operation of multimillion-ruble, world-class resort hotels to the creation of local factories, shops, and restaurants. As a consequence of these and other differences, most East-West joint ventures in China are between Western business entities and Chinese enterprises controlled by ministries, provinces, municipalities, or districts, while many East-West joint ventures in the Soviet Union involve privately owned, for-profit cooperatives as the Soviet partner.

In addition to structural differences, there are substantive differences between the joint venture laws and practices of China and the Soviet Union. China, for example, promulgated in 1986 a law providing a variety of mechanisms for balancing the foreign exchange requirements of Chinese-foreign joint ventures located within its territory. A similar body of law does not yet exist in the Soviet Union.

In general, the laws of both China and the Soviet Union require that all joint ventures generate sufficient foreign exchange from their own operations to meet their foreign exchange needs. Certain joint ventures, such as Western-style hotels located in China or the Soviet Union, have no problem meeting these needs because virtually all of their sales are to foreigners who pay for their services with convertible currencies. Manufacturing joint ventures, however, generally have to obtain foreign exchange through the foreign sale for convertible currency of their manufactured goods. These Chinese- or Soviet-based manufacturing joint ventures typically require foreign exchange to import necessary parts, materials, and components that cannot be obtained locally, to pay in foreign exchange the salaries of Western employees based in China or in the Soviet Union, and to expatriate in foreign exchange the profits allocable to the foreign partner. The requirement that a joint venture in China or in the Soviet Union generate its own foreign exchange has proved to be a major obstacle to foreign investments in both China and the Soviet Union, because Western companies are often not anxious to create competitors in the East for a Western marketplace already fully engaged by the Western partner. While some Western companies are willing to use China or the Soviet Union as a second source for their products, most Western manufacturers are, instead, motivated to explore opportunities in these countries principally by a desire to develop new markets, or protect old markets, for their products. Accordingly, foreign exchange balancing provisions tend to select against companies that do not require additional sources for their products but wish only to develop new market outlets in China, the Soviet Union, or elsewhere.

With this in mind, China's foreign exchange balancing provisions were amended in 1987 to provide that a joint venture engaged in the manufacture of products that have historically been imported into China over a long period of time may apply to have its products approved as "import substitutes" by the "department in charge of the joint venture," as that term is used in Article 6 of the 1983 Implementation Regulations on joint ventures.[4] Only a handful of East-West ventures located in China have applied for designation as joint ventures whose products are import substitutes. These companies have found the process of approval tedious and burdensome. In many cases they have found the process of implementation to be both frustrating and impractical. In one case of which I am specifically aware, the Chinese initially attempted to implement the import substitution concept by requiring each proposed purchaser of the joint venture's import substitute products to apply to the central government for foreign exchange with which to acquire those products. Because the products were relatively inexpensive (selling in the range of one to two thousand dollars per unit), the process was fatally inefficient, duplicative, bureaucratic, and time consuming. In addition, this particular manufacturer also suffered from the strongly embedded attitude that all things made in China (including those made by East-West joint ventures) are inferior to goods made abroad and, further, that goods made abroad are more attractive because inspection trips to the manufacturer's facilities are more interesting to prospective Chinese purchasers when those manufacturing facilities are located outside of China rather than, for example, Shanghai.

The Soviets have not yet adopted a law that specifically permits buyers in the Soviet Union to receive hard currency allocations from the central government to acquire products manufactured in the Soviet Union by East-West joint ventures where such products were previously imported into the Soviet Union. On the other hand, the Soviet Union has allowed certain state enterprises and agricultural collectives to use some of their hard currency earnings to buy goods for hard currency wherever those goods may be produced. Presumably a joint venture within the Soviet Union should be able to manufacture quality goods for distribution within the Soviet Union at a lower price than the "landed price" of comparable goods manufactured abroad. Buyers in the Soviet Union, however, are also suspicious of the quality of goods manufactured within the Soviet Union.

Under its 1986 Foreign Exchange Balancing Rules, China permitted joint ventures to obtain direct foreign exchange allotments from an applicable government authority where the joint venture provides highly sophisticated products produced with advanced technology, or provides products of superior quality—to the extent that such products are urgently needed in China and are internationally competitive. In these instances, the Chinese government is authorized to approve the direct allocation to the joint venture (most likely through central government loans or central government investment of foreign exchange) to cover the projected foreign exchange needs of the joint venture. Again, no similar law exists in the Soviet Union, although I am personally aware of proposals that would result in the investment by a Soviet partner in a proposed East-West joint venture of substantial foreign exchange to cover all, or some part of, the start-up foreign exchange requirements of the joint venture.

Other provisions available in China for foreign exchange balancing by East-West joint ventures include the export of Chinese products by the joint venture, even where such products are not produced by the joint venture. This device is more difficult to implement than it may appear because Chinese producers of internationally marketable products are often unwilling to sell those products to a Chinese-based joint venture for local currency when they are aware that the joint venture is selling them abroad for hard currency. It may take forceful intervention by the Chinese government to require such Chinese sellers to continue selling their products within China for local currency when there is obviously an external market for these products in hard currency. The problem becomes even more difficult if the products originate in a different industry, geographic area, or ministry from the one that controls the joint venture. Again, similar provisions do not exist in the Soviet Union, although barter agreements within the Soviet Union are common, and the Soviet Union has had some experience dealing with the exchange of raw materials for consumer goods with both Eastern European and Western nations.

The Chinese foreign exchange balancing laws also permit related joint ventures to aggregate their foreign exchange and local currency accounts for the purposes of determining foreign exchange surpluses or deficiencies. The result of this provision is that joint ventures with foreign exchange deficiencies often seek to become related to joint ventures with foreign exchange surpluses (such as tourist hotels), so that the foreign exchange surpluses of one can offset the foreign exchange deficiencies of the other. Again, the Soviet Union has no similar law, although it appears that foreign exchange will soon be freely transferable among East-West joint ventures in the Soviet Union with the approval of the USSR Ministry of Finance.

China also has two other provisions that are useful in permitting foreign exchange balancing within a joint venture. First, joint ventures that are long on local currency and short on foreign exchange are permitted to reinvest their local currency in other for-profit enterprises within China. While this device may not produce additional foreign exchange, it at least offers the prospect of converting excess local currency into hard assets, which may, at some future date, be convertible into foreign exchange. Additionally, certain joint ventures in China are permitted to compute the price of their products and so settle accounts within China for foreign currencies when they sell products to Chinese enterprises that have foreign currency balances, but only to the extent that such sales are approved by the State Foreign Exchange Control Departments. This provision extends the right to engage in foreign currency transactions within China to joint ventures located outside of the Chinese special economic zones or the economic and technological development zones of the coastal port cities, where, presumably, foreign currency could previously be used as an accounting unit without the prior approval of the State Foreign Exchange Control Department.

Within the Soviet Union, East-West joint ventures may sell their products to Soviet enterprises for foreign exchange after both the joint venture and the enterprises have registered with the USSR Ministry of Foreign Relations and have received from the ministry, and possibly other agencies, all necessary approvals. Similar provisions do not exist under Chinese law, although in effect the Chinese foreign exchange balancing provisions described above may permit a China-based East-West venture to obtain foreign exchange for local sales on a case-by-case basis.

PROBLEM OF SUPPLY AND DISTRIBUTION

Perhaps the most significant impediment to East-West ventures in either China or the Soviet Union is the virtual lack of the established, entrepreneurial, market-based support systems that exist throughout the West. Because of the lack of an established support system, the process of negotiating, structuring, registering, and commencing the operations of an East-West joint venture in either the Soviet Union or China is really the smallest part of establishing and conducting a successful business enterprise. More often than not, established joint ventures in either country find themselves adrift in a vast and trackless sea of commerce within which neither supply channels nor distribution channels have been clearly defined. Basic problems like obtaining necessary raw materials, supplies, machinery, equipment, labor, and services become oppressively burdensome and inhibiting. Even when these problems are overcome, Chinese- or Soviet-based joint ventures often flounder in their attempts to identify distribution channels within their host country, to obtain market information, to sell their goods across geographic or ministry boundaries, or to otherwise develop or tap into distribution systems.

Both the Soviet Union and Chinese production systems are evolving from a long-standing central planning system, which, for at least forty years, has provided incentives for local managers to meet centrally mandated quotas in order to be successful within the economic system. This single-minded definition of success has caused managers to develop manufacturing systems vertically integrated to an extent undreamed of in the West. For example, I have visited a railroad car production facility in the Soviet Union that included a steel production factory, a forging plant, a woodworking shop, and a textile dying plant. Because each of these ancillary functions was created for the sole purpose of supporting the railroad car assembly function (the plant produced only one hundred railroad cars per month), each of these ancillary functions operated at well below maximum capacity—in some cases, at only 20 to 30 percent of their available capacity.

From pig farms that make pork chops and pigskin pocketbooks to aircraft factories that operate aluminum smelting mills, Soviet and Chinese industries have taken on a vertical component directly in response to economic systems that harshly punish the failure to meet centrally dictated production quotas, reward managers for making quotas without any significant accountability for quality, and virtually ignore capital costs in the formulas for determining the success or failure of a venture. Accordingly, confronted with a system that defines success or failure almost exclusively in terms of the number of units shipped per year, local managers have historically gone to great lengths to assure their access to essential supplies, parts, and raw materials by developing captive sources for these items—cost, efficiency, and quality notwithstanding.

As a result, when a newly formed Soviet- or Chinese-based East-West joint venture goes looking for a forging factory to manufacture parts for the joint venture's products, for example, it is likely to discover that there are no independent forging plants willing or able to produce the desired parts. Any existing forging plants are likely to be captive operations that supply forgings exclusively to their parent company and will likely be unable to contract independently with outside manufacturers, to define or control their costs, or to obtain raw materials for outside manufacturing activities. The joint venture may, therefore, be required either to buy the required parts abroad for foreign exchange (which upsets the foreign exchange balancing laws) or to establish a very inefficient local production capacity of its own to produce the required parts. Moreover, the systems of vertically integrated industries that have evolved in China and the Soviet Union have created inconsistent standards among industries, with the result that parts produced within one ministry or industrial groups are unlikely to be compatible with parts produced in another.

Similarly, on the distribution side, most of the Soviet and Chinese factories I have visited have had only one customer and, therefore, have not found it necessary to develop a nationwide, or even a regional, distribution network. As a result, Soviet and Chinese industries often hold within a single management and economic unit all of the functions and ingredients necessary to manufacture, assemble, package, service, and transport their products. East–West joint ventures situated in the Soviet Union or China may therefore find it virtually impossible to tap into wholesale distribution networks for products because, for the most part, those types of networks have not evolved within the Chinese or Soviet single-customer systems.

CHINA AND THE SOVIET UNION: AN AMERICAN'S PERSPECTIVE ON REFORM

Both Chinese and Soviet experts commonly go to great lengths to explain that there are enormous differences between the Soviet Union and China. These experts therefore conclude that prescriptions for one will not necessarily cure the ills of the other. There is no denying that there are vast cultural differences between China and the Soviet Union, but it also is clear that these two economic systems have significant similarities that have created similar problems, and that these problems must be confronted and resolved in both countries for their respective reform movements to succeed.

In both countries, virtually all of the means of production have been owned by the state for several generations. It is true that there is a tradition of private ownership in China that existed within the lifetimes of many living Chinese citizens, but that experience involved a free-enterprise system more like present-day South American economies than the economies of Western Europe and the United States. In fact, most older Chinese citizens do not have fond recollections of the conditions that preceded the Communist take-over in 1949, because the experience in China from the date of the Boxer Rebellion in 1900 through Mao Zedong's "liberation" was one of disruption, invasion by foreign powers, uneven distribution of wealth, scarcity, and instability. China, therefore, has a vestigial recollection of capitalism and entrepreneurialism but lacks the tradition of the carefully organized and legally controlled systems of capitalism and free markets that exists in the West today.

Similarly, the Soviet Union has had a tradition of shortages and instability, from the overthrow of the tzars in the early 1900s and continuing through the purges of the 1920s and 1930s, World War II, to the current day.

Now that Communist rule is lifting throughout Eastern Europe and is being challenged in the Soviet Union and, less openly, in China, some of the old fears of insecurity, civil war, anarchy, and chaos are re-emerging among the local populations. The experiences of the late 1980s have indicated that these fears are not entirely unjustified. As the absolute power of the Communist party is abrogated, ethnic tensions have come to the surface. Uncontrolled entrepreneurialism has given rise to fears of exploitation and grossly inequitable distribution of wealth as well as to uncertainties with respect to the structure and composition of the new political systems that may arise to replace the old. Perhaps no single issue lays more heavily on the minds of responsible government officials in both China and the Soviet Union than the fear that the two systems might collapse into anarchy before attempts to reform and rejuvenate the underlying economic and political infrastructure can take effect.

While the Soviet and Chinese experiences are different in many respects, and while the two cultures are clearly and substantially different, the greatest challenge currently confronting reformers in both countries is the problem of managing an orderly transition from a highly regimented, centrally planned, single-party system to one in which individual initiatives are both valued and rewarded, market forces rather than central planning play a larger role in determining the allocation of resources, and political systems are more responsive and accountable to citizens. The transition from one system to another will invariably involve massive dislocations, potentially devastating inflation rates, periodic shortages of essential goods, social and political unrest, and a general culture shock to masses of people suddenly forced to reject the teachings of decades in favor of economic concepts and political ideologies previously forbidden as morally repugnant. Cultural changes of this magnitude generally have not been made in the recorded history of humankind except through violent revolution.

The year 1989 was a year in which Eastern Europe governments were changed, economic systems were scrapped, political structures were radically revised, and ideological beliefs were fundamentally challenged and altered. The impact of these changes has been to leave vast areas of Eastern Europe and the Soviet Union and People's Republic of China in a state of uncertainty, insecurity, and instability. These changes and uncertainties pose an enormous threat to the stability of both China and the Soviet Union and, therefore, to the desirability of these countries as places for investment or business activity. It goes without saying that civil war, anarchy, and ethnic violence are detrimental to national stability, individual health, and business prospects. It is, perhaps, entirely consistent with capitalistic notions that those areas of the world that today appear to offer the greatest possibilities for new markets and long-term profit also present a very high level of risk and uncertainty. These areas combined present a new market of more than 1.5 billion eager consumers and combined resources of materials, trained labor, and underutilized production facilities not available anywhere in the world. In addition, these societies have an urgent need for Western technology, management skills, and processing information for which they are willing to pay in raw materials, finished goods, and, as available, real money.

All of this potential benefit, however, has to be measured against a downside that some analysts have described in extremely dire, even apocalyptic, terms. The downside scenarios range from years of unrest and uncertainty to outright civil war between factional units of national armies equipped with everything from poison gas to atomic weapons. In my view, even the mildest downside scenario in either China or the Soviet Union will not benefit Western societies if allowed to persist over extended periods of time, and certainly Western governments must exert enormous energy to avert the apocalyptic downside scenarios. In the meantime, Western businesses continue to establish beachheads in these emerging market areas, and the tempo of new business activity, while presently somewhat measured and reserved, is assuredly picking up.

RECOMMENDATIONS

The process of developing business relationships in Eastern Europe and China is extraordinarily complex and not made easier by the rapid pace of economic, political, and social change in these regions. Perhaps the simplest part of the business planning process for Westerners seeking to expand into the Soviet Union or China is reading the new laws and regulations that are proliferating within these countries and designing a business structure that, at least hypothetically, conforms to the requirements of these new laws.

All of the nations within these regions are competing strenuously to attract Western technology, capital, and management skills. Accordingly, an analysis of the individual tax laws, customs, and duties' concessions and the government incentives and subsidies of each of these countries generally reveals a highly competitive marketplace for foreign assets (capital, technology, or management skills) available to Westerners interested in East-West business transactions. If the analysis stops with this simple structural and pricing review, however, the more important factors that will ultimately affect the success or failure of any proposed East-West business transactions will not have been considered.

More significantly, a Western business person proposing to do business in Eastern Europe or China must focus on the relationship that the proposed new business will have with the entire commercial structure within which it will be embedded. The analysis must focus on the source, price, availability, and quality of goods, supplies, parts, components, labor, and equipment necessary for the proper function of the proposed business. In addition, the Western business person must also focus on the distribution channels available to the proposed business, including mechanisms for obtaining market information within the host country, the availability of local transportation and warehousing facilities, access to mechanisms for advertising, marketing, and servicing products within the available marketplace (assuming that the marketplace can be identified), and mechanisms for servicing products once they are in the hands of end users.

A study group funded by Eastern and Western European governments is currently exploring key issues of monetary policies, price supports, consumer subsidies, capital accumulation, privatization of industry, housing, environmental matters, and other factors ultimately affecting social stability and the availability and equitable distribution of goods within reforming socialist countries. The very existence of this study group is compelling evidence that policymakers in both East and West recognize that these problems must be resolved by the Eastern European and Chinese governments before there is any real prospect for long-term stability or economic progress within these regions. In the meantime, Western businesses continue to work to establish economic relationships in or with Eastern European nations and the People's Republic of China within existing structures and within the existing environment of rapid and unpredictable change.

There are many very good reasons to commence or expand business activities within Eastern Europe and the People's Republic of China at this time despite the uncertainties that exist. The process, however, must be undertaken cautiously and with a full appreciation of the nonbusiness risks that may affect the ultimate outcome of the proposed business activity. This analysis breaks down roughly to an analysis of political risk—dealing with the political and social uncertainties in each of the respective nations—and of supply and distribution—dealing with integrating the proposed business into the available sourcing and distribution networks within the target host nation.

I have recommended to several multinational Western businesses that an association be created to pool the collective influence, investment potential, foreign exchange balancing capabilities, technologies, and skills of these companies to create a consortium that, in turn, would negotiate with policymakers and business people in each of the proposed target nations to develop legal, accounting, and physical structures designed to enhance the prospects for success of the individual business endeavors undertaken by each of the association members. By pooling resources; focusing investments within specially designated areas; setting aside relatively small amounts of money (for example, 5 percent of the aggregated proposed investment pool) to finance the creation of local, entrepreneurial support industries within the designated development zones (creation of an East-West venture capital fund designed to encourage the development of local entrepreneurial support industries); pooling collective foreign exchange balancing capabilities (i.e., the buyers generate foreign exchange credits for the sellers in the group); and negotiating with policymakers to create a system of laws and incentives that would permit this process to occur, I believe that Western business people could help to shape and create the supply and distribution channels so necessary to the success of their business investments within the host countries. Through this effort, Western business people would also ease the economic impact of the reform as perceived by local populations and encourage local entrepreneurs to learn the new rules of the road.

Based on my experience, I have the following recommendations for companies seeking to establish joint ventures in China or in the Soviet Union. These recommendations are necessarily general in nature, but they apply equally to ventures in China and in the Soviet Union and must, of course, be more specifically defined with respect to any particular proposal.

1. Begin any project in China or the Soviet Union with a realistic and disciplined statement of objectives. Projects may be justified for a wide range of reasons that may or may not include such obvious and traditional measures as short- or even long-term profitability or returns on investment. Significant and highly productive (in the sense of achieving objectives) ventures have been formed in both China and the Soviet Union for reasons of obtaining access to raw materials and technology, establishing a marketing or market-share beachhead in an emerging market, and protecting or expanding a pre-existing sales base within China or the Soviet Union.

2. Deal with the proper entities and individuals within the target country in order to best achieve the objectives. If, for example, the principal objective is a short-term return on investment or immediate profitability, deal with local plant managers (rather than ministry-level officials) who can promptly deliver a relatively efficient manufacturing capability. If, on the other hand, the objective is to protect a pre-existing sales base or to establish a nationwide foothold within the relevant market, deal with higher-level officials who may be helpful in achieving these more generalized objectives.

3. Carefully analyze the entire scope of the proposed business project to become

aware of all of the supply-side and distribution-side services that it will require to be successful. Assume nothing. Avoid disappointment by assuming only that it will be virtually impossible to obtain necessary raw materials; tap into an existing distribution network; obtain essential parts, components, supplies, and personnel; or obtain access to essential advertising, marketing, and other consulting services. In structuring the proposed transaction, take all of these factors into account during the negotiations and build into the agreement reasonable safeguards, both to assure access to these essential items and, where assuring access is not possible, to provide alternatives (such as foreign exchange reserves for importing such items) should such access become unavailable. In going through this process, it may be important to bring to the table some outside, independent third parties, who may control access to essential raw materials or to distribution systems, in order to enhance your prospects for success.

4. Try to enlist, both in the agreement and in practice, key officials who can be of assistance when the inevitable obstacles arise. It is impossible to predict in advance the multitude of problems that arise in the daily routine of a rather ordinary business in China or the Soviet Union. For example, a U.S. company doing business in China was recently threatened with local criminal sanctions because it painted its corporate name on the side of one of its delivery vans operating within the city of Shanghai. Local authorities impounded the truck and attempted to impose penalties for illegal advertising, which was banned not by national, economic, or business law but by a local criminal code. Other companies have nearly collapsed over battles to install telephones and telefax machines, or even issues relating to entry and exit visas for key people. A local official who has the clout to cut through bureaucratic impediments and local traditions can help avoid entanglements with corrupt officials who may view operating difficulties as an opportunity for personal profit.

5. Be a good local citizen within the host community and provide more than minimal training for employees to help them understand the basic economic concepts that underlie the for-profit and free-market mentality. Winning converts among the work force and local management may be one of the best ways to increase the odds of achieving objectives in the face of obstructive and even corrupt local regulations and practices.

Doing business in China and the Soviet Union is never easy, but it is also never dull.

NOTES

1. The Civil Law of the People's Republic of China, adopted 12 April 1986 by the First Session of the Sixth National People's Congress, chapter 1, article 1.

2. Law of the People's Republic of China on Industrial Enterprises Owned by the Whole People, adopted 13 April 1988 at the First Session of the Seventh National People's Congress, chapter 3, article 19, section 3.

3. M. Ivanova, "Kooperatsiya: itogi godi," *Ekonomika i zhizn* 12 (March 1990): 5.

4. Regulations of the State Council Concerning the Balance of Foreign Exchange Income and Expenditure by Sino-Foreign Joint-Equity Ventures, promulgated 15 January 1986 by the State Council of the People's Republic of China, article 5.

Part III

Western Investment and Trade in the
USSR: Analysis and Prospects

Chapter 6

Economic Activity in the Soviet Union and Restructuring of Foreign Economic Activity

Igor G. Doronin

The years that have passed since the announcement of economic reforms have not brought with them the expected changes in the condition of the Soviet economy. Moreover, the economic situation in the country continues to worsen, despite attempts to consolidate cost accounting, increase enterprise independence, legalize and stimulate the cooperative movement, and reorganize the banking system.

Did the idea of economic reforms fall through altogether? If judged by the results of economic activity (including a significant drop in the growth of the economy, increasing inflationary tendencies, growing imbalances, and growing foreign debt), then the failure of the latest reforms undertaken becomes evident. However, if the reforms are evaluated in terms of promoting a step away from the administrative command methods of supervision and of developing market relations, then we may justifiably conclude that the reforms have not really even begun. Even if the strategic course of the economic reforms was chosen correctly, the measures that were taken in implementing certain decisions had a superficial character and did not touch the very bases of the system that was created.

STRATEGIC TASKS IN ECONOMIC REFORM

Of course it would be very easy to attribute everything to the mistakes and miscalculations of the administrative apparatus. It is significantly more difficult to realize the very essence of economic reform and to create a mechanism for achieving the most important goal—transition to a regulated market economy. Up until today, the whole notion of economic reform has not been separated from the ideological burden, and ideology figures more prominently than economics in those arguments that concern the final ends of reform. For example, when passing the final document during the Conference on Economic Cooperation in Europe in Bonn in April 1990, the Soviet delegation, while completely agreeing with the idea of transition to a market system, had nevertheless insisted that the terms *principles* and *market economy* be replaced by *goals* and *market-oriented economy* respectively.

Today, notions such as private property, hired labor, and exploitation provide an allergic reaction even from a number of Soviet lawmakers. In 1922, the civil code pronounced the right of any citizen of the Russian Republic to private property and to found and own a private industry or business, and the land code consolidated the right of individual peasant households and the right to rent land and hire labor.

That which was evident and natural only a short time ago today still continues to provoke discussion. This can account for the endless arguments about the relationship of the market with the plan and about their priorities, while in Eastern Europe and in China this question was decided in favor of the market, and that the market is governed by the state has gained wide publicity.

And yet, whether fast or slow, changes in consciousness are taking place. The most important evidence for this is that from the idea of perfecting production processes and improving the mechanism of directing economic and social processes we have come to understand the necessity of forming a new economic model, founded on revolutionary transitions in terms of private property.

Today it is becoming clear to many that the transition to the market system assumes certain necessary preparatory measures, the significance of which lies in creating an infrastructure of a market: a new policy in terms of finances, credit, money, currency, prices, a new banking system, and a principally different system of social security. Ignoring that last demand of economic reform would have serious consequences.

First of all, the recent Law on State Enterprises and the Law on Cooperation have proven ineffective due to the absence of elementary market relations. The declared principles of self-financing, self-compensation, and self-management have not acquired a realistic content since a wholesale market has not been created, liberalization of prices have not been implemented, and a financial market is absent. In and of itself, the passing of the Law on State Enterprises could not bring about changes in the governing mechanism. The ministries have not only reserved their right to redirect financial resources but have also remained the main managers of material funds and limits. Enterprises began to receive state orders through the ministries. In the field or in foreign economic ties, dictation by branch ministries has brought about an increase in barter trade and reduced the professional level on the foreign market.

Adoption of the Law on State Enterprises had a series of negative consequences. Monopolistic tendencies in the economy were intensified by enterprises that belonged to a branch (branch monopoly) and individual enterprises that were the sole producers of certain goods in the national economy. In both cases there was the same result: an increase in prices, reduction in the volume of production, deterioration in quality, and a change in the variety of goods available because the cheaper items were dropped from production.

The absence of a market infrastructure has not only preserved the methods of relations between enterprises and higher organs of management but has also created serious problems in the relations of Soviet republics and regions, which have been tensing up in the past few years. It is becoming more evident how unrealistic it is to attempt to solve the problems of the economic independence of the republics and regions outside the system or market relations. At the current stage of administrative command rule the disintegrational tendencies are leading toward a replacement of the departmental monopolism by the monopolism of republican regional organs of management, an economic segregation of republics and regions, and a determination to localize the resolution of economic problems. Nevertheless, the way of self-isolation is not a solution to the existing situation. Thus, the task of creating an infrastructure of market regulations is present not only on the national but also on the republic and regional levels.

The economic independence of republics and regions under the conditions of forming a market infrastructure assumes first of all a separation of the duties of national organs and those of the Soviet republics and regions in regulating economic activity. Together with a single state policy of monetary transactions, crediting and taxing, there must exist programs of economic and social development for republics and regions that are tied to the system of regulating the economic activity of the corresponding republic and region. Such an approach would permit the greatest degree of integration of the interests of all sides involved. However, at its base must lie the principle to maximum possible freedom in the trade of goods and the flow of financial resources and the labor force.

It follows that national structural and investment policy must necessarily include the component of foreign economic relations. This policy should not be limited only to the creation of export-oriented manufactures or replacing imports, but should also encompass the possibility of the republics obtaining foreign loans and credits to carry out a policy that would attract foreign capital in order both to create manufactures that would help solve local problems and to create zones for free joint businesses on their territories.

The simultaneous participation of the republics and regions in the national and international division of labor is not mutually exclusive, but mutually complementary. The more integrated a Union republic's economic complex is in the national system of economic ties, the more extensive will be its opportunities for cooperating within the system of foreign economic ties. The development of a republic and region's international ties and international specialization and cooperation will in turn increase its cooperation with other republics and regions.

Thus, the solution of many problems rests upon the creation of market infrastructure and the developing of market relations. One wonders how soon the necessary measures can be taken. A certain retardation in resolving long-time problems is quite apparent. To a significant degree it is caused by the insufficient preparation of the common popular conscience rather than by the resistance of conservatory forces.

The current radicalization of the popular conscience in the Soviet Union is a direct result of dissatisfaction with the progress of economic reforms as well as of the drop in the standard of living of the people. Growing political activity illustrates the limited capability of the members of society to fully realize their physical and spiritual potential in producing and creating, or to receive a just reward for the amount of work they do and thus raise their standard of living.

The circle of problems that surrounds the economic reforms can be distinguished with ease. It includes restoring economic balance, bringing money demand into line with the supply of goods, and developing the infrastructure of a market economy. The only difference lies in the approaches to these problems and in the degree to which the proposed measures are radical.

The transitional period has its own logic of development. The thesis stating that a market can function effectively only when the economy is balanced provokes no objections. Yet the assertion that achieving proportionality in economics is possible only with the help of market instruments is no less justifiable. These two views were placed at the conceptual core of the economic reform of the Soviet Union and in the programs of extraordinary measures to act as the main component in the initial stage of the transition to a market. The ineffectiveness of the extraordinary measures, which became apparent only several months after their implementation, proved once more that it is impossible to solve economic problems without going outside the framework imposed by the administrative command system.

The situation emerging in the economy is objectively pushing toward the implementation of more decisive measures in the sphere of economic reforms. Mainly, these are the measures that call for limiting demand and widening supply. Among the first are conducting a policy of limiting the growth of incomes, partially freezing the growth of wages, monetary reserves of enterprises and the savings of individuals, and raising wholesale and regular prices. All of these measures were more or less discussed in the Soviet press and naturally did not provoke any general approval. However, the objective situation in economics forces one to undertake these socially unpopular policies. At the same time, to compensate for the general dissatisfaction, measures directed toward widening supply are necessary. They involve the removal of limits on and encouragement of enterprising activity, simplification of the procedures for new workshops, and intermediary bureaus that function on a commercial basis, including those in the area of joint venture activity. Thus we are talking about developing the nonstate sector of the economy, creating objective prerequisites for using market instruments that regulate economic activity, and forming the infrastructural basis of the market.

The achievement of macroeconomic equilibrium using market instruments does not exclude but rather presupposes conducting active structural policies. Amid the quite wide range of problems facing the Soviet economy, the one deserving the most attention is the question of agriculture and of encouraging small- and medium-scale industrial businesses.

Evidently, the increase in the effectiveness of the agricultural sector of the economy is capable of becoming a serious factor that would stimulate the market transformation of the economy, promote the achievement of equilibrium, and reduce the social tensions. For that deep land reform is needed, as well as the transfer of land to private ownership, its sale to those who can and want to buy it, and its availability for leasing with the right to purchase.

Agricultural reform is capable of causing a chain reaction in many spheres of activity related to preserving and processing agricultural products and giving a push to the development of numerous small- and medium-scale enterprises.

Changes in the structure of agricultural production are capable of putting serious pressure on other economic structures loosely tied into the branch (including food and light manufacturing, chemical manufacturing and machine building) or through other branches. It is difficult to foresee the full impact of this pressure and the possible resulting changes in economic relations. Most importantly, the ongoing process of structural reforms will have a self-perpetuating character. It will inevitably draw into the process questions of the effects of prices on agriculture, crediting and financing farmers' activities. Demand to restructure the trading of goods that facilitate agriculture (like technology, fertilizers, and building machines) will grow. As a result, an infrastructure of market relations will develop. The growth in the volume of supply and the increase in the effectiveness of agricultural production in their turn will not only eliminate the deficit in food and raw materials for processing industries, but will also provide a base for developing small- and medium-sized enterprises.

It is necessary to see the effect of structural policies on linking the market forces to the system of interrepublican and interregional economic ties. Raising supply above demand first in agricultural and then in industrial goods would eliminate the deficits and considerably lower the international ethnic problems.

FOREIGN ECONOMIC RELATIONS IN THE TRANSITIONAL PERIOD

Today practically no one doubts that it is virtually impossible to construct an effective modern market-oriented economic system without large-scale cooperation with the West in various forms: import of consumer goods, capital, technology, managing experience, and scientific exchange. However, it is also understood that the West would be prepared for such cooperation only if it sees an equal partner in the Soviet Union, one that is capable of effectively mastering modern technical achievements, actively participating in the system of international division of labor, and conducting open politics. Naturally, such an approach coincides with the long-term interests of the Soviet Union.

The absence of real progress in the internal economic transition to market conditions has had a dual negative effect on the development of foreign economic ties. First, trade imbalances have grown significantly due to the stronger role of foreign economic ties in compensating for planning miscalculations and disproportions in the economy. As a result, foreign economic relations have ended up in a situation no less difficult than the economy.

Second, reform of the mechanism of overseeing foreign economic activity, which basically called for using market instruments, was virtually blocked. Although thousands of Soviet enterprises and organizations have entered the external market, overseeing foreign economic ties is still done by administrative means.

Forming market economic conditions in the foreign sphere requires, first of all, an economically based rate of exchange for the ruble. This was not done in past years. The system of differential currency coefficients has seriously complicated internal accounts in export and import operations and thus rendered itself lifeless. At the present time, it is recognized as expedient to considerably increase the role of the exchange rate for the ruble in order to make it the link between domestic and international prices. This should stimulate transition to a market economy inside the country and guarantee statewide interests under the conditions of a more open economy. This course would allow the dismantling of the system of administrative regulation to begin, including the system of subsidizing exports and imports. This may bring about a series of unpleasant consequences, particularly with a rise in import prices for the consumer. Yet this will challenge all Soviet citizens to use the imported goods more rationally and effectively, force enterprises to measure their financial capabilities with import needs, and help bring the structure of internal prices closer to international ones.

The transition to a real rate of exchange for the ruble would force a reevaluation of the current internal system of crediting and financing import-export operations and would pave the way for changes in the banking system. It would also demand the reorganization of foreign currency policy by making it a part of monetary policy with the application of mechanisms of regulation, and it would become the factor in forming an internal financial market. It is imagined that a realistic appraisal of the exchange rate of the ruble, as compared to other foreign currencies, would alleviate several problems tied to the inflated value of the ruble, including the realistic appraisal of the value of capital invested in joint ventures by the foreign partner and the reorientation of joint venture activity to the outside markets.

Chapter 7

Soviet Priorities in the Development of Joint Ventures

Vyacheslav O. Maslov

The condition of the national economy in the Soviet Union by the late 1970s and early 1980s made it clear that the old methods of building the economy have exhausted themselves, and if they are to be used further, the economy of the country will be deadlocked. For this reason, a transition to a new economic mechanism has been initiated. This transition is connected with a shift in orientation in socioeconomic development that primarily aims to make considerable social achievements. One of the elements of the new economic mechanism is the creation within the Soviet Union of joint ventures, joint stock, or mixed companies, and zones of free entrepreneurship. These forms of foreign economic activity naturally result from broadening and deepening the internationalization of the economy.

Countries that accept joint ventures pursue aims oriented toward drawing and using foreign capital. Each stage in the development of the national economy must set up its goals and tasks to this end, which then prompts the selection of a particular system for encouraging foreign investors.

Within the framework of Soviet economics, several levels of goals and interests in creating joint ventures can be singled out, particularly national economic priorities, regional priorities, and branch priorities. This network of priorities is completed by the added system of economic levers that enable joint ventures to coordinate the interests of enterprises, regions, and branches with economic interests.

The legislature defined general goals for setting up joint ventures in the Soviet Union. These goals are: to meet the needs in particular kinds of industrial products, raw materials, and food products; to draw advanced foreign technology, know-how, management experience, and additional material and financial resources to the national economy of the Soviet Union; to speed up the practical realization of Soviet scientific and technical achievements; to build up the country's export basis; and to reduce 'irrational" imports.

These goals reflect a clear-cut orientation in the development of the Soviet economy at this stage. To achieve these goals, the Soviet legislature stipulates a system of certain priorities.

In order to explain the system of Soviet priorities we should start with an analysis of the system for making decisions on establishing joint ventures. At the initial stage of developing joint entrepreneurship in the Soviet Union, permits for joint ventures were to be obtained from the USSR Council of Ministers. This practice was made legal by the USSR Council of Ministers' Decree 48 of 13 January 1987. Permits were given to enterprises only after they had been approved by the ministries and departments of the Soviet Union, councils and ministries of the Union republics, the state planning agency USSR Gosplan, the USSR Ministry of Finance, and other ministries and departments in charge. In practice, this routine was too complicated, time consuming, and generally inefficient.

Thus, the right to make decisions regarding joint ventures in the Soviet Union was given to USSR ministries and departments and to the Councils of Ministers of the Union republics. Later, such decisions were made at the level of state enterprises, societies, and organizations willing to create a joint venture approved by a higher governing body. Cooperatives set up joint ventures after receiving approval from the council of ministers of a Union republic where there are no regional subdivisions, or from the council of ministers of an autonomous republic, the executive committee of a territorial or regional council, or from the executive committee of the Moscow city council or Lenigrad city council. There are cases where a cooperative can be established with the approval of the ministry in charge. This shows a shift in the national economic permissive priorities toward liberalization of the process of setting up joint ventures. This also shows a transition of joint ventures from one level to another, that is, a transition from a national economic level to a territorial and branch level.

When considering national economic priorities aimed at attracting foreign capital, it is worth mentioning a change in the size of the possible share for foreign participants in the charter fund of a joint venture. The practice established by the USSR Council of Ministers' Decree 49 of 13 January 1987 strictly limited the share of foreign partners to 49 percent. This restriction was later lifted. Currently the shares of foreign and Soviet partners in the charter fund of a joint venture can be negotiated and agreed upon by the partners concerned. In this context another important priority is worth discussing. This priority concerns foreign firms and the use of their experience and knowledge in the management and production of a joint venture. This can be accomplished only if the management of a joint venture is in the hands of its foreign partner, namely the general director of the joint venture representing the foreign firm. This also is stipulated in the new Soviet legislation.

There are other important Soviet legislative acts stimulating foreign investments in Soviet economics. Among them are customs priorities. In particular, a priority is given to equipment and material values imported to the Soviet Union as a contribution of a foreign partner to the charter fund of a joint venture. Such imports are free of customs duties. In addition, a minimum customs duty may be imposed on any commodity imported to the Soviet Union by a joint venture to meet the needs of production or such commodities may be entirely duty-free. In addition, the Chief Administration of State Customs Control under the USSR Council of Ministers was instructed to extend customs tax privileges to the foreign staff of joint ventures.

An important national economic priority of the Soviet state is to provide the nation with consumer goods as well as different kinds of services. Therefore the state is also interested in the creation of joint ventures capable of widening the assortment and improving the quality of goods and services supplied to the public. If these goods are to be produced domestically all over the country as a whole, this will lead to a reduction of currency spendings for imports. Thus, the population can receive additional consumer goods while the country is saving currency.

From this point of view foreign investors also enjoy certain priorities. There is a 30 percent state tax on profit from joint ventures set up on Soviet territory. There is also a 20 percent state tax on transfer profit, which may be different for different countries. The Soviet legislation has a provision regarding the general approach to priorities for joint ventures that allows the USSR Ministry of Finance to change the size of the tax on profit and its transfer and make it lower than the established norm. Under this provision, the Ministry of Finance is free not only to reduce the size of the tax on the profit exported from the Soviet Union, but also, for a certain period of time, not to impose tax at all on part of the profit due to the foreign partner of a joint venture. It goes without saying that not every joint venture can enjoy this right equally. This privilege is granted mostly to joint ventures engaged in the production of consumer goods, medical equipment and medicines, and products for research with potential vital national economic importance. In this way, the system of government priorities is extended into the social sphere, where these products are given first priority.

The Soviet state currently pays much attention to the system of national health care, which is also closely connected to the system for environmental protection of the population now and in the future.

It is already possible now to talk about the differentiation of taxation in practical terms. However, not until the USSR Council of Ministers adopted Decree 1405 on 2 December 1988 were there any criteria formulated in the legislature regarding the differentiation of taxation according to the kinds of products or services of a joint venture, its export orientation, the size of its profit in free-convertible currency, or its location. Unfortunately, such differentiation of taxation is equal for both the joint ventures that make their products entirely on their own, or partially complete them with components made by a Western partner and sell them on the Soviet market (often spending the hard currency of Soviet enterprises on this), and the joint ventures that use the intellectual and industrial property of their Soviet participants as well as raw materials and complete domestically produced components to produce export and import-replacing goods.

In addition to this, from the point of view of progress in science and technology, state priorities can support some especially important directions, including: technological supply on the basis of biotechnological production of food products (the so-called "Green Revolution"); implementation of new and environmentally safe sources of energy; production of new construction materials; use of high-temperature superconductivity; and, finally, the introduction of information and computer engineering in all the spheres of economics and the communal economy.

The technical and technological level of joint entrepreneurship can be considerably raised by means of the conversion of the military complex. The conversion currently underway can also be attributed to state priorities, since it can have considerable impact on the improvement of the scientific-technological and production potential of the national economy, and on re-equipment of some of the branches of industries, particularly in the medical branch. This conversion can also affect the agroindustrial complex and food services, as well as the sphere of consumer goods. The national economic priorities that concern foreign investments in the Soviet Union are realized through the general system of state control of export and import.

In April 1989, the Soviet Union introduced a system of licenses for goods to be exported and imported. The basic idea of licensing is to stimulate the export of finished goods and to reasonably limit the export of raw materials. The system of licensing also concerns joint venture operations. Favorable conditions for the development of export potential in the processing industry have been created because the export of finished goods does not require licenses, with the exception of consumer goods and technically sophisticated products. As far as basic raw materials are concerned, they are included in the lists of commodities, the exports of which do not require licenses. Such measures encourage joint ventures to process raw materials in order to get finished or semiprocessed products of superior quality. As a measure to stop any speculative transactions in raw materials, the operations of joint ventures acting as dealers in raw materials have been considerably limited in this sphere. In order to act as dealers, all joint ventures are now required to have the permit of the USSR Ministry of Foreign Economic Relations.

The past as well as the current requirement is that all joint ventures created on the territory of the Soviet Union are to be registered with the USSR

Ministry of Finance. Only then can they acquire the status of a juridical person, which enables them to register with the Ministry of Foreign Economic Relations as participants of foreign economic activity. On the basis of technical economic calculations, the Ministry of Foreign Economic Relations issues licenses for the export and import of goods necessary for the activities of joint ventures, provided these commodities are on the list of licensed commodities.

We have already mentioned the relationship between health care and the environmental protection of the population. In recent years, environmental protection has become the foremost problem in all the countries of the world, and the Soviet Union is no exception. It has become a priority in the national policy of the Soviet Union to solve environmental problems as part of its economic and social structure.

Likewise, the activity of each joint venture must meet environmental standards and, in its production process, ensure an effective system for protecting the environment from industrial pollution. The cost of this measure alone amounts to a considerable sum and makes up 20 to 25 percent of the total investments in the project.

National economic priorities for the environment are realized through regional interests. Soviet law requires territorial legislative bodies to give permits to all projects involving new construction or reconstruction planned or carried out by the joint venture.

This is where territorial priorities switch in. The problems of regional development only begin to receive attention under the heading of territorial self-sufficiency. The establishment of such priorities is effected in particular by a further strengthening of the economic and political independence of Union republics. The policy of territorial priorities is getting more and more important. The policy is devised directly by republican bodies and based on observing the interests of a particular territory and the population living in it. Thus, there is great interest in the role of joint ventures in attracting foreign capital to various regions of the country.

Decree 1405 of the Council of Ministers states some preferential conditions for the operation of joint ventures. This decree also provides for a reduction of the tax rate to 10 percent for joint ventures operating in the Far East economic region. This measure allows tax preferences to be used as a tool for the realization of regional priorities. Under this resolution, the Ministry of Finance is temporarily free not to tax the part of the profit due to a foreign participant if this part is to be transferred abroad, or to reduce the amount of the tax. This resolution applies only to joint ventures located in the economic region of the Far East.

Therefore, the reduction of tax rates on the profit made by a joint venture and the extension of a tax-free period are effective elements of regional adjustment of a joint venture. For the Far East economic region, for example, this tax-free period can be as long as three years.

One means of delineating territorial priorities is the development of special economic zones in different regions of the Soviet Union. A zone of joint entrepreneurship is a territory where all the Soviet laws are in force. It is a territory with Soviet executive and legislative bodies and Soviet enterprises and institutions. However, this particular territory is supposed to create more favorable conditions for foreign capital by means of granting most-favored-nation treatment—that is, granting more privileges in customs duties, rent payments (in some cases not charging at all), or creating the necessary production and social infrastructures.

These zones should not be exclusively export enclaves, as is often the case with developing countries. These zones should be the basic suppliers of products to the domestic market. No doubt, they should also make a contribution to the export market by increasing the degree of processing of raw materials intended for export and by exporting part of their manufactured products. Such zones can be created first of all in the Far East, like in Nakhodka. It is very promising to develop such zones, which, with foreign capital investment, could contribute significantly to the scientific-technological achievements of Soviet science. One of the possible options is to create such a zone near Leningrad. Zones of free entrepreneurship are based on vast regions that are part of a complex network of joint entrepreneurships. On the other hand, the creation of tourist zones, special recreation centers, and health clubs should correspond to the climate of particular areas. The creation of tourist and recreation facilities can increase currency returns for such regions of the country as the Black Sea coast of the Caucasus, the Crimea, the Novgorod region and the city of Novgorod, the Pacific coast of the Soviet Far East, and others.

Apart from national economic and regional priorities, it is very important for joint ventures to take into consideration the priorities of particular branches of the economy. Often the interests of these branches do not coincide with national economic and regional interests. Only with the help of state management is it possible to coordinate the interests at different levels and to determine mutually advantageous spheres for joint venture operations. Moreover, the interests of a certain branch of the economy may differ from the interests of particular enterprises. The enterprise is interested in receiving currency that it can use at its discretion to purchase know-how and equipment, additional raw materials, and complete sets of products, as well as consumer goods to cover the needs of its staff. At the same time, the branch represented by a ministry or department is anxious to fulfill planned assignments. The partial use of the production potential on the Soviet side as an installment for the charter fund can delay fulfillment of the plan. This may create additional difficulties both for the branch of the economy as well as for the enterprise.

To resolve similar contradictions we should analyze and consider the interests and prospects of a particular region. Temporary problems in the fulfillment of the plan can be turned into future technological advantages in the production of an existing joint venture. It can also result in an increase in production output and a further rise of ruble and hard currency returns. It is clear from experience that we can solve these contradictions only if we have the right understanding of our long-term projects.

With economic reform underway in the Soviet Union, a branch-oriented structure includes various types of economic relations, such as rent-based relations and joint stock ventures. The Law on State Enterprises has a provision on freedom and independence of ventures within a particular branch of economy. This provision allowed for many different methods of management to be applied in economics. It is in many respects thanks to this factor that the creation of joint ventures has been intensified.

Joint enterprises as well as joint stock companies and other forms of associations and societies contribute to making the activity of different branches more intensive. The interest of a particular branch of the economy in developing a joint entrepreneurship should be reflected in a system of economic standards. This is accounted for by the fact that there exists a certain system of settlements between a Soviet state enterprise and the ministry in charge. Should the creation of a joint venture have a favorable effect on the economics of the branch as a whole, the joint venture will get priority consideration from the branch in material and technical supply. Other forms of possible preferential treatment are reducing the tax on profits made by the joint venture, extending tax-free periods in the sphere of product sales on the domestic market (including sales for currency), and providing different social services for the staff of the joint venture with the view of reducing the venture's own expenses on these services.

Branch priorities and the motives of Soviet partners are interwoven with the opportunities stemming from the new openings and subsidies of joint ventures in the Soviet Union and abroad. Soviet law provides for establishing branch offices and subsidiaries. On Soviet territory, the decision to set up branch offices and subsidiaries is to be made by the board of a joint venture. Subsidiaries are supposed to promote vast territorial expansion and differentiation of activities of joint ventures. Considering the huge territory of the country and its multibranched economic structure, the creation of subsidiaries serves as an important tool in integrating joint ventures and Soviet producers.

There are two ways to create subsidiaries of joint ventures on Soviet territory. The first is when a subsidiary is allowed to have a juridical status and its own independent balance. In this case the subsidiary operates on the basis of self-repayment and self-refinancing, both in rubles and in foreign currency. However, in case of difficulties arising in the sphere or ruble or hard-currency financing, the subsidiary can count on its headquarters.

The relationship between the subsidiary and the state budget or local executive bodies can be resolved within the balance of this particular subsidiary. If the output of a subsidiary is considerable in terms of cost and physical volume, then the subsidiary can pay taxes to the state budget from its profits in the usual order existing for joint ventures. In this case, the subsidiary's profit is not considered a profit of the head joint venture and is therefore not taxed additionally.

The second way to create a joint venture subsidiary is when a subsidiary does not have juridical status or an independent balance. In this case, all the expenses and profits of the subsidiary are to be shown on the accounts of its head joint venture. It is understood that the profit of the subsidiary is reflected in the balance of the head venture as part of the overall profit received. Thus, the size of the tax taken from the head venture reflects the relation between the joint venture subsidiary and state budget.

Such an approach is characteristic of subsidiaries that are smaller than their head joint venture. Trying to centralize the activity of the joint venture as a whole may provide the grounds for creating subsidiaries with no balances of their own. The need for this often arises in the very first stages of creating a joint venture. Such subsidiaries have limited freedom both in making decisions and realizing them. This limited independence may in the long run lead to differences between the head venture and its subsidiary. Subsidiaries without balances of their own are most often set up in the spheres of the head joint venture's sales of finished products or services, postsale service, publicity, and the supply of certain kinds of raw materials and complete products. When a subsidiary begins multiple activities or starts its own production of goods and services, it is then reasonable to grant to it economic and managerial independence.

The prospects expected from a joint venture will no doubt be related to the expansion of a network of subsidiaries and branch offices of joint ventures on the Soviet territory.

Soviet law also provides for the creation of subsidiaries on foreign territories. Decree 412 of the USSR Council of Ministers, approved 18 May 1989, regulates the system of creating joint ventures on the territory of foreign countries. This resolution established the order of creating foreign subsidiaries of joint ventures functioning on Soviet territory.

The decision to create a subsidiary abroad is made by the board of a joint venture. Such a decision should take into consideration all the details of legislation of the country where the future subsidiary is to be set up, especially that regarding the juridical status of a foreign subsidiary. It is important to consider the problem of taxes for a subsidiary and the system of allocating a share of the profit of the joint venture registered in the Soviet Union, as well as of its named Soviet participant.

Priorities in the development of joint ventures in the Soviet Union should be taken into account and related, in practical terms, to the methods of calculating the economic effectiveness of would-be joint ventures. Certain steps in this direction have already been taken: Decree 1405 developing and implementing "temporary standard methods of determining economic efficiency of joint ventures created on the territory of the Soviet Union."

Not claiming universal and absolute value, these methods emphasize that there is contained in them an attempt to tie together the interests of the Soviet partner and the interests of the economy as a whole. It is necessary to make technical-economic calculations taking into account the profit of all the partners concerned. Only a detailed analysis of the results will enable us to draw a conclusion about the efficiency of a joint venture and facilitate the decision to create a joint venture.

The further development of entrepreneurship will require more detailed criteria for specifying the priorities. Thus, the general information on the economic branches involved in research and production needs a more detailed analysis. In the future, we would need an approach more clearly specifying the priorities connected with the engineering complex and new production based on advanced know-how. This know-how should be developed by Soviet producers within the industrial complex and in processing agricultural products.

Chapter 8

The Internationalization of the Soviet Economy

Philip Hanson

To speak of the internationalization of the Soviet economy may make Soviet foreign trade reforms sound both grander in scope and more successful in implementation than they have so far been. But integration into the international economy is a necessary ingredient in successful market reform. The radical economist and statistician Grigorii Khanin has remarked that "International integration is the chief strength of the Western economy."[1] That oversimplifies the issue a little, but the insight is a fundamental one: the market mechanism in the West operates in an international setting, with considerable freedom of trade and capital movements among nations. In a large part of each Western economy, the competition is international.

The aim of this chapter is to identify and describe the links between domestic market-oriented reform and the foreign trade reforms, and to consider some analyses of the foreign trade reforms from this perspective. The first section briefly summarizes the state of the foreign trade reforms at the end of 1989. The second section is an assessment of the key problems hindering further progress with these reforms. The third section considers what developments in the domestic economic system are needed in order to make further progress in opening up the Soviet economy to the rest of the world. The fourth section offers some comments on the chapter by Igor Doronin. The final section is a consideration of what Western governments might do to help. The role of joint ventures will be emphasized throughout, but there is little sense in considering them in isolation from the other elements of the foreign trade reform process, and I shall not do so.

The starting point for this chapter is a familiar but still important observation: the relationship between domestic and foreign trade reform is a reciprocal one.

On the one hand, the internationalization of the economy requires market reforms on the domestic front: Soviet manufacturing enterprises are unlikely to make much progress as exporters in competitive markets unless they are driven to innovate and cut costs by a domestic environment of sink-or-swim competition (hard budget constraints); joint ventures are unlikely to prosper on any substantial scale and across a wide range of activities as long as they are grafted onto an economy dominated by centralized supply allocation, shortages, prices that have little economic meaning, and related phenomena; nonresident convertibility of the ruble requires that ruble prices reflect relative scarcities, at least approximately, and that the ruble automatically provides command over Soviet goods and factors; and so on.

On the other hand—and this side of the relationship is less frequently discussed—domestic reform without an opening up to the world economy is also, if not impossible, at least very difficult and likely to be flawed. The monopolistic structure of Soviet production is a serious obstacle to successful market reform. It results both from the existence of branch ministries and from the huge average size of Soviet enterprises (there are about twice as many manufacturing establishments in the much smaller economy of the United Kingdom as there are in the Soviet Union). The view that import competition will be needed at an early stage in reform should be taken seriously. Adaptation to a market regime also requires expertise in matters that range from market research to the collection of income tax. There are many ways in which that expertise can be, and already is being, acquired, but an opening to foreign direct investment is probably the most effective.

These generalities do not of course take us very far. The real problems have to do with the details and timing of reform measures. However, the notion of a reciprocal relationship between foreign trade and domestic reform will serve as the theme around which this chapter is organized.

CURRENT STATE OF FOREIGN TRADE REFORM

There have been four periods of substantial change in the Soviet foreign trade system: the creation of the traditional system in a series of measures spread between 1918 and the early 1930s, the acquisition and organizational shaping of a Soviet trading bloc of state-trading nations in the late 1940s and early 1950s, the opening up of trade with non-communist countries between the late 1950s and the 1970s, and the present period of liberalization. The present wave of change, if it is not reversed in the near future, will rank with the first in fundamental importance.

One feature of the present reforms is their incremental nature. They began earlier and have been subject to more continual amendment than the reform measures affecting the domestic economy. The first group of measures was approved by the Politburo in August 1986. More detailed measures covering joint ventures were approved in December of that year. There were some further amendments in September 1987, and a radical extension of the reform measures was made public in December 1988. That in turn was followed by legislation that set out a system of import and export licensing.[2] In addition, there have been a number of lesser decrees and laws that helped to create the new framework, such as the new regulations on foreign travel by Soviet citizens for business purposes, the beginnings of the establishment of Special Economic Zones (SEZs), and detailed guidelines for the first currency auction, on 3 November 1989. (The hard currency sales at the first two auctions were tiny: if they were held monthly with the same volume of transactions, the amount of hard currency that would change hands in the course of a year would be less than a half-percent of the Soviet annual hard currency import bill.[3])

The chief objectives of these measures are the following: to diffuse the right to negotiate foreign trade deals widely among Soviet enterprises (including cooperatives), instead of restricting it almost exclusively to specialist foreign trade organizations (FTOs) subordinate to the USSR Ministry of Foreign Economic Relations (MFER, formerly the USSR Ministry of Foreign Trade); to allow and encourage the inflow of foreign equity investment from both socialist and capitalist partners, extending now to majority ownership by the foreign partner; to facilitate direct and extensive personal contact between Soviet producers and the outside world, and to move in stages toward ruble convertibility.

Administrative control by the central authorities over the total and composition of imports is not so far being removed, but the means of exercising it are shifting toward a mixture of direct instructions, licensing, and foreign currency controls. Soviet banking officials estimate that the source of finance for hard currency imports in 1988 were: 10 to 15 percent in enterprise retained hard currency earnings, 20 to 25 percent in bank credits, and 60 to 70 percent in central allocation.[4] Movement toward these objectives has been limited, but there have been some real gains in commercial cooperation with the non-communist world.

Perhaps the most favorable development is the almost total change in the atmosphere surrounding East-West trade. Reporting and discussion of Western economies and of Soviet trade with them have changed dramatically in tone: similarities and common problems are stressed; the adversarial language that used to be normal has disappeared. Travel and contacts have become vastly easier. Information that was previously secret is beginning, slowly, to be released. ("Slowly," however, is the operative word. We still do not have official data on the current account of the balance of payments, or on gold and foreign currency reserves. What has been said by Prime Minister Nikolai Ryzhkov about Soviet external debt is unclear and hard to reconcile with Western estimates.[5] The figure of 34 billion rubles, or 54 billion dollars, that he gave in June for external debt is presumably gross debt but even so is well above Western estimates. His forecast of 12 billion rubles or 19 billion dollars debt-service payments in 1989 must again be gross but, even so, seems high.) Detailed official data on outstanding indebtedness of socialist and Third World countries to the Soviet Union were published in 1990, but the hard currency debt situation has not been officially clarified.

In general, the official position in Moscow now is that East-West business relations should become normal. This shows up in a great many new phenomena, including Western management training for Soviet executives, consultation between Soviet and Western specialists, and so on.

One manifestation of this change in Moscow's stance is potentially of great importance: the new policies on international economic organizations. There have been two important decisions: to seek membership in the General Agreement on Tariff and Trade (GATT) and to negotiate a trade and economic cooperation agreement with the European Community (EC), on the basis long insisted upon by the EC, namely, that it would negotiate such agreements only with individual member countries of the Council on Mutual Economic Assistance (CMEA), not with CMEA itself—though under the umbrella of a loose framework agreement with the latter.[6] Toward the International Monetary Fund (IMF) the Soviet attitude is more guarded. It is clear that the existing voting rules in the IMF, which give the United States a veto, are seen in Moscow as constituting an obstacle even to seeking membership. The standard IMF formula, according to Robert Manning, would give the Soviet Union 6 percent of the vote. On the other hand, expert consultations with IMF officials are regarded in Moscow as desirable and have in fact started.[7]

The rapid growth of joint ventures is on the face of it another favorable indicator. By the end of 1990 over twelve hundred were registered.[8] But the average size is small and the cumulative foreign investment in them (insofar as that can be denoted by the foreign partners' contributions to initial capital) over a span of nearly two years is equivalent to well under 1 percent of total annual Soviet investment.

There has been some progress in information policy. The statements by Ryzhkov mentioned above about Soviet external debt and the debt service ratio, though still not adequately defined or issued on a systematic basis, are a step toward official Soviet release of such information.[9] Gold and foreign currency reserves data and balance of payments numbers are at the time of writing still secret. It is inconsistent with present Soviet policies to go on withholding this information. Perhaps it is being kept back to provide the Soviet Union with a bargaining point in negotiations with GATT and the IMF.

There has also been a limited advance toward creating SEZs. On 19 September 1989 Ivan Ivanov, the first deputy chair of the State Foreign Economics Commission, announced that three SEZs would be established during 1990: in Vyborg on the Finnish border, Nakhodka on the Pacific coast, and Novgorod in north-central European Russia. At the same time, Estonia, Latvia, and Lithuania have their own schemes for SEZS, independent of Moscow.[10] The Baltic schemes apart, what is being planned at present stops well short of the open sector scheme proposed by a group of foreign specialists under the aegis of the Soros Foundation and discussed with Soviet officials in late 1988 and early 1989. Again, however, these are only small beginnings.

The steps taken toward linking domestic to world market prices and making the ruble convertibility have been the following:

• The announcement of a gradual adjustment during 1991–95 of internal wholesale prices for fuels and materials to the level and structure of their world market equivalents;[11]

• A confused and confusing series of attempts to create automatic links between internal and external prices of traded goods: first abandoning the use of internal prices (with or without special markups) in transactions between foreign trade organizations and end users of imports or producers of exports in favor of a set of several thousand differentiated valuta coefficients (DVKs), with respect to about 10 percent of Soviet experts;[12] and then planning to abandon DVKs in favor of a single exchange rate valuing the ruble at half its present level trade purposes during 1990, after which there is supposed to be a new, realistic single conversion rate reflecting purchasing power parities after the revision of internal wholesale prices.[13]

• The creation of a new tourist rate of ten times the official trade rate (in rubles per foreign currency unit), still well below the black market rate; this is merely a device to reduce the leakage of hard currency into the black market.[14]

• The first internal auction of foreign currency for rubles, already mentioned. This is the start of a new arrangement which, substantially expanded, could eventually provide guidance on a realistic exchange rate.

• The official adoption of Nikolai Shmelev's idea of paying for increments of import-saving domestic output of hard wheat and oilseeds in hard currency, providing another linkage between the domestic economy and world prices.[15]

These small steps toward openness have been supported by similarly small improvements in the infrastructure of foreign trade activities: telefax machines, though rare, do now exist in some Soviet institutions; procedures for Soviet executives to get exit visas for business travel have been simplified and speeded up; banking links across Soviet borders have been somewhat strengthened.

KEY PROBLEMS

Efficient trading activities among Western countries are facilitated by features that are taken for granted in the West but are absent or severely restricted in East-West trade. A consideration of these features illustrates the key problems that confront the Soviet reformers who are trying to integrate the Soviet Union into the world economy. In what follows, the

West is defined geographically rather than politically. Japan and the newly industrialized Asian countries may perhaps represent an alternative model of international economic integration that the Soviet Union might follow. This will be considered separately.

First, the bulk of import and export decisions in the West are taken by profit-seeking firms in the light of the prices that are expected to affect their financial position. By and large, in Western Europe and North America, if a good can be bought more cheaply from abroad than from a domestic supplier, it will be. If a good can be sold abroad profitably, it will be. It is true that in practice there are many market imperfections. In the presence of monopoly power and administered prices, there may be quantity rationing—by delivery times, for example. Governments influence the terms of international transactions in a variety of ways, usually to the detriment of efficient outcomes, by tariff and nontariff barriers, by including the exchange rate, by preferential domestic sourcing of military hardware and some other public sector acquisition of tradeable goods, and so on; but they do not normally intervene in particular microeconomic decisions to export and import. In addition, there is considerable free movement of capital around the developed world in search of high rates of return.

In general, with imperfect information, monopoly power, and state intervention, there is plenty of room for misallocation of resources and for instability. But there is no doubt that available information is more effectively used than it is in foreign trade under traditional central planning. Adaptation of production and trade to changes in costs and demand is likely to be more flexible.[16]

The reforms in the Soviet foreign trade system up to late 1989 still leave that system closer to traditional state trading than to market-driven trade. Internal prices for importers and exporters do not provide reliable guidance to the cost-effectiveness of foreign as against domestic transactions. Those prices neither reflect domestic relative scarcities in the semi-isolated Soviet economy nor resemble even remotely the structure of world market prices. Because of the divergence of structure, there is no single exchange rate that could correspond to ruble-dollar purchasing power parity in traded goods generally (see Table 8.1).

The bulk of resources are still centrally allocated by planners, so enterprises have only limited choice with respect to trade anyway. Moreover, the incentives for state enterprises to trade efficiently would be weak even if they were faced with meaningful internal prices and could make their own foreign trade decisions. This is because of the general weakness of incentives to enterprises to cut costs and to innovate: losses are not threatening because the state enterprise expects to be bailed out of financial trouble by its higher authority; profits are not a strong positive stimulus because the state enterprise has no confidence that its higher authority will not simply appropriate any profits it makes in an arbitrary fashion.

Table 8.1
The Structure of Internal and World Market Prices (price of 1 ton of crude oil = 1.00, 1987/88)

	Current Soviet Wholesale Prices	Planned 1991 Prices	World Market Prices*
Electricity (1000 kwh)	.61	.37	.21
Quality steel (1 ton)	4.70	2.70	2.16
Ammonia (1 ton)	3.47	2.00	.60
Wheat (1 ton)	4.33	2.93	.65
Screw-cutting lathe	190.00	85.50	48.70

Source: N. Astrakhantseva, V. Kuznetsov, "Ot koeffitsientov--k real'nomu kursu," *Ekonomicheskaya gazeta* 35 (1988): 21. I am grateful to Dr. Kuznetsov for providing some background information on the sources and definitions of these data.

*Prices faced by the Soviet Union on Western markets with respect to either imports or exports.

Some of the new animals on the Soviet business scene—cooperatives and joint ventures in particular—are better motivated. Their creation and their ability to engage in trade amount to a significant change. Over fourteen hundred cooperatives and seven hundred joint ventures were registered as foreign trading entities by 1 October 1989.[17] But they are still very small in total size and handicapped by the shortage economy environment in which they operate.

There is therefore no reason to expect that the strong tendency to import bias and export aversion of the part of Soviet state enterprises is appreciably less of a problem than it was in the early 1980s. (It is less of a problem in primary product activities than in manufacturing. For primary product producers, world markets do not present the formidable challenges of quality control, marketing, and after-sales service that they do for Soviet manufacturers. This difference is implicitly acknowledged by Soviet authorities in the setting of much lower hard currency earnings retention shares as export incentives for the former than for the latter.[18])

In general, the rules of the game for market-driven foreign trade still do not apply in the Soviet Union. Here are some examples of the pathology that results. A deputy minister of MFER, Vadim Shestakov, has recently given the undercutting by one Soviet organization of another Soviet organization's export price as an example of an action that flouts the "state interest"; this, he says, is the kind of thing that justifies tighter control by his ministry over export pricing.[19] This maintenance of the monopoly power of the old state trading system is incompatible with the development of competitiveness in Soviet exporting generally.

If there were some uncontroversial and easily identifiable national interest, and if central planners were good at spotting it, this approach would make sense. But, notoriously, these conditions do not prevail. Indeed, high officials in the Soviet Union are increasingly accused these days not just of trying to do something inherently impossible, but of outright laziness and corruption and contributing to inefficient patterns of trade. This has been argued, for example, with respect to the grain import lobby.[20]

The microeconomic intervention of the central authorities in trade is still inconsistent and unpredictable. Recently, for example, the Minister of the USSR Fisheries Industry was reprimanded, and his first deputy severely reprimanded, for licensing exports of large amounts of fish when deliveries to the domestic market were well below plan.[21] Perhaps there was more to this story than was revealed in the press report, but there is no indication that any guidelines were violated. It looks more as though the central policymakers, having panicked about domestic food shortages, were looking for any scapegoats they could find. At all events, the episode shows that foreign trade decision makers still operate in an environment of quantity rationing, with ad hoc microintervention from above.

The curious episode of the allegedly unlicensed exports or attempted exports of military items by the ANT state cooperative concern illustrates the confused and unsystematic nature of trade liberalization. According to the minister of the aviation industry, ANT had special dispensation to export military-related items without any sort of license.[22]

The adverse effects on incentives are not confined to conventional trade, but extend to the absorption of imported technology and the working of industrial cooperation and joint ventures. Normally, Western business partners of Soviet organizations do not air these problems publicly, for obvious reasons. A remarkable exception was a Soviet press article by P. van den Tempel of the Dutch agribusiness cooperative, Sebeco.[23] His firm is engaged in a project to raise crop yields in one district (*raion*) of Moscow region (*oblast*). The original Soviet approach to Sebeco came in 1982. An agreement was not signed until February 1987.

Van den Tempel says that progress since then has been small, and indicates the reasons as he sees them. First, the competent specialists on the Soviet side are not the people who make the Soviet decisions. Second, nobody on the Soviet side has been worried by delays. This lack of interest and misuse of know-how, says van den Tempel, has produced gross errors on a scale his company has not encountered before, "even in the depths of Africa."[24] The company complained of all this in a letter to the USSR Council of Ministers. After several months without a reply, they took the matter to *Izvestiya*.

The Soviet reformers would find the internationalization of the Soviet economy politically easier if export performance could be radically improved without domestic production being exposed to competition from imports. The institutional changes made so far are, in fact, oriented in this direction. Import licensing and central control of hard currency leave only limited scope for decentralized import decisions, while diffusion of formal foreign trade rights, the creation of joint ventures, and the reduction of barriers to East-West contacts facilitate export growth. In this correction, it might be thought that the Japanese model would be attractive to them.

It may be doubted, however, whether it is a useful model for Moscow. Japan's resistance to import penetration is based on a number of factors, both institutional and cultural: a costly and complicated internal distribution system that is hard for outsiders to work with; close, informal cooperation between government and industry; cooperation both within and, on occasion, between the *keiretsu* groupings of companies that would be regarded as collusion in the United States; and what seems to be a polite but firm resistance in Japanese society to foreigners becoming insiders. All of these have their counterparts in the Soviet Union, but the Soviet equivalents are part of a social system inimical to high levels of productivity.

There is a parallel in the case of job security. Japanese workers inside the permanent employment system have a high degree of job security that makes them less immobile among employers than is the case in the Soviet Union, but they are still highly mobile geographically and occupationally motivated to work. A deliberate attempt to follow the Japanese model in foreign trade would probably only help to entrench features of the Soviet system that make it unconstructive.

NECESSARY DOMESTIC REFORMS

The basic problems of information and incentives, of course, all come from the economic system as a whole and are not specific to the foreign trade system. There is no need to expound the connections at length, as they are well known. They can be briefly summarized as follows.

First, if Soviet state enterprises are not motivated to reduce costs and increase profits over the long term in the light of information available to them, there is no reason to expect them to seek to export and import in cost effective ways. Second, if decisions on what, when and how to trade are retained by ministries and central planners, they will as a general rule be more poorly informed then if they were made by producers. Third, if domestic prices do not reflect domestic scarcities or—even roughly and as a second best—average costs plus a standard rate of return on capital, the available price information will be misleading, whoever uses it.

Fourth, predominantly centralized supply allocation renders money incapable of providing command over resources in the domestic economy. So far, therefore, the ruble is not money in the usual sense even inside the

Soviet Union. Still less can it be converted into goods by nonresident holders of rubles. This circumstance makes nonresident convertibility of the ruble for trading purposes impossible.

Fifth, any kind of automatic linking of domestic to foreign prices is ruled out by the previous two circumstances. It should, it is true, be possible for central policymakers to adjust the structure of centrally set domestic prices so that it more closely resembles that of world market prices at any rate for broad product groups and as a one-time exercise. That would allow the establishment of a single exchange rate for the ruble that permits consistent translation of the ruble into foreign prices for tradeable goods. But in the absence of decontrolled domestic prices and an international market in rubles, it is doubtful if the rate could be kept realistic for long because of the massive information problems of centralized price adjustment.

Sixth, chronic internal excess demand is generated by the traditional system—Janos Kornai's "shortage economy." It is therefore likely that decontrol of prices and the exchange rate would lead to the ruble falling continuously, with no built-in mechanism for achieving balance in the external payments.

Finally, all these difficulties affect industrial cooperation as well as conventional trade. Asset valuation, repatriation of profits, quality control, and the acquisition of material inputs all remain problematic for joint ventures and other forms of firm-level cooperation on Soviet soil. It follows—and the conclusion is uncontroversial to the point of banality—that the creation of a competitive domestic market must either precede or be carried out more or less at the same time as the genuine decontrol of trade decisions and the creation of a convertible ruble.

It is impossible, I believe, to demonstrate that opening up to the world economy must be simultaneous with domestic reform. It will have to be simultaneous if the structure of domestic production is so monopolized that domestic decontrol without freedom to import would fail to produce an environment of workable competition. If that is not the case, integration into the world economy can come after domestic marketization. I suspect, but know of no strong evidence, that import competition will in fact be needed if a competitive regime is to be established inside the Soviet Union. If that is so, the difficulties of the reform process are even larger than they would otherwise be.

Two questions arise from recent policy discussions. First, is there some maximum viable transition time and, if so, what is it? Second, if something other than a shock therapy approach is feasible, and the transformation could be spread out over several years, is there a role for a gold-backed ruble at an early stage in the process of change?

The transition process at present proposed is staged over six years.[25] Domestic competition and external convertibility would begin to be phased in during 1993–95, after financial stabilization has gone quite far and a new legal and administrative framework has been put in place during 1989–92. Is this too slow? The tests by which one might usefully assess different timetables do not exist. My guess is that the step-by-step transition supported by Leonid Abalkin is feasible, and shock therapy is not obligatory. But this guess is not worth much, even in inconvertible rubles.

Viktor Belkin advocates beginning with a special ruble that is internally convertible (into goods). This would be the enterprise revenue derived, directly and indirectly, from sales to the population rather than to other enterprises.[26] This approach is compatible with the Soros open sector idea of marketization and limited external convertibility, starting in one segment of the economy and extending to the whole economy over a period of a few years. This kind of staged approach may well be workable, but it need not follow that the shock therapy approach is not.

The second questions concerns the idea of U.S. Federal Reserve Board Governor Wayne Angell that the ruble should be made internally convertible into gold as a first step toward internal marketization and external convertibility. The scheme would entail Soviet citizens being able to get gold for their ruble notes on demand, and this would be the case for ordinary rubles, not for a special, parallel currency.[27]

The crucial result that Angell expects from ruble convertibility into gold is that the Soviet government would be forced to control the money supply, because, otherwise, Soviet citizens would convert their currency into gold at an indefinitely increasing gold price until the state had sold off all its gold. When faced with the impending loss of all gold reserves, the Soviet government would certainly wish to control the money supply. Whether it could in fact do so in the face of the traditional, passive behavior of the Soviet banking system is not so clear. Shortage economy pressures on the banking system to finance whatever enterprises "need" to do are strong, and the main banking network is still not divided between a central bank proper and commercial banks.

In general, there seems to be no clear way forward in integrating the Soviet economy into the international economy except by starting with financial stabilization and marketization of the Soviet domestic economy.

COMMENTS ON SOVIET WRITINGS

In the light of the account I have just given, it seems that many Soviet writers are too optimistic about the impact of joint ventures. They envisage improved export performance and a hospitable economic environment for joint ventures without the necessity of fundamental changes in the domestic economic system. For instance, current Soviet commentaries often envisage the economic branch ministries as part of the Soviet economic landscape for the foreseeable future, while joint ventures flourish and export performance improves. Yet the continued existence of government ministries held

responsible for specific outcomes in whole branches of the economy is incompatible with a market economy. This is not because ministry officials
are for some mysterious reason incompetent. On the contrary, the drive and
business acumen of some branch ministers and their deputies in the Brezhnev
era (Leonid Kostandov, for example, who presided over the modernization
of the Soviet chemical industry) were highly regarded by the senior Western
executives with whom they dealt. The incompatibility is due to the inherently
inefficient nature of the structures of information and motivation in a giant
hierarchy, and this is the fundamental reason why the Soviet chemical industry—to continue with the same example—was substantially modernized
but still never caught up.

Similarly, Soviet commentators characteristically see government regulation as the answer to conflicts of interest between economic branches, on
the one hand, and the nation or particular regions on the other. This, too,
places economic policy in the framework of a planned, not a market economy. It is true that in a market economy there are usually organizations
that articulate branch and regional interests: trade organizations, city, state,
or provincial governments, and the like. But in a market economy these
actors are usually fairly weak and never part of a larger administrative
hierarchy. The major actors in industry-government relations are on the
one hand firms that operate or could operate in several different branches,
and, on the other hand, a government that sets general rules of the game.

For the reasons given in the previous sections of this chapter, I do not
see a glittering future for joint ventures in the Soviet Union, for Soviet
exports, and for Soviet integration into the world economy generally, unless
and until the Soviet Union becomes a market economy.

This is exactly the point that Igor Doronin makes in Chapter 6. In general,
I very much agree with his analysis. There are only two observations I wish
to make.

First, I am uneasy about his confident choice of a transition strategy: a
managed adjustment to a "civilized market" rather than a shock therapy
approach. I do not meant o say that he is wrong; I just do not know how
he can be so confident that he is right. Earlier in this chapter, I raised the
question of whether there is a maximum feasible transition period and, if
so, what it is. The question is a serious one, because careful managed reform
in stages can so easily become institutional stagnation: witness Hungary for
most of the 1970s. It could be, after all, that there is in fact no alternative
to shock therapy. Doronin seems sure that there is. I agree with him that
a soft landing is better than a hard one. The question is whether the soft
landing is an available option; I fear that it may not be.

Second, there should be more discussion of specific measures and their
timing. One simple prescription that follows from the discussion above is
that branch ministries must be abolished. Like the reduction and eventual
removal of agricultural subsidies in the EC and the United States, this is,

of course, easier said than done. But in order to do it one probably has to say that it needs doing.

THE QUESTION OF WESTERN AID

There are a great many issues to do with Western assistance for Soviet economic and trade reform. I shall confine myself here to making two points of a general nature. The first concerns trade expansion and technical co-operation as higher forms of aid. The second has to do with the historical analogy of the Marshall Plan.

To begin with, several Soviet spokespersons have expressed the view that technical assistance, training, and the like are more important than large credits, and that the latter are not being sought from the West by Moscow. This seems to be the official Soviet position. There is no good reason to question it. In the absence of reform, large credits will be poorly used. Training and technical assistance, including, for example, assistance with the collection and analysis of economic procedures, with the running of a modern tax system, and so on can help the reform process itself. Throwing money at an unreformed economy will, if anything, help to delay reform.

Government policy in the West can also help by expanding Soviet trade opportunities. This would include facilitation of step-by-step Soviet entry into GATT, some rationalization of the Coordinating Committee on Mul-tilateral Export Controls embargo and reasonably liberal terms in the trade agreement now under negotiation between Moscow and the EC.

Marshall Plan assistance from the United States to war-damaged Western Europe in 1948–52 has been evoked as a model for aid now to Eastern Europe and the Soviet Union. For the Soviet Union, at least, it is inappropriate.

The disequilibrium in Europe that the Marshall Plan was meant to reduce had highly specific causes: they included shortage of domestic capital and therefore distorted factor proportions in Europe as a result of wartime destruction and the nonreplacement of obsolete equipment, redistribution of income that reduced savings ratios and losses of overseas assets. The disequilibrium showed up most conspicuously in the late 1940s in a West European current account deficit with the United States equivalent to around 4 percent of West European GNP, Marshall Aid deliveries were intended to prevent that balance of payments deficit blocking a rapid growth of investment and the restoration of output levels.[28]

The effects of Marshall Aid are uncertain, partly because the Korean War provided a boost to economic growth anyway, before the Marshall Plan had been in operation for long. But the logic of the Marshall Plan does not apply to the Soviet Union. In postwar Western Europe there was a potentially very high return to additional capital, because of the distortions of labor-capital ratios that had arisen from the war. Skills, attitudes, and economic institutions were in place: once some crucial bits of the European economic machine were replaced, it could roar into life. In the Soviet case, it is not a critical spare part or two that is needed; rather, a whole new machine has to be designed and built. That brings us back to domestic economic reform.

NOTES

Constructive comments by an anonymous referee are gratefully acknowledged.

1. In an interview entitled "My esche mozhem uchit'sys," *Nauka urala* (5 April 1989).

2. "Politburo TsK KPSS," *Izvestiya* (17 August 1986): 1; "O merakh po ko-renomu sovershenstvovaniu vneshneekonomicheskoi deyatelnosti," *Pravda* (24 September 1986): 1; "O merakh po sovershenstvovanniyu upravlenie vneshneekonomicheskimi svyazami," *Ekonomicheskaya gazeta* 4 (1987): 3–6; *Ekonomicheskaya gazeta* 6 (1987): 15–18; "Poryadok osuschestyleniya obedine-niyami, predpriyatiyami i organizatsiyami SSSR pryamykh proizvodstvennykh i nauchno-teknicheskikh svyazei s predpriyatiyami i organizatsiyami drugikh stran—chlenov SEV," *Ekonomicheskaya gazeta* 9 (1987): 23; *Ekonomicheskaya gazeta* 10 (1987): 23; *Ekonomicheskaya gazeta* 11 (1987): 23; *East-West (Fortnightly Bulletin)* 422 (12 November 1987); "V sovete ministrov SSSR," *Izvestiya* (10 December 1988): 2; "O merakh gosudarstvennogo regulirovaniya vnesheekonomicheskoi de-yatelnosti," *Ekonomicheskaya gazeta* 13 (1989): 21; *Ekonomika i zhizn* (1990): 9.

3. "Kliuchevoe zveno ekonomicheskoi reformi," *Izvestiya* (2 September 1989): 2; "Zoni sovmestnogo predprinimatelstva," *Izvestiya* (20 September 1989): 3; "Val-yutniye auktsioni v USSR," *Ekonomicheskaya gazeta* 40 (1989): 23.

4. *Business Eastern Europe* (10 April 1989): 113.

5. "Sluzhit intersom naroda," *Izvestiya* (8 June 1989): 1–3 and *Financial Times* (10 June 1989): 2. The debt figure probably refers to May 1989. The CIA estimates of Soviet debt at the end of 1988 are $41.7 billion gross and $27.3 billion net, with net interest payments of $2.4 billion. CIA/DIA, "The Soviet Economy in 1988: Gorbachev Changes Course," report presented to the U.S. Congress Joint Economic Committee Subcommittee on National Security Economics, 14 April 1989. The Vienna Institute of International Economic Comparisons (WIEW) estimate for end–1989 is $49.2 billion for gross and $34.4 billion for net, *Newe zuercher zeitung* (19 April 1990).

6. See Anders Aslund, "The New Soviet Policy towards International Economic Organization," *The World Today* (February 1988): 27–31; P. Hanson and V. Sobell, "The Changing Relations between the EC and the CMEA," Radio Free Europe Research RAD/73 (3 May 1989); interview with Vladimir Chemiatenkov, the new Soviet Ambassador to the EC, *Le Soir* (3 March 1989).

7. For the Soviet view see the interview with Gosbank board member Yurii Ponomarev, "Neobkhodimy korennye reformy," *MMI* 3 (1989): 45–46. For a tough Western view see Robert R. Manning, "Soviets in IMF—What's in It for the West," *Wall Street Journal* (8 May 1989): A16.

8. *Izvestiya* (26 January 1990): 3.

9. Perhaps, as Mikhail Berger has suggested ["Kak valyutu tratim," *Izvestiya* (20

June 1989): 5], the surprisingly high debt-service ratio quoted by Ryzhkov departs from standard international practice by including repayment of short-term borrowing. In any case, an authoritative definition is needed.

10. "Zoni sovmestnogo predprinimatelstva," *Izvestiya* (20 September 1989): 3, earlier statements are in G. Alimov, "Svobodnye ekonomicheskie zoni: sovetskaya model," *Izvestiya* (17 June 1989): 2 and, on Novgorod, V. Groyanovskii "Biznesmeny na novgorodchine," *Izvestiya* (30 August 1989): 1. On Estonia: AP from San Juan (13 June 1989).

11. A semiofficial statement by the organizing committee of the "scientific-practical" conference on economic reform set for 13–15 November 1989, Yu Prokuryakov, "Ot tsenogo k kursovomu mekhanizmu," *Ekonomicheskaya gazeta* 29 (1989): 18.

12. Prokuryakov, "Ot tsenogo k kursovomu mekhanizmu," 18.

13. But see the criticism of the proposed new price structure by N. Astrakhantseva and V. Kuznetsov, "Ot koeffitsientov—k real'nomu kursu," *Ekonomicheskaya gazeta* 35 (1988): 21.

14. TASS, "Gosbank SSSR soobshaet," *Izvestiya* (25 October 1989): 6, and "Byulleten kursov inostrannikh valyut," *Izvestiya* (31 October 1989): 6.

15. See interview with V. V. Nikitin, by B. Gavrichkin, "Pravo vuibora dolzhno ostavatsya tolko za krestyaninom," *Izvestiya* (7 September 1989): 2.

16. For the classic arguments, and some evidence, see Franklyn D. Holzman, *Foreign Trade under Central Planning* (Cambridge, Mass.: Harvard University Press, 1974); Peter Wiles, *Communist International Economics* (Oxford: Basil Blackwell, 1969); Thomas Wold, *Foreign Trade in the Centrally Planned Economy* (New York: Harwood Academic Publishers, 1988).

17. Interview with the deputy minister of foreign economic relations, V. N. Shestakov, "Predpochtenie proizvoditelyu," *Ekonomicheskaya gazeta* 42 (1989): 20.

18. Given Soviet enterprise incentives, these biases arise from the relative ease of buying and the relative difficulty of selling on world markets as against the domestic market. For a fuller version of the argument, see Hanson, *Trade and Technology in Soviet-Western Relations* (New York: Columbia University Press, 1981), Chapter 7. The hard currency retention rates go from 90 percent for exporters of computers to 2 to 3 percent for exporters of oil and gas [*Business Eastern Europe* (10 April 1989): 113–114]. Joint ventures are not, at least initially, an exception. Their imports from January to September 1989 exceeded their exports [D. Manasov, "Sovmestnie predpriyatiya," *Vestnik statistiki* 3 (1990): 67] by $258 million against $70 million.

19. Shestakov, "Predpochtenie proizvoditelyu," 20.

20. See Berger, "Kak valyutu tratim."

21. P. van den Tempel, "Priklyucheniya gollandstev v kashire," *Izvestiya* (21 October 1989): 2.

22. A. Propenko, "ANT i drugie," *Izvestiya* (27 March 1990): 3, interview.

23. Propenko, "ANT i drugie," 3.

24. Propenko, "ANT i drugie," 3.

25. 13–15 November Conference Organizing Committee, "Radikal'naya ekonomicheskaya reforma: pervoocherednye i dolgovremennye mery," *Ekonomicheskaya gazeta* 43 (1989): 4–7.

26. See Viktor Belkin, "Konvertiruennyi rubl': kogda i pri kakikh usloviakh," *Izvestiya* (4 August 1988): 2.

27. Mikhail Berger's interview with Angell, "Zolotoi standart, a ne zolotoi chervonets," *Izvestiya* (7 October 1989): 4.

28. Immanuel Wexler, *The Marshall Plan Revisited* (Westport, Conn.: Greenwood Press, 1983); Charles P. Kindleberger, *Marshall Plan Days* (London: Unwin Hyman, 1987).

Chapter 9

Legal Aspects of Establishing Joint Ventures in the Soviet Union

Natalya L. Platonova

HISTORICAL BACKGROUND

Various legal forms of association of Soviet and foreign partners for conducting joint economic activity, both on Soviet territory and abroad, were applied for the first time in the 1920s. This was a period of significant activization of the country's economic life on the basis of widespread development of market relations, including the foreign economic sphere. A decree of the VTsIK[1] on foreign trade, dated 13 March 1922, gave the People's Commissariat for Foreign Trade the right, with the approval of the Council on Labor and Defense (STO),[2] to create joint stock companies (Russian, foreign, and mixed) either in the Soviet Union or abroad. In mixed companies, the share of the Soviet side—the People's Commissariat for Foreign Trade or its agencies—had to comprise no less than 51 percent of the stock capital.[3]

The civil codes of the Russian Republic (RSFSR) and the other Union republics contained chapters devoted to partnerships (simple partnership, full partnership, partnership with limited responsibility, and joint stock company). On 27 August 1927, the USSR Central Executive Committee[4] and the USSR Council of People's Commissars (SNK)[5] adopted the All-Union Statute on Joint-Stock Companies.

Regardless of the organizational and legal form selected, the actual economic activities on Soviet territory of mixed companies were carried out on the basis of special permits and concessions granted in accordance with the provisions of a 23 November 1920 RSFSR Council of People's Commissars decree concerning general economic and legal conditions for concessions. Overall direction in attracting and admitting foreign capital into industry and trade within the country was entrusted to an organization formed for these purposes, the Main Committee for Concessions (GKK). A treaty on concessions and a special decree of the GKK and the SNK were the legal documents that formed the basis for the right of a foreign legal or individual person to participate in economic activities, including the creation of mixed companies.

At that time the purpose of using foreign capital was to restore a national economy destroyed by war and to achieve a further acceleration in its growth. Specifically, the Council of People's Commissars decree of 23 November 1920 spoke of "attracting technical and material industry resources of developed states both for the purpose of restoring one of the principal raw material bases of the entire global economy, i.e., Russia, and for developing its productive forces, which had been undermined by world war."[6] V. I. Lenin touched on this matter in his pamphlet entitled "On the Food Tax": "In 'propagating' state capitalism in the form of concessions, the Soviet government is stengthening large-scale production as against small-scale; advanced technology as against backward technology; machine production as against manual labor; it is increasing the quantity of major industrial products in its hands (royalty), strengthening state regulatory relations as a counter to petty bourgeois-anarchist relations."[7] In other words, in addition to the goals of receiving modern technology and additional capital, the task was set of enlarging production, of lifting it to a qualitatively higher level.

However, despite these advantages, the process of attracting foreign capital, including by means of the creation of mixed companies, did not develop very far and did not last long. According to published data, there were twelve mixed companies with foreign participation in the country as of 1 January 1925, but the process of liquidating them began as early as 1929–30.[8] It appears that the main reason for this was the unbridgeable gap between economic practices within the framework of this form, on the one hand, and the policy of economic construction being carried out by the country's leaders, based on certain ideological postulates, on the other hand. Lenin noted the existence and essential role of these contradictions. In "On the Food Tax," he wrote: "A determination of the measure, and of those conditions under which concessions are advantageous rather than dangerous to us depends on the correlation of forces, is decided by a struggle, since a concession is also a form of struggle, a continuation of the class struggle in another form, and by no means a replacement of the class struggle."[9] Within the country, as we already know, policies developed along the lines of a complete rejection of private forms of economic management, including those in which foreign capital was utilized.

During subsequent decades Soviet organization participated actively in creating and operating joint ventures in a number of foreign countries, principally in areas of trade and the fishing industry. Such companies were not created on Soviet territory.

The decree on joint stock companies, which had long gone out of use, lost its validity when the Fundamentals of Civil Legislation of the Soviet

Union and Union republics were adopted in 1961. We should note, however, that neither the Fundamentals of Civil Legislation nor the civil codes that the Union republics adopted subsequently included norms contained in that decree, and they did not propose a new variant for legal regulation of such relations. This deficiency in legislation reflected the absence of the corresponding economic practice.

PRESENT STATE OF SOVIET LEGISLATION CONCERNING JOINT ENTERPRISES

At the present stage of Soviet economic development, the legal prerequisites for organizing joint ventures with foreign participation on Soviet territory appeared when the Presidium of the USSR Supreme Soviet adopted a 26 May 1983 decree entitled "On Procedures for the Work of Joint Economic Organizations of the Soviet Union and Members of the Council for Economic Cooperation on the Territory of the Soviet Union." It should, however, be noted that this decree regulated only a limited number of issues of cooperation concerning one group of states and could not therefore serve as a real basis for developing this form of international economic ties. That became possible only after the elaboration and adoption of a series of documents that varied in juridical force and that formed, in their totality, the legal basis for implementing projects that presumed that joint ventures would be created.

At the present time there is no single law in the Soviet Union regulating the legal position of the joint ventures created on Soviet territory with the participation of foreign capital. Various documents adopted by government agencies and authorities define some of the most important aspects of the work of joint ventures, from procedures establishing them to the solving of problems associated with liquidating enterprises.[10] A peculiarity of legal regulation is that legislators make a distinction between joint ventures created with the participation of Soviet organizations and firms from capitalist and developing countries and those with participants from the Soviet Union and other member countries of the Council for Mutual Economic Assistance (CMEA). A number of normative documents contain regulations affecting one or the other group of joint ventures, while the remainder, primarily instructions from ministries and departments, are of a universal nature and are applied to all joint ventures regardless of the differences noted above.

This differentiation originated from the fact that, during the decades since the Council for Economic Cooperation was formed in 1949, there arose a multitudinous system of legal regulation that reflected the special features of economic development among member states, mainly in their planning and in the extensive use of intergovernmental documents within the CMEA framework. It was precisely these features that were reflected in the special regulation affecting the position of joint ventures, international associations, and organizations formed by partners from CMEA member countries. The economic, political, and organizational reforms that are taking place both in the council itself and in its individual member states require that such an approach be rejected and that working procedures of these two groups of joint ventures operating on Soviet territory be made uniform. It should also be made clear that legislation regulating relations with firms from capitalist and developing countries also applies to cases of trilateral cooperation, such as the establishment on Soviet territory of joint ventures with the participation of partners from countries with a different socioeconomic orientation, along with Soviet organizations.

Legislation of a general nature—civil, administrative, labor, and land use—is applied in matters not covered by special legal regulations (*lex specialis*) relating to joint ventures. Among documents of this type, the most important are the Fundamentals of Civil Legislation of the Soviet Union and the Union republics, as well as the republic civil codes adopted in accordance with them. It should be pointed out that certain questions are dealt with in different ways in different codes, and there are a number of internally conflicting norms in Soviet legislation as a result.

Aside from the sources of regulation already mentioned, there are also many other documents of all-Union and republic importance. One example is the Law on Property in the Soviet Union, passed 6 March 1990, which contains a section touching on the question of the property of joint ventures that, though brief, is essential to the regulation of their legal position. In general, the process of elaborating and introducing new regulation of foreign economic relations and decisions on problems related to them are proceeding at a brisk pace.[11]

As envisaged by the USSR Council of Ministers Decree 1405, a new special ruble exchange rate for certain operations has been in effect since 1 November 1989. This step has weakened criticism directed at the state-regulated relationship between the ruble and freely convertible currencies, especially in payments for consumer goods and services. Its introduction makes it possible (though not obligatory) for joint ventures to compute the wages of their specialists in accordance with the new exchange rate. It is not necessary to recompute the shares of Soviet and foreign participants in an enterprise. However, it is possible that future changes in the exchange rate will also affect trade operations.

There has recently been a general trend toward consistent and essential liberalization, as well as making earlier adopted statutes more specific in developing the normative basis for the work of joint ventures in the Soviet Union. One should note here the rejection of the obligatory minimum 51 percent share for the Soviet partner, the foreign partner's access to one of the two key positions in managing an enterprise, the application of a number of tax privileges depending on specific terms of capital investment, and much else. Many foreign specialists have considered these innovations to be of great value.

At the same time, the general exacerbation of the economic situation in the Soviet Union and the growing deficit in a number of consumer goods and goods important in production have forced the government to embark on a series of temporary restrictions in foreign trade, which has resulted in a substantial increase in the share of licensed, or state-controlled, Soviet export. This was reinforced by the adoption of a series of acts by governmental and administrative agencies—in particular, the USSR Supreme Soviet Decree of 20 November 1989, "On Additional Measures to Stabilize the Consumers' Market and Strengthen Government Control over Prices," which deemed it expedient to introduce licensing for the export of consumer goods and for the main types of raw material used in consumer goods production by all participants in foreign economic ties. On 11 December 1989, the USSR Council of Ministers adopted Decree 1104, "On Additional Measures of State Regulation of Foreign Economic Activities in 1990," in order to implement the earlier decree as well as to overcome certain negative phenomena in foreign economic relations, particularly the export of types of raw materials in short supply on the domestic market. One of the principal innovations was the requirement that only after the receipt of licenses from authorizing organizations could contracts be signed and products dispatched abroad in all types of foreign economic activities involving goods subject to licensing. Earlier, the signing of a contract usually preceded receipt of licenses from authorizing organizations. This decree also contains a number of restrictive provisions. These decrees do not seem to have a major influence on the work of joint ventures proper, they can materially limit only their intermediary operations. It should once again be pointed out that they are of a temporary nature.

PROSPECTS FOR LEGAL REGULATION

The rapid growth of joint ventures and practically raise the prospect of further changes in the legal regulation of these relationships. Specifically, 1990 plans were to complete legislation on stock companies, on rules for competition, on the protection of consumers' rights, and on a number of other questions. However, it is an easy matter to predict the results of legislative activity. Unfortunately, there have recently been cases of failures in this area, when a draft bill has lost its vitality and no longer responds to the requirements of reality as a result of lengthy consultations and compromises among departments.

One of the most important and as yet unresolved problems is that of the legal status of joint ventures. Completion and subsequent adoption of joint stock legislation should, in conjunction with legislation adopted earlier, give a complete picture of the regulation of the work of virtually all subjects of economic relations in the Soviet Union, including those that have attracted foreign capital. The numerous blank spaces still existing in legal regulations will be eliminated. In the process, some decisions will be given a more solid basis, with reliance on world legislative practice. This applies, for example, to procedures for creating an enterprise, to the way participants deposit their shares into charter funds, to procedures for liquidating an enterprise—a very important matter from a practical point of view—and some other aspects.

The process of preparing this legislation is not a simple one. Its authors confront the problem of adapting particular forms accepted abroad, or used earlier in the Soviet Union, to the new social and economic realities of the early 1990s. The task consists not so much in creating classical models as in developing an effective mechanism capable of regulating and ensuring optimum economic relations among participants in civil society (*oborot*). The internal duality of the Soviet economy, expressed in attempts to liberate market relations while still forced to preserve the *diktat* of administrative methods of management, materially hampers this process.

THE ROLE OF INTERSTATE REGULATION

Interstate and intergovernmental agreements can play a vital role in regulating the work of joint ventures. USSR Council of Ministers Decree 49, of 13 January 1987, states that the work of joint ventures with the participation of firms from capitalist and developing countries is subject of Soviet legislation "with exceptions set forth in interstate and intergovernmental treaties with the Soviet Union."[12] Specifically, a treaty between the Soviet Union and another state may provide rates for assessing taxes on the profits to be transferred abroad by a foreign participant in a joint venture that are different from the rates set by Soviet legislation.

The Soviet Union has concluded intergovernmental agreements on preventing double taxation with nineteen capitalist countries and with all CMEA member countries. In accordance with them, partners from Austria, Great Britain, Cyprus, and Finland that participate in joint ventures in the Soviet Union are completely exempt from paying taxes on profits.

Intergovernmental agreements providing for mutual protection of investments have been concluded but not yet ratified, with seven states, including Finland, Belgium, the Netherlands, and several others. The process for working out such agreements is continuing. However, that such agreements are being concluded does not eliminate the need for internal legislative acts.

PRIVILEGES ACCORDED TO JOINT ENTERPRISES

In permitting and encouraging the creation of joint ventures with foreign capital on Soviet territory, legislation does not restrict the sphere of activity of joint ventures to particular branches of the economy. However, present procedures for establishing such enterprises, which require the approval of the higher-ranking management body of a Soviet participant, presuppose that such control will be exercised to preserve state interests.

In order to encourage the growth of branches of the economy that are of priority importance to the Soviet Union, in particular the production of consumer goods, medical technology, medicines, and high-tech products, the USSR Ministry of Finance has the right either not to assess taxes for a certain period of time on a portion of the profits due to an enterprise's foreign partner when it is transferred abroad, or to reduce the amount of the tax.

The Soviet state grants the most important privileges to joint ventures formed in the Far Eastern economic region. These enterprises are exempt from paying a tax on profits for the first three years after receiving such profits, instead of the two years prevailing in other parts of the country. In addition, the tax on profits of joint ventures in the Far Eastern economic region has been reduced from 30 percent to 10 percent. Regulation of foreign investments could be carried out on the basis of a law that provided for a more differentiated regime of capital investment, depending on the state's interest in applying foreign capital to a particular sphere.

ON THE CONCEPT OF A JOINT ENTERPRISE

Soviet legislation does not define the concept of a joint venture. An analysis of existing legal documents makes it possible to list the following distinguishing features of such a joint formation:

- the presence of two or more partners;
- joint capital investments in the enterprise;
- joint assumption of risks;
- joint participation in profits, with profits being divided according to the partners' share in the capital;
- joint management of the enterprise;
- the imparting of the status of a legal person to the enterprise;
- delimitation of the obligations and responsibility of a joint venture from the obligations and responsibility of the founding (*uchreditel'nyy*) organization; and
- limitation of the joint venture's responsibility according to its obligations in proportion to the property belonging to the enterprise.

Some of these features are also characteristic of joint ventures, a form used in foreign practice. According to some American legal experts, this concept signifies the association of two or more persons to carry out a project in the sphere of joint ventures, which does not presume that a long-term relationship will be established among the partners, as distinguished, for example, from a partnership.[13]

When creating a joint venture in the Soviet Union, the goal is to achieve stable and long-lasting relations among the partners so that the enterprise itself will be secure and have good prospects for its work. One feature that distinguishes a joint venture from a partnership is that, in U.S. business practice, the work of a partnership is not subject to taxation. Profits are divided among the partners and taxes as the income of an individual.

A joint venture established in accordance with Soviet law is a juridical person, which distinguishes it from a partnership under the law of West European countries. This gives it the opportunity to conclude agreements; obtain property rights and other personal, nonproperty rights; incur obligations; and become a plaintiff or defendant in court or in arbitration court. Joint enterprises have independent balances and accounts in various banks, and their work is subject to taxation.

One essential feature that distinguishes joint ventures located in the Soviet Union from many foreign partnerships is the Soviet legislative requirement concerning the legal status of founders from the Soviet side. They may only be juridical persons. As for a foreign partner, in accordance with the Law on Property in the Soviet Union, foreign citizens may also be recognized as such. Another important requirement of Soviet legislation is that, besides an agreement, a charter for a joint venture must be drafted and registered with the state in the prescribed manner, and this makes it possible to include the enterprise among statutory associations.

At present Soviet legislation does not set a minimum or maximum amount for the charter capital or the relation of shares in the capital of individual participants. These questions are decided by agreement among the partners. Certain draft legislative acts provided for limiting the aggregate capital invested by foreign participants in a joint venture, defined as a rather modest sum (expressed as an absolute sum, and not as a percent of the total charter fund). It is difficult to agree with this idea, since it would lead to artificially limiting the scale of an enterprise. In practical terms, it would be applicable only to small-scale enterprises. Instead, it would be useful to follow the Chinese example, by introducing a minimum rather than a maximum amount of capital that a foreign partner can invest (in China it is 25 percent of the charter capital), and to establish the procedure whereby a foreigner can invest his or her share.

PROCEDURE FOR ESTABLISHING A JOINT ENTERPRISE

A single authorizing procedure for establishing joint ventures is in effect in the Soviet Union. The right to decide to create joint ventures with foreign participation is granted to all state enterprises, associations, and organizations. The Soviet participant must first obtain the agreement of its higher-ranking administrative body. Production cooperatives create joint ventures by agreement with the Council of Ministers of a Union republic, and when it does not have oblasts (territories), by agreement with the Council of Ministers of an autonomous republic, the kray (regional) executive committee, oblast executive committee, Moscow City Executive Committee, or the Leningrad City Executive Committee, depending on the location of the cooperative, or by agreement with the Ministry (department) of the enterprise (organization or institution) where the cooperative was organized.

Proposals to create joint ventures are made by interested Soviet organizations to their higher-ranking administrative bodies. A technical-economic substantiation (TEO) and draft founding documents, which consist of an agreement on creating the joint venture concluded among the participants, and a charter must all be submitted simultaneously. These documents are prepared by the enterprise participants themselves. It is also possible to bring in organizations to provide consultation and other services. The USSR Trade and Economic Council, which has access to a wide range of qualified consultants, can be of great assistance.

The charter is confirmed by enterprise participants. It defines the object and purposes of a joint venture's work, its location, participants and their shares, size of the charter fund, structure, composition and competency of an enterprise's management bodies, procedures for making decision, and the range of questions that must be resolved by unanimous agreement, as well as procedures for liquidating the enterprise. The charter may also include other points, as long as they do not conflict with Soviet legislation and reflect the special features of the work of a joint venture.

A very essential part of the process of creating a joint venture is its registration with the USSR Ministry of Finance, accomplished in the Ministry's Combined Department of State Revenues. The registration is done in accordance with instructions issued by the Ministry of Finance on 24 November 1987. The documents required for registration are a covering letter, a document reflecting the agreement of the appropriate administrative body to the creation of the joint venture, and notarized copies of the founding documents signed by the participants.

Data concerning the newly founded joint enterprise are added to the State Register of Joint Enterprises of the USSR Ministry of Finance. The registration is attested to by a certificate. At this moment the joint venture becomes a juridical person. Only after the enterprise is registered will Soviet banks open payment and current accounts, issue monetary funds, and conduct credit payment operations with it. Joint enterprises operate on the basis of full self-accounting, self-responsibility, and self-financing.

Registration is also required of the branches of joint ventures created on Soviet territory. They may be opened if their organization is provided for in the founding documents of their joint ventures. Branches are registered in the USSR Ministry of Finance.

MANAGEMENT OF A JOINT ENTERPRISE

A board and managing staff provide the leadership of a joint venture. The board is the higher body of a joint venture. It consists of persons designated by the participants of an enterprise. The procedure by which the board makes decisions is determined by its founding documents.

Management, which includes Soviet citizens and foreigners, guides the day-to-day activities of an enterprise. It is headed by a general director, who may be either a Soviet citizen or a foreigner, according to Soviet legislation. This is also the case with the board's chair. However, Soviet legislation does not permit both of these leading positions in a joint venture to be occupied by foreign citizens. In practice, these bodies may be formed by agreement of the parties.

OWNERSHIP OF THE PROPERTY OF A JOINT ENTERPRISE

Ownership of the property of a joint venture established with the participation of firms from capitalist and developing countries has, for a long time, not been clearly addressed by legislation. The absence of specific instructions has reflected a certain political and economic timidity on the part of lawmakers. Decree 49 only indicated that a joint venture has the right to own, utilize, and dispose of its property in accordance with the purposes of its activity. This left room for doctrinal interpretation. Some authors considered property to be owned by the enterprise, while others used the idea of fiduciary ownership as a possible compromise. The property of joint ventures formed with the participation of CMEA members was defined by the Council of Ministers Decree 48 of 13 January 1987 as general Socialist property.

The 1990 Law on Property in the USSR contains a principled solution to this problem. Article 27 of the law, entitled "The Property of Joint Enterprises," states that joint ventures established in the Soviet Union "may own property required for carrying out the work provided for in its statutory documents."[14] No distinction is made among different groups of joint ventures. Thus, instructions on the powers of possession, use, and disposal of the relevant property now finds culmination in their definition as comprising the right of ownership of a joint venture.

PERSONNEL OF A JOINT ENTERPRISE

In accordance with Soviet legislation, the personnel of a joint venture must consist mainly of Soviet citizens. Foreign specialists may be hired on the basis of individual contracts made with them. A trade union organization is created at a joint venture, and the administration is obligated to conclude a collective agreement with it. Its content is determined by Soviet legislation and by its founding documents. The basic legal document in this area is the "General Document on Procedures for Concluding Collective Agreements," confirmed by decree on 24 September 1984 by the All-Union Central Council of Trade Unions and the USSR State Committee on Labor and Social Questions.

A joint venture, in the form of its management bodies, has the right to decide independently all questions connected with the hiring and firing of personnel and workers, the form and amount of payment for their labor, as well as material incentives in Soviet rubles. Individual contracts determine questions of leave and pensions for foreign citizens working at joint ventures.

Deductions for the state and social insurance for Soviet and foreign personnel, as well as deductions for pensions for Soviet personnel, are deposited in the Soviet state budget at rates established for Soviet enterprises. Payments toward the pensions of foreign personnel are transferred in accordance with the funds of those countries where they are permanent residents and in the currencies of those countries. Wages received by foreign personnel of a joint venture are subject to income tax. Any part of a foreigner's wages that remains unspent in the Soviet Union may be transferred abroad in foreign currency. Customs privileges are extended to foreign personnel.

PRODUCTION ACTIVITIES

A joint venture carries out its statutory work according to a program that it develops and confirms independently. It should be emphasized that, in accordance with Soviet legislation, it is not included in the system of planning that operates in the Soviet Union. Compulsory state planning tasks are not assigned to it. Sale of the products is also not guaranteed.

However, this does not exhaust the subject of the legal regulation of relations between joint ventures and Soviet organizations, relations that are varied and extremely important to their work. More detailed regulations of these relations are contained in Decree 1074, as well as in a decree of the USSR State Committee on Material and Technical Supply dated 4 June 1987, "Procedures for the Material-Technical Supply of Joint Enterprises Created on the Territory of the Soviet Union with the Participation of Other

Countries and Foreign Firms, and the Sale of Their Products," and the 4 November 1987 decree that supplemented it.

Earlier, in accordance with Decree 49, deliveries among joint ventures were carried out with payment in rubles through the appropriate Soviet foreign trade organizations. This created a situation in which there were always the same, or several of the same, foreign trading organizations acting in the intermediary role between a joint venture and a Soviet partner, and it was always necessary to pay a commission for their services. This was not always convenient for organizations operating on self-accounting and self-financing principles. The existence of such a multistage system complicated the structure of relations, and delayed and reduced the certainty of fulfilling the agreement obligations.

This decision was partially rescinded by Decree 1074. In accordance with it, joint ventures have the right, in agreement with Soviet enterprises and organizations, to determine the type of currency in accounts for products sold and commodities purchased, as well as the procedures for selling its products on the Soviet market and delivering commodities from this market.

That legislation has granted joint ventures the legal right independently to carry on the export and import operations required for its work is very important. These operations may also be performed by agreement with Soviet foreign trading organizations or through the marketing network of foreign participants.

It should be emphasized that the system of regulation of foreign economic relations extends to joint ventures, in accordance with Council of Ministers' Decree 203 of 7 March 1988, including:

• registration of participants in foreign economic relations;
• declaration of commodities and other property moved across Soviet state borders;
• procedures for exporting and importing commodities of state importance; and
• measures for the operative regulation of foreign economic ties.

In accordance with this decree, joint ventures created on the territory of the Soviet Union may export only products—including services—that they produce, and may import products only for their own requirements. Intermediary operations require the permission from the USSR Ministry of Foreign Economic Relations.

On 20 March 1989, the USSR Council of Ministers' State Foreign Economic Committee approved "Regulations on the Procedure for Licensing Operations in the Foreign Economic Relations of the Soviet Union," based on decrees adopted previously by the Council of Ministers. The regulations state that licensing for both export and import is applicable for certain periods of time for transactions carried out within the framework of export and import limitations, and is a precautionary measure with respect to those participants in foreign economic relations who have engaged in unfair competition and have inflicted harm on the Soviet state by their operations.

The procedure established for licensing also applies to joint ventures as participants in foreign economic ties. Licenses may be general or one-time licenses. General licenses permit the export and import of commodities for a period of time, generally one year. One-time licenses permit the export and import of commodities for one particular transaction and are issued for the period required to accomplish it, but not longer than one year. Licenses may be extended if a valid request is submitted.

It should be emphasized that licensing extends to all types of import-export operations, including commodity exchange.

Earlier we partially touched on the reasons why a licensing system was introduced. Such systems exist in many countries, in each case serving purposes related to a specific economic situation. However, we could not agree to the unjustified extension of licensing to cover types of activities as well as commodities. For example, at present, intermediary activities can be performed only with permission from the USSR Ministry of Foreign Economic Relations.

PROCEDURE FOR DISSOLVING A JOINT ENTERPRISE

The circumstances under which a joint venture may be dissolved, and the procedure for liquidation are determined by enterprise participants themselves and are set forth in its founding documents. Soviet legislation includes only one obligatory norm relating to the liquidation of a joint venture: an enterprise may be dissolved by decree of the USSR Council of Ministers if its activities do not correspond with the goals and tasks set forth in its statutory documents. Soviet legislation includes only one obligatory norm relating to the liquidation of a joint venture: an enterprise may be dissolved by decree of the USSR Council of Ministers if its activities do not correspond with the goals and tasks set forth in its statutory documents.

The joint venture's documents indicate reasons for dissolving it. Reasons may include the expiration of the period established by the agreement for the enterprise's operations, or written agreement by the parties to dissolve, specifically if the joint venture is unprofitable.

A joint venture ceases to exist in the legal sense from the moment that fact is registered at the USSR Ministry of Finance. From the day of such registration, the enterprise loses the status of a juridical person and ceases its activities. The process of liquidation begins. The main role in this process is played by a liquidation commission created for this purpose.

Upon the liquidation of a joint venture, or upon leaving the enterprise, the foreign participants have the right to reclaim their monetary or commodity contribution in its residual form at the time the enterprise is dissolved, after meeting any obligations to other participants or third parties. A report on the liquidation of a joint venture is then published in the press.

CONCLUSION

This chapter presents a brief sketch of current regulations in the Soviet Union regarding the process of establishing and operating joint ventures in which foreign partners, especially those from capitalist countries, participate.

The current state of legislation in this field corresponds, in our opinion, to the situation that has arisen in the country, in its economy and domestic policy, and in the sphere of social relations. The first attempts at economic management under new conditions have provided acute problems, with no indication of a way to solve them swiftly and effectively. At the present time an active and sometimes intuitive search is underway at all levels of government and administration to find a way out of a multitude of complicated situations, including some in the sphere of foreign economic relations.

It must be admitted that a unified, integral concept of development is not yet evident in the legislative regulation of this important area. An adequate basis has not been laid for working out the ever-multiplying individual laws that, in draft, do not systematically ensure the optimum development of the foreign economic complex in coordination with the development of internal state economic relations. The question of the relations between administrative regulations and freedom in the activities of economic units, including joint ventures, is a very pressing one but has also not been sufficiently thought out. It seems that economic reform is entering a decisive phase that, if successful, will largely determine the future both of the Soviet Union as a whole and of its individual republics and territories, all of which have their own interests and ideas about prospects for further development.

NOTES

1. The All-Russian Central Executive Committee of Soviets (VTsIK)—the supreme legislative, executive, and supervisory body of the Russian Republic (RSFSR), acting on the basis of the RSFSR constitutions of 1918 and 1925. A presidium fulfilled its functions in the intervals between VTsIK sessions.

2. The Council on Labor and Defense, created in 1920, is subordinate to the RSFSR Council of People's Commissars in the field of securing the country's defense and economic construction.

3. Collection of Statutes of the RSFSR, No. 24 (1922), 226.

4. According to the USSR Constitution of 1924, the supreme body of state power in periods between all-Union sessions of the Soviets.

5. Until 1948, the supreme legislative and executive body in the Soviet Union.

6. Decree on Concessions, adopted by the Council of People's Commissars on 23 November 1920 (Petrograd, 1921).

7. V. I. Lenin, "On the Food Tax (The Importance of the New Policy and Its Conditions)," *Complete Works* 43 5th ed. (Moscow), 224.

8. *Bol'shaya sovetskaya entsiklopediya* 2, 1st ed. (Moscow), 119.

9. Lenin, "On the Food Tax."

10. The most important acts regulating the group of relationships described above are the Edict of the USSR Supreme Soviet Presidium of 12 May 1978, "On Income Tax from Foreign Juridical Persons and Individuals" (with respect to individuals, the new Law on Income Tax of USSR Citizens, Foreign Citizens and Stateless Persons was adopted 23 April 1990 and went into effect on 1 July 1990); the edict of the USSR Supreme Soviet Presidium, "Concerning Twenty Matters Relating to the Creation on the Territory of the Soviet Union and to the Work of International Associations and Organizations with the Participation of Soviet and Foreign Organizations, Firms and Administrative Bodies"; the USSR Council of Ministers Decree 49, adopted 13 January 1987, "On Procedures for Creating on the Territory of the Soviet Union and for the Work of Joint Ventures with the Participation of Soviet Organizations and Firms from Capitalist and Developing Countries"; Decree 1074, of the Central Committee of the Communist Party of the Soviet Union and USSR Council of Ministers dated 17 September 1987, "On Additional Measures to Improve Foreign Economic Activities under New Economic Conditions"; the USSR Council of Ministers Decree 1405, dated 2 December 1988, "On the Further Development of the Foreign Economic Activities of the State, and Cooperative and Other Public Enterprises, Associations and Organizations"; and, last, the USSR Council of Ministers Decision 203, dated 7 March 1988, "On Measures for State Regulation of Foreign Economic Activities," which proposed introducing a system for licensing import-export operations in the Soviet Union. The main propositions in this last decree were subsequently expanded and made more specific in legal acts adopted by the Ministry for Foreign Economic Relations, the USSR Council of Ministers and the USSR Foreign Economic Bank.

A series of instructions concerning the establishment and activities of joint ventures with foreign participation has also been adopted by Soviet ministries and departments, specifically the 12 February 1987 instruction from the USSR Ministry of Finance, "On the Procedure for Registering Joint Enterprises, International Associations and Organizations Established on the Territory of the Soviet Union with the Participation of Soviet and Foreign Organizations, Firms and Administrative Agencies"; the joint instruction of the USSR Ministry of Finances and the USSR Central Statistical Administration (now the USSR State Statistical Committee) dated 7 February 1987, "On Introducing Accounting (*uchet*) and Book-keeping at Joint Ventures, International Associations and Organizations Established on the Territory of the Soviet Union."

11. Aside from Decree 203, a statute on the import, export, forwarding and transfer into and out of Soviet borders of Soviet currency, foreign currencies, and other monetary and nonmonetary valuables was adopted in 1989 (confirmed by Decree 266 of the USSR Council of Ministers on 13 March 1989). The program of legislative work outlined by the government is thus being implemented.

12. USSR Council of Ministers Decree 49, *Subranie postanuvlenii pravitel'stra SSSR* 9 (Moscow, 1987), item 40.

13. *Black's Law Dictionary*, 5th ed. (St. Paul, Minn.: West Publishing Co., 1979), 753.

14. "Law on Property in the USSR," *Pravda* (10 March 1990): 4.

Chapter 10

New Soviet Laws on Property and Land Ownership and Their Approach to the Issues of Joint Ventures

Natalya G. Semilutina

The presence of separate property is not only one of the most important features of a "legal person," but also a necessary prerequisite for normal activities of joint ventures. According to the Soviet Law on Property in the Soviet Union approved 6 March 1990, "The merging of property, under the possession of citizens, legal persons, and the state, is permitted, as well as the establishment of mixed forms of property, including property of joint ventures with the participation of Soviet and foreign legal persons and foreign citizens."[1] In Article 4, it is established that "the state creates the conditions necessary for the development of diverse forms of property and provides for their protection." It is also stipulated in Article 31 that the "state is under obligation to provide citizens, organizations and other property owners equal conditions for the protection of their property rights."

The statements quoted above contain the major principles relating to the regulation of the legal code of ownership of joint ventures in the Soviet Union. First among these principles is the inclusion of joint ventures in the list of possible property owners, along with Soviet citizens, state, cooperatives, and other organizations that were granted the rights of a legal person. There are also provisions for equal opportunities in the development and protection of all forms of ownership in the Soviet Union.

Moreover, in accordance with Article 27 of the Law on Property, in a section dealing with the ownership rights of joint ventures, foreign citizens, organizations, and states, it is stated that joint ventures "are allowed to own property necessary for the conduct of their businesses as described in their charters."

It is important to mention that the property of joint ventures is not uniform. All valuables in the possession of joint ventures can be divided into two categories, according to the legal basis of their ownership: property that the organization is entitled to use, and property that is fully owned by the organization. The first category, as described in Article 21, includes land, water, natural resources, and other resources that can be defined as public or national property. All other property, in accordance with the above-mentioned section of the Law on Property, is considered to be under the possession of the organization.

Soviet state enterprises, cooperatives, and other organizations are legally entitled (for example, in accordance with Article 29 of the Law on State Enterprises, or Article 28 of the Law on Cooperatives in the Soviet Union) to form joint ventures with the participation of foreign firms in the Soviet Union and to grant rights to use this public property. It is obvious that in order to be able to grant such rights, state enterprises, cooperatives, or other organizations should fully possess the right to use the property. Also, such rights have to be viewed as alienable, so that the owner can transfer them to the joint venture. Thus, there must be a situation where rights of use are separated from the rights of ownership belonging to the state, represented by its agencies. However, the Law on Property does not answer directly the question of whether or not the rights of use, as distinct from the right of ownership, can go through further alienation and thus be transferred by joint ventures themselves. In other words, there are questions as to whether or not joint ventures are entitled to extend their rights of use, granted by their Soviet partners, and whether or not such rights can be used as collateral. In our view, by allowing the option of alienation and transfer of utilization rights at the moment they are granted to the joint venture by the Soviet partner, it would be completely logical to give the joint venture itself the opportunity to transfer these rights.

In addition, the foundations of the legal code of the Soviet Union and Soviet Republics, passed on 28 February 1990, give the land user the right to "transfer on a temporary basis the parcel of land or a portion of it." Article 6 of this act mentions joint ventures, with the participation of foreign and Soviet parties, as possible users of the land.

The granting of the right to transfer utilization rights to property, owned exclusively by the state, is important not only for joint ventures operating in the Soviet Union, but for all national enterprises and organizations engaged in business activities. In our opinion, it will make it possible to inject a necessary dynamism into transactions involving the use of national resources while preventing the squandering of such resources.

The state, as an entity, licensed through its organizations and agencies to manage the property that falls under the definition of "property of the people," should, in our opinion, establish regulations for the transfer of rights of use from one party to the other. In this transfer, an approval of the appropriate government organization supervising this type of property will be required.

It is essential to stress the importance of the chapter of the Law on Property dealing with the issues of guarantees and protections of the rights of ownership. The information in this chapter concerns all the property owners in the Soviet Union, including joint ventures. In Article 31, it is stated that "the state guarantees the stability of property relations defined by the present law." The law offers the property owners protection against violations of their rights, even though they might not be threatened by the loss of ownership, according to Article 32. The law offers protection of the rights of people who are not considered owners, yet possess property and the right to use it. In this case such persons are entitled to defend their possessions even against the owner.

The Law on Property, in addition to guarantees to the owner, defines the reasons and conditions under which the right of ownership can be revoked in Article 33. Among such conditions are the seizure of property during the procedure for recovery of such property in cases specified by the legislation of the Soviet Union and Soviet Republics, or the requisition and confiscation of property by court order, state arbitrage, or any other competent government body. In the case of confiscation, the owner is compensated for the value of the property. We should emphasize that the Law on Property does not include nationalization as a method for eliminating the rights of ownership. In our opinion, the failure of the government to mention this alternative does not signify that the government is committing itself not to nationalize property. The right of the state to nationalize property, including that which belongs to foreign enterprises, is considered a sovereign right of the state and one means for conducting a state's economic policy.

The renunciation by the state of the option to nationalize foreign-owned property is, in principle, pointless. Nationalization of foreign-owned property should be viewed as a measure that is either provøked by particular economic interests of the state, or a defensive measure against the activities of the foreign enterprise, undermining the economy of the state.

In our opinion, the Law on Property should define the rights of the state in the case of nationalization, in terms of the following: conditions under which such actions are considered justified; the obligations of the state regarding compensation; and the procedures for arbitrage in case of a nationalization. A distinct feature of the nationalization of foreign property, including property of joint ventures, should be a special procedure for compensation to the foreign participants. This compensation should be made fully or partially in foreign hard currency, taking into account the initial investments.

It is significant that international agreements providing for the encouragement and protection of direct foreign investment include articles dealing with the nationalization of foreign property. Thus, the standard form of intragovernmental agreement on mutual protection of investments, approved by Decree 1353 of the USSR Council of Ministers on 27 November 1987, provides the following wording in Article 3 for articles dealing with the issues of nationalization of foreign property: "Neither side will attempt to take coercive measures for the withdrawal of capital investments (such as nationalization, confiscation, etc.) made on its territory by the investors of the opposite side, with the exception of the cases when such steps are needed to protect the interests of the state, under conditions that these steps will comply with the legal code of the country and that compensation will be paid to the property owners. Such measures will be non-discriminatory and the compensation will be paid promptly, without delays and in hard currency that can be easily transferred from one country to the other."[2]

Similar provisions were included in Article 4 of the agreement approved 8 February 1989 by the governments of the Soviet Union and Finland, "Encouragement and Mutual Protection of Investments," as well as in Article 5 of the 9 February 1989 agreement between the Soviet Union, Belgium and the Grand Duchess of Luxembourg, "Mutual Encouragement and Mutual Protection of Investments."

NOTES

1. All excerpts of the Law on Property may be found in "Law on Property in the USSR," *Pravda* (10 March 1990): 4.
2. Taken from an unpublished xerox copy, available from the author.

Chapter 11

The Legal Foundations of Soviet Joint Ventures: A Comment and Critique

William E. Butler

In the chapter "Legal Aspects of Establishing Joint Ventures in the Soviet Union," Natalya L. Platonova ably and succinctly sets out the legal foundations of joint ventures under Soviet legislation in their formative period. She is especially perceptive in reminding us of the legal heritage of the 1920s in the Soviet Union. In the sphere of foreign investment, as in so many other domains of Soviet life, the 1920s have an enormous amount of relevant experience and wisdom to offer. It is no wonder that Soviet social scientists, including lawyers, are constantly having recourse to that period for inspiration.

More than three years have elapsed since the legislation of 13 January 1987 formally setting in place the flexible and rudimentary legal foundations of joint ventures. Although those foundations required alterations and additions in 1988 and 1989, the essential philosophy of the joint venture and the flexibility offered by the original legal framework remained more or less intact.[1] By early 1990, three years later, Soviet authorities felt the time had come to begin to evaluate what had been accomplished and what remained to be done. More than two thousand joint ventures had been registered by spring 1990. A few have been deregistered for violations of Soviet legislation of various kinds. In a very few cases, criminal proceedings have been brought against individuals for serious offenses.[2] But whatever activity of this nature may have existed, by all accounts it has been an extremely minor aspect of foreign investment and pales in comparison with analogous activities in the cooperative sector of the Soviet economy, where, by all press accounts, speculation, bribery, organized crime, and other types of offenses have been endemic.

The numbers of joint ventures registered have not been criticized in and of themselves. Registration being a permissive procedure, the Soviet authorities are at liberty to select among the applications made for registration and screen out those that do not meet the standards of the foundation legislation or are not consistent with domestic economic priorities. Figures on the rejection of applications are for these reasons unfortunately not available. Indeed, criticisms of the low levels of registration would be difficult to make when applicants themselves complain so often of the delays in effecting registration. While it is impossible to judge whether the flow of registration is now satisfactory, it is certainly the case that the process has been both decentralized and considerably accelerated. The Soviet government is mindful, however, of the profile of joint ventures registered and the amounts of capital nominally and actually invested, as well as of the numbers of joint ventures actually in operation as compared to those registered.

The evaluation of total capital investment by foreigners represented in joint ventures, as disclosed in public comments by Soviet authorities and the media, reflects a certain naiveté. There seems to be a presumption that large is good in entrepreneurial terms. And there seems to be an expectation that investment will flow simply as a consequence of the signature and registration of deals. The Western concept of using corporate structure (i.e., the holding company, companies created solely for tax purposes) as a vehicle for a vast range of entrepreneurial activities still is not fully appreciated in Soviet legal and financial circles. While it is wholly understandable that large investments would be welcome, the ultimate contribution to the Soviet economy of low capital and possibly of high technology or know-how by small firms ought not to be lightly dismissed.

It has become fashionable in the economic media of the Soviet Union to speak about the average capital investment of foreigners. This is a highly misleading figure because it simply amounts to the division of the total amount of foreign investment in joint ventures as stated on paper by the numbers of joint ventures actually registered. In and of themselves, such ratios say very little. In particular, they offer no insight into the reasons that the parties to a joint venture have for fixing their respective capital contributions, nor do they address other collateral reasons that may be present in the intentions of the parties or in their ability to invest on a large scale.

This is particularly the case where the parties, in order to make a substantial investment, must borrow from outside sources, whether Soviet or foreign financial institutions. There remain significant legal obstacles in Soviet legislation to effective project financing of joint ventures. This has become especially evident in the sphere of services, where it has been possible for Soviet and foreign partners to come to terms rather quickly on the construction of hotels and tourist complexes in light of the enormous demand for such services. Few foreign companies are in a position—or would find it desirable—to finance by themselves the construction and early operational costs of such facilities. Bank loans for this purpose are effectively available if appropriate legislation on pledge (mortgage or pawn) and enforcement procedures can be devised to satisfactorily protect the lender's interests. Soviet legislation of late 1989 and early 1990 on leasing, land, and ownership in some measure addressed these concerns and especially with respect to leasing, alleviated certain apprehensions of the foreign financial community with regard to the security of land tenure and the protection of leasing interests.[3] But the machinery for satisfactory protection, as would ordinarily be expected in Western financial circles, is still not entirely in place. The law of pledge,[4] for example, is not satisfactory, nor is it clear, when state assets are involved in such transactions, precisely where state ownership is affixed or precisely who has the right to convey title to either a joint venture or, in the event of default, to lenders.[5]

Legal considerations are also adversely affecting the launching of joint ventures into operation. In many situations Western investors have simply underestimated or not appreciated the obstacles imposed by Soviet conditions upon the effective organization of a joint venture. Where the construction of facilities has been required, for example, difficulties in obtaining construction materials or a skilled labor force in the Soviet Union for the joint venture have been formidable. Many joint ventures, expecting to finance this aspect of their existence in local currency, have found themselves either unable to obtain the required material or labor skills, or wait in the massive queue for such items together with other Soviet enterprises and organizations. In a very few cases the Western partner has been able to import these components and find a way to cover the hard currency expenditure. Even in these instances, however, the Western partner has found the original calculations concerning the joint venture inaccurate. While these at first may seem to be bureaucratic constraints, they inhere in fact in the legal framework of the planned economy and can be comprehended only by mastering Soviet legislation on capital construction, labor, and finance.

Enough experience has been accumulated in connection with joint ventures to justify serious changes in the original legal foundations for joint ventures. Whether the changes will be sufficient to give effect to the desired transition to a market economy, and whether the domestic political costs associated with such changes will be tolerated by the Soviet people and the foreign investment community, are matters only the future can determine. Economic and financial theories along these lines cannot succeed, however well conceived, unless the legal foundations are adequate to their ends. Already there are strong indications as to what the next legal reform must accomplish. In the world of project financing, the sovereign or state guarantee of financial transactions will become increasingly rare, not only because it is inconsistent with the economic and legal values of perestroika, but also because the financial ability of Soviet ministries, state committees, and large economic and legal conglomerates will be evaluated, and must be so, by the lending community separately and individually.[6]

This means that a ministerial guarantee can no longer be taken at face value but must be measured against the hard currency earnings of the ministry concerned and its hard currency budget appropriations. In short, the ministry's ability to pay is no longer being lightly assumed, nor is it being accepted without question in the absence of appropriate supporting documentation of pre-existing hard currency obligations to other lenders and the anticipated receipts of hard currency from other sources. Some Soviet ministries and state committees are impressive earners of foreign currency, such as the USSR Ministry of the Oil and Gas Complex, the USSR Ministry of Civil Aviation, the USSR Ministry of the Maritime Fleet, and others. Local government will increasingly be a substantial earner of foreign currency throughout various local concessions and other leasehold arrangements with joint ventures and other forms of foreign investment. Their ability to lend to joint ventures will consequently not depend upon guarantees, as such, but their own assets and exposure to liability for indebtedness.

The joint venture might be described as a favorite channel for the foreign investment community. That is to say, those who form joint ventures receive a special legal status, certain tax concessions, and other privileges conferred upon the joint venture.[7] It has been, and will remain, a key point in debates about economic policies whether these privileges and concessions conferred on joint ventures are adequate to their purpose, and whether they are discriminatory against other forms of economic organizations in the Soviet economy. Those who have invested in joint ventures must expect continuing pressure in the 1990s to equalize the legal status and privileges of other forms of Soviet economic organization with the joint venture. Soviet joint stock companies with foreign investment, or even entirely owned by foreigners, will become the most obvious source of pressure of this nature. Likewise, special concessions negotiated in the foundation documents of joint ventures will come under pressure as their full economic implications unfold in the larger context of perestroika.[8] Inducements offered in the late 1980s to attract a particular foreign investor may by the mid–1990s appear to be excessively generous or unfair. Especially in the realm of taxation, the pressures will be strong to eliminate tax holidays or reductions that are not justified by economic performance and are at variance with the general range of such concessions accorded by legislation.

The same may be true of the preferential position enjoyed by certain joint ventures in the manufacture and marketing of goods and services. This will be generated by the investment philosophy underlying joint ventures. The rationale for a permissive procedure in the registration of joint ventures lies principally in their desirability for the national economy and their anticipated contribution to economic development. As the pressures accumulate to allow market forces to play their natural role in this respect—that is to say, to increase competition within the Soviet economy—the quasi-monopoly rationale underlying many original joint venture schemes will disappear. This has already become evident on another front. Many early joint ventures secured rights in their foundation documents to manufacture and export, or in some cases simply export, valuable raw materials and finished products from the Soviet economy. As the domestic demand for these items has intensified to epidemic proportions in light of domestic shortages, some joint ventures are finding their right to export without licenses, or their right to export at all, being circumscribed in the interests of other economic policies.[9]

In conclusion, it is appropriate to consider the implications for joint ventures of the devolution of political and economic power with the Soviet Union itself. In the Baltic republics, as early as fall 1989, special legislation was introduced in the form of what we would traditionally call "company law." This legislation contemplated the introduction of wholly or partially owned foreign companies operating on those territories just as domestic companies would operate. In many respects the joint venture framework would become irrelevant.

There is a normal and understandable foreign reaction to Union republic legislation on matters affecting foreign investments. That is to say, we are inclined to look upon devolution and local initiative as creating opportunities for differentiation, competition, and more favorable conditions. This is not an unreasonable assumption, for undoubtedly local competition will lead to some areas or authorities attempting to introduce an investment package that attracts not merely the foreign investment community, but also the Soviet investment community outside their own territories. But this preoccupation with the competitive dimension of devolution should not blind us to the other side of the equation. One of the principle attractions of the Soviet market for the foreign investment community is its vast size and resources, and a population whose short- and middle-term demands for the most elementary consumer goods appear to be almost infinite. To reach that market, however, will require not merely appropriate production skills and financial resources; it will require a market—a legal environment in which the flow of goods and services is possible with minimal constraints. It is consequently wholly understandable that Soviet legislation concerned with the demarcation of powers between the Soviet Union and the Union and autonomous republics, and legislation regulating the exercise of economic autonomy by the Union republics, should direct attention to the all-Union market. The Union republics are to be constrained in their ability to introduce tariffs, quotas, or any other import or export restrictions within the Soviet Union itself, or to introduce pricing policies that would amount to unfair competition.[10] While these provisions are to be found in the legislation, precisely what they mean in practice and how they are to be implemented will become one of the critical questions of perestroika policy in the 1990s.

What we are witnessing is the embryonic emergence of regulatory legislation within the Soviet Union intended to give effect to the market economy on more or less the same lines that we regulate such matters. But that legislation will be required to function in a transitional situation, during which price policies and their rationale will be obscure and contradictory, and the canons of fair competition will be worked out on virtually a day-by-day basis as experience accumulates. Joint enterprises that produce for the domestic market, or for that matter any Soviet entity in which foreign investment is represented, will need to come to terms with this emerging legal framework rather rapidly if they are to survive.

When evaluating the legal foundations for foreign investment in the Soviet Union it should be borne in mind that the country possesses certain advantages that either do not exist at all in Eastern Europe or exist on a vastly smaller scale. The raw material resource base is one of the most prominent advantages in this respect. It is not merely that the Soviet Union is rich in raw material resources and has the capacity to export them fairly rapidly in order to earn hard currency; rather, it is that the Soviet Union is in a position to attract foreign investment on a truly massive scale, including foreign investment in the social and economic infrastructure of the country's remote regions, which have been most disadvantaged economically by the policies effected before 1986. As in other parts of the world, when the foreign oil industry decides to attract investment on a substantial scale, the financing in the short term of perestroika can be assured on a scale inconceivable for other socialist economies making the transition to regulated market economies. The legal foundations of foreign investment of this character will require adaptations to Soviet circumstances and Soviet adaptations, legally and economically, to the scale of the investment and the risk being undertaken by the investor. One or two such deals are capable, in the amount of money involved and the rapidity of return, of dwarfing all other joint venture projects, oil and gas, for example, presently underway in the Soviet economy. Developments of this order of magnitude will require creative thinking about the long-term direction and substance of the legal foundations of foreign investment and rapid responses to those circumstances that, to date, have not been characteristic.

NOTES

1. The decree of 13 January 1987 was amended on 17 March 1988 (unpublished) and 6 May 1989. For a consolidated text in translation, see W. E. Butler, *Basis Documents on the Soviet Legal System* (New York: Ocena Publications, 1990), 475–84. The amendments incorporated changes introduced by the decrees of 17 September 1987 and 2 December 1988 on the improvement of Soviet foreign economic relations.

2. No information is available about convictions. The alleged crimes had to do with currency, customs, and accounts violations, including embezzlement.

3. For example, land is now available on lease. The lease is a civil law relationship, rather than an administrative command relationship as in the case of the

old land grants. This means the local soviet concluding a lease is subject to suit in court in the event of a violation. Most leases allow subleasing, and the foundation is being laid for the pledge of leases to secure project financing.

4. A draft law on pledge was drafted in July 1990 by a working party headed by this writer for submission to the USSR Council of Ministers.

5. The USSR State Property Fund, created by edict of the president of the USSR on 15 August 1990, may help alleviate the difficulties. Apparently it will be vested with title to many state assets and have the right of complete disposition. See Butler, *Soviet Legal System*, 283–84.

6. Perestroika requires that economic ventures be self-supporting, profitable, and not subsidized. Borrowers are fully accountable for their liabilities out of their own assets. The lender, in turn, evaluates carefully and monitors closely the capacity of the borrower to repay. With a state guarantee, the lender has little interest in how the monies are used.

7. This status, of course, is the heart of the entire joint venture scheme. It is possible to create other types of joint ventures—joint stock societies, limited responsibility societies, partnerships—and one-person companies. For the texts of relevant Soviet legislation, see Butler, *Soviet Legal System*, 323–44. The Soviet government is expected to legislate further on foreign participation in these entities, and it remains to be seen whether joint ventures will retain their special privileges or be assimilated to other Soviet entities.

8. Soviet tax legislation, for example, is abolishing the tax holiday on profits for joint ventures, although a five-year loss carry forward is allowed. For the tax law, see Butler, *Soviet Legal System*, 433–62.

9. A U.S.-Soviet joint venture enjoying the right to export gold, platinum, and similar products—a right laid down in its registered foundation documents—was forestalled by export restrictions subsequently introduced by the Soviet government as an emergency measure for 1990–91.

10. See the Soviet legislation on the delimitation of powers between the Soviet Union and the Union and autonomous republics adopted in April 1990. Translated in Butler, *Soviet Legal System*, 45–50.

Chapter 12

The Status of Joint Business Ventures in the Soviet Union

Zinoviy M. Eventov

The process of the formation of joint business ventures on Soviet territory began in 1987. The first Soviet-foreign joint venture, Littara-Volanpak, was established by the Lithuanian enterprise Littara and the Hungarian association Volanpak and registered in the USSR Ministry of Finance on 12 May 1987. Then, from May to December 1987, twenty-three joint ventures were formed. Two U.S.-Soviet joint ventures were among them: Pris, with the participation of the U.S. firm Combustion Engineering, and Dialog, with the participation of the U.S. firm Management Partnerships International.

Later, the pace picked up as the number of joint ventures increased substantially, reaching 168 by the end of 1988, including 11 U.S.-Soviet joint ventures. In 1989, an average of 90 joint ventures were formed every month; overall, 1,083 joint ventures were formed in 1989. The increase was due, in part, to the fact that many joint ventures take a year or more to negotiate and an additional period of time to finalize and register. Thus, it would be expected that the number of registered joint ventures in the initial years would be quite small and increase rapidly after the first year or two as the start-up period passed (see Table 12.1). In addition, there is often a delay between the registration of a joint venture and the time that it is actually put into operation. Therefore, the data provided in this chapter, which is based on registered joint ventures, overstates the actual amount of activity. The USSR State Committee for Statistics is developing information on the number of joint ventures actually operating.

As a whole, firms from sixty countries participate in joint ventures with Soviet enterprises. See Table 12.2 for a list of countries that have participated most actively in the formation of joint ventures. The data for this table, and for the chapter as a whole, is complete up to 1 April 1990.

Most joint ventures are bilateral, with 1,201 in all, but 73 are multilateral, including the Soviet-Franco-Italian joint venture Interkvadro, the joint ven-

Table 12.1
Joint Venture Formation over Time

Time Period	Number of JVs	%	Initial Capital (mln rubles)	%
TOTAL	1465	100	3767.79	100
1987	23	1.57	159.37	4.23
1988	170	11.60	667.48	17.72
1989 (total)	1076	73.45	2695.15	71.53
I quarter	176	12.01	386.21	10.25
II quarter	320	21.84	909.67	24.14
III quarter	256	17.47	468.01	12.42
IV quarter	324	22.12	931.25	24.72
1990 (total)	196	13.38	245.80	6.52
January	92	6.28	120.95	3.21
February	62	4.23	77.43	2.05
March	42	2.87	47.42	1.26

ture Sterkhavtomatizatsiya, which has Soviet, U.S., and Austrian partners, and the joint venture Soyuzforminvest, which has 14 different participating partners, including firms of the United Arab Emirates, Sweden, Greece, Austria, Oman, and 9 Soviet businesses and organizations.

The total value of investments in the charter fund of these ventures exceeds 3,350 million rubles.[1] The Soviet contribution is 58.9 percent, and the investment of foreign partners is 40.1 percent. In dollar terms, the investments of foreign partners from capitalist and developing countries in the charter fund of joint ventures exceed $1.9 billion.

The geographical distribution of joint ventures is quite wide (see Table 12.3). The majority, 953, are situated in the Russian Republic, with 647 of those in Moscow and 99 in Leningrad. There are many joint ventures in Estonia and the Ukraine (87 and 78, respectively). There are substantially fewer joint ventures in the remaining republics. Georgia, for instance, is home to 33 joint ventures, while there are only 31 in Latvia, 22 in Byelorussia, 12 in Lithuania and Moldavia, 10 in Uzbekistan, 9 in Armenia and Azerbaijan, and 8 in Kazakstan. There are only a few joint ventures located in the remaining republics.

Joint ventures have been established in various branches of manufacturing: machine building and appliance assembly (including the manufacture of machines, processing centers, robotics, sensory and laser technology,

Table 12.2
Distribution of Joint Ventures (JVs) within Soviet Territory by Country of
Foreign Partner (1 April 1990)

Country	Amount of Foreign Participation		Joint Initial Capital		Foreign Investment	
	Number of JVs	%	mln rubles	%	mln rubles	%
TOTAL	1558	100	4392.62	100	1510.96	100
Socialist Countries	186	11.94	717.37	16.33	212.50	14.06
GDR	1	.06	5.00	.11	2.50	.17
Vietnam	5	.32	4.28	.10	1.49	.10
Czechoslovakia	5	.32	30.49	.69	7.50	.50
North Korea	8	.51	31.02	.71	14.17	.94
Poland	54	3.47	124.56	2.84	33.34	2.21
China	19	1.22	39.73	.90	18.03	1.19
Bulgaria	37	2.37	204.82	4.66	51.49	3.41
Yugoslavia	28	1.80	182.38	4.15	53.97	3.57
Hungary	29	1.86	95.09	2.16	30.01	1.99
Capitalist Countries	1256	80.62	3500.29	79.69	1243.48	82.30
Australia	21	1.35	151.67	3.45	70.10	4.64
Austria	99	6.35	272.38	6.20	67.83	4.49
Belgium	21	1.35	67.51	1.54	25.00	1.65
England	96	6.16	190.94	4.35	70.80	4.69
Greece	7	.45	7.53	.17	3.30	.22
Denmark	3	.19	3.14	.07	.98	.06
West Berlin	30	1.93	32.17	.73	11.65	.77
Ireland	5	.32	17.00	.39	8.15	.54
Spain	21	1.35	53.69	1.22	17.97	1.19
Italy	95	6.10	510.74	11.63	167.31	11.07
Canada	37	2.37	111.51	2.54	44.97	2.98
Liechtenstein	17	1.09	17.32	.39	8.55	.57
Luxembourg	6	.39	2.11	.05	.86	.06
Netherlands	20	1.28	50.74	1.16	23.02	1.52
New Zealand	2	.13	1.50	.03	.60	.04
Norway	5	.32	4.65	.11	1.15	.08
United States	172	11.04	359.47	8.18	173.02	11.45
Turkey	1	.06	1.75	.04	0	0
Finland	175	11.23	367.40	8.36	116.31	7.70
FRG	214	13.74	548.22	12.48	158.92	10.52
France	54	3.47	370.23	8.43	146.45	9.69
Sweden	58	3.72	194.74	4.43	60.90	4.03
Switzerland	69	4.43	107.09	2.44	35.93	2.38
Japan	27	1.73	56.54	1.29	29.61	1.96
Portugal	1	.06	.25	.01	.10	.01

Table 12.2 (continued)

Country	Amount of Foreign Participation		Joint Initial Capital		Foreign Investment	
	Number of JVs	%	mln rubles	%	mln rubles	%
TOTAL	1558	100	4392.62	100	1510.96	100
Developing Countries	116	7.45	174.96	3.98	54.98	3.64
Argentina	1	.06	.56	.01	.28	.02
Afghanistan	1	.06	2.24	.05	1.09	.07
Bangladesh	1	.06	.20	0	.03	0
Bolivia	1	.06	.65	.01	.09	.01
Brazil	4	.26	23.54	.54	4.58	.30
Venezuela	7	.45	2.73	.06	1.11	.07
Hong Kong	2	.13	.43	.01	.21	.01
Egypt	2	.13	6.40	.15	1.92	.13
India	26	1.67	52.71	1.20	12.89	.85
Jordan	3	.19	4.05	.09	1.65	.11
Iran	1	.06	.02	0	0	0
Cyprus	17	1.09	17.38	.40	7.01	.46
Columbia	1	.06	1.25	.03	.50	.03
Kuwait	4	.26	3.45	.08	1.69	.11
Lebanon	4	.26	5.63	.13	1.46	.10
Mauritania	1	.06	.10	0	.05	0
Pakistan	2	.13	13.72	.31	4.26	.28
Panama	4	.26	2.55	.06	1.22	.08
Oman	1	.06	1.15	.03	0	0
Malta	2	.13	2.00	.05	.44	.03
UAE	3	.19	4.15	.09	1.50	.10
Saudi Arabia	1	.06	.15	0	.07	0
Singapore	12	.77	14.84	.34	7.80	.52
Syria	11	.71	13.88	.32	4.61	.31
Thailand	2	.13	.16	0	.07	0
Phillipines	1	.06	.52	.01	.20	.01
South Korea	1	.06	.50	.01	.25	.02

Note: Figures are based on 1478 of 1542 registered joint ventures.

Mixed joint ventures -- ventures with partners from more than one foreign country -- are registered in each country. Therefore, the total sum of the joint ventures indicated here and their initial capital is greater than the corresponding registered data.

unpiloted lifting cranes, equipment for installing and strengthening machine parts, commercial refrigeration equipment, computers, shoe soles, sports cars, and electronic telephones); in the chemical industry (the manufacture of ethylene glycol, preservative compounds, hermetics, dyes, and synthetic organic products); in the wood-processing industry (the manufacture of pulp materials, furniture frames, and parts); in construction; and in light and food industries (the manufacture of footwear, consumer goods, and the

Table 12.3
Geographic Distribution of Joint Ventures within the Soviet Union

Republic	Number of JVs	%	Initial Capital (mln rubles)	%
TOTAL	1459	100	3648.67	100
Azerbaijan	10	.69	29.33	.80
Armenia	10	.69	48.27	1.32
Byelorussia	27	1.85	65.52	1.80
Georgia	41	2.81	116.70	3.20
Kazakhstan	10	.69	14.74	.40
Kirgizia	2	.14	.72	.02
Latvia	39	2.67	45.05	1.23
Lithuania	18	1.23	50.24	1.38
Moldavia	14	.96	47.99	1.32
Russia including:	1072	73.47	2864.90	78.52
Leningrad	113	7.75	164.07	4.50
Moscow	717	49.14	1655.23	45.37
Tadjikistan	1	.07	.50	.01
Turkmenia	1	.07	4.00	.11
Uzbekistan	11	.75	47.99	1.32
Ukraine	99	6.79	196.25	5.38
Estonia	104	7.13	116.47	3.19

extraction and processing of fish and other sea products). Joint ventures have also been established in other spheres, as in the manufacture of computer software and video products, engineering and consulting services, advertising and publishing, medicine, hotel and restaurant services, and film and concert activities.

Most enterprises have formed in the areas of engineering, the manufacture of computer programs, informational consulting, and project construction activities—in other words, those sectors of the economy that do not require substantial start-up investments (see Table 12.4). Thus, 27 percent of joint ventures are related to engineering, consulting, intermediary activities, scientific research, and experimental design; 13 percent are related to the manufacture of personal computers and software; 6.5 percent are in printing and the organization of entertainment enterprises; and 5 percent in medicine and health care. All told, more than 50 percent of joint ventures have been formed in these branches.

Nine enterprises were formed in metallurgy and nine in the fuel-energy complex. Five percent of joint ventures have been formed in the chemical-

Table 12.4
Joint Venture Specialization

Sphere of Activity	Number of JVs	%	Initial Capital (mln rubles)	%
TOTAL	1447	100	3653.83	100
Fuel and energy complex	16	1.11	89.74	2.46
Metallurgical complex	21	1.45	167.50	4.58
Chemical-lumber complex	97	6.70	450.61	12.33
Heavy machinery	91	6.29	307.92	8.43
Production of personal computers and software	208	14.37	276.21	7.56
Construction and building materials	117	8.09	461.60	12.63
Transportation and communication	27	1.87	33.97	.93
Agro-industrial complex	91	6.29	375.60	10.28
Trade and public food service	71	4.91	100.55	2.75
Toirism, hotels, transportation	87	6.01	227.19	6.22
Health and medical care	56	3.87	174.62	4.78
Education	2	.14	2.35	.06
Light industrial manufacturing	53	3.66	117.45	3.21
Consumer goods	123	8.50	331.04	9.06
Film and video	34	2.35	35.10	.96
Concert activity	22	1.52	13.47	.37
Printing and publishing	43	2.97	56.94	1.56
R&D	71	4.91	43.89	1.20
Engineering	58	4.01	75.92	2.08
Consulting and intermediary services	149	10.30	304.84	8.34
Personnel training	10	.69	7.23	.20

forestry and machine-building industries, 4.4 percent in agriculture, 7.6 percent in construction and building materials, and 10.4 percent in light industry and consumer goods production.

There are few large joint ventures. Only slightly more than thirty enterprises (approximately 3 percent) have charter funds of over 20 million rubles (see Tables 12.5 and 12.6). In addition, about sixty enterprises (approximately 5 percent) have charter funds from 10 to 20 million rubles. The larger part—more than 770 enterprises (60 percent)—have charter funds of 1 million rubles or less, and more than two hundred enterprises (15 percent) have funds of less than one hundred thousand rubles.

U.S. firms characteristically follow the same patterns of capital investment as do other foreign participants in joint ventures. The largest group of joint

Table 12.5
Initial Capital in Joint Ventures

Range of Initial Capital	Number of JVs	%	Initial Capital (mln rubles)	%
TOTAL	1478	100	3776.74	100
0--0.5 mln rubles	695	47.02	129.29	3.42
0.5--1 mln rubles	225	15.22	144.55	3.83
1--5 mln rubles	381	25.78	771.23	20.42
5--10 mln rubles	86	5.82	556.80	14.74
10-1000 mln rubles	91	6.16	2174.87	57.59

Table 12.6
A Sample of Joint Ventures with Largest Initial Capitalization

Joint Venture	Initial Capital (mln rubles)	Activity
Intervin	98.0	Champagne, wine
Krovtekh	48.1	Roofing canvas
Khomatek	47.7	Machine building
Konakerskii Aluminum Plant	41.0	Aluminum foil
Usol'efarm	40.0	Organically synthesized products
Al'tair	40.0	Construction of space research center
Sovbutital	38.3	Synthetic rubber

ventures with the participation of U.S. firms is in research and development, engineering and consulting services, and the social complex (medicine, printing, film and video production, food service). U.S. firms so far tend not to participate in spheres that may require a lengthy period of time before becoming profitable.

The basic financial foundation of U.S.-Soviet enterprises is not large: in more than 65 percent of U.S.-Soviet joint ventures, the joint venture's charter fund is less than 1 million rubles.[2] There are enterprises that have charter funds of only fifty, twenty, or even twelve thousand rubles. There are a few exceptions where joint ventures with U.S. firms have charter funds of over 10 million rubles.

This testifies to the fact that Americans, like the majority of foreign partners, have been hesitant to invest heavily in joint ventures on Soviet soil. Evidently, the regulations of the Coordinating Committee on Multi-

lateral Export Controls (COCOM) that are currently in place have a pro-
hibitive effect on joint ventures that involve technology transfer, as do U.S.
restrictions on the introduction of high technologies as contributions to the
charter fund or in licensing agreements.

As previously discussed, the profile of activity created over the past two
years of joint ventures testifies to the fact that foreign partners do not actively
pursue the creation of joint ventures in branches of the economy—machine
building, electronics, the chemical industry, agriculture, and others—on
which the Soviets place a high priority and where a substantial investment
and long periods of nonprofitability may be necessary. This has resulted in
foreign interest in joint ventures that do not require substantial capital
investment, such as engineering joint ventures, and joint ventures in the
service sector, where the return on investment and profits are made in a
shorter period of time (see Table 12.4).

Under the circumstances, it would be useful to stimulate the establishment
of joint ventures in priority branches by differentiating the level of taxation
of profits, as it done in regions of the Far East.[3] For such industries it would
be necessary to oversee and prioritize the order of the material and technical
supply.

While joint ventures characteristically have a small level of investment
(in the sphere of engineering, computer programming, and the service
sector), firms from some countries have actively invested capital and resources in the initial stage of joint venture activities on the basis of yielding
a more effective return but over a longer time period and with the intention
of introducing themselves to the Soviet market, hoping in the future to
occupy a more important position, even in high priority branches.

The most active firms have been from the Federal Republic of Germany.
On 1 June 1989, German firms took part in the creation of approximately
ten important joint ventures, three of which were for machine building, one
for building large, portable cranes, one for producing technical electronic
equipment, and two for wood processing. There are also German enterprises
for manufacturing petroleum products, and for processing agricultural products.

Italian firms also participate in important joint ventures in the manufacture of grain-harvesting machinery, switches and consumer electronics, synthetic rubber, and plastic products. French firms participate in the important
project of building an international space research center, and also in a large
joint venture for the production of aluminum foil. Spanish firms cooperate
in the manufacture of electronic communications technology and in non-
ferrous metallurgy, and Yugoslavian firms participate in the manufacture
of turbine equipment and polymer materials. Firms from other countries
have entered into joint ventures for the production of dyes and other chemical products (Switzerland), organically synthesized products (Bulgaria),

copper wire (Austria), veneers (Finland), and automobile moldings (Canada).

Only a few important joint ventures have been formed with the participation of firms from the United States, except in the field of computer programming. An important project tied into the cooperation of the Soviet and U.S. consortia could fundamentally change the role of U.S. firms in joint venture participation as a whole; yet, this project will require some time before the effects are felt. At the same time many U.S. firms could. cooperate on a parallel basis with Soviet partners, in their own time finding a place in the Soviet market. For the time being, other Western firms fill the gaps left by U.S. firms.

Because of this, and in connection with the short period of time that has passed since the appearance of this form of cooperation, products and services of joint ventures do not yet occupy a substantial relative share in the general exchange of production in the Soviet Union. At the same time, the growth in numbers of joint ventures in different branches and recent discussion of a few important projects (Tengizpolymer, on the base of the Tengiz oil complex, with the participation of the U.S. firm Occidental Petroleum Corporation and a number of Italian and Japanese firms; or the U.S.-Soviet consortium with the participation of major U.S. firms) can lead to the conclusion that joint ventures will become more important to the Soviet economy in the near future.

The future, then, will show the direction of the development of joint business ventures on Soviet territory. At the same time it is now possible to say with assurance that this process will expand, Soviet legislation regulating these issues will improve, new zones permitting advantageous conditions for joint ventures will appear in some form or another, and all this will aid not only the expansion of foreign economic relations of the Soviet government, but a strengthening of the economic potential of the Soviet Union.

NOTES

1. Calculated at the acting commercial exchange rate of the USSR State Bank (Gosbank).

2. For comparison's sake, 51.7 percent of the total number of joint ventures in the Soviet Union have initial investments of less than 1 million rubles.

3. USSR Council of Ministers, Decree 1405 (2 December 1988).

Part IV

Joint Ventures in the USSR: Practical
Problems

Chapter 13

General Trends in the Development of Joint Enterprises in the Soviet Union: A View through the Lens of Survey Research

Tatyana M. Artemova and Alan B. Sherr

In February and March 1990, the editors of this book conducted a survey of a sample of U.S.-Soviet joint ventures to obtain firsthand information on the problems and successes they had experienced. The survey was conducted by means of an extensive questionnaire that explored motivations for entering a joint venture, problems in negotiation, problems in operations, and views of future prospects. Because opinions on the experiences of joint ventures in these areas have been based almost exclusively on subjective impressions or very small samples, it was hoped that the results of this survey would contribute significantly to understanding the real prospects for this form of foreign direct investment.

The questionnaire was developed by specialists from the Center for Foreign Policy Development at Brown University, the Institute for World Economy and International Relations of the USSR Academy of Sciences, and the All-Union Scientific Research Institute of Foreign Economic Relations of the State Foreign Economics Commission under the USSR Council of Ministers. It was completed by 48 Soviet representatives of U.S.-Soviet joint ventures and 18 U.S. representatives out of a total of 172 such joint ventures registered as of 1 April 1990. All of the joint ventures surveyed were chosen in order to represent a range of sectors and activities. A breakdown of the areas of production represented by the joint ventures surveyed is shown in Table 13.1.

We believe that the selection of joint ventures used for this survey reliably reflects the overall picture of operating joint ventures. Small- and medium-size enterprises predominate. There were relatively few large joint ventures with charter funds in excess of 10 million rubles represented in the survey—only 6 percent of the total number of registered joint ventures—although their share in the total amount of charter funds was 38 percent. In the initial phase this is to a large degree natural, but it is clear that the transition to

Table 13.1
Sphere of Activity of Surveyed Joint Ventures

Sphere of Activity	Soviet	U.S.
Fuel and energy complex	1	0
Metallurgical complex	1	1
Chemical-lumber complex	1	1
Production of personal computers and software	9	1
Construction and production of building and transportation materials	1	1
Agroindustrial complex	2	1
Trade and public food service	2	1
Health and medical care	4	0
Consumer goods production	4	1
Production of film and video products	5	1
Printing and publishing	2	2
R&D, engineering, intermediary consulting services/personnel training, marketing	16	8
TOTAL	48	18

the creation of larger joint ventures is going slowly. It is also obvious that there are relatively few joint ventures actually producing commodities. We should point out that small enterprises continue to appear in the sphere of consultative and various other services of a nonmanufacturing nature. It may be that the demand for such joint ventures has already been met. There may be increased competition among them as new ones become active. (Many such joint ventures are "recruiting personnel"; they are registered but have not yet begun to operate.)

U.S.-Soviet joint ventures, both those surveyed and all of them in general, should be viewed through the lens of the overall conditions under which the Soviet economy and its foreign relations are developing. One of the most important aspects is foreign companies' evaluation of the risk accompanying investment in joint ventures in the Soviet Union. It is hard to reflect this problem fully through questionnaire results, which can only provide a snapshot. Ongoing research is needed here. But certain factors can be caught, even by a one-time questionnaire.

There is no question that the risk factor manifests itself mainly in relation to the foreign partner's share in the charter fund and in the total volume of investments in a joint venture. Considering the potential opportunities for U.S.-Soviet cooperation, the present scale of joint U.S.-Soviet production activities clearly falls short of its potential. It is therefore easy to conclude that U.S. corporations view the risk accompanying the creation of joint ventures in the Soviet Union to be rather high. (We will not deal here with the other obstacles complicating the process of forming joint ventures in the Soviet Union.)

However, evaluations of the various risk factors are not immutable, and there are structural movements in the assortment of these factors. At first, many factors were evaluated abstractly, due to a lack of practical experience. As experience was acquired, estimates became more precise. Evaluations of the general state of the Soviet economy, of its immediate prospects, and of the potential situation in the country and in particular regions have also changed.

Since the end of 1989 a conviction has emerged in the Western business world that the risk accompanying investment in the Soviet economy is substantially increasing and taking on new features, conditioned in the first instance by growing political instability. Many business people have spoken frankly about the expediency of playing a waiting game, particularly after they have discovered the difficulties that Soviet organizations have experienced in paying for imported deliveries. It is also well known that most joint ventures registered on Soviet territory still exist only on paper and have not actually begun to operate.

However, figures released in September 1990 by Goskomstat, the USSR State Committee on Statistics, based on the first returns from a new system of mandatory reporting by joint ventures, indicate that the percentage of operating joint ventures is actually significantly higher than has usually been assumed. Goskomstat reported that of the 1,754 joint ventures registered through the first half of 1990, 541 (or 30.8 percent) were actually operating and producing goods or services. An additional 162 joint ventures (9.2 percent) were not producing goods or services but were paying their workers. Thus, the number of joint ventures that could be said to be operational was 703, or 40.1 percent of the total registered.

It took Soviet public opinion a long time to realize that the process of establishing joint ventures was running into serious difficulties. Since far from all Western businesses were scared off by the heightened degree of risk accompanying business activities in the Soviet Union, and since the number of Soviet enterprises and organizations interested in finding partners to set up joint ventures increased substantially with the decentralization efforts of 1988 and 1989, new joint ventures continued to appear. This fact was reported by the mass media with accuracy and goodwill, with only a few exceptions. Soviet citizens in general, and enterprise managers in particular, formed the impression that everything was going well in this area. All the more so, because there was material evidence to support that optimistic view: some joint ventures in the production field, from among those established in the first wave, began operating and producing goods. Naturally, quantities were small in relation to the size of the Soviet domestic market, but what was important to the public and to Soviet factory directors was that a new type of production had appeared in the Soviet Union, not just in words, but in reality.

Thus, increased skepticism in the West coincides with the opposite trend in the Soviet Union, where interest in joint ventures continues to grow. They have become fashionable, and there were references to joint ventures in virtually every spoken or written comment by economists who are lobbying for a radicalization of economic reform and who view them as one of the main ways to achieve the desired goal of activating foreign economic ties. The same can be said, incidentally, about other forms of foreign economic activity new to the Soviet Union. Debates about whether or not to create free economic zones have grown more and more heated, without any reference to the stance of Western businesses, and without considering their actual interest in such zones.

The heightened degree of risk associated by Western business people with investment in joint ventures on Soviet territory lends special relevance to a study of factors that might favor the success of existing joint ventures, or at least enable them to survive. The more common approach is one that exhaustively studies the factors that hinder the creation of joint ventures or prevent ones that are already registered from commencing operations. But that approach needs to be supplemented by another directed toward joint ventures already in operation. This concept had a major influence in the preparation of the questionnaire for our survey.

It would be useful to take a look at the types of organizations that have founded the joint ventures in the survey. In general, they can be described as varied and as including a broad spectrum of enterprises and organizations interested in joint economic activity with U.S. partners. Perhaps one could even say that the range of joint venture activity is diverse to a fault and includes a number of activities of dubious value.

Before pursuing this subject, we should note that the Soviet founders of the enterprises surveyed include industrial giants, rank-and-file enterprises both large and small, scientific research institutes of the industrial branch type, universities, academic scientific research institutes, cooperatives, foreign trade organizations within the system of the Ministry of Foreign Economic Relations, department stores, and public organizations. At first sight, one can only welcome such an array of the most varied participants. However, such an attitude is only appropriate if the large circle of participants indicates good prospects opening up for U.S.-Soviet economic cooperation in general, and for joint ventures in particular.

Unfortunately, one could also reach the conclusion that joint venture participants are too varied, and that this has happened because interest in creating joint ventures has been exaggerated due to the underdevelopment of other forms of cooperation. Indeed, why are such diverse enterprises and organizations from widely differing fields of activity suddenly trying to participate in joint ventures? The same form has turned out to attract a variety of founders of joint ventures. Quite probably, some of the reasons motivating Soviet founders had only an oblique and distant connection with joint production activity as such. For example, Soviet founders could have seen joint ventures as the best (or even only) opportunity to enter the foreign market or to establish contacts with foreign colleagues. Sometimes the drive to set up joint ventures seems to have become fashionable, a mass enthusiasm. But then it follows that joint ventures may decline in relative importance as other forms of foreign economic activity improve. That will mean that the foreign economic activities of Soviet enterprises and organizations will be divided more equally in various directions.

A comparison of Soviet and U.S. founders leads to yet another observation: on the Soviet side there are often several founders, whereas there is generally only one U.S. founder. This is not accidental. It seems to relate to certain general features of the Soviet economy. In the first place, one should keep in mind that the Soviet economy is still organized mainly on the principle of narrow branches: all, or almost all, enterprises of a particular type are subordinate to a ministry (department). In the second place, the enterprise is still the primary economic link, the economic cell (although, in fairness, one should also note the existence of a large number of associations, also largely of one branch). An enterprise is the primary link in precisely the original meaning of the word: a factory or plant taken by itself.

A high degree of monopolization is also characteristic of the Soviet economy. Many enterprises are the sole producers of their particular commodities. These could be finished products with a high degree of complexity requiring the cooperation of dozens of enterprises in various branches for its production. Or they could be simple component parts needed by many consumers to make a variety of finished products. But in any case the enterprise, being a monopoly, possesses powerful levers of pressure and becomes a subcenter of economic power.

Nevertheless, paradoxically enough, the economic opportunities for such an enterprise may be limited. Economic power and limited opportunities go hand in hand. Enterprises may find power in relations with consumers, who have simply nowhere else to go for such goods, yet still face weakness in, for example, developing new types of goods and putting them into production. An enterprise does not have its own research base, it has no opportunity to carry out experimental designs on an extensive scale. As noted above, this is a result of the low degree of aggregation at the primary link level, with the enterprise as a single factory, a single plant, even though a large one. It also follows that enterprises do not have their own marketing network, which they are even less likely to have outside of the country.

The result is that a single enterprise is often unable to cope with the tasks confronting joint ventures. An association of two or more Soviet participants is necessary. For example, a scientific research institute and an industrial enterprise, or an industrial enterprise and a foreign trade association, appear as founders on the Soviet side. In both cases, the founder on the U.S. side is a corporation that has within its structure either a research subdivision and production links or production links and a strong marketing service.

The need to combine the efforts of several Soviet participants to create joint ventures introduces certain complications into the process of organizing and operating them. However, it seems certain that new, multibranch structures will emerge in the course of the structural reorganization of the Soviet economy, that they will far surpass existing enterprises in their possibilities, and that they will become the basic economic links in the national economy. The opportunities for such multielement, diversified associations to organize joint ventures will be correspondingly greater.

By relying on the results of the survey and an analysis of general trends in the development of joint production activity in the Soviet Union, one could make a rather convincing argument that the particular form of joint venture cooperation now present in the Soviet economy, rather than being firmly grounded in economic and commercial factors, is a result of arbitrary and artificial forces. That is, the process of joint venture development has not yet run its course to an economically rational conclusion. In a certain sense, artificial factors still play an important role, though they are of secondary importance from the viewpoint of objective, long-term prospects. An example of such an artificial factor would be the chance to form a contact with a Soviet partner with an office, telex, or telefax at its disposal. Such factors are especially important for relatively small foreign firms making their first attempts to break into the Soviet market.

Though it might seem strange at first glance, one could even consider joint ventures that are founded by foreign companies with years of experience in contacts with Soviet enterprises and organizations as motivated purely by artificial factors. The experience of the foreign partner on the Soviet market was acquired in the past, when trade was the principal form of foreign economic relations. Moreover, the mechanism of foreign economic relations was different and presupposed a different model of conduct by partners and a different horizon of interests. Such past experience has little relevance to demands on joint venture partners who must now operate under a commercial relationship that presumes a different set of goals, another mechanism, and another structure of interrelations with the domestic economy.

All this is certainly not said to offend Soviet and U.S. partners, who are working together despite numerous obstacles and complications. No one should minimize the services of enthusiasts in any good cause. However, for the sake of objectivity one must still take into account the play of chance, the confluence of relatively unimportant circumstances, that leads to the appearance of a joint venture. It could not be otherwise in a situation where the choice of partners is complicated by:

- the lack of data about most promising potential areas for establishing joint ventures and possible participants;
- the lack of free access by all Soviet economic units to the foreign economic sphere;
- distortions introduced by the heritage of the former administrative methods of managing the Soviet economy; and
- a reflection of the distortions and disproportions existing in the Soviet economy, which have worsened in the recent period.

In this situation the mechanism for forming joint ventures can give rise to extremely paradoxical results. Let's take an example. The view that ruble inconvertibility is a principal obstacle to forming joint ventures is generally accepted, and is indeed the case. However, there is another aspect: there are joint ventures that owe their existence to ruble inconvertibility. If the ruble were convertible, their activities would be simply unnecessary. This applies mainly to those joint ventures that perform intermediary or quasi-intermediary functions, supplemented sometimes by a symbolic amount of production activity. Naturally, this occurs in areas where the inconvertibility of the ruble and the gap between the price structure in the domestic market on the one hand and the price structure in the world market on the other have caused exchange proportions to take on a clearly asymmetrical character. The activities of joint ventures in such cases are in fact oriented toward outmoded component elements of the former economic mechanism of the Soviet economy, elements destined to be dismantled: the inconvertible ruble and an unsupported price structure. Can it be said that such joint ventures help promote the rejection of old methods of organizing economic life on the macroeconomic level and help speed the transition to a new economic mechanism; specifically, an adequate concept of a regulated market economy? To some degree, of course, that is so. But their role in this respect should not be exaggerated.

After the liquidation of the administrative command economic mechanism, the purposes for which some joint ventures were created may disappear. It will be found that such joint ventures are of an essentially transitory nature. There is nothing bad about this process, of course. The transitional period through which the Soviet economy is now passing cannot possibly be a short one, like a blitz chess match. Such joint ventures will therefore last quite a while. Still, one should not overlook the fact that the existing group of joint ventures is of a transitional nature when judged by numerous parameters, such as the types of participants, areas of activity, and scale of operations. Only the future will show and determine which trends in joint activity will be defined by primarily economic factors, which will bear a long-term character, or which will strengthen interaction between the two countries' economies.

What has been said above about the specific nature of the parameters defining the totality of joint ventures relates to projected ones, as well as to those already in existence. In this connection, we would like to mention one more specific circumstance. As is well known, a high degree of centralism, resulting, among other things, in the desire to carry out large, showy, and advantageous projects, is inherent in economic management on administrative command bases. Apparently this passion for gigantism, which is fed by an administrative command type of structure, has also affected the sphere of joint ventures, One indication of that is the scale of the design at the basis of the well-known American Trade Consortium and its Soviet counterpart. It has a difficult road ahead: any concrete results are still a long way off and the plans of its initiators are still on paper. It would seem that such schemes are also of a transitory nature; they reflect the specific character of a transitional period. One should note that this is true on both sides: on the Soviet side, because links in the previous economic mechanism can perceive such supersize projects as one advantageous method of prolonging their existence and demonstrating their usefulness, and, on the U.S. side, because participants in trade and economic ties with the Soviet Union have traditionally been large corporations capable of carrying out major projects and accustomed to dealing with traditional administrative structures in the Soviet economy. Moreover, these participants are accustomed to placing a high value on their contacts with these structures and know from experience that the degree of success of many projects is directly proportional to the level of the hierarchy at which they have managed to establish businesslike relationships.

However, in the future this approach will be less suited to the decentralization of economic decision making in the Soviet economy and to the appearance of a large number of newly independent participants in the economy. The possibility cannot be excluded that even major projects that are objectively necessary will be affected. The excessive popularity of major projects may be replaced by the other extreme—a blindly negative attitude toward them. One should also not fail to consider that, when the economy is in a transitional period, the difficulty of coordinating all the components of major projects inevitably increases.

In short, it is hard to dispute the fact that present joint ventures are oriented to the structure of the Soviet economy as it now exists, implying that defects in this structure have influenced their formation. That is quite natural. But something else must become natural as well: the growing strength, and then the domination, of an orientation toward the future structure of the Soviet economy. That orientation will be for long-term and genuinely bilateral cooperation. At present, this strategy, pointed toward the future, still looks weak.

It would be no great exaggeration to say that, for many U.S. corporations, participation in the organization of joint ventures is simply a continuation of trade operations, a form of trade in their products. Indeed, in creating joint ventures on Soviet territory, U.S. corporations make use of what they have already achieved; they rely on whatever level of competitiveness they had attained outside any contacts with Soviet partners. In such cases, the future competitiveness of a U.S. founder of a joint venture will also not generally depend (or almost not depend) on joint activity with a Soviet partner. True, for the latter, the creation of a joint venture may serve as an important link in its economic strategy. But, in any case, it is hard to speak of the appearance of a joint strategy; the partners continue to go their own ways even after forming a joint venture.

It is a different matter when the partners jointly develop commodities with which they will enter the consumer market in five or ten years and that will largely determine both their ability to compete and the financial rewards of both Soviet and U.S. participants. In that case, the matter truly affects the economic strategy of the partners and leads to joint, long-term goals. Such a joint venture certainly cannot be called artificial, and its activities will not, as is the case now, remain on the periphery of the operations of joint venture partners. But is there reason to believe that such joint ventures will occupy a prominent place among U.S.-Soviet joint ventures and give them a qualitatively different character?

We think there are such reasons. In principle, joint ventures are capable of becoming a form of interaction between the scientific-technical potentials of the two countries—interaction leading to interpenetration. For a host of reasons (including psychological and historical-cultural ones), development along these lines may be more likely in U.S.-Soviet trade and economic ties than in Soviet economic relations with other countries.

The results of the survey, as well as the work of U.S.-Soviet joint ventures as a whole, confirm that the present state of affairs is still far distant from the proposed scenario. Nevertheless, it would seem to be possible, particularly judging by the fact that the Soviet Union has many potential partners whose cooperation would be viewed by U.S. corporations as important in helping them succeed in the competitive struggle on world markets. The creation of a joint venture on Soviet territory will then be what it should always primarily be—a method for joining the scientific-technical potential of the Soviet Union to the international division of labor, in this case, via interaction with U.S. partners.

In this connection we would like to touch on one particular and important problem. Familiarity with the activity of U.S.-Soviet joint ventures demonstrates that Soviet managers, engineers, and other specialists are interested in obtaining work at joint ventures. At joint ventures, they receive wages that are in effect quite comparable to what they would receive if they were working abroad.

According to Goskomstat data, nearly all workers in Soviet joint ventures are Soviets. Out of a total work force of 66,600 people accounted for at

Table 13.2
Average Wages of Employees of Joint Ventures

Sphere of Activity	Average Monthly Wage (in rubles)	Percentage of National Average (257 rubles)
Industry	535	208%
Construction	678	264%
Trade and public catering	789	307%
Scientific research and project construction	644	251%
Other branches of the national economy	705	274%
Cooperative	742	289%

the end of June 1990, approximately 65,500, or 98.4 percent, were Soviet citizens. The average monthly wage in the Soviet Union for blue- and white-collar workers was 257 rubles at the end of the first half of 1990. As shown in Table 13.2, the wage rates for Soviet joint venture workers were thus substantially above the national average—up to three times as much.

Scientific personnel would be in an analogous position, if they were able to obtain work at joint ventures. It is well known that many people in the Soviet Union are concerned by a potential brain drain. A partial solution to this problem could be found by speeding up the development of high-tech joint ventures making use of Soviet scientific and engineering potential. Soviet scientists who work in applied science, or who have achieved results suitable for transfer to the stage of applied research, could solve many of the questions that prompt them to look for work in foreign scientific establishments.

Quite naturally, it is hard to predict the course of events connected with the Soviet Union's brain drain problem. If a brain drain takes on truly tangible proportions in a country possessing the world's largest contingent of scientific personnel and numerous scientific schools that have enjoyed a solid reputation for many years throughout the scientific world, it is possible that a kind of competition to attract Soviet scientists will develop among Western countries. The United States will undoubtedly be the chief center of attraction for scientists leaving the Soviet Union to look for work—the chief attraction, but not the only one. It may well turn out that other Western countries will be more competitive with the United States than would seem likely today, especially if they are the first to appreciate fully the potential of joint research work and increase the importance of this factor in the overall motivation to form joint ventures.

This question of motivation was directly addressed by our questionnaire. Results of the survey among Soviet respondents show that in most cases the initiative in creating joint ventures came from the Soviet side (according to 19 out of 41 respondents) or was mutual (18). Only 4 respondents reported that the initiative came from a U.S. company. As 24 of the respondents reported, some administrative personnel were opposed to initiating negotiations on the creation of joint ventures; in 5 cases there was serious opposition, while in 16 there was moderate opposition.

Explanation of this result is not so simple, since it was often not a matter of opposition to the founding of a joint venture but a struggle among different opinions and interests. Apparently the problem is that in many cases (according to 13 of 43 Soviet respondents), negotiations with the U.S. side were initiated by the ministry to which the founding enterprise was subordinate, while the enterprise itself initiated the negotiations in only 11 cases. Moreover, the founding enterprise often did not itself conduct preliminary research or act as the principal author of documents (in 28 cases out of 43). This laid the basis for conflict in the positions of the various interested parties, such as the ministry, enterprise, or initiating group. We think that differences of opinion among an enterprise's administrative personnel will be much reduced at the start of negotiations as the economic independence of enterprises grows and becomes real rather than declarative, since the idea of creating a joint venture will spring from the enterprise itself, not from outside, as is often the case now.

The questionnaire results indicated that most joint venture partners, after several months or more of operation, have not significantly changed their views on the merits of the joint venture approach. On the one hand, this may be due to the relatively short time that joint ventures have existed and to the lack of such changes in the Soviet economy that would seriously affect joint ventures while major changes were occurring in other areas. On the other hand, the relative stability over time in the ranking of factors motivating the creation of joint ventures testifies to the fact that the founders understood the situation rather well and judged it correctly. We should note that this was not necessarily a great insight on their part. The state of the Soviet market is such that it is often easy to choose a sphere of activity in which the joint venture will become virtually the only supplier. A fine analysis of the factors influencing economic activity is far from always necessary for such a supplier, especially when there is such a high level of demand.

Most of the Soviet respondents, and 7 of the U.S. respondents, noted as important factors—in both initially creating joint ventures and in continuing with the operation as of the date of the survey—the Soviet partner's opportunity to participate in the production of goods, to sell them on the Soviet market, and to export them to the West (the latter was mentioned by 26–27 Soviet respondents, more than half of which pointed to this factor as being number one or two among important factors, and considered most important by 4 of 18 U.S. respondents). U.S. respondents also rated such factors as the expectation of profit (4), the expectation of good return on investment (5), and the import by the joint venture of the U.S. company's product (5), as the most important reasons for undertaking joint ventures. These responses generally reflect the different perspectives of Soviet and foreign partners—the latter focusing in particular on the potential for breaking into the huge Soviet market.

It might seem puzzling that only one Soviet enterprise cited the opportunity to gain a foothold in the world market, which would appear to be closely related to the highly popular export factor. In fact, however, there is no contradiction. Rather, it is evidence of an unfortunate tendency common to many joint ventures. The export of goods and services by joint ventures to Western markets is of a subsidiary nature—but not optional in the sense that the joint venture may decide whether or not to export. They must export, if only to secure hard currency self-financing. That is an important goal under conditions of ruble inconvertibility, but it is not a strategic goal. It is characteristic that joint ventures soberly evaluate their potential and recognize that their export base is too weak to pose the question of a solid entry onto the world market. The export of products and services by joint ventures therefore simply serves the principal sphere of their activity and enables them to grow, and that sphere is, as before, the domestic market. In and of itself, there is nothing wrong with that. Still, the establishment of an export base should proceed in parallel fashion.

An important question in the questionnaire asked the respondents to evaluate a list of potential factors that may have been considered during the negotiation of the joint venture. Those factors were to be judged important, moderately important, or not important, viewed both at the time of negotiation and at the time the survey was conducted. Not surprisingly, there were more Soviet respondents who viewed the repatriation of profits as vital at the time of the survey than who had during the negotiating period (28 and 26 respectively). It is odd that several Soviet respondents considered that factor unimportant during the negotiating period (7) and continued to think so (4). Apparently, those Soviet respondents count on increasing the use of freely convertible currency in domestic economic turnover within the Soviet economy. So far this policy has justified itself, but it is also clear that this cannot become the rule for most joint ventures.

Evaluation of the importance of securing reliable deliveries has not changed to any important extent (39 Soviet respondents replied to this subpoint, of which 18 continued to consider it a vital problem while 15 considered it of little importance). We should not be in a hurry to interpret this result. Problems with the supply of component parts and raw materials have become especially severe in the Soviet economy during the summer of 1990—that is, since the survey was held. However, one should not exclude the possibility that joint ventures will continue to evaluate the problem of deliveries in the same way, even though production in the Soviet economy has continued to drop since the first quarter of 1990. Everything would seem to depend on the supply mechanism that was chosen when the joint venture was established. If the joint venture pays for deliveries from Soviet enterprises either partially or fully in hard currency, then the supply will remain reliable. We should also note an increase of importance at the time the survey was administered, as compared to the time of negotiation, with respect to such factors as control over management and the adoption of decisions, distribution of shares of the charter fund among participants, status of a partner, evaluation of payments, evaluation of intellectual property, and introduction of bookkeeping calculations. Consequently, all these questions should be given heightened attention during negotiations.

Judging by answers to subpoints of that same question, such factors as quality control, hiring of Soviet workers, financing through Western sources, sale of products in the Soviet Union, political risk, and customs duties and tariffs have become more important to Soviet managers in the operation of joint ventures than was expected before they began to function. The number of Soviet respondents viewing ties with local government agencies as a vital part of their activity doubled, from twelve to twenty-four. Curiously, evaluation of support from high-level organizations or branch ministries remained virtually unchanged. Thus, changes in the political structure of the Soviet Union, an increase in the authority of local government agencies as the influence enjoyed by traditional departmental branch structures has declined, are leaving a noticeable imprint on the work of joint ventures. These trends, one must suppose, will continue to be evident in the future.

The perspective of U.S. respondents on these matters was generally consistent with that of the Soviet respondents. The U.S. respondents were asked to rate 39 potential negotiating issues according to whether they had perceived each as important, moderately important, or unimportant to the negotiation, and whether the resolution of each had proven to be difficult, moderate, or easy. The most unambiguous assessment was made with respect to addressing the problem of the inconvertibility of the ruble; it was deemed to be important by almost all the respondents (15 of 17) and difficult to resolve by 10 out of 17.

Other negotiating issues frequently cited by 17 U.S. respondents as both important and difficult to resolve included: quality control (15 important, 5 difficult), obtaining office and work space (12 important, 8 difficult), management control and decision making (13 important, 6 difficult), and financing from Western sources (9 important, 5 difficult).

Some negotiating issues were viewed as important, but not particularly difficult to resolve. These included: agreement on business objectives (13 important, 4 difficult), valuation of contributions (11 important, 3 difficult), partnership share (10 important, 4 difficult), protection of intellectual property (10 important, 2 difficult), financing from Soviet sources (9 important,

3 difficult), figuring input prices (9 important, 2 difficult), and figuring output prices (9 important, 1 difficult).

Finally, there were some issues not seen as important by as large a proportion of the U.S. respondents as the previous categories, but did present difficulties to a significant number of them. These included: guarantees or approvals of central agencies (6 important, 6 difficult), housing and schooling for foreigners and dependents (5 important, 6 difficult), document handling (6 important, 6 difficult), customs duties and tariffs (5 important, 5 difficult), marketing outside the Soviet Union (7 important, 5 difficult), and bookkeeping and accounting (7 important, 5 difficult).

One issue—identification of the proper partner—has often been cited as an important and difficult one with respect to the negotiation process, but did not stand out when put to the survey respondents. Only 7 of 17 U.S. respondents indicated that this was an important issue, and only 1 stated that it had proven to be difficult to resolve. One reason for this surprising result may be that Western partners tend to be too easily satisfied with respect to Soviet partners. Perhaps somewhat daunted by the job of finding the right partner in view of the gross lack of information about potential partners and great difficulties in communication, many Westerners appear ready to sign on with the first reasonable candidate that appears. This tendency is reinforced by the fact that a central ministry or other central agency often has been the initial contact for the Western side, and this central authority then has decided which Soviet entity to tap as the operational partner. However, as central authority diminishes and enterprise independence grows, this directing function will decline. As alternatives to state enterprises—such as cooperatives, other joint ventures, joint stock companies, and other forms—develop as potential partners for Westerners, the question of finding the right partner may loom larger in the initial calculus on the Western side.

It should be remembered that the preceding figures do not indicate whether the issues mentioned turned out to be significant with respect to the operation of the joint venture. The question was whether the issues were considered to be important during the negotiation stage, and whether difficulties were encountered in dealing with the issues in the drafting of the founding documents. Another set of questions probed the sources of problems encountered by joint ventures during the operational stage.

As it turned out, problems in operation often had been presaged by difficulties in negotiation or the perceived importance of addressing particular issues during negotiation. In particular, many respondents (16 of 48 Soviet, and 7 of 18 U.S.) pointed to accounting and bookkeeping as a source of difficulty in view of the lack of a special, comprehensible accounting system convenient to both partners in a joint venture. Eight Soviet and 11 U.S. respondents noted difficulties in management. At least from the U.S. side, this reflected a concern that Soviet managers did not fully appreciate the importance of free-market concepts (such as profit or price) and were having trouble changing gears from a command-driven to a market-driven approach.

There was some ambiguity introduced by answers to various questions. Though a large number of respondents (27 of 48 Soviet, and 7 of 18 U.S.) pointed to difficulties with material-technical supply, few considered the guarantee of supplies as a vital factor in organizing their work. Still, it would seem that such responses can be reconciled. The term "difficulties in supply" was understood to mean problems of a general nature—the lack of a developed wholesale market and the exclusion of joint ventures from the state supply network. It is clear that directors of joint ventures do not expect a wholesale market to develop rapidly. Joint enterprises still must make sure of their supplies on an individual basis, so to speak. In future, naturally, they will raise the question of the need for a transition to other principles of supply on the basis of a wholesale market.

A considerable number of respondents (14 Soviet, 5 U.S.) noted difficulties in relations with Soviet administrative bodies. Here again they had general problems in mind, primarily the absence of clear legal regulation. There are good reasons to suppose that this problem is in the process of being solved—as a matter of fact, even while the survey was being held, administrative bodies, as well as joint ventures themselves, recognized the need to work out a legal document regulating the work of joint ventures.

There was also mention of a higher-ranking ministry that had put the brakes on one joint venture's operations. Again, it should be noted that many joint ventures have been pioneers. The influence of branch ministries has diminished, while the work of joint ventures has acquired its own dynamic, has picked up speed and demonstrated its usefulness.

Of course, branch ministries are far from being the only part of the higher administrative echelon with which joint ventures have contract. It is instructive that in evaluating the investment climate in the Soviet Union, many respondents characterized their dealings with the Ministry of Finance (21 Soviet, 2 U.S.), the Ministry of Foreign Economic Relations (15 Soviet, 3 U.S.) and the Council of Ministers' State Foreign Economics Commission (1 U.S.) as having an unattractive aspect. Such evaluations probably also arise because of the lack of a single, clear legal document regulating the work of joint ventures.

As one might expect, the majority of respondents characterized service in the Soviet Union, in virtually every area, as unsatisfactory. This applies in particular to communications, transportation, hotel service, and food. As a whole, translating and visa services were evaluated positively. The factor deemed most detrimental to the investment climate in the Soviet Union was the availability of supplies, materials, and spare parts.

It was also not hard to predict that the matter of providing information about markets would be described as poor. Respondents also gave low marks to banking services. This proves yet again that reform of the entire banking sphere must continue. Work in this direction is indeed proceeding.

It should be noted that, as their number and scale of operations develop, joint ventures themselves must be seen as a factor influencing the evolution of the economic environment in the Soviet Union. They do not simply provide a demonstration (although that is important). The classic formula—demand creates supply—is effective. Since joint ventures are generally regarded as attractive business partners by Soviet enterprises and organizations, there is an effort to satisfy their requirements. Joint enterprises are also influencing the evolution of management culture. On the whole it may be said that joint ventures have succeeded in becoming a notable phenomenon in the Soviet economy, despite all the difficulties and complications they have encountered. Moreover, their growth is proceeding at a rather rapid tempo, a fact not always reflected subjectively. After all, quite recently, joint ventures were perceived as being quite exotic. Now they are perceived as, if not quite ordinary, then as a rather common phenomenon.

What then are the future prospects for joint business activities on Soviet territory? It may be assumed that there will not be important changes in the next few years in the array of factors stimulating Soviet and Western partners to participate in creating joint ventures. Judging by the answers to the questionnaire, the acquisition of hard currency is considered the most important factor in creating joint ventures (33 out of 39 Soviet, and 14 of 18 U.S. respondents). Access to Western markets was in second place (30 Soviet, 9 U.S.), though this is more likely to be a way to obtain hard currency rather than an independent factor. Other important motives were access to modern technology (28 Soviet, 8 U.S.) and improving the quality of the goods produced. In addition to these factors, U.S. respondents attributed Soviet interest in joint ventures to such factors as obtaining technological know-how (11), obtaining the benefits of flexibility and preferential treatment offered by joint venture laws and regulations (10), and obtaining managerial know-how (9). Confirming the above-mentioned effort of many Soviet enterprises and organizations to create a joint venture merely because it is the economic unit enjoying most favorable status, a large number of respondents (23 Soviet) pointed to that as a motive. One may suppose that this factor will most likely lose its importance as the organization of foreign economic relations improves. Such a development can only be welcomed, since it will provide greater stability and purposefulness to the process of creating joint ventures.

Most U.S. respondents indicated that the opportunity for Western companies to participate in joint business activities was moderate and even strong for selected companies (10 of 18). But the respondents also reacted with reserve to a question about the general prospects for Western investment in the Soviet Union during the next five years. Most respondents described such prospects as uncertain (26 of 40 Soviet, 7 U.S.). Significantly, there were more optimistic evaluations (10 Soviet, 13 U.S.) than pessimistic (4 Soviet, 0 U.S.). Business people should be restrained in their judgment, as is natural to people who value their reputations. But at the same time, business people prefer specificity and clarity. Of particular importance, therefore, is the question that asked whether the respondent proposed to increase its investment over existing obligations within the next five years. An absolute majority (29 out of 33 Soviet, and 13 of 18 U.S. respondents) replied affirmatively. Hopefully, conditions in the Soviet economy will develop in ways to justify this expectation. Both Western and Soviet participants should extend every effort to ensure that they will.

Chapter 14

Problems of Formation and Function of Joint Ventures

Tatyana M. Artemova

Participants in each joint venture encounter their own particular problems and difficulties. However, an analysis of the problems arising with joint ventures makes it possible to see the regularities they share in common.

To achieve the goals set for them by the Soviet side, joint ventures must organize the production of goods and services within the Soviet Union. In view of the enormous Soviet market and the currently existing imbalances, this opens up practically unlimited opportunities for the production of goods and services. But the real limiting factor in production today is the problem of material and technical supply, which is one of the necessary elements for integrating joint ventures into the Soviet economy. What is this now becoming the first and foremost problem?

Traditionally Soviet producers have been supplied through the centralized supply system of the Soviet Union. Joint ventures are not included in the system of centralized planning, nor, consequently, in the system of centralized distribution of resources. It is just these difficulties of integration that make obtaining resources from the domestic market the greatest problem for every joint venture. Foreign partners as a rule have to worry about timely shipments and quality of the goods.

In general, difficulties in this sphere result from the incomplete restructuring of the domestic economic mechanism. At present, joint ventures have three sources of supply: branch supply, wholesale trade, and Soviet foreign trade associations.

Joint ventures can be supplied by industrial branches only with the full cooperation of both the Soviet partner and its superior agency. The main difficulty is finding branch resources for production outside the plan of a joint venture. It is possible to develop opportunities for branch supply by including joint venture products in the system of state orders. It is on a purely voluntary basis that joint ventures' governing boards must decide whether they want to accept state orders or not. If joint ventures decide to accept state orders, they have the opportunity to receive supplies from industrial branches at the prices agreed upon with government bodies as well as the chance to sell their products via state channels, thus receiving a guarantee of a certain volume of sales.

Therefore the question of priority supply to joint ventures is a fully justifiable one and, of course, should depend on the degree to which particular products are of national economic importance. Here it is proper to think of state orders that would include those products needed by joint ventures. If the matter is approached without prejudice, in principal there are no obstacles to such a step. Past stereotypes are dissolving both in the course of radical economic reform and in the process of the functioning of joint ventures as foreign partners encounter Soviet economic practices. There is every reason to believe that the pragmatic desire of joint ventures' foreign partners to see their enterprises functioning in a normal and profitable way will not only remove any possible objections they might have to being supplied under some plan, but will even make them very interested in such a course of supply.

The fact that deliveries to joint ventures are included in the orders does not mean that the problem of setting prices for these deliveries has been solved. Depending on a particular situation, the regime of price formation can be made more or less preferential. Deliveries can be fully or partially paid for at contract prices, in hard currency or in other ways. Since joint ventures are an organic part of the Soviet national economy, there is every reason to prevent any unwarranted increase in the cost of their products, as well as any arbitrary increase in their profits.

Wholesale trade offers an ideal channel of supply for joint ventures, from both theoretical and practical points of view. The experience of the past two years is certainly not indicative, since this has been an initial period in forming a wholesale trade mechanism within the Soviet economy.

There are plans for the coming years to radically expand the wholesale trade market, but at this point many of the details of these plans are sketchy. The wholesale trade market is a convenient and natural channel for joint ventures, but at present it is still underdeveloped.

Joint ventures have been supplied by foreign trade organizations to a certain extent, but this channel is of limited use. These foreign trade organizations are interested in supplying joint ventures for hard currency, while joint ventures are interested in obtaining intermediate goods and materials for rubles. Moreover, foreign trade organizations are able to sell only a limited product profile, and a joint venture cannot count on being fully supplied by its foreign trade intermediate partner. One positive aspect in obtaining material and technical supplies from foreign trade associations is that joint ventures can impose greater quality control, and deliveries are made on time more often than in other cases.

Currently, joint ventures cannot, as a rule, confine themselves to one channel of supply. They have to use several, which complicates the process of supply, makes for an unwieldy system of services to this section, and may lead to higher prices and expenses. Therefore, the partners of joint ventures should work out these problems in detail at an early stage, when the feasibility study and founding documents are being prepared.

In general, supply needs to be improved not just in particular ways, but by making a basic change in the very approach to the position that joint ventures occupy in the system of relations among enterprise suppliers and enterprise consumers.

Under the present approach, joint ventures are supplied, voluntarily or not, on a residual basis. This, apart from anything else, forces them to look for foreign sources of supply, thereby reducing the benefit they might bring to the national economy and diminishing the potential of their hard currency earnings. These currency earnings could otherwise be used by the joint ventures to modernize production and purchase new equipment and licenses, for example.

The integration of joint ventures into the Soviet economy is closely connected with the general problem experienced by all the joint ventures: the need to observe the principle of hard currency self-financing, an element in the self-financing of joint ventures as a whole. This means they must fully meet their hard currency needs, consisting of expenses such as purchases of equipment, intermediate goods, and materials necessary to perform their statutory operations, plus part of the profit (in hard currency) due to foreign partners as their share. The joint venture may cover these expenses by exporting products or providing services for hard currency in the foreign partner's country or in a third country. Of course, the inconvertibility of the ruble was and remains a more general reason for the fact that joint ventures must be self-financing in hard currency. However, it should be pointed out that orientation to the need to export parts of goods or services arises not from ruble inconvertibility itself, but from the need to ensure high-quality products in conformity with world standards. It is quite well known that a product's competitiveness cannot be determined by conjecture. The only criterion for a product to meet world standards is that it sell on the world market. The Soviet side therefore considers export to be an essential condition for the functioning of joint ventures as a certain guarantee that their products are not out of date and are keeping pace with demands on the world market.

The problem of hard currency self-financing for joint ventures is a complicated one but is completely solvable. Current legislation permits joint ventures to sell products and services for hard currency on the domestic market as well as on the foreign one. As part of the reform of foreign economic activity in the Soviet Union, enterprises were given the opportunity to open hard currency accounts in the USSR Bank for Foreign Economic

Relations. Soviet enterprises, organizations, and cooperatives can use these funds at their own discretion, and they can also use them to buy products from joint ventures. It is often more advantageous for Soviet producers to buy these commodities from joint ventures than to import them directly, since in this case they save on such expenses as transportation or packing. Thus, one way of achieving hard currency self-financing is to promote sales on the domestic market for hard currency.

The data (available for nine months of 1989) on sales of joint ventures' products on the domestic market for hard currency basically concern ventures that have already started serial production. Among them: Cranload (production of cranes), Lenvest (footwear), Tirpa (equipment for the production of footwear), Dialog, Interkvadro, Variant, Serveko, Conpan (computers and software), Sterkhavtomatizatsiya, Pris, and YATIG (engineering). The overall volume of sales for hard convertible currency on the domestic market amounted to about 80 million rubles in foreign currency. A considerable amount of consumer goods was also sold for hard currency on the territory of the Soviet Union. This accounted for 20 million rubles, or 25 percent of the overall hard currency returns of joint ventures in the Soviet Union.

Another trend that may help expand the close limits of hard currency self-financing is the creation of consortia. Consortia may consist of a group of joint ventures working in different areas. Some of them produce goods solely for the domestic market, others only for export, and a third for both the domestic market and foreign markets. Therefore, some joint enterprises need rubles for their normal functioning, while others need hard currency. A consortium may establish a general ruble fund and a general hard currency fund, with both rubles and hard currency circulating within the consortium. A consortium of this kind was established on the basis of the Soviet Foreign Economic Consortium and the American Trade Consortium. Major American firms, such as Chevron Corporation, Eastman Kodak Company and Archer Daniels Midland, Johnson and Johnson, Mercator Corporation, and R.J.R. Nabisco are participating in setting up and operating these consortia. Soviet participants in creating joint ventures include enterprises and associations of the USSR Ministry of Geology, Ministry of the Medical and Microbiological Industry, and the Ministry of the Oil and Gas Complex.

However, the consortial form of organization is not being used adequately. One possibility is to establish consortia by setting up groups of joint enterprises, linked together in a technological chain, where suppliers could work on a ruble basis, while manufacturers could export part of their finished products to foreign markets so as to cover the cost of hard currency expenditures for the entire consortium.

In addition to the above measures, the solution of the problem of hard currency self-financing lies in ruble convertibility, which first requires the stabilization of the entire economy.

Among the goals we have set in developing joint undertakings is to gain access to advanced technologies and management experience, and also import substitution. Regarding import substitution, deliveries must be not merely reliable but also closely coordinated with the future development of Soviet enterprises, the consumers of these products. Enterprises that become suppliers of import substitute products for joint ventures cannot remain passive either. They must adapt to current and future demand for their products from joint ventures. We do not mean some kind of imposed commands, but production efficiency in both the joint ventures themselves and the enterprises associated with them. Active interrelationships between import-substituting joint ventures and their suppliers and consumers will naturally lead to their becoming closely involved in the fabric of the Soviet economy.

We also need to take a new look at prospects for forming multibranch joint ventures. Such ventures deserve special support. They are not only more suited to meeting the fluctuating requirements of branch markets, but are also capable of ensuring a more efficient introduction of advanced technologies by shifting financial and material resources in a timely and flexible manner and by setting up production in closely related fields in their operations. The task of widely disseminating advanced technologies and management experience in the national economy calls for a serious approach to interbranch coordination among successfully operating enterprises, including joint ventures.

The question of the size of joint ventures is part of any analysis of the process of their formation. Indices of size, though provisional in a sense, may be obtained by looking at charter funds.

The charter funds of joint ventures vary a great deal in size. Besides the substantial charter funds of such large enterprises as the Khomatek machine-building joint venture (about 50 million rubles); the Usol'efarm joint venture, which makes organic synthetic products (40 million rubles); and Sovploastital (about 24 million rubles), there are ventures with relatively small charter funds of around 100,000 to 360,000 rubles (Dinamika and Interyunis, which make computer parts; the Moskva-Ashok Company with its Delhi Restaurant; the Leningrad Chaika Company, which also has restaurant services; and the ERF Video Joint Venture, which prints videotape; and others).

A large number of the enterprises with small charter funds are in R&D, consulting, computer and software production, and personnel training. The emergence of such a number of small joint ventures is related to the development of market relations in the economy. They are capable of giving a quick and flexible response to market demands, such as the demand for computer technology and personnel training. These fields do not require large capital investments and are highly profitable in hard currency as well.

The creation of large joint ventures in the spheres of machine building,

metallurgy, and transportation is dependent on solving the problem of material-technical supply, which at present operates as a brake.

Foreign partners from developed countries have refrained up until now
from making large-scale investments; it is easy to understand why this is
so, but it can hardly be called a long-term orientation. Still, the total sum
of all joint venture charter funds registered by 1 April 1990 amounts to 3.7
billion rubles. Investments by foreign partners from developed countries
amount to about 1.5 billion U.S. dollars. However, not all of these investments are located on Soviet territory; this is only the size of the charter
funds agreed upon in their founding documents. Actual receipt of funds is
usually known to the partners and is the result of calculations made and
agreed upon jointly. The charter fund may be formed in stages, depending
on the development program of the joint venture.

The size of the charter fund certainly testifies to the size of the enterprise
and the scale of its operations. However, it is very difficult for the partners
to agree about the question of funds when negotiating the technical-economic basis for the joint venture.

The difference in price formation on the Soviet and world markets makes
it impossible to use the usual ways of estimating the elements of investment
to the charter fund. These elements can be rent for land, buildings and
structures, equipment, transfer of rights to industrial property, and funds.
Soviet legislation provides that partners should evaluate the elements of the
investment as well as the whole investment to the charter fund by contract
prices on the basis of world market prices. This means that when the partners
evaluate their investments, they can consider not just the cost of the investment but also the significance of the investment made in the fund by
each partner.

This can be illustrated with an example. One partner pays to the charter
fund the rent for some land or a building, or the cost of some considerable
part of the needed equipment, or supplies of raw materials for the first year
of the joint venture's functioning. At the same time the other partner pays
for only an inconsiderable part of the equipment cost, or technology, or
special tools to be used in the production. When compared by the current
world price, it turns out that the investment of the first partner is equal to
90 percent of the cost, while that of the other is only 10 percent. However,
the production of any competitive product without this 10 percent is absolutely impossible. It then is quite realistic to suppose that the contract
prices must enable the partners to balance the proportions of costs in such
a way that they would truly reflect the significance of the size of investment
to the charter fund (for running the whole process of the production of
goods and services). In the above example this would mean that the share
of the second partner could be evaluated as 20 to 25 percent, depending
on particular circumstances.

This problem will be solved much more easily as progress is made toward
ruble convertibility and setting a realistic exchange rate. However, at present

it is very important for both Soviet and foreign entrepreneurs to clearly see the Soviet as well as the world markets, and to conduct market research more actively.

In forming charter funds, partners run into the problem of evaluating the right to use land or mineral resources—in other words, the problem of rent. Western partners have expressed dissatisfaction with the fact that this question has not been resolved. However such decisions have already been made with respect to rents in Moscow. Appraisal committees operating under local authorities are better prepared now than they were previously. All questions relating to new construction or large-scale reconstruction in setting up joint ventures are solved with the consent of territorial administrative bodies. This measure, strengthened by law, has the goal of exerting real control over the solution of ecological and other land-use problems.

However, the whole question of the size and introduction of rents should be resolved in a way appropriate to the needs of this type of foreign economic activity. The procedure worked out by the Moscow Soviet, for example, does not take full account of the specific features of joint ventures.

In our opinion, the following system of paying rents for land use would be an expedient one (an analogous procedure could be followed with mineral resources, depending on the specific characteristics of the joint ventures). A Soviet participant would make rent payments for land use for a certain period of time as a contribution to the charter fund. Payments would be made in a lump sum and in rubles. The joint venture would begin to pay rent from its own funds as production becomes established.

Depending on the hard currency balance, part of the rent (for example, 30 to 40 percent) could be paid by the enterprise in hard currency and, in some cases, depending on hard currency receipts by the joint venture (such as hotels for foreign tourists, or the use of natural resources for producing commodities for export), local authorities could receive an annual rent solely in foreign currency. Revenues to local budgets could be used to buy and build purifying equipment and technology and to develop infrastructure.

Another problem for joint ventures on Soviet territory is the problem of relationships between joint ventures and Soviet enterprises currently using new forms of management and administration: leases, cooperatives, or state cooperatives. Therefore it is absolutely necessary to develop the mechanisms that would enable joint ventures to invest in associations, concerns, trade centers, or consortia. This will be a logical part of the adjustable market.

Problems of creation and function of joint ventures are related to the position of a Soviet participant in the general structure of the economic mechanism. They result from the insufficient economic independence of state enterprises. Obstacles preventing a state enterprise from participating in a joint venture arise from the following:

• State enterprises have state orders. The size of these orders usually depends on the production capacity of a particular enterprise; therefore, in order to use part of this capacity as a contribution to the charter fund, the enterprise has to increase the pressure on its remaining capacity (which is technically impossible), or it has to reduce the state orders (which can be decided by the higher body).

- State enterprises are hardly interested in searching for new technologies and improving their products in a deficit market (consumers' requirements are not high at all, as the products on the market are either unavailable or insufficient in quantity).
- State enterprises do not have sufficient means to form charter funds. In such a case, state enterprises have to turn to ministries for help, so that in fact the ministries manage the joint ventures while the enterprises' participation in joint ventures is just a formality.
- The profit gained by the Soviet participant enters into its revenue and is then redistributed in accordance with the existing norms. Part of it goes to the centralized funds of ministries and other higher bodies, the other part goes to the state budget. As a result of this situation, state enterprises are not interested in joint ventures.

In my opinion the following measures could provide an incentive to joint entrepreneurship: State enterprises that create a joint venture using their own accumulated capital should be independent and free to use their profits, making the necessary payments only to the state budget. In cases where the joint venture has been created with the consent of the higher body, and where part of its production capacity was transferred to the charter fund, the volume of state orders to be fulfilled by this venture should be reduced. These provisions must be stipulated in special legislations.

Any consideration of the problems of joint ventures in the Soviet Union deals with the period of their initial formation and activities. New problems may appear in the course of operations, but the experience already gained with existing joint ventures shows that it is possible to find solutions to problems, to go forward together to develop mutually advantageous cooperation, and to jointly formulate goals and the ways to achieve them.

Chapter 15

The Human Factor: Management and Personnel Issues in East-West Joint Ventures

Noah E. Gotbaum

As Eastern European regimes crumble and the traditional central role of the state diminishes, East-West joint ventures are riding the slippery economic crest of change, a balancing act that requires perseverance, creative problem solving, and a surprising amount of interpersonal skill and management. As is only recently being noted, East-West joint ventures are unpopular with many local citizens and public officials, who either view such partnerships as perpetrators of destabilizing, unwanted change or as the source of growing jealousy between those who are and those who are not employed by them. This problem is further exacerbated by an Eastern work force that often lacks experience in the independent initiative and decision making needed to make the venture work. Such an environment can breed enough internal bickering and external strife to ruin any partnership. "Signing the papers that establish joint ventures is easy," says Michael Levett, a longtime participant in U.S.-Soviet trade. "Getting people to work together is much more difficult."[1]

The tensions created by this lack of acceptance and free-market knowledge show up clearly in all levels of East-West joint ventures' managerial and personnel relations: between government officials and the joint venture management, between Eastern and Western managers, between management and workers, and finally, and perhaps most importantly, between the joint venture and the general population of the host countries. Such tensions can ultimately threaten investments by creating bureaucracy and increasing costs while at the same time decreasing output and regulations. This is because joint venture investors and operators may receive two or three different and often conflicting answers from Eastern government officials on legal questions of joint venture policy. "Trying to figure out the business law around here is like on-the-job legal training for both the government and for us," said one exasperated American executive. Even where guidelines appear steadfast, actual operations vary widely. In short, existing joint venture practice, and not necessarily the written laws, often defines what operators can and cannot do.

Certainly, human resource and managerial issues vary by industry. Perhaps more significantly, they differ based on the joint venture's host country. Joint ventures in Prague operate in a different environment than those in Budapest or in Moscow. Where significant differences in legal and operating policy exist by country, they have been documented. Yet, in all cases, East-West joint ventures represent the difficult but fascinating integration of the controlled and free-market systems. Or, as put more succinctly by PC World-USSR board member Frank Cuttita, "combining the two systems is like inviting tuxedos and leisure suits to the same party." As such, similar policies and problems arise and make sharing techniques and experiences valuable.

METHODOLOGY

The information used in this chapter was collected between July 1988 and December 1989 and updated July 1990. It was gathered almost exclusively through free-form interviews with some seventy-five joint venture managers, employees, shareholders, government officials, and other experts, representing twenty joint ventures located in the Soviet Union, Bulgaria, Czechoslovakia, Hungary, and Poland.[2] Because of the sensitivity of their positions, some respondents would discuss certain issues only when granted anonymity. The twenty joint ventures, like the joint venture representatives, were chosen to provide as broad a range of experiences as possible. They include production, service, and retail joint ventures in fields that range from tourism and publishing to high technology and heavy manufacturing.

The case study selection and interview process provided an operational focus and a richness of experience that a more structured methodology could not accommodate. Thus, while this chapter originally was to focus solely on labor and human resource issues, during research the focus was expanded as joint venture operators revealed that managerial questions often play a critical role not only in setting human resource policy but also in determining the viability of the entire joint venture. Because most of the joint venture operators could not be reinterviewed, this study does not try to describe the evolution of these issues over time but merely documents the operational situation as it stood between mid–1988 and late 1989.

The next section of this chapter provides some background on the partners that form East-West joint ventures and the top managerial structures they utilize: the board of shareholders, the advisory board, and the management board. The chapter then looks into the range of issues affecting the joint venture's top Eastern and Western managers, respectively, and analyzes these issues as they relate to the joint ventures' rank-and-file employees.

BACKGROUND

Because the focus of this chapter is on joint venture management and labor questions, the issues surrounding the joint ventures' partners are investigated only in the context of their direct impact on the joint venture's daily management and human resource policy. Yet some brief background on the initial roles and tendencies of the Eastern and Western partners is helpful to understand the complexities faced by the joint ventures' full-time employees. These partners, in conjunction with the Eastern host government officials, not only define the purpose, scope, and feasibility of the venture but also build its operating structure and select its management.

Partners

Eastern partners in East-West joint ventures are almost exclusively government ministries or major enterprises and other business establishments under the supervision of a ministry. In some cases research institutes, banks, foreign trade organizations (FTOs), as well as smaller enterprises or cooperatives have received equity for the expertise, resources, or personnel they bring to the venture. Partnerships that cross enterprise and ministry lines can pool resources and speed approvals in even the most highly segmented, planned economies. In a few instances, Eastern governments have also given some of their citizens with close relationships to Western business people a free hand to establish and operate joint ventures around those relationships; in return, however, the ministries and factories that formerly employed these citizens usually receive some ownership stake in the joint venture.

On the Western side, partners range from large multinational corporations to individual entrepreneurs. Western partners of East-West joint ventures are almost exclusively for-profit institutions. Unlike their Eastern counterparts, partners from free-market countries generally have not teamed up with other Westerners when establishing joint ventures. This may be changing, though, as groups of corporations, like the American Trade Consortium, have recently come together to pool complimentary resources and contacts.

The factors that brought together the twenty Eastern and Western partners in this study were as varied as the businesses ultimately undertaken (see Table 15.1). Some major companies, like Siemens and Honeywell, had extensive previous experience with their Eastern partners; for them the joint venture was simply an extension of that previous involvement and an attempt to secure and expand their market shares in the East. In other instances, Western partners with specific business propositions but no prior experience in the East were directed by host country government officials or trade organizations to the proper Eastern ministry and officials. In a few cases, Eastern ministries or enterprises initiated the contact either by directly

Table 15.1
Case Studies of Joint Venture Respondents

Joint Venture	Year Founded	Major Eastern Partner	Major Western Partner	% Equity Share East-West	No. of Employees East-West	Type or Branch of Activity
Bulgaria						
APV Bioinvest	1985	Bioinvest	APV Paracal (UK)	55%-45%	9E 0W	Consulting and engineering in biotechnology and food services
Fanuc Machinex	1981	ZMM Production Enterprise	Fujitsu Fanuc (Japan)	50%-50%	2W	Maintenance of numerical controller (NC) systems for machine tool industry
Sheraton Balkan*	1986	Interhotel Bulgaria	ITT-Sheraton	NA	536E 8W	Hotel operation via management contract
Systematics	1984	Chemical Ministry	Honeywell Corporation (USA)	60%-40%	25E 0W	Design, engineering and marketing of automated control systems
Czechoslovakia						
Avex	1987	Tesla Consumer Electronics	N.V. Phillips (Netherlands)	80%-20%	350E 0W	Production of videorecorders and cameras
Tessek	1987	Tesla Laboratory Equipment	AS Senatek (Denmark)	51%-49%	120E 0W	Production and marketing of liquid chromatography equipment

Hungary

Babolna McDonald's	1986	Babolna Agrarian	McDonald's Corporation (USA)	50%-50%	420E 0W	Restaurant operation
OTP-Penta Tours	1983	Hungarian National Savings Bank	Penta Tours (Austria)	60%-40%	74E 1W	Tours and travel agency
Sicontact	1974	Remix Radio Technical Corporation	Siemens AG (FRG)	51%-49%	115E 1W	Computer sales, service and software development

Poland

Hanna-Barbera	1987	PP Studio Bielska Biala	Hanna-Barbera Productions	51%-49%	90E 0W	Animation and film production
ITHK	1987	Kosciusko Steel Mill	Industrie Tech. Walzwerksanlgn.	51%-49%	360E 0W	Processing of metallurgical wastes
LIM	1987	LOT Polish Airlines	Marriot Company (USA)	52%-48%	1000E 10W	Build and operate airline terminal, hotel and office space

Soviet Union

AES-Pris	1987	Ministry of Oil Refining and Petrochemicals	Combustion Engineering (USA)	51%-49%	45E 5W	Service and manufacture of NC systems for petrochemical industry
Dialog	1988	KamAz Factory	Management Partners International (USA)	79.2%-21.8%	600E 2W	Service and assembly of personal computers and information systems

Table 15.1 (continued)

Joint Venture	Year Founded	Major Eastern Partner	Major Western Partner	% Equity Share	No. of Employees	Type or Branch of Activity
Interkvadro	1987	Moscow Aviation Institution	Amiral Utec (France) Delta Trading (Italy)	75%-25%	170E 2W	Service and assembly of personal computers and information systems
PC World USSR	1989	Radio I Svyaz Publishing	International Data Group (USA)	51%-49%	20E 2W	Computer magazine production and publishing
Perestroika	1988	Mosinzhstroy Engineering Enterprise	Worsham Group (USA)	80%-20%	8E 1W	Office and apartment building, construction and renovation
Petrovoith	1988	Petrozavodsk Machine Enterprise	J.N. Voith AG (Austria)	51%-49%	9E 2W	Develop and manufacture machinery for paper and pulp industry
Symbol (in formation)	1989	Cooperative	Story First Entertainment (USA)			Clothing design and production for Soviet and Western markets
Sporthotel Gudauri	1988	Georgia Tourism Ministry	Austrian Tourism Consultants (Austria)		111E 1W	Operation and marketing of ski resort
Sterch Controls	1988	Ministry of Mineral Fertilizers	Honeywell Corporation (USA)	51%-49%	48E 2W	Service and manufacture of NC systems for fertilizer industry

Sources: Interviews; Economic Commission for Europe, *East-West Joint Ventures* (New York: United Nations, 1988).

*Not a joint venture

soliciting a specific Western company or through a "request for proposal," or "tender" process as it is known in the Soviet Union.[3] Finally, some of the most successful joint ventures have evolved simply from chance meetings between like-minded Eastern managers and Western business people at trade fairs or other similar events.

Despite beliefs to the contrary, prior working experience with one's joint venture partner doesn't always help ease internal problems once operation gets under way. Certainly an understanding of the host country's operating environment and trust at both the partnership and managerial level is important. Nevertheless, both sides find that joint ventures create greater internal tensions than previous trade relations, especially in the management and personnel realm. Thus, and often to their surprise, experienced partners seem to have as much trouble working together as newly organized relationships. In part, this may be because those Western partners with prior host country experience often are large organizations that attempt to establish equally large and complicated joint ventures that can be very difficult to govern.

Governance

Both large and small joint ventures normally employ the same basic managerial superstructures, which include a board of shareholders, a management board, and a supervisory or advisory board. Recent changes in host countries' joint venture laws have all but eliminated previous socialist government regulations over these superstructures. Governmental requirements regarding the size or nationality and professional origin of the board members have been abolished. In all five countries analyzed, foreigners are now allowed to chair any of the three boards and may also serve as the joint venture's general director, overseeing daily operations. Notably, in order to counterbalance the potential for greater Western control brought on by the deregulation, a Soviet decree in December 1988 stipulated that major decisions made by the board of directors must be unanimous. However, what is considered a major decision is left up to the joint venture.[4] (As is the case for almost all East-West joint ventures, all the general directors in this study were Eastern citizens. Western managers, when they existed, normally served as a deputy general director, or in other top managerial positions.)

When the negotiating concludes and all agreements have been signed, the joint venture's management board and other full-time employees are often left on their own to make the joint venture work. Yet, by most accounts (including, ironically, those of shareholders on both sides), negotiating partners consistently underestimate both the philosophical and logistical difficulties that East-West joint ventures will encounter in trying to mesh two very different economic systems. In the words of one Western deputy general director: "They set it up, and then they forget about it." The following is a look into what happens to the joint venture's management and other full-time personnel after the partners have walked away.

EASTERN MANAGEMENT IN JOINT VENTURES

According to Franz Silbermayr, a member of the board of directors of the Austrian-Soviet joint venture Petrovoith, "Eastern managerial development, more than repatriation, capital or other questions, is the most critical issue facing East-West joint ventures today." Silbermayr is not alone in his belief. By most accounts the top Eastern managers, and specifically the general director, are the joint venture's most important employees. Because of the host countries' difficult business environments and traditions, internal managerial requirements, and the unfamiliarity of Western partners in operating in this new environment, top Eastern managers often control both the joint venture's external and internal relations. When these Eastern managers actively and independently work to promote the profit-making goals of the joint venture, success often follows. When instead they are too closely tied to the Eastern partner, or are too steeped in the traditions of the centralized economies, difficulties arise.

Roles and Importance

The roles and importance of the Eastern managers hinge on a number of factors. First, the Eastern host countries clearly lack the service, legal, and personnel infrastructures that many Western business people have come to rely on. Standard services from employment agencies to car rental companies are usually impossible to come by. Add to this the still strong control of the centralized planned economic systems and it is easy to understand why H. Michael Mears, former U.S. Commercial Counselor in Moscow, warns Westerners planning to work in these areas to be prepared to enter "not just another country but another planet." Within these conditions Eastern managers are often heavily relied on to use their contacts and experience to guide the joint venture through the external problems faced by the joint venture, be they supply bottlenecks, pricing problems, or superfluous government regulations. Igor Faminsky, Director of the All-Union Institute for Foreign Economic Relations of the USSR State Foreign Economics Commission, said that, despite Western wishes to the contrary, "It would be hard to imagine a foreigner playing the leading role as a general director because few foreigners are familiar enough with the inner structure of the economy and the interaction between [Eastern] enterprises and ministries."

Eastern managers also often dictate the joint venture's internal operations. This has much to do both with the roles assigned by the partners and the joint venture's location in the East. With the overwhelming number of joint venture employees coming from the host country, Eastern managers are normally asked to oversee personnel policy and, as explained in the follow-ing sections, to hire, fire, and oversee day-to-day administration. In contrast, Western managers are normally responsible for technical oversight, export marketing, and quality control. In some cases there are no full-time Western managers even employed by the joint venture. Certainly, exceptions to this structure exist, but, according to one Western manager, for most joint ventures analyzed, "the Eastern general director sets the tone . . . and every-body knows that he's the boss."

Performance

According to Western partners and managers, the performance of these joint venture bosses has been mixed, with some getting high reviews and others vilified. About one in three Western joint venture representatives interviewed had serious problems with their top Eastern managers; in four cases the Western shareholders were working to replace the general director or had already done so.[5] Complaints generally centered around the man-agers' lack of understanding of the free-market system and their dependence on hierarchical, bureaucratic structures. Claimed one Western deputy gen-eral director, "They're very autocratic around here. They don't like sub-ordinates making decisions." This tendency may further explain the Eastern managers' controlling role in the joint venture. It may also explain why some Eastern managers are afraid to make decisions without the blessings of their superiors. Said one Western shareholder regarding a Polish general director who has since been removed, "Every time he had to make a decision he'd pick up the phone and pass it by the ministry first."

This Eastern management dependence is based not only on a lack of experience in risk taking and decision making but also on an insecurity regarding the viability of new joint ventures. According to co-workers, some Eastern managers simply did not buy into the goals of the joint venture. Instead, they linked their personal fortunes to the stability of the Eastern partner and the host enterprise, whom they believed would be around far longer than the fledgling joint enterprise. Commenting on her joint venture's internal strife, a Soviet joint venture employee warned, "The General Di-rector had better start realizing that his interests are tied to this joint venture or we're going to have a disaster on our hands."

But it is not always the Eastern managers who run the ship aground; sometimes the joint venture's partners are also responsible for managerial difficulties. Either they do not allow their respective managers to operate independently, or they fail to work out their differing work styles and goals during joint venture negotiations. Often Western partners sought production and distribution primarily to expand into the internal Eastern markets, while the Eastern partners wanted to produce for third markets and immediately increase their hard currency receipts. Similar tensions arose over questions involving technology transfer. Western partners often sought to start the joint venture using less-complicated cooperation methods such as assembly and service, while Eastern partners wanted more sophisticated technological production introduced sooner. Joint ventures that worked out these incongruent goals in advance often had successful operations.

Interestingly, the most harmonious joint ventures often manifested a strong working relationship not only among managers but also specifically between the Western partners and the top Eastern manager. These relationships helped to set a precedent for balance and cooperation throughout the entire joint venture. In referring to the particularly successful U.S.-Soviet joint venture Dialog, the Commerce Department's Mears explained, "There is no question that the relationship between Joe Ritchie [the American partner] and Pyotr Zrelov [the Soviet manager] is the key to that joint venture's success."

Dialog, and other similarly successful joint ventures, often have another thing in common: independent Eastern managers with excellent managerial skills. From Poland to Hungary, such independence was made possible by partners on both sides who were not afraid to give their managers full operational decision-making power, in some cases making them partners as well. As for the special talents and qualities that partners might look for in top Eastern managers, they are varied and, by most accounts, not always easy to find.

First, a good Eastern manager must understand the workings and pitfalls of the changing socialist structure. The manager must also believe in the profit-making goals of the joint venture and be willing to work toward those goals. Furthermore, this manager should be, according to both Eastern and Western sources, an entrepreneur unafraid to take the risks required to navigate the joint venture through the difficult conditions of the Eastern market. Some experience in working in a free-market country usually helps here too. Does this mean that the manager must think and act "Western"? "No," says Zrelov of Dialog, "it is not Western thinking, it is simply logical thinking." Others would disagree.

By any name, the operating style of Eastern managers can have a significant impact on the bottom line of the joint venture. Are they hiring active, energetic employees, or disinterested castoffs from ministries under siege? Are they, as one Western joint venture manager describes, "creating a family atmosphere of cooperation" or re-creating an Eastern bureaucracy where employees are afraid to make decisions and voice complaints? Perhaps most importantly, are they pushing the limits of the existing system knowing which regulations are steadfast and which ones are malleable in order to get the most for the joint venture; or do they simply say, "It's not allowed"?

Hiring

Both types of Eastern managers—the traditional and the entrepreneurial—existed in all Eastern countries surveyed. Few of the managers surveyed, however, could be considered in between these two management styles. They either displayed an entrepreneurial common sense and energy, or they did not. Yet despite these large differences and the leading role played by the top Eastern managers, in two-thirds of the cases analyzed Western shareholders had little input into the Eastern management's selection and in some cases had not even interviewed them prior to their hiring. "The ministry simply told us one day that they had chosen the general director and the [Eastern] deputy general director," said one Western shareholder of a U.S.-Soviet joint venture. When asked about this lack of involvement, shareholders often explained that during the normally tense negotiating period other issues seemed more pressing. Instead, most of the Western partners generally trusted the candidates put forth by their Eastern counterparts and anticipated working out any potential problems through the board of directors.

With few exceptions, the top Eastern managers are brought into the joint venture directly from key positions in the ministry or enterprise of the host country's major partner. As former financial and deputy directors within an enterprise, or department directors within a ministry, most of these joint venture general directors and Eastern deputy general directors have held positions of reasonably high status and responsibility and have often worked closely with the Eastern members of the joint venture's board of shareholders. On rare occasions the joint venture placed public advertisements for top management positions. More frequently, top managers were part of the team that helped to initiate the joint venture and were hand-picked by the Eastern partners.

Wages

While Westerners often complain about the lack of available Eastern managerial talent, they can no longer point to explicit host government wage limits as the cause. Joint ventures now are almost completely unregulated in this respect. One notable exception is host government mandates that no hard currency be paid to Eastern citizens, except for per-diem payments when traveling abroad.[6] In explaining the regulation, one Polish official said, "If we allow joint ventures to pay our people in 'valuta' [foreign currency], then 'valuta' becomes the legitimate currency in our country."[7]

Nevertheless, some joint ventures have gotten around the hard currency prohibition in two ways: First, some pay a portion of their Eastern employee's compensation into a hard currency account from which the employee may draw when he or she travels to the West, ostensibly for training and other work-related purposes. This benefit can significantly increase the employee's purchasing power of coveted Western goods, since those lucky enough to travel to the West in the first place are usually allowed to exchange only small amounts of their local currency for Western cash. Second, some joint ventures and Eastern enterprises (including ironically, Vneshekonombank, the Soviet state bank that regulates foreign currency flow) pay a portion of their employees salaries in hard currency credits. These credits are then used by the Eastern employees to purchase selected Western goods, which normally can only be bought with hard currency.

Wages for the general director and other Eastern managers are usually established by the major Eastern shareholder despite the fact that most founding documents assign the task to the full board of directors. All the Western partners interviewed, however, felt that Eastern management compensation, usually at 20 to 40 percent above comparable managerial levels, was extremely reasonable. For example, a Soviet general director's base salary of 750 rubles per month (approximately two and a half to three times the average Soviet wage) translates to about twelve hundred U.S. dollars, with a deputy general director receiving about one hundred rubles less per month.

Not surprisingly, these salaries create jealousies between the Eastern joint venture managers and top-level Eastern bureaucrats. Few enterprise directors or deputy ministers can understand why their former subordinates should now earn more than they do. These former bosses may also object to losing a key employee, often without compensation, and may be bitter that they themselves have not been chosen for the joint venture. "For managers moving from a major enterprise or ministry into a joint venture," says Michael Volodarsky, a Soviet adviser to the PC World-USSR joint venture, "it is like going from the public to the private sector in the United States. Although you may have fewer people reporting to you in the joint venture, you are paid more, you have much more responsibility for the bottom line of the enterprise, and you usually have higher status."

In the cases where tensions arise, the top Eastern partner normally intervenes on behalf of the embattled joint venture managers in an effort to insure the cooperation of enterprise and ministry leaders. In a few instances, however, the Eastern partners offered no such help. Instead, the partners' relationships with the Eastern managers—with whom, in these instances, they had not worked previously—were acrimonious. A few explanations might be given for why these tensions exist: First, as the joint venture requires Eastern managers to answer to both Eastern and Western partners, the Eastern partners become unhappy about losing some control over Eastern managers. The partners may also be responding to managers whom they find too entrepreneurial and independent. Second, according to some sources, these partners are also unhappy that they are not as involved with the daily joint venture operations as they would like. And finally, some partners appear to have difficulty balancing their roles as head of two distinctly different and in some ways competitive entities. Ironically, in the few instances where problems between the Eastern partner and Eastern manager have arisen, the managers readily admit that they have become more closely allied with the Western partners. As one explained: "[The

Western partner] and I are close. Without him around I probably would have been replaced long ago."

WESTERN MANAGEMENT IN JOINT VENTURES

In many ways, looking into the human resource and managerial issues related to Western joint venture employees is more difficult than doing so for their Eastern counterparts. In part this is because there are simply not as many Western managers as Eastern, and partly because of the lesser roles they often assume. What is clear is that host country's rules, regulations, and difficult working conditions have a large and often negative impact on these Western joint venture employees. Such hindrances increase costs and, in turn, limit Western participation, sometimes even precluding full-time Western involvement.

Roles

As the key representative of capitalist partners in the unsettled business environment of the Soviet Union and Eastern Europe, Western managers often have an extremely difficult role to play. They are directly responsible for the successful transfer of complex technology or services into an unprepared and resource-scarce setting; they must work closely with Eastern managers and employees (many of whom have had little training or experience in Western business ventures); and they must intuitively understand what is allowed and not allowed in a setting where rules are both fluid and vague.

Due to the relative high cost of employing and providing an infrastructure for Westerners in planned economies, Western employees are almost always in top managerial and technical positions. The roles of the Western deputy general director and other Western employees may be formally stated in the joint venture's foundation documents or informally established over time. In most cases Western employees are asked to serve multiple functions within the joint venture. Beyond working with the Eastern general director on basic administrative supervision, standard roles for Western managers and engineers include training, technical supervision, and quality control of the joint venture's goods or services. Western employees also oversee home and third country marketing and sales if the joint venture is exporting from the host country.

Wages

Adequately reimbursing Western employees can be both enormously expensive and, within some Eastern countries, highly regulated. Only a few Eastern European and Soviet cities have the infrastructure and services—

including apartments, automobiles, and schools—that Western managers and their families desire. Thus, to entice competent and high-level workers as well as pay for the accommodations their managers desire, Western companies incur high costs. One partner cited an outlay of approximately $400,000 per year to employ a manager that would cost one-quarter to one-third of that in his home country.[8] Sometimes these high salary levels have resulted in an imbalance between the joint venture manager's payments and those of other managers in the home company. As one executive explained, "Compensation is so high that it is difficult for companies to fit the person back in the corporate hierarchy once they are finished with their assignment."[9]

The affordability problem is often exacerbated by the fact that the major portion of Western staff salaries are borne by the Western partner alone, not the entire joint venture. Although all full-time Western employees received a local currency (and sometimes a hard currency) salary directly from the joint venture, in twelve out of thirteen cases these salaries had to be supplemented by hard currency payments directly from the Western partner. These payments, which are often accrued and repaid to the Western partner when the joint venture earns hard currency profits, have become a sensitive issue for a few joint ventures whose earnings have not matched their projections.

Joint ventures that do not want to supplement Western salaries or have trouble doing so because of host country regulations, may simply forgo hiring Western employees. Of the twenty joint ventures analyzed for this study, seven had no full-time Western staff. The absence of Westerners varied according to the host country analyzed. Most of the Soviet- and Hungarian-based joint ventures in this study had at least one full-time Western staff member, while few of the Polish, Bulgarian, and Czechoslovakian joint ventures employed Westerners. In the latter countries, hiring has been limited due to laws or policies requiring that hard currency salary payments come only from the joint venture's hard currency earnings as well as currency exchange constraints, which make repatriation and thus savings of the hard currency almost impossible for Western employees.

Not all joint ventures have suffered without full-time Western managers. The Austrian-Soviet joint venture Sporthotel Gudauri, which is developing a ski resort in Soviet Georgia, used experienced Hungarian managers to replace their more expensive Austrian employees. Other joint ventures avoided regulations and lowered costs by hiring Westerners either on a contract basis or by using Western partners and employees as consultants to oversee the joint venture's start-up and training and, later, to monitor progress with planned monthly visits. In such cases the Western partner usually assumes the hard currency portion of the employees' expenses, with the host country partner or the joint venture paying for all local currency costs. Yet, unless the joint enterprise is fairly simple or there is unusual trust between the Western partners and the Eastern managers, such arrangements generally require too much Western shareholder involvement in daily operations to be desired by either party.

Beyond a few complaints from Czech officials, the disparity between Eastern and Western management wage levels caused little animosity within the joint venture. This may be due to the fact that Eastern joint venture employees are among the highest paid in their countries. It also may be a result of Eastern bloc tradition in which Westerners, and some highly privileged Eastern citizens, have been accorded "more equal" treatment. "Socialist country citizens," explained one Western deputy general director, "are used to having foreigners treated differently. Foreigners get off airplanes first, wait in fewer lines and are able to buy certain goods [with hard currency] that natives can only look at." He stated that Eastern employees are extremely reluctant to rock the boat even if they have been mistreated. This trend may be changing, however, in light of the East's recent political and labor upheavals.

To insure that their accrued benefits and seniority within the home country are retained, Western joint venture managers normally continue their existing employment contracts with the Western partner. The partner then contracts with the joint venture for the employee's services. Occasionally the Western employee signs dual contracts with the joint venture and with the Western partner. Explicit Eastern government approvals for full-time Western employees are no longer required, except in Poland. Still, joint ventures find it good practice to clear incoming Western employees through their major Eastern shareholders. Most originating joint ventures documents also include the names and numbers of their Western employees.

In rare instances, Western employees have been asked to join host country labor unions. Those interviewed declined since their pension, health, and vacation benefits dictated and provided by their Western employer were usually quite sufficient. Nevertheless, in the countries analyzed, the joint venture is required to make standard payments into its "social development" fund for pensions and health insurance for all employees.[10] With the exception of consultants, Western joint venture employees must pay standard income taxes in the host countries. Some Western shareholders have decided to reimburse their employees for taxes paid to host country governments, since there are few tax treaties between these countries and their free-market counterparts.

Hiring and Living and Working Conditions

Perhaps because they were able to bring in longtime, well-established employees for placement in major East European and Soviet cities, most joint ventures in this sample did not express difficulty in finding competent Western managers. Yet, by many accounts, such hiring is not always easy.

Recently an executive search firm found twelve suitable candidates for a top management job in a U.S.-Soviet joint venture on the Black Sea, only to have all twelve decline the job because their spouses refused to relocate.[11] Younger employees may be more willing to relocate to join joint ventures, but often companies seek managers with more developed skills. While increasing Westernization and interest in Eastern Europe could help, the problem could remain as joint ventures are now spreading to more remote, and less desirable, East European and Soviet cities.

A large part of this lack of desirability is that daily life is still not easy for Western joint venture employees in a region where Westerners have not always been welcome or common. This problem is especially acute in the Soviet Union and, until recently, in Hungary, where some joint ventures have been forced to rely on government agencies such as the Soviets UPDK (Upravlenyie Po Obsluzhivaniyu Diplomaticheskogo Korpusa) and the Hungarian PKI (Penz Intezi Kozpont), which procure consumer and business services for foreigners at hard currency costs that approach those in major Western cities.

To avoid these costs some joint ventures have begun to contract with newly formed cooperatives or other private ventures for services that range from translating to chauffeuring. Western employees who rely on the Eastern partner's pre-existing service infrastructure and contacts to assist their search, however, often come up either empty-handed or unhappy with results. Said the wife of one Western manager surveying their newly acquired Moscow apartment: "This may be luxurious by their standards—but definitely not by ours." And because consumer items in the East are far scarcer than the currency used to buy them, Western managers may also find that their Eastern comanagers are not as understanding about such living standard differences as they are about salary differentials.

Western managers also complain that resource scarcity and extensive regulation hamper the daily management of joint ventures. These problems are again most prevalent in the Soviet Union, where obtaining visas for international travel and re-entry and gaining government clearances for domestic travel must often be planned well in advance. Basic office supplies imported from the West, such as telefax and copy machines, may take months to clear customs. Despite recent legal revisions, some joint ventures still are forced to use hard currency to pay for items such as domestic air travel and visits from Western partners' representatives.

As has often been noted, one of the biggest managerial difficulties is the lack of office space. One Western manager is contemplating leaving the joint venture simply because he is too frustrated with trying to manage it out of his Moscow hotel room. Combustion Engineering's AES-Pris joint venture with the USSR Ministry of Petroleum Refining and Petrochemical Industries has some fifty-odd employees spread over three locations, one of which is a highly security-conscious federal office building. Andy Pechkovsky, the joint venture's Western deputy general director, noted that it may take him half a day simply to get clearance to see his employees. "[This is] a problem," he lamented, "which makes hands-on management somewhat difficult." Nevertheless, Pechkovsky seems to understand the constraints of doing business in a planned economic environment. "Would we ever let the Soviet citizens into the Pentagon or some our other government centers without proper clearance?" he asked.

Western partners that have had a representative office with foreign credentials, apartments, and other resources that predate the establishment of the joint venture have a valuable head start against their competitors. In addition to better contacts, these well-established Westerners also have a base of knowledgeable and trusted employees, both local and from abroad, on which they can build their joint venture's business. Shareholders on both sides must be aware, however, of the tensions that are likely to arise in the few cases where a joint venture manager continues to work in the region on business unrelated to the joint venture.

MIDDLE- AND LOWER-LEVEL EASTERN EMPLOYEES

While the workers of Eastern Europe and the Soviet Union have a reputation for being unproductive and difficult to motivate, many joint ventures have been pleasantly surprised. Within certain fields, Eastern joint venture employees, if thoughtfully hired, can perform excellent work at comparatively low wages. Joint ventures' special status and ability to pay higher wages makes hiring and motivating workers far easier than for standard Eastern European and Soviet enterprises. Yet, as with many issues of joint venture operation, this special status can be a double-edged sword also leading to tensions with host country partners, government officials, and fellow workers. With Eastern rank-and-file employees constituting by far the largest share of most joint venture payrolls, managers and shareholders must be aware of these impediments in order to take advantage of the opportunities.

Hiring

By most accounts, the hiring of the Eastern work force is one of the most critical roles of the joint venture's managers. It may also be one of their most sensitive. Although finding employees willing to join these new enterprises is often far easier than locating other joint venture "inputs," the source of these workers must be carefully attended to. Hand-picking employees from various sources almost inevitably incurs the jealousy of former employers. Yet, hiring directly from the Eastern partner on a large or small scale, while often speeding start-up and increasing flexibility in contracting out, may create its own tensions with the nonhired employees and even with the Eastern partner.

Part of the initial tension accompanying joint venture hiring is based in traditional socialist theory which has sought to protect its citizens from becoming expendable spare parts for capitalist gain. "You must realize," explains Mears of the Commerce Department, "that [Eastern] citizens working directly for capitalists is one of the great taboos in these countries." Thus, prior to the joint venture laws, Western businesses could only hire socialist citizens indirectly through contract relationships with organizations like the previously mentioned Soviet UPDK and the Hungarian PKI, which established most terms of employment. In the era of joint ventures, the proscription against a direct link between capitalist owners and socialist laborers has evolved into explicit warnings by Eastern governments against joint ventures that exploit, rather than train, the host country work force. In part, joint ventures have served to make employment between capitalists and socialists more palatable by insuring the mediating influence of the Eastern partner.

This mediating effect, however, does not appear to have moderated Eastern citizens' desires to attain the benefits that joint ventures can provide, as few of the joint ventures analyzed had difficulty in finding job candidates. Echoing many of his colleagues, Stanislav Holenda, technical director of the Czech-Dutch joint venture Avex, said, "I have people constantly coming in off the street."

At the Huta Kosciusko steel mill in western Poland, the ITHK joint venture was founded in an attempt to turn around an undesirable portion of the mill that could no longer find replacements for its exiting work force. After increasing salaries and adding minor capital investments, the joint venture is turning a profit within the previously unprofitable division. Now, with demand to work in the joint venture so high, ITHK's Eastern partners have forced the joint venture to sign an agreement not to hire any more employees from within the enterprise. And beyond the complaints of fellow Eastern employers, some government officials also fear the allure to Eastern citizens that joint ventures create. Says Anna Halustyik, an adviser to the Hungarian government on joint venture law, "I am worried that because joint ventures can provide better financial and professional conditions than our standard enterprises, they will artificially select employees and drain away the talent needed for our general economic reform."

The incentives to which Halustyik refers include training and access to high-tech products, upgraded work facilities, and, in some cases, the chance to travel and earn hard currency or hard currency bought items. Eastern managers and workers also cite the attractiveness of working within a less-hierarchical, freer Western management structure and style that may be the model for future Eastern enterprises. Finally, in attracting the Eastern work force, one must not underestimate the importance of money and joint ventures' ability to pay salaries that other Eastern enterprises normally cannot match. Says Karoly Csanadi of the Hungarian Chamber of Commerce, echoing the feelings of many joint venture operators: "While employees want experience with new technology, new organizations and new freedoms, higher pay is still the best incentive for workers to join joint ventures."

The hiring of host country citizens into joint ventures is, for the most part, the exclusive purview of the general director and the Eastern deputy general director, although some Western managers and shareholders have been very involved in the process. Most joint venture employees are usually hired directly through the main partner ministry or enterprise, or from the informal personal networks of the top management. In some cases, public advertisements and concourses—contests in which potential employees must solve a particular service or engineering problem—are also utilized. There also have been some instances where Eastern employees were hired through the contacts and the recommendations of Western managers. However, such a hiring procedure may be considered risky for the Eastern applicant in countries that remain highly security conscious.

As explained in the section on employee performance, hand-picking employees from various sources is often considered the best way to insure effective hiring. Yet those that do so may run into stiff resistance from ministries and enterprises that stand to lose their best employees and gain little in return. Says Paul Pfamitzer, partner and former deputy general director of the Hungarian-Austrian joint venture OTP-Penta Tours: "If the home enterprise finds out that one of their employees is out looking for a job, they'll kill the person." This resistance is especially prevalent in Czechoslovakia and the Soviet Union where there is no real tradition of labor market fluidity and where government protection of joint ventures against fearful bureaucrats has been inconsistent. In these cases, joint ventures may have to assure potential employees a job or, at a minimum, clearance from levels above their immediate bosses as a precondition for application. As explained by Vatslav Krotov, the Soviet general director of the AES-Pris joint venture, "People don't budge without instructions from the top, without the right political protection."[12]

Eastern governments are addressing these problems in different ways. In Bulgaria, and recently in the Soviet Union, laws have been passed that allow enterprises that provide intermediate inputs (including labor) to share the benefits of joint ventures by receiving some hard currency payments. Poland has taken a slightly different track; there, top government officials have lead interference through the roadblocks established by lower level bureaucrats. According to one Polish general director, this direct pressure has succeeded: "We used to be treated like dogs; now we are like cows in India." Respective of the country and the level of government support, however, Eastern partners and especially top management are usually still the first and last lines of defense in freeing joint ventures of bureaucratic and political resistance in hiring.

Hiring directly from the key shareholder ministry or enterprise, or contracting wholesale with shareholders' enterprises, which is standard in large production joint ventures, normally eases the hiring process and may provide flexibility. This reliance often significantly shortens the joint venture's start-up time. Guesswork is minimized as joint ventures are aware of applicants' track records before hiring. In instances where they may be dissatisfied with an employee's performance, the joint venture hiring directly from the Eastern partners sometimes returns those employees to their former positions.

A close connection with the Eastern partner may also make for a more flexible hiring policy. Honeywell's joint venture Systematics hires most of its employees on a part-time contract basis from its Eastern partner, the Bulgarian Chemical Ministry. When demand is strong, the joint venture hires more technicians. When demand is weak, the technicians return to their positions within the ministry. The Bulgarian partner benefits from its share of the joint venture's profits and from extra payments, some of which are in hard currency, for the loan of the employee. The ministry also gains an upgraded, better-trained work force. Honeywell benefits from a profitable joint venture that always matches its payroll with its demand.

In Hungary, a major challenge for public or private firms alike is to maintain worker productivity and allegiance in an economy where a large percentage of the work force holds a second job. Instead of working against this tendency, the German-Hungarian joint venture Sicontact has utilized it to their advantage. Sicontact has ceded its entire after-hours service department to a quasi-private company, or VGMK (Enterprise Business Work Unit), established and run by its employees. Reiner Schoning, the joint venture's German deputy general director, is extremely satisfied with the situation. Says Schoning, "With this arrangement I don't have to worry about the quality of Sicontact's twenty-four hour service. I also don't worry about the kind of second job that our employees are taking." The Mc-Donald's joint venture in Hungary is also adapting itself to the "second economy" as some of the joint venture's administrative staff have begun giving private English lessons to their floor workers during nonbusiness hours.

Despite the advantages, some Western representatives have noted that a few words of caution should precede a joint venture's hiring a majority of its employees from the major shareholding Eastern ministry or enterprise. First, Eastern employees may be less likely to put the independent interests of the joint venture ahead of those of their former employers (a tendency which, Eastern representatives point out affects Western employees as well). Second, employees hired from outside of the major partner's fold do not always receive the same treatment as their counterparts when it comes to salaries and promotion opportunities. In some cases these Eastern employees have turned in confidence to Western managers and shareholders for support, thereby creating potential internal divisions within the joint venture. Third, hiring a critical mass from an Eastern enterprise increases the chances that the bureaucratic procedures of that enterprise might pervade the joint venture as well.

Yet the biggest problem in a joint venture's strong connection with a large existing enterprise or ministry has as much to do with the joint venture's organizational layout as it does with its hiring policy. Frequently, Eastern shareholders and managers mention that jealousy of non–joint venture employees working next to or near their better-paid colleagues demotivates enterprise workers and threatens the joint venture's internal peace. To allay these tensions, Eastern partners often spread the fruits of the joint venture to its non–joint venture employees in the form of upgraded facilities and other hard-currency purchased benefits. Persuasion tactics may also be utilized. At the Kosciusko mill, management held a companywide meeting at which the joint venture's workers were asked to testify that their longer work days and meager benefits were a fair trade-off for their higher salaries. In spite of these and other peace-keeping efforts, most joint ventures have ended up simply having to physically separate their employees from the enterprise's standard work force.

Wages

While most shareholders agree that Eastern joint venture employees can be hired at bargain rates, in practice, setting these rates can be extremely tricky. Because equality of reward, irrespective of performance, has prevailed throughout Eastern Europe and the Soviet Union, public and private pressures against wage differentials and performance payments abound. To deal with this, all but a few East-West joint ventures self-regulate both the levels and the methods of paying their employees. "Don't think," warns Adriano Callegari, deputy general director of the U.S.-Soviet Sterch-Honeywell joint venture, "that you can walk in and structure salaries and bonuses like we do in the West."

In the long term, the consumer power of the 400-million-person Eastern European and Soviet market is often touted as the chief reason that Western companies brave the difficult world of East-West joint ventures. Yet, many joint ventures are finding that the East's inexpensive labor supply not only helps short-term stability but can also be a key to future export profitability. "At hourly wages of between $1.30 and $2.00 per hour fully-loaded," says economist Jan Vanous, "the Eastern labor market can compete with any around. And most are located within only 1500 kilometers from Central Europe." Vanous points out that highly skilled engineers and scientists can be hired at one-fifth to one-tenth of their cost in the West. "And comparative costs should be even less," he says, "as real effective exchange rates move downward in these countries."[13]

Below are a few examples of how some joint ventures take advantage of these wages and skills:

- Numerous joint ventures are using highly skilled Eastern engineers to replace their more expensive Western counterparts, thereby lowering the costs of products exported from the West. Systematics, among a number of other joint ventures, uses software designed by its Bulgarian employees to accompany its equipment sold around the world.

- Petrovoith, Honeywell, and other joint ventures find that by using Eastern instead of Western employees to service and install their products, they are able to charge their Eastern customers less hard currency, thereby retaining a competitive price advantage to expand their market share. Sicontact's Schoning says that his joint venture is providing "German engineering in Hungarian hands." It is also providing it at closer to local Hungarian prices.

- Eastern employees can also help to expand capacity and, with it, profitability. The Hanna-Barbera production company, which had difficulty hiring Western animators at any price, uses its joint venture in Poland to bring in "some of the best animators in the world."[14] Paying by piece, they have been able to hire almost one hundred new cartoonists for their North American and European productions at bargain prices.

While former government regulations on joint venture wage payments have diminished, informal pressures are felt by almost all joint venture managers. From Budapest to Leningrad, joint venture operators hope to avoid the public animosity and backlash that has befallen many cooperatives and other newly private institutions. Inside the work place, as explained, wage differentials lead to headaches for both the home enterprise and the joint venture. Government pressures to keep wages in line, while less overt, also exist. In Poland this pressure seems to be less intense, but other countries are not so open. For example, Bulgaria's Decree 56 recently ended any formal government role on setting Eastern joint venture wages and also allowed hard currency salary payments. When asked, however, if any joint ventures have taken advantage of the changes, a joint venture manager nodded toward a government official saying, "Are you kidding? In practice they still control us." And, even as Eastern governments nominally give joint ventures increased freedom to pay their employees as they please, some have started taking back control by implementing highly regressive income tax schemes that severely undercut the usefulness of allowable wage hikes.

In walking this thin line between backlash and acceptance, joint ventures have carefully, and sometimes creatively, structured their employee payments to increase paychecks. These salary schemes, which are normally determined by the shareholders in smaller joint ventures and by the management board in the larger joint ventures, can be segmented into three major groups: The first, which is made up of the most numerous and the highest-profile joint ventures, normally set base salaries within approximately 20 percent of comparable levels for regulated enterprises and later add discretionary bonuses and profit sharing where possible. These joint ventures may further disguise bonus payments under terms such as *functional allowance* and *additional expense requirements*. The second set of joint ventures, which are usually smaller, less visible, and not as sensitive to outside pressures, sets base salaries at 20 to 70 percent above comparable government standards, again adding bonuses and profit sharing above that. Finally, a small minority of joint ventures, mainly in Poland, set piece-rate levels usually offering little or no bonus. Commission payments do not appear to have hit the planned economic world as yet. With the payment of higher salaries, joint ventures generally do not pay overtime except to low-level factory workers.

Discretionary bonus payments, normally less visible to outside parties, often constitute the major salary differences between joint venture and standard host country salaries. These payments may be equivalent to three or four months standard salary payments before profit sharing is considered. To understand this bonus implementation, a bit of background on standard host country bonus procedure is helpful.

Generally, in Council on Mutual Economic Assistance (CMEA) countries, enterprises make payments into a "material incentive fund" for bonuses, which theoretically rise or fall based on an enterprise's profitability.[15] Each employee's portion of the fund is then determined by a committee made up of managers and labor union and employee representatives. Since most socialist enterprise revenues have been predetermined by government, however, and since Eastern economies have bred a tradition of equal pay regardless of performance, little variation exists among different enterprises' bonus pools or among their employees' shares of that pool.

Joint ventures generally use the material incentive fund procedure for bonuses, except, unlike standard Eastern enterprises, they base their overall fund allocation on profits instead of government mandates. Normally the board of directors determines the overall bonus pool, and the management board sets individual bonuses. According to joint venture managers, the various members of the joint venture's material incentive committee then rubber-stamp these apportionments. Despite their more market-oriented structure, however, joint venture bonus policies in practice are still a far cry from the profitability- and performance-based systems that many Western companies utilize. Once again, tensions rising from socialist traditions are the cause.

In the Soviet Union for example, some joint venture shareholders have complained that the government forces them to place most employee compensation within more visible base wage payments by making bonuses non–tax deductible (government officials dispute this, however). Other joint venture officials explain that since most Eastern employees are used to receiving a bonus regardless of their enterprise's performance, joint ventures are under extreme pressure to make payments into their material incentive funds regardless of profitability.

Traditions of equality have also made the tracking of, and the compensation for, individual employee performance nearly impossible. Says OTP-Penta's Pflamitzer, "I can't run a business without determining profit centers, and I can't determine profit centers without monitoring and evaluating employee performance. Yet when I tried to set up an in-house evaluation system within the joint venture, I almost caused a riot." Other Western and Eastern managers recount having asked middle-level colleagues to distribute bonus pools based on employee performance only to find out later that the fund had instead been divided equally or that the distributions had been based on seniority. As one Western manager explains: "These people have been taught their entire lives that they are all equal; how the hell can we now expect to walk in and get them to believe that some are better than others and that the better ones should be paid for it?"

Benefits, Labor Unions, Party Influence, and Contracts

Although higher salaries and bonuses are by consensus the most important motivating factors for the host country employees, material fringe benefits are critical, and traditional, compensation in countries where shortages of consumer goods prevail. With the exception of those in Poland, most joint ventures have found it necessary to match the social benefits, such as housing, vacation accommodations, and even schooling for employees' children, that traditional Eastern employers have provided. At the joint venture's outset, these benefits are usually provided through the pre-existing infrastructure of the major Eastern partner and its labor unions, although some of the larger joint ventures have started to build their own benefit network. As stated, some joint ventures have recently begun distributing hard-to-find consumer items, purchased with hard currency, to their workers.

Through their ownership of parts of this infrastructure, and through their distribution of the holdings of the joint ventures' "social funds," which pay for these benefits, labor unions have in some cases assured themselves a role in East-West joint ventures. Like standard socialist enterprises, joint ventures in the East are required to make payments into these funds and, with the exception of Poland, they are also required to form a labor union to help in the distribution. The speed with which joint ventures have obeyed these government mandates has varied however. Most joint ventures initially use the existing unions of the major host enterprise or ministry. However, a number of Soviet joint ventures have established a joint venture labor union.

Yet, beyond providing the service infrastructure and serving as administrative organs for distribution of the material, sickness and pension benefits, Eastern unions are largely seen as formalities with little authority over the joint venture's economics. One Hungarian labor union official complained that unions were in a state of "complete disaster." Perhaps noting this, some Polish joint ventures are now abandoning both unions and the socialist tradition of providing many benefits and little salary. "Our people," says Hanna-Barbera Poland's general director Wojciech Trzcinski, "get no free coal, no free vegetables, no rent assistance, no nothing... just far better salaries. And we don't have a union." Still, until Eastern citizens are able to buy more goods with their salaries and joint venture regulations are relaxed, the Hanna-Barbera model will probably not spread.

Like most Eastern enterprises, many joint ventures have had an internal Communist Party apparatus so employees who are party members can meet and discuss issues of their choosing. Nevertheless, the party apparatus appears to have had little direct involvement in the joint venture management in the past, and should have even less as the party loses control over governments throughout Eastern Europe. Few top Eastern joint venture managers interviewed were party members and, in most cases, the party had neither a formal nor an informal role in hiring or operations. A notable exception has been in Czechoslovakia, where the upper management of the country's few joint ventures were formally approved by party officials.

When moving into positions with joint ventures, most Eastern employees are mandated by law to provide their former employers with at least two months' notice. All joint ventures established formal probation periods of two to six months for their new employees; yet, workers were rarely let go after such periods, in part because the joint ventures were satisfied with their work. Yet, most joint venture managers (outside of a few consumer service joint ventures) also admitted that true probationary periods were unrealistic, and that, as previously explained, longer employment commitments were required for joint ventures to hire the employees they wanted.

Once hired, host country employees are normally party to two contracts with the joint venture. The individual contract establishes the employee's pay scale, seniority level, and specific duties. The "universal" or "collective" contract is signed with the shareholders on behalf of all the joint venture employees. The universal contract is negotiated by worker representatives and, where they exist, labor unions. It establishes working hours, termination policy, and general medical, meal, and vacation benefits. The term *negotiated* should be used loosely, as national labor law dictates much of its content.

A few joint venture operators in the Soviet Union have also quietly mentioned that illegal mafialike organizations or rackets have been vying to fill the influence vacuum left by the diminishing roles of the Party, the state, and the unions. These rackets prey on cooperatives, some joint ventures, and their employees by demanding "protection" money from those who "earn too much." Those who refuse to pay may have their premises vandalized, their Western possessions stolen or destroyed, or worse. According to the victims, Soviet officials offer little relief from these rackets. "When I called the police and identified the racketeers," said one Soviet joint venture operator, "they laughed at me and told me that compared with the unrest in the republics, my problem is too small to deal with."

Performance, Efficiency, Bureaucracy, Firing

The accessibility and affordability of Eastern employees to joint ventures clearly means little if these employees are unproductive. Yet, many joint ventures, including approximately three-fourths of those surveyed here, have been quite satisfied with their Eastern rank-and-file employees. In part joint ventures have found that good performance and productivity is simply dependent on finding the right individuals. But other factors, such as the economic sector in which the joint venture is active, how the joint venture motivates its employees, and whether the joint venture can avoid the internal inefficiency and bureaucracy that plague many Eastern enterprises, are also critical in getting the most out of the rank and file.

Despite the work force's reputation as unmotivated and unproductive, most joint venture employees are, according to many sources, mechanically well skilled and enthusiastic about working with Western technologies. Thus, many joint ventures that design, assemble, service, and install low-tech and medium-tech products like computers, office automation systems, and automated control systems are extremely happy with their employees. "They're better than back home," says Combustion Engineering's Pechkovsky. These joint ventures are taking full advantage of the Eastern economies' strong educational focus on engineering and technical management in which, according to Interkvadro deputy general director Mario Germondari, "the price of good minds is being subsidized by the government."

However, joint ventures dependent not on their employees' technical finesse but rather on their understanding and adaptability to market- and consumer-oriented services, receive no such benefits. Thus, managers of joint ventures in the tourism and restaurant field, for example, complain that employees must often be pushed to be responsive in environments where the consumer has traditionally had lower standing and no alternatives beyond the government. "I don't know how many times I have tried to teach [the employees] to put the ashtrays in front of the customers instead of in front of the empty chairs," laments OTP-Penta's Pflamitzer.

Despite the problems, partners and managers say that with some effort, and the correct means, Eastern employees in all sectors can be trained and motivated. First, the example provided by a hard-working and open-thinking management board can be critical. Some Western managers have mentioned that the remnants of the socialist hierarchies have left middle- and lower-level employees distrustful of their superiors. Thus, when managers roll up their sleeves instead of simply giving orders, much progress can be made. In this regard, informal meetings and firmwide social outings have also been helpful. In part this effort also hopes to show workers that they are employed by a special type of enterprise that can provide them with special opportunities. Explains ITHK partner Joachim Sombert: "We have imported a new spirit and approach... which means a work trial period, piece work and performance-related payments. The offices and halls were modernized and equipped Western-style. All this has naturally motivated the work force."[16]

As Sombert mentions, the motivational effects of material incentives are also not to be denied. Herbert Kapellar, a manager with the Ilbau Construction Company responsible for building the LIM-Marriot Hotel in Warsaw, noted that he could tell which of his subcontractors paid their Polish employees higher than state-mandated wages simply by looking at the productivity differences. Where employees directly received the piece payments that Ilbau was paying the subcontractor, Polish productivity approximated that of the Western workers on site. But when the subcontractor, often state controlled, held Polish wages down, the productivity differences could be as great as four to one. "One must remember," mentions Kapeller, "that [these] employees have proven themselves to be excellent workers in other countries. The incentives and the employment environment must be right, however."

These environmental issues often revolve around the quality and age of the tools and machinery with which Eastern employees work, as well as the administrative efficiency of their work place. In terms of the former, most joint ventures, recognizing that obsolete or faulty machinery will hinder the productivity of even the most highly motivated and trained workers, have brought new technology and machinery as part of their initial contribution to the joint venture's start-up capital. Surveying the results of new machinery and materials installed into his plant, one Eastern joint venture manager mentioned that it was difficult to compare his former work place to his new one: "It's as if before our products were handmade; now they are machine-made."

Administrative changes also have a large impact on this transition, and in the East bloc that usually means reducing bureaucracy. At Hanna-Barbera, for example, administrative staff now make up 10 percent of the employees, whereas for the non–joint venture portion of the same factory, administrators make up almost 60 percent of the work force. Many other joint ventures cite similar disparities. "The result," says Hanna-Barbera's Trzcinski, "is that work that used to take four months now takes two weeks."

Of course, critical to motivating Eastern employees and reducing bureaucracy is hiring employees that are open to the new working conditions that joint ventures pose. Says Sheraton's Jensen: "Many of the workers are great, you just have to find them." For most joint venture managers, finding the right employees often means looking once more for what many call "entrepreneurs": employees eager to take on varied roles and work harder and longer than the average citizen, thus enabling the joint venture to hire fewer employees. In seeking such workers, joint ventures often limit their applicant pool to younger citizens. Says one Russian joint venture manager: "Age is definitely a factor—older citizens are a product of a seventy-year-old stagnant system." Georgy Prityko, chair of the board of the Sterch-Honeywell joint venture, agreed: "We won't hire anyone over forty. Otherwise they are just too difficult to train. Joint ventures are, and have to be, a matter of the future."

Yet, even when hand-picking employees from a limited applicant pool, finding employees capable of thriving under the new conditions is not easy. "A lot of it is just plain luck," says Kapellar. Because of this, many joint ventures, especially those in the consumer service sector, have resorted to what they call the "shakedown" process. They hire more employees than they need, find the ones that are competent, and then over the course of approximately one year reduce the work force size and increase pay levels. The McDonald's joint venture in Budapest, for example, started with 300 full-time and 120 part-time employees, but may eventually end up with half as many.

This weeding-out process partially benefits from what Leonid Govoryut-kin, deputy general director of the AES-Pris joint venture, calls a "natural selection," whereby Eastern workers that don't have the flexibility or desire to put in the hours that the new enterprises require leave the joint venture of their own volition. In some cases, these workers were simply not motivated or adaptable and wanted out of the joint venture as soon as they realized that their higher wages would not come easily. Yet other, seemingly excellent employees are also part of the shakedown, often leaving after burning out from the hectic early days of the joint venture. Says one employee of a service joint venture located in Moscow: "I've been working twelve- and fourteen-hour days for the last three months, and I'm still waiting for my bonus. Even if it's huge it can't be worth this work." She has since left that joint venture to work with another Western company.

Certainly, not all joint ventures have been able to control administrative numbers like Hanna-Barbera, or to shakedown their work force through natural attrition. As discussed later, some joint venture managers have had to coerce or fire Eastern employees that they do not need or approve of, each with varying degrees of success. And some Eastern managers never intend to reduce the number of employees but instead hope to re-create former bureaucracies. "They just want big," complained one Western joint venture manager. To combat this, some Western companies have had hiring limits and administrative quotas written into their joint venture's founding documents.

Not surprisingly, some Eastern government officials have also "wanted big," as more than a few joint ventures have come under pressure to hire along the lines of traditional socialist enterprises. Heinz Chytil, the Austrian deputy director of the Sporthotel Gudauri joint venture, mentioned that he "had to fight like crazy" with local officials for the right to expand his employees' work week from forty to fifty hours, thereby avoiding hiring an extra shift. Sheraton's Jensen had similar problems: "The Bulgarian government wanted me to hire one person just to pick up empty bottles in the hotel. At first, no other employees were allowed to do that." Eventually, both Chytil and Jensen got what they wanted, but both they and others warn that joint ventures must be willing to compromise when seeking flexibility from external and internal pressures.

Firing

Except during the start-up phases of the consumer service joint ventures, there was surprisingly little staff turnover in the joint ventures analyzed. In large part this is a result of competent hiring, the favorable benefits accorded to joint venture employees, and the aforementioned self-selection process. Yet, in the few cases where unsatisfactory joint venture employees have remained, the situation becomes considerably more complicated. While all operators said that firing was possible, few had done so, and in no cases were there large-scale layoffs. Internal pressures, as well as government guidelines, often hindered the termination process. Because of this, joint ventures' abilities to fire employees seem to hinge on the will and determination of management to make the move and on the Eastern director's ability to carry out that decision.

Joint venture managers mentioned that they receive pressure against firing joint venture staff from all sides: other employees, the public, and especially Eastern government officials. While the termination process in Bulgaria, Poland, and Hungary seemed looser than in the Soviet Union or Czechoslovakia, it was with a few exceptions viewed as a very difficult and touchy subject. "You have to prove that they stole something," mentioned one Western manager. Because of such tensions, this manager and many of his counterparts often use less direct methods than firing to sever the relationship between the joint venture and the employee; "We've learned to force people out," he explained. A Soviet manager using similar methods seemed unfazed by the constraints on outright termination; "Coercion," he says, "can be very effective."

Part of the difficulty encountered in firing is that, except in Poland and Hungary, joint ventures are responsible for finding terminated employees new jobs to their satisfaction. Sometimes an employee can be sent back to the former employer, but this is not always easy, even when that employer is the Eastern partner. And, while host countries are only now establishing unemployment insurance systems, most have mandated severance pay systems. These regulations, like most that are dictated by general host country labor law, are in a state of flux due to the political and economic changes in the East and should be closely monitored.

According to partners and managers, the policy key regarding the firing of Eastern joint venture employees is to do so selectively, but with determination. When this is done the unions, local councils (in Hungary), and party officials (in Czechoslovakia) that must be notified often put up a minimum of resistance. "I haven't fired many," says Interkvadro's general director Lev Weinberg, "but when I do it, I do it with the speed of light." Weinberg mentioned, however, that confidentiality breaches, and not incompetence, were his major grounds for termination. When the determination to fire on the grounds of incompetence is made, the initiative often comes from the Western side, especially in the consumer service joint ventures. Regardless of how the policy decision to terminate an employee is made, however, in no case did Western managers or shareholders directly fire Eastern employees. Instead, it was Eastern managers, because of host country sensitivities, who were fully responsible for firing Eastern joint venture employees.

Training

Despite the desire on all sides that East-West joint ventures play a key role in training Eastern employees in Western business skills and the ways of the free market, actual results in this area have been mixed. Certainly, joint ventures have helped to transfer some modern technical skills to the East as well as train many Eastern citizens in some of the operational facets of modern Western consumer service businesses. Many joint ventures as well have used host country government-aided training opportunities to improve hiring, product quality, and profits. Ultimately, however, joint ventures may be too isolated within the larger controlled economic systems to be relied on to capably train Eastern citizens in such areas as accounting, finance, marketing, and overall free-market organization.

Of the case studies analyzed, approximately two-thirds held some formal training for their management and lower-ranking employees, and ten of the twenty sent some hand-picked Eastern employees back to the Western country for training. These workers, in turn, were relied upon to train their fellow Eastern joint venture employees back in the host country. In most cases, Western trainers were also brought in for short intervals.

A few joint ventures, building on their host country government's desire to upgrade its work force, innovatively used the existing power structure and the centralized economic infrastructure in their training efforts. Some examples:

• In Czechoslovakia, the government placed a closed-down textile factory complete with its former employees at the disposal of the Avex joint venture for its video-recorder production. As part of the initial joint venture contract, the Western partner, Phillips, was paid hard currency by the Czech government to spend a year retraining many of these workers for the joint venture's consumer technology production. After eight months of activity, 170 of the initial 190 retrained employees were successfully working with the joint venture, and the government had avoided a potentially difficult unemployment problem.

- In Poland, Hanna-Barbera has set up an exclusive contract with the renowned Polish Academy of Fine Arts to train artists for its joint venture. The joint venture partners have been able to design a training program to their specifications, with a minimal initial capital investment.

- In Bulgaria, the government has given the Honeywell-Systematics joint venture unusual leeway in overall personnel policy because of the perceived benefits of the joint venture's excellent high-tech training center there.

Despite these examples, however, few employees, even at the managerial level, were given any type of overview either of the Western company or of more generally transferable market economic operations. With training costs high and start-up difficult, broader training is usually delayed. As AES-Pris's Govoryutkin explains: "Perestroika demands technical and managerial expertise. Unfortunately, the latter must wait." Instead, most joint ventures trained their Eastern employees only in skills specific to the roles that they were asked to perform. And due to profit and expediency considerations, the most critical free-market business roles, such as export marketing and quality control (which are also the most foreign in the East), are often given to the few Western representatives with experience in these areas.

The problem also lies partially in the fact that many Western companies simply do not view their East-West joint ventures as similar to their other enterprises. Thus, they may not attempt the same type of management and control mechanisms. which in turn limits the training possibilities and experience of the joint venture's Eastern employees. When, for example, the Eastern financial director of a long-standing and profitable joint venture asked for standard home company turnover goals and quotas, he was rebuffed. "We are making money for them," he complained, "yet we're still treated like stepchildren."

Further limiting training possibilities are host country government regulations and conditions that make joint venture operation as a truly free-market company almost impossible. Because, for example, all Eastern host countries demand that joint ventures use planned economy accounting systems, opportunities for Eastern employees to learn and use Western control systems are limited. Similarly, with hard currency and banking systems still tightly held by Eastern governments, training in Western financial management methods is almost impossible. And while some joint venture managers can help to create an open "Western" feeling in joint ventures, their daily operations for the most part must necessarily be a hybrid of Western and

Eastern systems in order to handle the internal and external tensions of operating in a distinctly non-free-market environment. Until the host countries' overall economic systems move further toward the free market, East-West joint ventures cannot be counted on as a major training ground for Western business techniques.

CONCLUSIONS

With the economies of Eastern Europe and the Soviet Union in transition from the still-powerful influence of their planned economic past to efforts to becoming more free-market oriented, East-West joint ventures are challenged to find the difficult operational balance between these stages. Joint ventures must be autonomous enough to shield themselves from the pervasive external social and political tensions while at the same time maintaining good outside relations with the public, government officials, and suppliers. Inside these joint enterprises, new and more flexible business structures must be established while still recognizing the limitations presented by incomplete infrastructures and few training opportunities.

To attain such a balance, joint ventures must put stock in what are likely the most reliable assets in the East's tumultuous business climate: independent and innovative joint venture employees. While governments fall, laws change, and old attitudes give way to new, competent workers, especially at the managerial level, can provide a consistent anchor for joint venture operations. Because of this key role, joint venture partners, especially those in the West, should be more active in personnel matters. Specifically, they must seek out entrepreneurial Eastern managers who are as loyal to the joint venture as they are to those in power at the moment, find employees who understand the rewards and benefits of a market economy and believe in the joint partnership, and recognize the myriad of pressures on daily operations and the need for flexibility in such operations.

For Western partners, such focus can help to balance power and in some cases even allow them to control the joint venture—this despite a lack of majority equity ownership and sometimes without any full-time Western employees. In a few joint ventures in Poland, Hungary, and even the Soviet Union, operators on both sides noted that all major decisions were made by the West. This was achieved either because the Eastern partners intentionally took a back seat, or because operations were controlled by managers that tried to model their enterprises after Western businesses or looked to the West for overall guidance. While such instances were not the rule, the point remains: daily operations can make or break joint ventures, and employees, not ownership percentages, determine those operations.

Looking to the future as most East-West joint ventures move beyond early operational phases, internal and external pressures are likely to remain strong. After start-up, joint venture growth often creates added bureaucratic levels and makes personal interaction and problem solving more difficult. Says Michael Levett, "With the changing situation in the [East], small- and medium-sized joint ventures are definitely more flexible and much easier to operate than larger ones. In smaller joint ventures, there aren't as many forces vying for influence—and when you do have problems you can usually straighten them out person to person." Developing joint ventures will also face added managerial and personnel pressures as they move from simple cooperation methods, like service, installation and assembly, to more complicated technology transfer and production methods. "Things are going fine now," said one general director about a rival joint venture, "but they may not be so happy with their workers when they start trying to produce those black boxes from scratch instead of just installing them."

Finally, most operators mentioned that the larger a joint venture becomes, the more closely it is watched by the government and the public and thus the more it is subject to external demands and jealousies. Yet, opinion was mixed as to how these external pressures would develop in the future. Many felt that public and government resistance to joint ventures and free-market reforms in general would abate within a few years in Poland, Hungary, Bulgaria, and Czechoslovakia. Few, though, were as sanguine about the possibilities in the Soviet Union, with many suggesting that the environment there would get worse before it got better. Regardless of the country, however, over the next few years change will be an important constant for joint ventures throughout the former Eastern bloc: change the opinions of host country citizens and officials, change in their acceptance levels, and change in their knowledge of free-market structures. Operators that stay aware of the human factor, both inside and outside of their joint enterprises, will have a leg up on these future developments.

NOTES

This chapter was researched and written with the generous support and assistance of the International Institute for Applied Systems Analysis (IIASA), and of Professor Mike Uretsky, director of New York University's Management Decision Laboratory.

1. The quotations used in this chapter are taken from the author's conversations with joint venture participants, government officials, and other experts, between July 1988 and December 1989.

2. The case study of Sheraton's Hotel Balkan, while not a joint venture, was also used.

3. For further information on the tender process see I. Soloviev, "Guidelines of Foreign Partner Selection in the USSR," International Institute for Applied Systems Analysis (IIASA) working paper WP–80–02 (January 12989).

4. The new Bulgarian Foreign Investment Decree 56 stipulates that joint venture founding documents must explain the board of directors' decision-making process.

5. This frequency of Eastern management turnover was similar to Soviet joint ventures as a whole. According to Lev Weinberg, president of the Soviet Union's

Joint Venture Club, six of the first thirty Soviet joint venture general directors were replaced within eighteen months. Of course reasons beyond Western shareholder dissatisfaction may have caused this turnover.

6. Bulgarian Degree 56 is alone in allowing hard currency payments to Eastern citizens working in joint ventures. To date, Czechoslovakia has controlled all joint venture wages; Hungary imposes wage controls only on ventures with less than 20 percent foreign ownership and with a capitalization of less than 5 million forints.

7. Interview with Kazimierz Kalinowski, director of the Department of Wages and Remuneration, Polish Ministry of Labor and Social Policy, summer 1988.

8. "Joint Misadventure," *Time* (10 April 1989): 84.

9. "A New Supply Problem: Executives in East Europe," *The International Herald Tribune* (14 December 1989).

10. Hungary requires these payments only if the employee uses the system. In the Soviet Union payments made for Western employees may be reimbursed when the employee leaves the country.

11. "New Supply Problem."

12. "Perestroika's Yankee Partner: Inside Combustion Engineering's Joint Venture," *New York Times Magazine* (11 June 1989): 20.

13. Comments made at the Malenta, West Germany Symposium on East-West relations (16 October 1989).

14. Conversation with Jerzy A. Schon, Chair of the Hanna-Barbera Poland joint venture supervisory council, summer 1988.

15. The Council for Mutual Economic Assistance (CMEA) is a trading alliance that includes the five countries analyzed in this study as well as Cuba, Romania, and Vietnam.

16. From "Auf Schrott gebaut," *Unsere Wirtschaft*, the Dusseldorf Chamber of Commerce and Industry (November 1989).

Chapter 16

Joint Ventures in Banking

Lyudmila S. Khudyakova

Until the end of 1989, when the International Moscow Bank was established, there had not been a single bank in the Soviet Union that had a joint account with a foreign bank, although the number of joint ventures in the sphere of industry and services had already reached one thousand. This situation, for all its specific reasons, did not depart from the world tendencies. On the one hand, Western multinational banks, in their attempts to expand internationally, usually tend to follow their clients—multinational corporations. On the other hand, it was only in the 1980s that foreign direct investments in banking began to grow so fast within the world community of industrialized countries. At the same time, the national policy of these countries is becoming more and more liberal concerning the access of foreign banks to national credit markets.

Although the trend toward greater openness of national financial systems and the growing globalization and interpenetration at the micro level since the mid–1980s is gradually encompassing the East European countries, including the Soviet Union and China, it is evident that the scale and character of its development is different there than in the West. In many respects, this development depends on how well these countries are prepared for a transition to market-oriented economies, as in the readiness of their particular economic units and changes in their foreign economic strategy.

These processes are slower in the Soviet Union than in Hungary or China, where foreign capital attracted to the banking sphere is part and parcel of the general reform of the credit-banking system which is being carried out there now. The basic share of joint stock banks' operations in both Hungary and China is oriented toward financing foreign trade and other international transactions, as well as toward servicing joint ventures.[1] However, in the future it is expected to expand the participation of joint stock banks within the framework of traditional activities of national commercial banks. Thus, in December 1985, a joint stock bank, Citibank Budapest, was established in Hungary. Eighty percent of this bank's assets is owned by the biggest U.S. bank, Citibank New York, and 20 percent is owned by the National Bank of Hungary. From the moment this bank was set up it was given all the power of a Hungarian national commercial bank except for the right to process current accounts. In addition, it was given the right to carry out operations in convertible currencies. At the present time, Citibank Budapest accepts deposits and gives credits (in forints as well as in foreign currency) to Hungarian mixed companies. It also grants leases and renders various consulting services.[2]

At about the same time, a joint stock bank, China International Finance Company, was set up in China in the city of Chengzhen. The company is aimed at conducting credit-financial operations not only in specially designed economic zones as it used to do, but also all over the country.

In 1979 the first offshore bank in Eastern Europe, Central European International Bank, was set up in Hungary. Thirty-four percent of this bank's assets are owned by the National Bank of Hungary. The remainder is owned by the world's biggest banks, including: Banka Commericiale Italiana (Milano); Societe Generale (Paris); Long Term Credit Bank of Japan (Tokyo); and Tai Kobe Bank (Kobe). This joint stock bank conducts operations in convertible currencies only, it does bookkeeping in U.S. dollars, and it is not subject to the national banking adjustments of Hungary—the country in which it is located. The basic sphere of the bank's activity is financing Hungary's foreign trade. The other aspects are leases, forfeits, and the opening of deposit accounts in convertible currencies for foreign clients (private persons) and corporations.[3]

It is also interesting to mention the Hungarian experience of setting up a joint stock bank in 1986. One of the stockholders of this bank is a specialized branch of International Financial Corporation.

For some past years, China has been successfully using the experience of setting up financial companies with a narrow specialization. Especially popular, in particular, have been leasing companies specializing in renting out machinery and equipment to Chinese and joint ventures. In addition to Chinese banks, their participants are the banks of France, the United States, Japan, Italy, and Siangan.

Until recently, foreign banks in the Soviet Union have been represented solely by their branches engaged in collecting information or establishing business contacts. However, they were not authorized to conduct any banking operations. At the present time about forty of the world's biggest banks have their representatives in the Soviet Union.[4]

Since the late 1980s, many leading international banks have been displaying a growing interest in participating in the process of economic perestroika in the Soviet Union. Also, both Soviet and foreign partners felt an urgent need in banking consulting services. In this connection, the government bank (Gosbank) and the Bank for Foreign Economic Relations (Vne-shekonombank) of the Soviet Union started developing a new form of cooperation: they concluded a number of agreements with Western banks on rendering assistance to joint ventures. As of November 1990, there were twenty protocols on such cooperation. We have such agreements with the banks of France, Italy, Germany, England, Austria, and others. The protocols provide for rendering various consulting and managerial services to joint ventures including: giving a business and financial profile of its participants, finding the best sources of financing for joint ventures, and estimating the credit and currency risks involved. On the basis of protocols, joint working groups have been established. They are engaged in working out concrete procedures for providing consultations by Soviet and foreign banks.

The next step here could be the creation in the Soviet Union of a joint specialized consulting or financial company with the participation of foreign banks—something like the leasing companies in China. These questions are currently being investigated. So far, one step has been taken: in November 1989, the International Bank Moscow was established in the Soviet Union. This is the first bank in the history of the Soviet Union to have joint assets with foreign banks. Its charter was registered by Gosbank as "Charter of a Joint Commercial Bank #1." At the same time, it was registered by the USSR Ministry of Finance as Joint Venture 1000. The International Bank Moscow has been established as a joint stock company with assets of 100 million rubles, and it is going to conduct its operations on the basis of principles of full economic accountability and currency self-financing. Among the foreign investors of International Bank Moscow (with the investment contribution in foreign currency amounting to 60 percent of the bank's joint stock) are such large European banks as Banka Commerciale Italiana, Credit Lyonnaise (France), Kreditanstalt-Bankverein (Austria), Cansallis-Osake-Pankki (Finland), and Bayerische Vereinsbank (Germany). No doubt the experience and international reputation of these foreign banks' stockholders will be valuable for the joint stock bank.

The participation of the three specialized national banks—Vneshekon-ombank, the Bank for Industrial Construction (Promstroibank), and Retail Savings and Credit Bank (Sberbank)—their knowledge of local conditions and the current financial situation, and their ability to accurately evaluate the creditworthiness of Soviet borrowers are also important guarantees of success.

International Bank Moscow has been set up as a credit-financial establishment of a broad profile. It is authorized to carry out operations both in rubles and in foreign currency. Along with traditional banking services, such as bookkeeping, statements, accounts, and settlements, International Bank Moscow will render many other financial services, including assistance to Soviet and foreign companies in finding the best partners, preparing the technical-economic foundation for projects, conducting leasing and factoring operations, and handling trust operations. It is expected that 10 percent of the bank's staff will be represented by highly qualified foreign specialists.

The International Bank Moscow is to be controlled by Gosbank, which will control its liquidity and solvency on the basis of proper recommendations provided by the international body, Basel Committee on Control over Banking Operations. This concerns the bank's transactions made in foreign currency. It is to be controlled by participants from foreign banks. The International Bank Moscow's operations in rubles are to be controlled by Gosbank in accordance with the standard procedure established for transactions made by international banks.

The establishment of International Bank Moscow is an important step toward the improvement of the currency financial service of joint ventures that have received access to the world market. So far, this has been solely in the hands of the USSR Vneshekonombank. The International Bank Moscow has become its first competitor. Thus, the first step has been taken to break the structure of monopoly in the banking system of the Soviet Union. The access of the International Bank Moscow to world financial markets will help the Soviet Union to overcome the existing limits in crediting only one borrower, in the practice of Western banks. Such rules limit the potential size of foreign loans for the Soviet Union in cases where the only borrower on behalf of the Soviet Union is, for example, the Bank for Foreign Trade (Vneshtorgbank).

We hope that the creation of International Bank Moscow is just the beginning of the whole process of creating a network of joint stock banks with foreign assets. Also, this network seems to be essential from the point of view of reconstruction of the whole system of banking in the Soviet Union. This reconstruction should involve various aspects of banking: broadening the sphere of rendering credit-financial services, enhancing the sphere of competition, bringing in the latest methods, and raising the efficiency of the bank staff. At this early stage of perestroika, we find this form of creating joint stock banks or other credit-financial establishments in the Soviet Union quite appropriate for attracting bank capital. However, in the future, at the advanced stages of economic reforms, we will have to think of creating branches and subsidiaries that will be controlled or totally owned by foreign banks. In our opinion, branches and subsidiaries of large transnational banks are capable of having a stimulating effect on raising the efficiency of the national credit-banking system. The only factor to be controlled is the manner of adjusting them to local conditions.

However, let us return to joint stock banks. These banks have not been long in existence in East European countries and China much less in the Soviet Union: the International Bank Moscow has served Soviet and foreign clients, specializing in foreign trade and project financing, only since fall 1990. As a result, no serious conclusions can be made regarding their activity or their role in the development of national economies and the processes of internationalization in the sphere of international credits. However, the very fact of existence and expansion of such credit-financial establishments with foreign capital in them is significant for the Soviet Union.

The national policy of countries regarding the attraction of foreign bank capital depends in many respects on how the official authorities assess the balance between the possible positive and negative consequences (net benefits) of opening a domestic market for foreign banks. Until recently, the arguments of the opponents of foreign capital's access to Soviet banking prevailed in the Soviet Union. Actually, their arguments are very close to those put forward by supporters of banning, or strictly limiting, foreign capital in other countries. First of all, they doubt the expediency of allowing foreign bank capital into the sphere of credits and currency, since those are the keys to adjustment and control functions in the national economy. Because of the inconvertibility of the national currency (ruble), the question arises of hard currency guarantees of the repatriation of foreign banks' profits. Also, fear is expressed that the foreign banks with more developed banking techniques and advanced technology will become strong competitors to national banks and, therefore, will handle the biggest and most profitable part of banking operations. Some countries—members of the Organization for Economic Cooperation and Development (OECD)—would use the same argument about the protection of national competitiveness in order to justify their discriminatory measures regarding certain operations of foreign banks. The other fears expressed in this connection are that foreign banks may more easily escape observing the requirements of national monetary policy as well as financial discipline.

In the Soviet Union all these worldwide fears are aggravated by the ideological aversion to foreign capital in general—the ideology that strengthened during the long years of the Cold War. At the same time, the experience of prerevolutionary Russia gives evidence of the possible positive effect of foreign banks' capital on the development of national credit systems. Karl Marx wrote: "It was thanks to foreign capital that Russia succeeded in establishing a mechanism of exchange (banks, credit companies, etc.), something that took the West long centuries to do."[5]

The first influx of foreign capital into Russian banking took place from the 1860s to the 1880s. The basic part of it then originated from Germany. French capital started to come in the 1890s. At approximately the same time, the shares of Russian commercial banks began to gradually switch over from Germany to France.

E. Agad studied the banking system of Russia and his data was later widely used by V. I. Lenin in "Imperialism as a Higher Stage of Capitalism."[6] Agad noted that by the end of 1913, eleven out of nineteen of the biggest banks of Russia were actually based on foreign capital. Two of them were based on German capital, two on British capital, and five on French capital. The active, or "working," capital of all the nineteen banks amounted to 4 billion rubles. V. I. Lenin wrote: "over three-quarters of it, i.e. more than three billion is in fact the share of the banks that actually are subsidiaries of foreign banks."[7]

There was a really tough policy toward attracting foreign capital into the banking sphere during the postrevolutionary period. The evidence of this is the fact that in the 1920s, during the New Economic Policy (NEP) period and in particular during the time of foreign concessions, foreign banks were not allowed to take part in banking in the Soviet Union. They were not allowed, though this question was brought up by Narcomfin (People's Commissariat of Finance) before the Soviet government on 6 July 1925. A note from Narcomfin, dated 28 July 1925 and addressed to A. I. Rykov, president of the Council of People's Commissars (SNK), stated that this question should be considered in order to improve the currency-financial situation in the Soviet Union. The note said that "foreign banks no longer present any danger to either our finance or our money circulation and credit. At the same time it can do a lot of good to the Soviet economy, as it will strengthen our ties with the international monetary market and will broaden our opportunities in terms of drawing foreign capital."[8]

At the present time there are more and more supporters of the theory of reasonable openness in the Soviet economy, in particular in the credit-financial sphere. In the international as well as in the Russian experience, there are many examples of efficient measures of control over foreign banks' operations. This control is supposed to reduce the risk of possible negative consequences and to increase the payback for the national economy. The arguments below speak in favor of allowing foreign capital in the banking sphere of the Soviet Union (some of these arguments have already been illustrated by the example of the International Bank Moscow). The allowance would:

- break the monopoly structures and raise the level of competition in the banking business, which will consequently raise the efficiency of the national credit system;
- bring into the country new methods of banking, advanced experience, and the latest technology, which would also contribute to raising the quality of Soviet banking;
- broaden the range of international banking and financial services rendered in the Soviet Union to Soviet and joint enterprises;
- assist in creating and developing an interbanking market, which practically does not exist in the Soviet Union;
- provide an opportunity to draw additional foreign capital into the country from international financial markets;
- integrate Soviet economics into world economics, in particular into the international financial system, by taking certain steps toward liberalizing policy regarding foreign banks' access to the national market.

Many Western countries, in particular the countries of the European Community (EC), would take into account the principle of reciprocity when considering the question of issuing licenses to foreign banks. Besides, the question of liberalization of trade through international banking and financial services is on the agenda of the General Agreement on Tariffs and Trade (GATT), with whom the Soviet Union is planning to cooperate in the near future.

On the whole, one can say that among economists, bank workers, and representatives of official authorities, the idea of attracting foreign capital into the country is gaining more and more support and understanding. Thus, at a meeting with representatives of business and financial circles in Italy in December 1987, the possibility of creating joint stock banks in the Soviet Union was raised.

However, the aim of attracting foreign capital (even allowing that it is taking place at the highest echelons of power) is not sufficient to ensure that the process receives widespread development and becomes truly useful and mutually beneficial for both sides. The decisive factor here is the establishment of a proper legal-contractual basis, as well as the creation of a favorable economic and social climate. At the present time such an environment is virtually absent in the Soviet Union: there is no truly competitive market for bank credits. The level of development of banking infrastructure and banking systems is quite low. The system of guarantees is developed poorly. There is a lack of highly qualified financiers with a good knowledge of market conditions and a capacity to adjust to them.

Thus, if judged from the point of view of traditional neoclassical theory, the rating of the Soviet market is rather low. Capital is supposed to be driven to areas where profit is highest and risk is least. However, we believe that, at the present time, large companies or banks are basing their strategy on many other criteria, particularly on globalizing their policy and maintaining a high level of international competitiveness.

It should be stressed that the current situation cannot be considered fixed. Perestroika of the whole economic system, including the credit-banking system of the Soviet Union, is underway. Though its progress is often very much like the traditional stop-and-go policy, some positive changes are obvious.

An important step toward creating a legal-contractual base for joint entrepreneurship in the banking was taken 11 December 1990 with the passing of the USSR Law on the State Bank and the USSR Law on Banks and Banking Activity.[9]

New banking laws legalize and set the rules for creating foreign banks or joint banks invested with foreign capital on Soviet territory. Under the Law on the State Bank, licenses for such banks are distributed by the central banks of the republics, whereas all-union commercial banks receive licenses from Gosbank. However, during the transitional period, foreign and joint banks are licensed by Gosbank. The Central Soviet of Gosbank cedes the right to license banks only after the creation of appropriate conditions.

Founders of stockholders of commercial banks can be juridical entities and citizens, but when establishing a foreign or joint bank, one of the foreign founders must be a bank. In order to receive a license, a foreign or joint bank needs additional documents, which are specified in the Law on Banks and Banking Activity. In addition to the legislation on banking, all-union and republican legislation on foreign investment also regulate the activity of foreign and joint banks, and of affiliated banks of other countries.

The growing openness of the Soviet banking system is apparent in the rejection of the currency monopoly and centralization of currency operations, and in the expansion of the rights of commercial banks in this area. According to the Law on Banks and Banking Activity, commercial banks can conduct foreign currency transactions under the license of Gosbank or a central republican bank. The rules for awarding licenses to operate in foreign currency are established by Gosbank.

In January 1991, more than ten commercial banks received domestic licenses from Gosbank for conducting foreign currency transactions on Soviet territory. The licenses only allow relations with Soviet clients. By early 1991, eight more commercial banks had received general licenses for foreign currency transactions. The latter banks have the right to conclude agreements with foreign partners and to open corresponding accounts in foreign banks.

The system of guarantees is essential for foreign banking capital, especially guarantees of preservations of property, expropriation of profits, and other guarantees against any kind of economic and political risk or risks of nature. It is also important to have not only legal guarantees but an adequate system of national and private insurance institutions. Such a system is just beginning to be established in the Soviet Union. Neither do we have a system or an institution similar to those in Western countries (for instance the U.S. Federal Depositors' Insurance Corporation), that protects the interest of bank depositors.

There is much more to be done to establish a proper socioeconomic environment favorable for joint stock banks to function and support a really effective market structure. It is especially important to restructure the whole credit-banking system of the Soviet Union. The key objectives of this restructuring, in our opinion, are: to overcome national monopoly in banking, to start a transition to the joint stock form of running credit institutions, to create a credit market, and in every possible way to encourage competition in banking, to change the role of the central bank, and to transfer to economic methods of regulating the credit-financial sphere. In this connection it would be interesting to mention the interview that a correspondent of the newspaper *Izvestiya* took from F. V. Cristians, president of the Deutsche Bank's supervising board. When answering the correspondent's question of whether the Deutsche Bank would be able in the near future to open its branches in the Soviet Union, Cristians said, "The development of banking services would depend on how quickly the business of banking in the Soviet Union will be activized."[10]

The basic task now is to train a highly qualified banking staff capable of acting professionally on a competitive market and recognizing the risks of a project undertaken, and, at the same time, possessing the expertise and knowledge of how to insure banking against the basic risks that may arise under the current conditions.

Another necessary condition is the introduction of a realistic ruble exchange rate and the transfer to at least partial convertibility through the regulation of the hard currency transactions of enterprises and private citizens. The future of credit-financial institutions in the Soviet Union will depend on the restructuring of the whole foreign economic strategy of the Soviet Union and on its involvement in the world economy, that is, its partners of the first joint stock bank on the territory of the Soviet Union. At the same time, the role of the United States in the international credit-financial system as well as many other factors are responsible for the necessary prerequisites that have made a broader cooperation between Soviet and U.S. banks possible in recent years. The other factors contributing to this were a high level of technology and internationalism of U.S. banks and operations, and positive changes in U.S.-Soviet relations.

In conclusion, we would like to stress that the creation of joint stock banks and other credit-financial institutions uniting the shareholders from the Soviet Union and Western countries is an important factor of stabilizing economic and political relations between East and West. Therefore, any promotion of this process will be in the interests of both sides.

NOTES

1. In these countries, similar preferential orientation on international transactions is not a specific feature of banks with foreign capital. According to the research done by OECD, it has become a practice of most of the banks functioning in the member countries of OECD to make transactions with their partners in foreign currency. R. M. Pechioli, "Les Pouvoirs publics face a l'internationalisation bancaire," OECD (Paris, 1983), 87–88.

2. M. Friedlander, *Hungary's Banking Reform* (Wien: Wiener Institut fur International Wirtschaftsvergleiche beim osterreich, 1988), 13.

3. Friedlander, *Hungary's Banking Reform*, 13.

4. Foreign (European) banks in the Soviet Union whose representatives have been accredited by USSR Gosbank: Barclais Bank PLC, Midland Bank PLC, National Westminster Bank (Great Britain), Credito Italiano, Banka Commerciale Italiana (Italy), Pariba, Credit Lyonnais, Société Generale (France), Dresdner Bank AG, Deutsche Bank AG, Commerce Bank AG (FRG). Among the accredited U.S. banks are: Bank of America, Chase Manhattan Bank, and others.

5. K. Marx, *Friedrich Engels Collected Works* 19 (Moscow: Gospolitizdat), 401.

6. The data are taken from the book by A. G. Dongarov, "International Capital in Russia and the USSR," *International Relations* (Moscow: Miezhdunarodnyie otnosheniya, 1990), 14–15.

7. V. I. Lenin, *Collected Works* 27 (Moscow: Gozpolitizdat), 360.

8. Dongarov, "International Capital," 145.

9. See "USSR Law on the USSR State Bank" and "USSR Law: On Banks and Banking Activity" in *Izvestiya* (19 December 1990): 3–4.

10. E. Bavkun, "Vnutrennye i vneshnye rezervy perestroiki," *Izvestiya* (8 May 1990):17.

Chapter 17

Financing of Western Trade and Investment in the Soviet Union

Jan H. Kalicki

Financing presents one of the most serious practical difficulties faced by Western companies that engage in commercial relations with the Soviet Union. With the broad decline of the Soviet economy and the increasing volatility of the domestic political situation, Soviet credit ratings, which were once among the highest outside the Organization for Economic Co-operation and Development (OECD), have plummeted. The inconvertibility of the ruble, delays in payments on hard currency contracts, disruptions of production facilities, a declining infrastructure, and confrontations between the central government and the republics exemplify the extremely serious problems that will face Soviet authorities and Western investors alike over the next decade.

When approaching the Soviet market, a potential investor must always bear in mind the above factors. It will not be business as usual. New and creative sources of financing must be sought. To be successful in the near term, companies need to identify niches in which they can generate hard currency returns despite a generally adverse economic environment. Over the longer term, the more successful companies will be those prepared to adopt a broad-based investment approach, tapping the enormous natural and human resources of the world's largest country, and to help raise the economic and social standards of Soviet citizens despite somewhat lower returns.

Two examples illustrate the value of the latter approach. Since 1974, Pepsico has exported Pepsi concentrate to the Soviet Union as part of a barter deal for Stolichnaya vodka. In 1990, Pepsico began accepting Soviet ships as well as vodka, both of which can be sold for hard currency, as part of its barter deal. These arrangements, coupled with increased investment generated by Pepsico in the Soviet food service and ship-building industries, allowed Pepsico to expand substantially its exports to the Soviet Union.[1]

Second, as a result of changes in U.S. export controls, IBM has launched a fifteen-year program of sales of personal computers, and related software and accessories to the Soviet Union. This program was catalyzed by initial contributions of personal computers to Soviet schools and universities.[2] In each case, the companies were willing to adopt a flexible and long-term approach to trade and investment, whereby short-term revenues in the millions are likely to develop into long-term revenues in the billions.

Initially, most U.S. companies were slow to recognize the value of a more flexible long-term strategy. The result was that European companies, in particular German, Finnish, French, and Italian, began aggressively establishing business ties in the Soviet Union and leaving their U.S. counterparts far behind. American companies, however, soon caught up. As of March 1990, although the number of German and Finnish joint ventures exceeded that of the U.S., the United States was the world leader in total capitalization, with investments totaling $288 million.[3]

SOURCES OF FINANCING

Sources of financing have evolved significantly in response to changes in the Soviet Union's domestic and international environment. Traditionally, the Soviet Union had been able to finance projects and other imports through its own hard currency earnings, through countertrade deals, or through Western credits based on guarantees from foreign export agencies or from the Bank for Foreign Economic Affairs (Vneshekonombank or BFEA), the state organization that has controlled all foreign currency transactions in the Soviet Union. These mechanisms and the state's monopoly on foreign trade made possible maintenance of strict Soviet control over foreign trade and investment. This strict control, however, severely limited the level of investment and insulated enterprises from normal market conditions.

In order to attract greater investment from the West, the Soviet government granted independent authority for negotiating trade and investment to Soviet ministries and other economic enterprises. It also offered incentives such as two-year tax holidays from the receipt of first profits and a subsequent 30 percent tax ceiling for profits from joint ventures, and enabled foreign partners to obtain majority shares as well as effective management control.[4] Effective 1 January 1991, foreign investors could acquire 100 percent ownership of business ventures in the Soviet Union.[5] At the same time, though, limitations on government hard currency reserves required joint ventures to be self-financing, that is, the joint venture's borrowings and other expenses must be repaid from its receipts, and BFEA guarantees must be denied to all but those projects of highest priority to the state. Consequently, joint ventures have been forced to rely on funds generated by the partners themselves rather than on allocations from central authorities.

In addition to employing their own funds, Western partners have looked to what can be termed "soft" and "hard" sources of financing. Soft financing sources provide the partners with funding at relatively favorable, often subsidized, terms of credit. These sources include, on the Western side, low-cost government credits and guarantees that finance exports of goods and equipment. Such credits and guarantees are now available in all OECD countries including, to a degree, the United States. In addition to goods and equipment, Western partners can contribute technology, managerial expertise, and know-how toward their capital contribution to the joint venture.[6]

On the Soviet side, sources of soft financing include real estate, production facilities, raw materials, and attendant rights to natural resources under their own control. It also includes ruble financing from newly established commercial banks as well as specialized state banks serving particular sectors of the economy, such as Promstroibank (the Bank for Industrial Construction), Agroprombank (the Bank for Agro-Industrial Complexes), Zhilsotsbank (the Bank for Housing, Communal Economy and Social Development), and Sberegatel'nyi Bank (the Savings and Consumer Credit Bank). Indeed, these state banks themselves are being transformed into commercial banks. Recent legislation now permits Soviet banks to provide both initial joint venture financing and ongoing working capital and construction loans of varying duration, and even to take equity interest in joint ventures.[7]

Hard financing sources provide the partners with funding on commercial terms of credit. Because of limitations on loans and guarantees from the state through BFEA, the partners must seek such commercial financing through their own resources. Western companies can obtain some of this financing through recourse to their own corporate credit or through the credit of a subsidiary, but they are generally reluctant to accept an additional liability on their own balance sheets. More frequently, the partners will seek such financing from banks and private investors on the basis of collateral in their projects and the hard currency that they generate. Successful examples of such asset-based project finance can be found in hotel projects, which generate high early returns on investment; ship and aircraft acquisition programs, where appreciating values of assets in non-Soviet jurisdictions provide excellent collateral; and natural resource projects, which guarantee foreign off-take of products.

The largest of such project financing attempted to date is the undertaking of Combustion Engineering (now part of Asea Brown Boveri) to construct a $2 billion petrochemical plant complex in a joint venture organized through the Ministry of Petroleum Refining and Petrochemical Industries in Tobolsk, Siberia. This project has experienced substantial organizational difficulties from its inception. Nevertheless, Western financing has been planned through a combination of government export agency credits and commercial bank loans, including a $900 million hard currency package organized by Credit Lyonnais (France), First Bank of Chicago (United

States), and Postipankki (Finland). Only one of the four loan tranches is to be backed by Soviet guarantee, which would be a ministerial, not a BFEA, guarantee. In addition, the Soviet financing is to be executed through $500 million equivalent in ruble loans and $600 million in equity contributions from the government. Western creditors share the risk that the plant's products (butyl rubber and thermoplastic and urethane elastomers), which will be sold to one of the joint venture's partners, Neste Oy of Finland, will generate sufficient revenues to cover the servicing of the debt.[8]

POTENTIAL FINANCING PROBLEMS

Western companies unquestionably face difficult financing problems in the Soviet Union. Due to the inconvertibility of the ruble, Western partners must develop a mechanism for generating hard currency. The most widely employed method is countertrade. In countertrade, foreign partners purchase Soviet goods for rubles and then export them to the West for hard currency.

The second problem is the growing decentralization of the Soviet banking system and the "war of the banks" beginning in mid–1990 between the State Bank (Gosbank) and the BFEA at the center, and their counterparts and the growing number of commercial banks in the republics.[9] Western investors are increasingly confused about which bank is in a position to give reliable credit support to future projects, resulting in growing caution about Soviet-related financing arrangements.

The third problem is the credit risk of the project. To the extent that the project is supported by BFEA guarantees, it will be considered equivalent to a sovereign credit. Despite the "war of the banks," such credits remain acceptable to Western banks and other creditors but at wider margins of interest because of an overall decline in the credit standing of the Soviet Union.

More frequently, however, the project will either receive only a partial BFEA guarantee, or a guarantee from a Soviet ministry or other authority at the republic or municipal levels. It must be noted, though, that guarantees by ministries or other bodies are not unconditionally supported by the state. The creditworthiness of their guarantees depends primarily on their own hard currency resources and the strength of the legal commitment between them and the parties for whom they provide the guarantees—much like the obligations of public authorities in the West.

On the other hand, Soviet ministry guarantees can imply the additional backing of the state treasury, if only to protect the overall credit standing of the Soviet state in the international markets. The argument here would be that the Ministry of Finance and Gosbank would be reluctant to permit a default on an obligation guaranteed by, say, the Ministry of Merchant

Marine, because of the likely adverse impact on present and future Soviet state credit.

Western financial institutions have yet to establish a standard formula for assessing the creditworthiness of ministerial, republic, and municipal guarantees. Currently, over twelve thousand Soviet enterprises and foreign trade organizations (FTOs) have been granted to the right to trade directly with the West.[10] If these enterprises are to be regarded as a private rather than a sovereign risk, then there is the added difficulty of determining a credit rating for an entity with little or no track record.

The Soviet environment can also compound the completion and performance risks traditionally associated with any venture or project. In general, joint ventures lie outside the centralized state supply system and therefore must rely on an underdeveloped wholesale supply network subject to numerous disruptions and delays. Legal commitments remain vulnerable in a climate of changing laws and less-than-predictable Council of Ministers' decrees at both the all-Union and republic levels.

These problems have been compounded by increasing reports of late payments by Soviet enterprises to their foreign trade creditors.[11] Soviet officials blame overcommitments by certain enterprises, and they are seeking to discipline them by delaying their access to hard currency. They also blame the delays on chaos resulting from a decentralization of the foreign trade system. While Soviet exports and imports used to be relatively simple and reliable transactions handled through several state-run trade organizations, now Soviet enterprises are taking advantage of their new-found independence from central control and are becoming overextended because of lack of experience and expertise. As of November 1990, the total trade credits overdue from Soviet enterprises were estimated to exceed $500 million. German and Japanese firms have already taken the first steps to claim export insurance. According to the Export Credit and Guarantee Department (ECGD), British firms, while not yet filing any claims, have made inquiries about recovering their losses.[12] Where new credit facilities have become available, notably Germany, as part of the financial package negotiated at the time of unification, drawings have already been made to bring Soviet payments up to date.

Thus far, transactions guaranteed by BFEA continue to be paid on a relatively timely basis. There is growing concern on the part of Western financial institutions, however, over the level of Soviet indebtedness and the likely difficulty of future debt servicing. Traditionally, the Soviet Union had always enjoyed the highest credit rating. It paid its debts on time and its huge natural wealth provided comfort to its creditors. Perceptions in the West of Soviet creditworthiness began to change in 1989, when, in the spirit of glasnost, Moscow disclosed that its foreign debt had grown from $42 billion to $51 billion. Despite these negative perceptions, the Soviet Union's ratio of debt service to hard currency earning is among the lowest in Eastern

Europe—somewhere between 21 percent and 25 percent.[13] The Soviet Union's willingness to use part of its vast gold reserves as collateral for selected credits has helped to bolster its tarnished credit rating.[14]

POSSIBLE FINANCING SOLUTIONS

The financing problems identified above can be solved in a number of ways, but the ability to implement the solutions varies greatly according to the nature of the project, its partners, and its priority for the Soviet government. Moreover, many projects are not susceptible to a single financing solution, but rather require some combination of the hard and soft financing approaches reviewed previously.

In order to generate hard currency cash flow, a venture will usually first seek hard currency sales in the Soviet market. If the joint venture can show that its project will save or generate hard currency through increased efficiencies, import substitution, or export promotion, its prospects for allocations of scarce hard currency reserves will be greatly enhanced. For example, a joint venture undertaken by Honeywell received hard currency allocations because it contributed to the automation and efficiency of hard-currency-generating facilities.

The next approach of the venture will be to seek compensation through countertrade—the purchase in rubles of commodities and goods that can be sold for hard currency—and to obtain authority to use any rubles in excess of local expenses to purchase such commodities. Generally, unless the state priority of the project is very high, the most fungible commodities—precious metals and oil—will be very difficult to obtain. If unable to obtain these commodities, the venture must then look to a wider spectrum of commodities and goods, ranging from ships to timber and pulp products, that may be more difficult to market. Depending on the security of the cash flow projected from these marketing arrangements, ventures can obtain needed financing from banks or the global capital markets on the basis of projected countertrade.

In the absence of any developed free market, the Soviet partners will have to assure access to the commodities and goods that are needed to help finance the venture. This also will be easier when it can be demonstrated that commodities are in excess of state requirements, or that the partners will invest in expansion of production to cover their hard currency requirements. It will be easier when the Soviet partner is directly responsible for the commodity in question, for example, the Ministry of the Merchant Marine in the case of ships, or the Ministry of Forestry in the case of timber. When that is not the case, more complex arrangements must be negotiated across ministries. For example, as part of Pepsico's recent barter deal, by which Pepsi concentrate is exchanged for Stolichnaya vodka and ships, Pepsico is establishing Pizza Hut restaurants jointly with the USSR Commission of Agriculture and Procurement and is arranging for a Bermuda-based Norwegian shipping company that is also marketing the Soviet ships to invest in upgrading six Soviet shipyards.[15]

To solve the problem of credit risk, more and more projects are using their own assets and cash flow derived from revenues as collateral. For example, the Soviet shipping company Sovkomflot and the Soviet state airline Aeroflot have been successful in raising large amounts of asset-based finance in the form of both leases and purchases and have required only secondary credit support from their own Ministries of Merchant Marine and Civil Aviation.[16]

Clearly, Soviet financing of joint venture projects will remain limited as long as such financing depends on scarce hard currency supplies and on excess commodities in the Soviet Union. For the near future, much of the credit support for East-West trade and joint venture projects will come from Western governments and international economic organizations. The $3 billion in German credit that the Soviet Union received in 1990 is just one example of the types of Western financing that will play a critical role in expanding credit supports for future projects.[17] Although these credits extended by Western governments will almost always be tied to exports from the originating country, they will help to alleviate pressure on other financing sources, which could be used to support projects with other countries.

FUTURE FINANCING TRENDS

Recent experience with financing solutions shows that a hybrid of hard and soft financing sources is now emerging that may significantly improve the future financing environment for Soviet ventures and projects. This hybrid, which might be termed cooperative financing, consists of increased institutional support for commercial financing, expanded countertrade arrangements, and new multinational facilities. All of these methods of financing involve cooperative approaches by the Western and Soviet sides.

As noted above, increased institutional support can be expected from Western banks as well as government credit facilities. This support, combined with an increased emphasis on project and asset-based finance, could catalyze expanded use of private funds generated from the global capital markets.

Expanded countertrade arrangements can help generate substantial amounts of additional credit based on commercial financing and alleviate the need to rely on sovereign guarantees, which have been unduly strained in recent years. Forward sales of precious metals and oil could be used to generate commercial credits well in excess of $1 billion for future use by Soviet projects and ventures.

New multinational facilities will also emerge, beginning with the newly established European Bank for Reconstruction and Development, which will grant limited credits to the Soviet Union as well as to the countries of Central and Eastern Europe. The credits from this bank will be used primarily to help finance the development of a private sector in these countries. The Soviet government has also initiated talks with the International Monetary Fund (IMF), which is likely to play a role in the Soviet economy when Soviet leaders embrace a complete transition to a free market, convertible currency, and privatization of state enterprise. Such a policy shift would also encourage U.S. financial support through import-export credits and increased participation in the European Bank, targeted at beneficiaries in the emerging private sector rather than the Soviet state sector.

Cooperative financing will require catalysts not only at the governmental level, but also in the private sector. Here investment banks can make an important contribution by advising Soviet enterprises and Western companies, identifying appropriate partners, and constructing workable financial structures to access the needed finance. With the support of its parent company American Express, Lehman Brothers is performing this function in the fields of health care, hotels, ships, oil, petrochemicals, and computer sales. In addition, Lehman Brothers has developed close cooperative relationships with BFEA and the Soviet state sectoral banks in order to provide needed institutional support for joint ventures and other Soviet projects.

With the assistance of investment banks, cooperative financing can also be expected to develop into consortia of companies rather than individual joint ventures. Consortia, such as the American Trade Consortium and the American Medical Consortium, make it possible to broaden access to necessary commodities as well as to pool hard currency arrangements among their participants. In addition, they provide leverage to attain additional financial benefits, such as longer tax holidays and more favorable treatment under future economic legislation. A variant developed by Lehman Brothers is to establish separate but complementary Soviet and Western consortia that can then operate on a project-by-project basis and receive the same incentives as the more traditional consortia.

These trends make it possible to build financial bridges between ventures operating within the present Soviet economic system and a future free-market structure that will be characterized by greater ruble convertibility and expanded commercial and financial flexibility of enterprises. An interesting indication of this shift to a free market is the hard currency auctions conducted to date in the Soviet Union and the decision to grant to joint ventures and duly registered foreign investors the right to participate, starting 1 January 1991 in such auctions or other currency exchange programs organized by the Ministry of Finance.[18] Hopefully, new financing mechanisms will hasten the day when the average Soviet citizen will at least reap material benefits from the fundamental transformation of the Soviet system instituted under President Gorbachev.

NOTES

The author gratefully acknowledges the assistance of Lisa Halustick and Mark Hayes in the preparation of this chapter.

1. "Soviets Swapping Ships for Pepsi," *Journal of Commerce* (10 March 1990): 5A.

2. "IBM Signs Pact with the Soviets," *New York Times* (2 June 1990): 37.

3. Jan Vanous, ed., "Soviet Joint Ventures: Developments through the First Quarter of 1990," *PlanEcon Report* (27 April 1990): 9–10.

4. Decree of the President of the USSR, "On Foreign Investment in the USSR," *Izvestiya* (26 October 1990): 1.

5. "Law of the USSR on Taxes on Businesses, Associations and Organizations," *ECOTASS* (30 July 1990): 7–8.

6. U.S. Department of Commerce, *Introductory Guide to Joint Ventures in the Soviet Union*, (Washington, D.C.: U.S. Department of Commerce, 1 January 1990): 18.

7. Decree 1015 of the State Bank of the USSR and Decree 149 of the Bank for Foreign Trade of the USSR, "Procedure for Crediting and Settlement of Accounts of Joint Ventures" (22 September 1987), cited in *Venturing in the USSR, Hungary and Poland: The Emerging Legal Framework* (Washington, D.C.: Fried, Frank, Harris, Shriver & Jacobson, 2 April 1990): 35.

8. "U.S.-Soviet Venture is Finalized," *Journal of Commerce* (29 November 1989): 7A. Also see Vera Turtianen, *Trade Finance and Banker International* (April 1990): 35; *Business Eastern Europe* (18 December 1989); Peter Montagnon, "Soviet Chemicals Venture May Secure $900M Loan," *Financial Times* (1 December 1989): 8.

9. "A War of the Banks in the Offing?" *Moscow News* (19–26 August 1990): 1.

10. Scott Kilman, "Soviet Union Keeps Buying Corn at 1989 Pace but U.S. Traders Worry About Its Financing," *Wall Street Journal* (8 May 1990): C14.

11. See Laurie Hays and Peter Gumbell, "Soviet Concerns Falling behind in Paying Bills," *Wall Street Journal* (6 March 1990): A3; Laurie Hays, "Payment Delays of Soviets Hurt Western Firms," *Wall Street Journal* (7 May 1990): A11; and "Plan on Paying Overdue Bills Set by Soviets," *Wall Street Journal* (23 May 1990): A20.

12. Hays, "Payment Delays," A11.

13. Stephen Fidler, "A Loser Hand in Moscow Worries Foreign Creditors," *Financial Times* (27 April 1990): 2; David Morgan, "The Soviet Union Faces Hard Times in International Banking," *The Reuter Library Report* (11 March 1990): 2.

14. Neil Behrmann, "Soviets Deposit Gold in Western Banks as Collateral for Easing Cash Squeeze," *Wall Street Journal* (4 June 1990): A3.

15. Anthony Ramirez, "Pepsi Will be Bartered for Ships and Vodka in Deal with Soviets," *New York Times* (9 April 1990): 1; Stephen Moore, "PepsiCo, Soviet Union Trade Pact Gives Opportunity to Norwegian Shipbuilder," *Wall Street Journal* (11 May 1990): A9.

16. Fidler, "A Looser Hand in Moscow," 2; *Trade Finance and Banker International* (June 1990): 52.

17. Ferdinand Protzman, "Bonn to Aid Kremlin Reforms with $3 Billion Bank Credit," *New York Times* (23 June 1990): 1.

18. Decree of the president of the USSR, "On the Establishment of the Commercial Exchange Rate for the Ruble to Foreign Currencies and Measures to Create an All-Union Currency Market," *Izvestiya* (26 October 1990): 1.

Part V

Conclusions and Recommendations

Chapter 18

The Future of Joint Ventures in the Soviet Union

Vladimir V. Ranenko

At the present time some basic features of joint business venture activities in the Soviet Union have already taken shape. This process has been notable for an accelerating rate of growth in the number of joint ventures and the expanding number of participating foreign countries, testifying to the growth of mutual interests on all sides.

The intensification of joint venture activity is fostered by such attractive characteristics of the investment climate of the Soviet Union as the scale of the unsatisfied market for consumer and producer goods, the scientific and technical potential of the country, and the availability of diverse supplies of natural and secondary raw materials as well as personnel.

However, the process of formation and operation does not fully meet such intended goals as saturating the Soviet domestic market with goods and services, attracting additional materials and financial resources, and expanding Soviet exports while reducing irrational imports. For instance, from January to December 1989 the average size of the joint venture charter fund declined from 4.1 million rubles to 2.6 million rubles, or more than one and a half times (150 percent).

Joint ventures increasingly concentrate on spheres of activity that do not require major initial investments, such as the social sphere; provision of various informational, consultative, and intermediary services; computer programs; and the production of personal computers. The relative share of joint ventures formed in the machine-building and chemical industries and in the agroindustrial complex is decreasing.

These trends cannot all be labeled negatively. They arise, on the one hand, from the structure of unsatisfied needs of the Soviet market in goods and services and by a natural desire for a more rapid return on investments by joint venture participants. The large number of small- and medium-sized joint ventures creates an atmosphere of healthy competition that helps to ensure the high quality of the goods and services they provide. The products of such joint ventures—like the Soviet-German Lenvest and Belvest (shoes), Soviet-Spanish Telur (telephones), Soviet-American Dialog (personal computers and computer programs), Soviet-Italian Sovploastital (plastic consumer goods), Soviet-Finnish Vneshkon'sult (consulting services for international trade), and many others among the four hundred existing joint ventures—are very competitive on the Soviet market. Such enterprises expand the market sector of the Soviet economy, thereby furthering the process of economic reform. Their activity provides positive experience and dispels the initial caution felt by Soviet and foreign partners toward this new form of close, long-term cooperation.

At the same time, an analysis of the scale and structure of investment and of the activities of joint ventures up to the present time shows that there are some serious problems and that the mitigation or elimination of these problems will depend on the future of joint venture activity in the Soviet Union. In our opinion, these problems fall into the following categories:

- the imperfect domestic market mechanism, as well as the incomplete status of Soviet economic reform;
- the limited nature of Soviet legislation regulating the attraction and use of foreign investment in the Soviet Union;
- the inadequate inclusion of joint ventures into the national economy and the absence of a system of multidirectional regulation of the structure of foreign and Soviet investment in joint ventures;
- the unrealistic exchange rate as well as the inconvertibility of the Soviet ruble;
- the underdeveloped production and social infrastructure of the Soviet Union; and
- the inadequate preparation of most Soviet officials and specialists to operate independently in the foreign economic sphere.

It is of paramount importance to find a solution to these problems, if joint ventures are to be formed more quickly and in greater numbers in the Soviet Union.

The prospects for joint undertakings in the Soviet Union are directly related to how well the country's national economic mechanism of production and distribution relations assures real economic independence for Soviet enterprises and organizations. The direction of change in the internal economic mechanism from a system of administrative management through vertical links to one of economic methods of management is marked by the plans of perestroika and the development and functioning of independent and equal commodity producers cooperating with each other on the basis of contractual relationships. The transition from extremely centralized management of the economy to a market-regulated economy is proceeding slowly and painfully. On the one hand, passage of the Law on State Enterprises and the Law on Cooperatives in the Soviet Union, as well as the repeal of many normative acts bolstering the administrative power of ministries and departments, has created a certain legal bias for the formation of free relationships among commodity producers. On the other hand, these laws did not free state enterprises from the dictates of the plan; from a system of distribution for raw materials, supplies, and semimanufactured goods prescribed by the fund; or from rigid price formation and the distribution of profits dictated from above. In a situation where raw materials, materials, and spare parts are not readily available, and in view of their long-standing custom of acting on the basis of orders from above, many state enterprises do not try to move to the market sector of the economy, where they will not have a guaranteed market for their products and where they will have to compete for orders and for the resources necessary to fulfill them.

Characteristically, the share of government-owned manufacturing enterprises as a total number of Soviet joint venture participants does not exceed 23 percent. These enterprises cannot receive acceptable profit margins on the investments in the joint venture if the existing practice of centralizing up to 70 percent of their balanced profits, including net profits, is preserved. Simple calculations show that even if that same joint venture has a profit margin of 50 percent the realistic profitability of the Soviet government enterprise as a partner in the joint venture, its profits cannot exceed 7 or 8 percent, taking into account the centralized government deductions.

The USSR Supreme Soviet and the government of the Soviet Union are formulating a system of legal acts that are creating a new base for manufacturing and distribution relations in the internal economic mechanism of the Soviet Union. A law on property, which acknowledges the coexistence and equality of the integration of government, cooperative, collective, and other forms of property was effected in March 1990. Laws have also been passed on leasing and leasing relations, on land and land use, and on the basic economic relations of the Soviet Union with Union and autonomous republics, which establish a definite order for using natural resources by economic links in the Soviet Union, including their use by joint ventures.

In the process of forming the law on a single taxation system for economic enterprises and organizations in the Soviet Union, there has been discussion of preserving, among other things, the preferential tax status of joint ventures to prevent the double taxation of the profits of Soviet partners in joint ventures. These laws will establish needed guarantees of contractual relations between different types of commodity producers, which in turn will provide an important stimulus for the intensification of joint venture activity in the Soviet Union.

Inasmuch as joint ventures are not included in the system of government planning and centralized distribution of resources in accordance with their present legal status, the weakening of this system and the strengthening of market relations in the Soviet economy means the formation of more favorable conditions for their activity. The reform of Soviet foreign economic activity creates favorable prospects for the attraction of foreign investment in joint venture activities on Soviet territory.

There has been a basic reorganization in the system of regulating foreign economic ties. In place of the earlier rigid monopoly over virtually all foreign economic operations exerted by the former USSR Ministry of Foreign Trade, as of 1 April 1989 all state, cooperative, and other public organizations gained the right to export their products independently and to make purchases on the foreign market. Currently, approximately fifteen thousand independent participants in foreign economic activity have been registered. They can use foreign currency they have accumulated to buy equipment and consumer goods directly. This greatly increases the opportunities for joint ventures to obtain hard currency by selling their products in the Soviet Union. Characteristically, in 1989 the turnover of goods and services of joint ventures for foreign currency gradually reached 200 million rubles and increased more than 700 percent in the second half of 1989. Apparently, until the ruble becomes convertible, one of the most important sources of hard currency revenue for joint ventures will be the sale of modern goods and services in the Soviet Union.

Soviet enterprises can now pool their money and efforts to operate on certain foreign markets or to carry out complex foreign economic programs by organizing consortia, trading houses, associations for business cooperation, and other similar associations. Such organizations can do more than provide their members with the information, consultative, and intermediary services they need, thereby facilitating cooperation with their foreign partners. They can also provide certain guarantees, risk insurance, and preferential credit operations for members and their foreign partners by drawing on their joint funds and commercial profits. Foreign enterprises and firms can now participate in such organizations also with Soviet legal personages, and, in this case, similar associative economic processes are formed under the same legal conditions created for joint ventures.

The nature of the reform planned in price formation is of cardinal importance for the development of joint ventures. Existing wholesale prices in the national economy for raw materials, semimanufactured goods, and manufactured goods do not correspond with the prices for analogous goods and services on world markets. On the one hand, diminished prices for raw materials and other goods, elevated prices for manufactured products, and the shortages of many types of commodities all prompt joint ventures in the direction of various trade operations that assure a high degree of profit by exporting raw materials and importing commodities in short supply, like consumer goods. A number of joint ventures are engaging in such activities, deviating from their statutory activity and violating established requirements to obtain a license for intermediary operations that discredit joint venture activities as a whole. On the other hand, it is virtually impossible for joint ventures to obtain raw materials and goods at low wholesale prices, since these resources are distributed through a centralized system among state enterprises. It is therefore difficult for joint ventures to compete with state commodity producers in cost levels. Because of shortages and the high quality of their products, joint ventures can reach a higher degree of production efficiency by raising prices on services and manufactured goods. In the future, when the majority of state enterprises move to real market principles of operation, joint venture activities will benefit from the new Soviet price formation system. This will help attract resources, materials, and energy-saving technologies into joint ventures and help them improve the quality of their products.

The future of joint business ventures in the Soviet Union depends on the establishment in the nearest possible future of a more valid exchange rate for the ruble for all forms of economic operations on a legal as well as a physical basis for Soviets and foreigners. The artificially high official exchange rate of the ruble for trade operations is the reason for many difficulties in relations between Soviet and foreign partners in determining contributions to the charter fund of the enterprise and balancing the joint venture's income, expenditures, and profits. The attainment of a convertible ruble is scarcely possible in the coming years under conditions of severe shortages and low labor, agricultural, service sector, and industrial productivity. At the same time, if a more realistic exchange rate for the ruble against foreign currency is imposed, accompanied by a reform in price formation, more objective relations will be formed between joint venture partners and also between those enterprises and Soviet manufacturers that stimulate the process of joint entrepreneurial activities.

The slow tempo of the influx of foreign investment in joint business ventures in the Soviet Union is closely tied to the absence of complex legislation to regulate the creation and practical activity of joint ventures in the Soviet Union or to establish guarantees, privileges, rules, and responsibilities for foreign investors in the Soviet Union. The only legal acts of the highest power—the decree of the Presidium of the USSR Supreme Soviet of 13 January 1987, a series of acts from the USSR Council of Ministers, and departmental normative documents—played their political roles in the beginning stages of joint business activities. Now this legal basis is acknowledged by both Soviet and foreign specialists to be inadequate for supplying an effective and guaranteed use of foreign investments in the Soviet Union. Many cases of prevailing normative acts are not sufficiently tied into the recent passage of laws on property, land and land use, or leasing and leasing relations, and there are currently laws on taxation, joint stock companies, and other economic societies and groups being delayed in the Council of Ministers and the Supreme Soviet.

Foreign investors should be given the opportunity to participate in new types of Soviet enterprises and organizations, such as joint stock companies, concerns, consortia, and others, and also to create enterprises with full foreign ownership. It is also expedient to expand the opportunities for attracting foreign investment for modernizing existing Soviet enterprises. In Soviet legislation on foreign investment there should be clearly defined spheres of priority for use with corresponding guarantees and priorities for taxation, credit, and the allocation for natural, material, and technical resources.

It is apparent that much attention should be directed toward the simplification of organizational procedures tied to the attraction and use of foreign investment in the Soviet Union. Starting in 1991, for example, the registration of joint ventures will be handled by the Soviet republics. As a result, it will not be necessary to go through Moscow from other cities and agricultural regions, which will make the registration of joint ventures less complicated. At their discretion local governments will be able to significantly simplify the process.

In the future, as business, including foreign business, develops in the country, the opportunity will certain arise to move away from the authorization process of registering joint ventures currently in use in the Soviet Union to a reporting process used in many countries of the world to register such ventures.

There is a series of particular questions not regulated by existing legal acts that leads to certain complications in the establishment and especially the operation of joint ventures:

- the diversification of the joint venture's structure, the formation of affiliates and new joint ventures with the joint venture's participation;
- statistical and required public accounting of organizations in which foreign investors actively take part;
- procedures for agreements on the establishment of joint ventures, and the responsibility of the organs of management for the objectivity and timeliness of decisions;
- the procedure and conditions for transferring the basic funds of Soviet enterprises to the capital fund for joint ventures;
- the procedure for selling the production of joint ventures in retail trade, including for foreign currency.

Part of these issues will be regulated by the changing norms of economic law in the Soviet Union, for instance, in legislation on economic societies and groups. Foreign investors taking part in these societies and groups will be subject to the same norms on a common foundation. Other related issues, specifically relating to foreign investors, will be regulated by a separate juridical act on foreign investment.

For the formation of more favorable prospects for joint ventures in the

Soviet Union, both the current reform of the internal economic mechanism and the development of legislation regarding the use of foreign investment have special significance, since they will facilitate the future integration of joint ventures into the Soviet economy. The isolation of joint ventures from the centralized distribution of resources, while it does not forge economic initiative for the joint venture, creates tangible difficulties in the supply of materials and in the supply of construction, transportation, and manufacturing services.

At the present time the system of management in the Soviet Union is changing with the result of expanding and strengthening the market not only for consumer goods and services, but also for technical and manufactured production. It is intended to bring about the regulation of economic processes, using such levers as priority credits, taxes, and leasing prices for land and other natural resources without direct interference in the activities of manufacturers and their horizontal relations. Naturally, the practical realization of such reforms in the Soviet economy will create better conditions for the inclusion of enterprises with foreign investors in the system of domestic economic relations.

The more complete inclusion of enterprises in the system of internal economic relations of Soviet producers will soften the problem of the hard currency self-financing of joint ventures. It is evident that the principle of hard currency self-financing will remain in Soviet legislation. Only a few exceptions from this principle can be expected, and the exceptions could be imposed on the basis of agreement between the Soviet Union and other countries on the mutual protection of investments. Therefore, the future of joint ventures, especially those oriented to the sale of their production to Soviet consumers, depends on the expansion of possibilities for receiving foreign currency.

Under a more complete inclusion of joint ventures in the mechanism of the internal economic life of the Soviet Union, the following possibilities could open up:

- participation in organizations, consortia, and associations in which joint ventures will be able to distribute profits in rubles and in foreign currency between themselves in accordance with individual strengths and needs (for instance, a hotel/tourist complex for foreign clients, with a joint venture in agriculture producing food products for the internal market, including its own partner in the given enterprise).

- participation in hard currency and in wholesale auctions, where the joint venture can find customers with hard currency;

- participation in the implementation of governmental social manufacturing and technical programs by means of the production of import-substituting production and the use of currency resources targeted toward financing this program.

The intensiveness of the development of manufacturing, a social infrastructure, and a net of productive services will have a particular influence
on the scale and tempo of the influx of foreign investment to Soviet economy.
At the present time the inadequate development of transportation (especially
automotive, to satisfy the growing demand for transporting small loads),
communications (especially telephone and telefax machines), mechanized
and automatized storage, hotel and modern living accommodations, medical
facilities, and other elements of the infrastructure have a negative impact
on the investment climate in the Soviet Union. Naturally, joint ventures
gravitate to the industrial centers of the country. More than 62 percent of
joint ventures are registered in Moscow, Leningrad, the Baltic states, and
the Ukraine.

The lag in the manufacturing and social infrastructure in the Soviet Union
will hardly be eliminated in a short period of time. The development of the
infrastructure of communications and housing and other social objectives
should be included in a number of important directions for utilizing Soviet
and foreign investment. It is expedient to stimulate the reinvestment of
profits from joint ventures and the development of manufacturing and social
infrastructures of designated regions of the Soviet Union in order to attract
foreign investment in the context of new forms of industrial cooperation.

One such new form is the formation of special economic zones in the
Soviet Union. Such zones are meant to supply the best possible conditions
for attracting and using foreign investments by providing the necessary
manufacturing and social infrastructure, in limited regions, and by imposing
a preferential tax, hard currency, and organizational conditions for the
activity of Soviet, joint, and foreign enterprises in these regions. As of late
1990, legislation for organizing special zones of joint business activity in
the regions of Vyborg in the Leningrad oblast, Nakhodka Primorskogo
Kraya, and other regions in the Soviet Union was being concluded. This
will create additional conditions for the attraction of foreign capital for the
formation of high-tech industries, the activities of which could contribute
to a growth of exports and a better supply to the domestic Soviet market.

The central problem for forming special economic zones is the financing
and formation of the manufacturing, social, and working infrastructure in
the regions. The financing of such programs from the Soviet budget, bur-
dened by the existing deficit, is rife with problems. It is necessary to rework
and realize a mechanism for attracting the investments of Soviet manufacturers, joint ventures, and foreign firms and organizations with this goal in
mind. It is important that an investment guarantee on funds invested in the
zone accompany this mechanism of financing, and that the surrounding
urban territory be leased by the foreign and Soviet entrepreneurs that will
conduct individual or joint manufacturing activities in these zones.

For all practical purposes, all basic problems curbing the flow of Soviet
and foreign investments into Soviet joint business ventures on Soviet ter-

ritory can be solved only by the successful and radical reform of economic management in the Soviet Union. Real economic independence of Soviet enterprises and organizations, realistic price formation, market relations among commodity producers operating on the basis of various forms of ownerships, legal guarantees for the protection of property, and fulfilled contractual obligations will create conditions favoring large-scale foreign investment in the Soviet economy and the profit functioning of joint ventures.

Chapter 19

Looking to the Future: Western Policy and Business Options

Alan B. Sherr

Most analyses of the future of perestroika begin with the assertion that economic reform in the Soviet Union depends first and foremost on the efforts of Soviet citizens and the responsiveness of Soviet institutions, as opposed to the influence of external forces. This is undeniably true, but the potential role of Western (shorthand for "developed capitalist") states is growing. In the early stages of Mikhail Gorbachev's economic reforms, the contribution to be expected from the West was minimized by Soviet officials and placed decisively behind domestic self-help and fraternal assistance from the socialist bloc.[1] However, the heady days of perestroika have passed and grim awareness of the difficulty of the domestic transformation has taken hold. Moreover, doubts about the capability and willingness of the East European states to help shoulder the burdens of perestroika have been eclipsed by the reality of their political and economic reorientation away from the Soviet Union and toward the West.

The increasing Soviet interest in Western economic involvement in perestroika is thus attributable for the most part to the failure of preferred alternatives. But there is also a positive element—the growing commitment to radical reform, by which is meant in large measure the introduction of free-market mechanisms. This commitment, which admittedly proceeds in fits and starts and is not universally shared, draws on Western models and is often facilitated by Western participation or advice.

Consequently, Western economic cooperation with the Soviet Union has assumed greater importance both for Soviet officials who increasingly desire it, and for Western officials who must assess whether it is in their best interests to provide it. However, the speed of economic and political developments in the Soviet Union and Europe has deprived Western policy-makers of an opportunity to fully explore the options, even while the apparent urgency of dealing with the upheavals has increased pressure to develop a clear policy.

The first step in assessing Western policy options must be to identify the desired goals. A wide range of sometimes contradictory objectives has been stated or implied by Western officials, business people, academics, and others. This chapter therefore examines a number of these suggested objectives and tests them against current Soviet conditions and trends. An assessment is made in each case whether the objectives are realizable and whether, on balance, achieving them would advance or hinder Western interests.

The final section of the chapter looks at the tools that Western governments might use to advance those goals that seem desirable and realizable. There is a particular focus on what is most likely the most intensive, and potentially effective, form of Western participation in the Soviet economy— direct investment. The prevalent form of direct investment is joint ventures, although other mechanisms are developing. It is contended that direct investment in the Soviet Union can significantly advance a coherent set of Western policy goals.

IDENTIFYING WESTERN POLICY GOALS

In view of the varying interests of the developed capitalist states, it is not possible to ascribe to these states a uniform set of goals. The following discussion proceeds primarily from the U.S. perspective, although the differences from the Western European or Japanese perspectives frequently involve questions of degree, rather than kind.

Certain themes commonly frame discussions of Western interests in the success of perestroika. Perhaps the most frequent is the encouragement of pluralism in the Soviet Union. Others include support for a reduced Soviet military threat and measures to bolster democratization and independence in Eastern Europe. Another strand to the discussion, which seems stronger in Western Europe and Japan than in the United States, is the economic self-interest of the Western country in expanding commercial ties with the Soviet Union.

There are also those in the West who see more to gain from the failure of perestroika than from its success. Their immediate objective is to encourage the political breakup of the Soviet Union. It is expected that this, in turn, will lead to greater pluralism (at least in gross terms involving the independence of regional or national groups), enhanced Western security, and greater freedom and prosperity in Eastern Europe.

Policy Goal 1: Encourage Pluralism in the Soviet Union

Political pluralism. The term *pluralism* is used in the context of Soviet reform to refer to a number of different concepts. One involves the development of a multiparty system, the formation of formal and informal interest groups, and meaningful citizen participation in the political process. Because this political form of pluralism depends entirely on the actions of Soviet governments, institutions, and citizens, its connection to Western economic involvement in the Soviet Union must of necessity be indirect. Conceivably, Western cooperation can be offered as an inducement for Soviet authorities to proceed with political reform, or it can be withheld as punishment for not moving fast enough or for backsliding. However, any such link would be very weak. Political reform arose in the Soviet Union primarily to provide dynamism and faith to a stagnant and cynical society, both by providing outlets for individual initiative and by breaking the strangling monopoly of the Communist Party. The forces involved in this domestic struggle far outweigh any influence that either a threat or inducement of Western assistance could exert.

Another possible connection is to view Western economic cooperation as a means of helping certain individuals or groups (often reduced to Gorbachev alone in the minds of Westerners) maintain themselves in power and thus allow the process of political reform to proceed during the next few crucial years. While more plausible, this linkage is more complex than is often assumed and, in some forms, is clearly unrealistic.

The linkage is weakest when it proceeds from the hope that the West can provide a quick fix to Soviet economic problems. Over a period of decades, Western economic cooperation can have a significant impact on Soviet economic development and thus on the stability of Soviet society. But political reform (democratization) in the Soviet Union is moving at a far faster pace than economic reform. Alternative political parties are being formed, and the political power wielded by the people is sharply increasing. It is doubtful that foreign economic assistance could arrive on the scene quickly enough and in sufficient quantity to fundamentally alter the political fortunes of any nationally important individual or group during this turbulent political phase.[2]

Notwithstanding such practical constraints, it is still possible that the mere appearance of a significant Western commitment to the economic reform of the Soviet Union could produce political benefits for the Soviet leadership. There would seem to be a strong analogy here to the early days of the Gorbachev era, during which progress on arms control negotiations with the United States, particularly with respect to the treaty on intermediate-range nuclear forces in Europe and the new leadership's well-received rhetorical positions (the "new ways of thinking") not only boosted the Soviet Union's international stature, but also bolstered Gorbachev's domestic political authority at a crucial time of political realignment. The leadership's foreign policy initiatives also gave it breathing room to address domestic concerns.[3] Similarly, it might be hoped that a dramatic underwriting of perestroika by the major Western states would immediately inure to the political benefit of the Soviet leadership, even though the effects of Western involvement might be transient at first and require many years to take hold.

The problem with this analogy is that Soviet society has changed enormously in the few years since the arms control debate held center stage. The attention of the Soviet population and of virtually all political and academic institutions has been directed sharply inward. The Soviet leadership has unfortunately expended a great deal of political capital on failed efforts to invigorate the economy at the same time that glasnost has exposed, and even magnified, the many problems of Soviet society. The prestige of summits, international agreements, and pledges of international cooperation are fine, but Soviet politics is now far more tuned to the condition of the economy and rapidly rising concerns about crime, corruption, and nationalist and ethnic antagonisms.[4] Thus, while a decisive Western economic commitment to perestroika could provide the Soviet leadership with some immediate moral support, it would not long divert attention from the compelling need to produce results on the home front.

Another salient consideration is the powerful process of decentralization of leadership—economic as well as political—in the Soviet Union. During 1990 in particular, the central role of the all-Union government ebbed dramatically as the initiative was grasped by leaders at the republic and even local levels. It is thus not so clear what person or group constitutes the Soviet leadership on a particular issue. Attempts by the West to bolster one group or another would seem inevitably to involve delicate and dangerous involvement in domestic politics.

If there is not a good basis for linking Western economic cooperation with enhancement of the process of political pluralism in the Soviet Union, is there reason to believe that the opposite tact—exacerbating the economic pressure on the Soviet Union—can have an effect? While none of the Western governments apparently consider this negative approach to be a feasible or desirable alternative, there remains an undercurrent of opinion in this direction that emerges at times of stress in East-West relations.[5] In its mildest form, the approach would consist of withholding all economic cooperation so that the Soviet Union is forced to proceed with fundamental political reforms. At its most extreme, the thrust is to tighten the screws so that the need for revolutionary change is inescapable.

Such views in all their manifestations are misguided and likely to be counterproductive. First, as noted above, the connection between Western economic cooperation and the process of political reform in the Soviet Union is tenuous at best. Where the connection might be the strongest—in having a marginal impact on the political survivability of the reformist leadership—the strategy of contributing to economic problems can only make matters worse. Moreover, it would be virtually impossible to organize a united Western front in an economic attack on the Soviet Union. Any country that attempted to do so would probably find itself isolated while other Western countries rushed to fill the vacuum.

Second, the very poor economic performance of 1989 and 1990 provided sufficient impetus toward fundamental economic restructuring, and it is unlikely that further economic pain can speed the process. Undeniably, the Gorbachev leadership has taken a long time to come to the realization that perestroika must be a radical process. Apparently buffeted by events rather than driven by a grand plan, perestroika has moved progressively through the stages of acceleration, intensification, resource reallocation, and piece-meal structural change. Intensive debate continued through 1990 on which of several reform plans should be adopted, with sharp divisions appearing not only along ideological lines but also on territorial and political lines, primarily between the all-Union government and the leadership of the Rus-sian Republic. Nonetheless, it can generally be said that 1990 ushered in a qualitatively new commitment to radical reform, and that a broad cross-section of the leadership now accepts the fact that the central apparatus is the chief villain, and that some form of a market economy is the only salvation.

To be sure, the specifics and timetable of the transition are still uncertain. The central leadership correctly sees that many Soviet political and economic institutions, as well as the people themselves, are unprepared to break loose from the past and enter the world of market competition, open unemploy-ment, and higher prices.[6] Moreover, there is a sharp debate in political and academic circles about the degree to which Soviet society could and should accept capitalist concepts, a principal of which is unfettered private own-ership,[7] and there is heartfelt disagreement regarding the possibilities for retaining socialist values and mechanisms.[8] Nonetheless, it is hard to see how antagonism on the part of capitalist countries at this crucial and un-certain stage can encourage the Soviet leaders and people to follow the free-market path and become more closely integrated into the world economy.

Constitutional separation of powers. This term identifies a particular aspect of political reform that has dramatically arisen in the Soviet Union in the wake of the East European revolutions of 1989. As recently as 1988, it seemed a far-fetched notion that the Soviet Union could soon move to a constitutional system of separation of powers in which the government, rather than the Communist Party, was paramount.[9] By early 1990, however, an executive presidency, including a functioning cabinet, had been created, and the legislative branch was beginning to assert itself in domestic and political affairs.[10] The contemporaneous repudiation of the constitutional guarantee of the Communist Party's pre-eminent role in society (and its monopoly of political power) cemented this shift of national leadership in favor of the government.

Notwithstanding qualms about the extraordinary powers invested in the president, Western governments warmly welcomed this transition, as well they might. A system of governmental checks and balances, together with a vigorous and independent press, have been among the traditional touchstones of Western political values.

At first glance, it would not appear that this central aspect of Soviet political life could be much influenced by the degree of Western economic activity in the Soviet Union. Indeed, the link is indirect, but it is not insignificant. Westerners doing business in the Soviet Union have been vocal in their unhappiness with the implementation of promising new commercial legislation. In particular, they have complained loudly about the common practice of Soviet administrative agencies (ministries, state committees, local or regional governmental bodies) to substantially alter legislation for their own purposes by means of promulgating restrictive regulations or orders.[11] This contrasts with the Western model, under which agencies simply implement laws or fill in the blanks in a manner consistent with the original legislative intent. Moreover, Western judiciaries and administrative review bodies have the power and expertise necessary to identify administrative transgressions and order that they be revoked, and citizens or corporations have the right (with appropriate restrictions) to hold the administrative agency accountable before the courts. This crucial layer of judicial or administrative review, and easy public access to it, are at a very early stage of development in the Soviet Union.

Western business people, as well as Western academics and consultants, are gaining the attention of Soviet leaders anxious to identify and eliminate the obstacles that have frustrated the implementation of progressive legislation. In addition, Soviet leaders are visiting the West with increasing frequency, often in the context of business discussions, and coming back with lasting impressions about the balance between the legislative and executive (administrative) branches of Western governments and the role of the judiciary in enforcing that balance.[12] Although many of the principles involved seem ordinary to Westerners and tend to be taken for granted, they are not at all obvious in the Soviet context and face strong opposition from the administrative bureaucracies. Expanded and sustained contacts with Western business people both in the Soviet Union and abroad are sure to have an influence on the Soviet debate over the division of powers within a newly powerful government.

Economic pluralism. The call for decentralization as the cornerstone of structural economic reform has been joined by increasing demands for denationalization (*razgosudarstylenie* is more literally translated as "de-state-ification"), meaning transfer of ownership over the means of production and associated resources from the state to joint stock companies, employee groups and other lease holders, cooperatives, and even private owners.[13] A third related component of economic restructuring is the withdrawal of the Communist Party from supervision of the workings of ministries, enterprises, and other economic units. Taken together, these three components promise a basic change in the locus of economic power in the Soviet Union—away from central government and party bureaucrats to a multitude of self-directed associations and individuals.

However, this promise is a long way from realization. There is little market infrastructure in place to support tens of thousands of independent economic units; allocation of supplies and distribution of goods is still largely controlled from the center, and working outside this system can be very difficult, time consuming, and expensive, as managers of cooperatives and joint ventures can attest. In addition, decentralization that has occurred at the all-Union level has often stopped at the regional or local level, where officials are gathering under their own control the assets released higher up.[14] Whether these officials will provide vital resources (buildings, utilities, or production inputs) to independent businesses, or allow others within their jurisdiction to provide them, is much in doubt. Moreover, although Soviet citizens appear receptive to the idea of a greatly diversified economic base and the competition it would engender,[15] they are ambivalent about becoming personally involved as entrepreneurs,[16] and, in any event, very few have any training or experience in the rudiments of running a business under market conditions.

It is very much consistent with Western interests to do whatever is possible to encourage decentralization, denationalization, and the full retreat of the Communist Party from direct involvement in economic affairs. As long as the central government or party controls economic power, there is a possibility of retreat from democratization and the other aspects of political pluralism. But if economic power eventually devolves on tens or hundreds of thousands of independent managers and entrepreneurs across the country, they (together with trade and professional associations, environmental and other public interest groups, an independent media, and others) will constitute a strong counterbalance to residual centripetal forces. Moreover, the emergence of widespread, independent commercial relations will require the development of commercial law to clearly define the rights and responsibilities of all participants and to provide recourse and remedies in case of failed responsibilities. A strong commercial law in the Soviet Union, buttressed by a judiciary capable of enforcing it, will replace the "telephone right" that has held sway in Soviet society.

Over time, the result of all these factors will be a far more balanced society in which domestic and foreign policy must be reached relatively openly through some form of large-group decision making and in which the state will be accountable to public opinion for its policies. This is not to guarantee that a democratized Soviet Union would not nevertheless embark on expansionist foreign policies or transgress human rights domestically or abroad. The tarnished record of Western liberal democracies amply demonstrates the potential in this regard. However, it is less likely that such turns will be taken suddenly and without an opportunity for alternative paths to be considered. It is also for the better to continue the transition from the traditional closed and tightly held Soviet decision-making process to one that is more transparent to the Soviet people and the world.

If one assumes, then, that economic pluralism is an important factor in achieving political pluralism in the Soviet Union, and that this result would be highly desirable for the West (as well as the Soviet Union), the more difficult question remains of how the West can help the Soviets overcome the obstacles noted above to achieving economic pluralism. One obvious mechanism is the training of managers, officials, and others in the ways of the market system. A number of joint ventures have developed in this area, and there are also management training programs established with the backing of the Soviet and Western governments, such as the one involving Germany. (There is actually no compelling need to style most of these training programs as joint ventures; they could as easily be conducted under a simple contractual arrangement between Soviet and Western institutes or businesses.) One of the problems of this approach, however, is that there is a world of difference between operating an efficient business in the West and operating an efficient enterprise, cooperative, or joint venture in the Soviet Union. The economic structures are entirely different, and thus techniques appropriate for one may be useless in the other.

A more direct approach is simply to encourage the development of Soviet-Western joint ventures in manufacturing, retail, service, and other sectors.[17] One of the main strengths of joint ventures (as compared to direct sales, licensing, turnkey arrangements, and so on) is that they bring Western managers and workers in close and sustained contact with their Soviet counterparts, thus vastly increasing the opportunities for transfer of skills and of management know-how. Just as important, a Western joint venture manager working in the Soviet Union must learn how to adapt his or her training and experience to suit Soviet reality, with the Soviet partner in most cases being the principal source of instruction in this regard. The result is a cooperative learning process in a real world environment—a good vehicle for bridging the gap between the two economic worlds.[18]

Ironically, this potential for a transfer of know-how is seen by Western officials, particularly those in the United States, as a difficult form of technology transfer to control under existing export control legislation and Coordinating Committee on Multilateral Export Controls (COCOM) practice, and one that is potentially inimical to Western interests.[19] There is some basis for this concern. The transfer of technical data, of which management know-how can be considered a subset, is among the most problematic area of export control policy. It is much harder to measure, assess, and keep track of the transfer of information, particularly in oral form, as is often the case with respect to management know-how, than to impose similar controls over materials, products, or licensed technology. Moreover, basic information about how to manage a system may be far more valuable than achieving access to pieces of machinery or technology that make the system work.[20]

Nevertheless, it makes little sense to lump all kinds of know-how transfer together in assessing risks to Western security. Few in the West would advise lifting barriers to the acquisition by the Soviet Union of Western technology and know-how that could legitimately be seen as weakening Western defenses. At the same time, it must be appreciated that other kinds of transfers—those that help Soviet managers think for themselves, build economically viable and independent businesses, and trade successfully with the West—can be good both for the West and the Soviet Union. Of course, there will be difficult lines to draw and judgments to make in some cases. But the vast majority of joint ventures clearly provide more in the way of inculcating free-market ideas and practices than of supplying militarily sensitive technology or information. Hopefully, the significant improvement in Soviet relations with the Western world—given particular impetus by the fact that the Soviet leadership lived up to its noninterference principle and other aspects of the "new ways of thinking" in the context of Eastern Europe—will continue to reduce the scope of militarily sensitive transfers and thus simplify the line drawing.

Policy Goal 2: Reduce the Military Threat to the West

Defense conversion. The effort of the Soviet Union to break out of the economic straitjacket of the centrally planned economy is frustrated by several contradictions: One is that it is extremely difficult to establish a free-market economy under conditions of acute shortages (of quality as well as quantity) and lack of competition among producers. At the same time, it is difficult to redress these shortages and break the monopoly position of producers without the benefit of market mechanisms. In a search for ways to escape this contradiction, Gorbachev has forced a process of converting some defense industries to the production of consumer goods.[21] The three principal goals in this regard would appear to be to improve the quality of consumer products (on the assumption that the historically higher-quality military production can be transferred to the civilian side), to increase the number of facilities producing those goods and thus engender competition (resulting eventually in better quality as well as larger quantity, lower prices, and greater attention to consumer demand),[22] and to help lift the burden of defense spending that contributes to the critical budget deficit problem and thus to inflation and shortages.[23]

From the Western perspective, a fourth goal of defense conversion (perhaps better described as an indirect consequence) is of at least equal interest—the demilitarization of Soviet society. This is a process that has encountered some resistance from the Soviet defense establishment—a reaction that for bureaucratic reasons would be expected under normal times and is substantially exacerbated by the enormous shock of the disintegration of the Warsaw Pact, the tension inherent in the need for Soviet armed forces to maintain domestic peace and be prepared for armed insurrection in some republics, the alarming rise in draft resistance and desertion engendered by separatist movements in the republics and generally lower esteem for the military, and low morale among officers and soldiers due to problems that their colleagues have faced in finding housing and employment after release from duty.

It is obviously in Western interests to see the process of Soviet defense conversion succeed and grow. In the political-military—as contrasted with the economic—realm, Western behavior can clearly have an impact. Continued good East-West political relations justifies what some in the Soviet Union see as a gamble by the Soviet leadership with the country's defenses in an attempt to compensate for blunders in the economic realm. On the other hand, any reversal in the perception of the West as relatively non-threatening to Soviet security interests could produce enough additional anxiety among conservatives and the military establishment to create a serious problem for the reformist political leadership and halt or reverse the conversion of defense industries.

The prospects for influencing defense conversion by economic means are more problematic. A potential mechanism, and one that is quite direct, is for Western governments to encourage the practice of creating joint ventures between foreign firms and defense industry enterprises.[24] As new mechanisms for foreign investment become available—for example, foreign stock ownership in purely Soviet enterprises—they can be applied to the same end. However, there are both positive and negative factors that must be considered.

On the positive side, defense-industry enterprises (or those formerly associated with the defense industry) are sometimes involved in higher technology activities and employ a work force with above average skills in science and technology. The expectations of the enterprise management and work force with respect to meeting quality standards may also be higher than average. Thus, the prospects for successful joint ventures—ones that can be run efficiently, and produce goods of value on the world market—may be enhanced. In addition, some government bodies have targeted defense conversion as a means for building local industry and services and for attracting foreign capital. For example, the government of Moscow in 1989 established a development fund, one purpose of which is to promote defense conversion projects involving the large number of defense industry enterprises in the area, some of which have been transferred to the city's control as a consequence of decentralization. Projects involving Western participation are all the more attractive as they present possibilities for earning hard currency, acquiring new technology, travel and training in the West, and all the other benefits usually ascribed to East-West joint ventures.[25]

On the negative side, the small number of joint ventures actually operating in the Soviet Union after more than three years of effort (according to figures released by the State Committee on Statistics, Goskomstat, 541 out of 1,754 joint ventures registered through the first half of 1990 were actually operating, and an additional 162 were paying their staff although not producing goods or services) attests to the marginal impact that joint ventures can be expected to have—absent a concerted effort by Western governments to encourage them—when considered against the complexity of restructuring the Soviet defense industry and the economy in general. In addition, Western qualms about the transfer of militarily useful technology are not likely to be lessened by the connection of the Soviet partner to the Soviet defense establishment. In particular, traditional concerns about high-tech joint ventures are likely to increase as a result of the apparent shift of emphasis by Soviet defense planners toward greater reliance on technology and modernization in response to the dwindling size of Soviet—and, more dramatically, Warsaw Pact—forces. The resulting reorganization of such bodies as the Ministry of Communications and the State Committee for Computer Technology and Information Science into the military-industrial complex in 1989 may cause additional concern for Western governments with respect to commercial transactions between those entities and Western companies.[26]

Rather than adopt sweeping generalizations about the desirability of joint ventures (or other Western investment or participation) in Soviet defense industries, line drawing based on the technology involved in each joint venture is again called for. The issue of export control must also be placed in the context of historic change in Europe, not only in Eastern Europe, but also in the process of West European economic unification. In particular, German reunification adds a new meaning to East-West technology transfer. In the longer term, the inevitably closer ties between the European Community (EC) and the more advanced East European states, and the continuing strong trade relationship of those states with the Soviet Union, will force a narrowing of export control regulation in order to focus only on the most crucial commodities and technologies. The more active involvement of Western Europe will also require that the United States keep pace. Failure to do so will only result in losing business to Western Europe with no appreciable accretion to U.S. security interests.[27]

Arms control and disarmament. Western economic activity in the Soviet Union also has some bearing on the disarmament process and thus on Western security interests. It was noted above that the domestic political value to the Soviet leadership of arms control agreements has diminished since the conclusion of the treaty on intermediate-range nuclear forces in Europe because of the growing inward focus of Soviet society. However, the linkage in the opposite direction has greater continuing force. Economic success and consequently enhanced political authority at home would free the Soviet leadership to achieve more in the disarmament realm, consistent, of course, with Soviet political-military objectives.

Specifically, a greater measure of economic success would strengthen the prospects for disarmament negotiations by means of at least two mechanisms: First, the Soviet central leadership in early 1990 was apparently severely distracted by domestic problems (many of which had economic underpinnings) and thus could not respond to Western disarmament initiatives as quickly or as positively as it had previously. Relief on the economic side would presumably provide an extra measure of time and confidence for addressing the disarmament issues. Second, economic problems provided powerful political fuel for conservative opponents and critics of reform, including those in the military, and may have required a hardening of position by the Soviet leadership in 1990 on disarmament questions to protect itself against this conservative force.[28] It follows that a reduction in the Soviet Union's economic problems—to a point at which serious reform of the economic structure could be handled in a noncrisis environment—would translate into a strengthening of the leadership's political position and thus allow it greater latitude in pursuing disarmament negotiations.

But even assuming that these conclusions are valid in principle, the reality is that there are severe limits on the impact that Western economic cooperation can have in the near term on Soviet economic problems. Nonetheless, special considerations apply in this context. For one thing, the process of arms control and disarmament is a long-term one. The transition from a military confrontation in Europe to some form of political and economic cooperation there has progressed far more rapidly than anyone had thought possible, but a complete transition to a security system based on law and on economic integration will take a great deal of additional effort and time. Moreover, it may be decades before strategic nuclear disarmament has largely been achieved. A growing Western commitment to Soviet prosperity during this period cannot help but support those in the Soviet Union who seek a demilitarized relationship with the West.

In addition, there is a positive feedback loop between domestic economic progress and disarmament. Reductions in the number of Soviet troops deployed (particularly outside the Soviet Union), as well as cutbacks in procurement, maintenance, and other elements of military spending, on balance improve the economic picture by reducing government spending and liberating resources. If Western economic assistance can have any positive impact at all on perestroika, perhaps over a period of five to ten years or more, then this may help set in motion a self-reinforcing trend in which economic confidence begets the political confidence to make further disarmament concessions, allowing reductions in military outlays, and so on. In the meantime, Westerners may be able to provide valuable advice on how to redeploy liberated resources to further the development of a market economy.

Viewed from the negative side, Western attempts to hinder Soviet economic development—or, more realistically, a merely halfhearted policy of cooperation—would likely complicate efforts to obtain the assistance of the Soviet Union in developing a secure economic system in Eastern Europe.[29] A stable economic system is probably a prerequisite for obtaining a broad new security arrangement and, in any event, is necessary for the long-term stability of any such arrangement.

Policy Goal 3: Support Democratization in Eastern Europe

President Vaclav Havel advised the U.S. Congress soon after his election that the most important thing that the United States could do for Czechoslovakia, and for freedom in Eastern Europe generally, would be to help the Soviet Union move toward pluralism and a market economy.[30] As strange as this suggestion first appears, particularly coming from a man who had been jailed for his defiance of communist rule, there is substantial merit to it. The main concern is not that the Soviet Union will revert to the Brezhnev doctrine, which has been convincingly renounced by the Gorbachev regime and could not be revived without catastrophic consequences. Rather, the issue is one of economic viability in Eastern Europe and the recognition that, for all the interest in revived trade with the West, the Soviet Union will continue to play a crucial role in East European economics for the foreseeable future.

That role can be constructive if the Soviet economy is itself on a firm footing, but could be a destabilizing one in the event that perestroika continues to flounder. On the positive side, the gradual disintegration of the Council for Mutual Economic Assistance (CMEA) as a trade organ among the Soviet Union and East European states marks an inevitable abandonment of international administrative economic mechanisms in favor of direct bargaining between enterprises in a widening market based on world prices and using free convertible (hard) currency. If the development of the Soviet economy with respect to foreign trade proceeds at or near the same rate as that of the more industrialized East European states (not including the formerly socialist part of a reunited Germany), then the Soviet Union will provide a crucial market for East European goods before they are fully competitive on the world market and will continue to be the most important source of materials and goods to that region. Rather than the West propping up Eastern Europe by means of large subsidies and loans, the Soviet Union can assume a large responsibility and allow the West to target its resources where they will do the most good—in longer-term investments in industrial and other infrastructure.

The downside potential is also a real possibility, however. The Soviet

Union has already paid a heavy price in Eastern Europe as a result of disappointments in perestroika. Gorbachev and other Soviet leaders probably hoped that a revitalized Soviet economy (together with an enlightened foreign policy and the "new ways of thinking") would refurbish the image of the Soviet Union in Eastern Europe and create a positive force that would counter the centrifugal tendencies that were gaining momentum in the latter half of the 1980s. However, the new ways of thinking helped Eastern Europe to distance itself from the Soviet Union before Soviet domestic economic reform could exert any positive influence. The result is a nascent "de-Sovietization" of Eastern Europe in which pre-existing preferences for trading with the West are being accelerated. In one respect, this trend has an advantage for the Soviet Union since it would provide the East European states with increased hard currency earnings to pay for Soviet oil and other energy resources.[31] In all other respects, however, the gradual disengagement of Eastern Europe from trade relations with the Soviet Union would deal another serious blow to perestroika.[32] Ultimately, Soviet economic failure could well lead to a conservative backlash in the Soviet Union and increased tension, if not outright hostility, with respect to westward-looking Eastern Europe.

It is reasonable for the West to take a special economic interest in the East European states, because most of them are further along the road of democratization and even economic restructuring than the Soviet Union, and their much smaller economies make it more likely that Western assistance can have an impact. However, in view of the relationships discussed above, it is inconsistent for the West to seek increased freedom and independence for Eastern Europe through an aggressive policy of economic cooperation while, at the same time, taking a relatively passive attitude toward economic cooperation with the Soviet Union.

Policy Goal 4: Economic Self-Interest

Because of the severe economic (as well as social) difficulties faced by the Soviet Union at the start of this decade, there has been a tendency to view economic cooperation as a one-way street in which the benefits flow to the East from the West. However, this is by no means a universal perception. Many Western business people take a long view and are seeking to establish relationships that will have solidified by the time the ruble is a convertible currency and the administrative obstacles to trade have been abolished. This point need not be belabored, as the hope of business people to establish a foothold in what is often called "the largest untapped market in the world" has been the primary generator of joint ventures, trade exhibitions, and a number of other highly publicized economic undertakings. It is worth noting, however, that Western governments also are taking this long view.

In particular, Germany took an early lead in pursuing government policies that somewhat cushion the business risk and enhance the prospects of developing long-term business relationships. In the former category are such measures as effectively underwriting political risk insurance and encouraging certain forms of credit arrangements.[33] In the latter category is a program in which the German government provides a modest amount of financial support to encourage Soviet managers to come to Germany to attend training sessions and visit firms. The value to the German business participants of establishing relationships with important Soviet figures is far greater than the cost of the program to themselves or to the government.

A number of German firms also have seen the Soviet market as important to their immediate, as well as long-term, financial and competitive position. Faced with stiff international competition and a saturated market, German machine-tool makers, for example, have found ways to lower costs and introduce competitive products by using components made by Soviet-German joint ventures.[34] To an extent, such arrangements are facilitated by the deeper economic cooperation with and, as compared with the United States in particular, the closer geographic proximity of Germany to, the Soviet Union. More generally, however, the unambiguously supportive policies of the West German (and now German) government have played an important role in allowing German firms to seek and establish profitable contacts in the Soviet Union.

The U.S. government has been among the least supportive of the Western states in this regard, for a number of well-known reasons, including its historical wariness of intervention in support of business, its principal responsibility for offsetting Soviet military power during the Cold War, and its sensitivity to human rights abuses in the Soviet Union. Now that the Cold War has been declared to be over, and glasnost and democratization have fundamentally altered Soviet society, the U.S. government is free to consider other aspects of the relationship with the Soviet Union. One possibility is that U.S. exports to the Soviet Union will someday play a role in easing what may be a long-term balance of trade problem for the United States. A not incidental corollary is that if and when the Soviet Union becomes an important market for U.S. goods and vice versa, there will be a real measure of increased security for both sides. Just as the United States and Japan are careful of upsetting what is a crucial economic relationship for both sides, the United States and the Soviet Union would likely think twice before jeopardizing important economic relationships, not to mention destroying a market in the most direct way possible—by nuclear attack.

IMPLEMENTING WESTERN POLICY

The preceding discussion has identified a number of areas in which Western-Soviet economic cooperation can contribute to attaining Western policy goals. Specifically, Western governments and business people may, in limited but not insignificant ways:

- enhance the constitutional separation of powers in the Soviet Union by helping to identify the need and means for effective judicial review of administrative and executive actions affecting commerce;
- encourage decentralization, denationalization, and the withdrawal of the Communist party from direct involvement in commerce by helping Soviet managers to understand and utilize (within the specific conditions of the Soviet market) formerly alien practices such as pricing, marketing, effectively motivating workers, and so forth, and by assisting in the conceptualization, drafting, and implementing of commercial law;
- strengthen the process of defense conversion now underway in the Soviet Union by actively pursuing the creation of joint ventures and other ties between Western firms and Soviet firms within the defense conversion program (with due regard to real problems of export control); and
- develop a long-term plan for economic cooperation that will help to gradually move Soviet society from a crisis state to one that is economically and politically stable, thus alleviating the domestic political pressures and distractions now endured by the Soviet leadership and thereby indirectly contributing to progress in international relations, including arms control and disarmament; opening the way for normal relations between the Soviet Union and Eastern Europe to the degree this is mutually advantageous; and cultivating a future market for Western goods and a source of supply for Western industry and consumers.

In all of these instances, however, the form of economic cooperation is important. New forms, such as joint ventures, wholly owned subsidiaries of foreign corporations in the Soviet Union, special economic zones, and direct investment through purchase of stock, are in various stages of discussion and implementation. Moreover, intergovernmental agreements and international economic and financial mechanisms may also play a major role in the development of the Soviet economy and its emergence into the world market.[35] It is not possible to predict how these approaches may be combined and applied to best effect, but it is useful to dispel false impressions about some forms of economic cooperation and to emphasize those with the most promise.

One proposal that is often discussed, because it is direct and holds out the hope of immediate results, is to provide massive infusions of Western consumer goods into the Soviet economy. Unfortunately, this is not a fruitful approach, whether conceived of in terms of Western largess or Soviet purchases.

The problems of the Soviet economy are so large that purchases of foreign goods sufficient to satisfy wholesale and retail needs would be prohibitively expensive for the Soviet Union and too costly for Western governments or international organizations to undertake as a matter of foreign aid under present political conditions. In any event, the effects of such purchases or gifts on the current stock of excess money would not address the underlying reasons for the continuing accumulation of excess money—principally the budget deficit and the excessive growth in Soviet wages.[36] In the absence of independent internal restructuring of the Soviet economy to address these two problems, the effect of Western imports would be to treat the symptom and not the disease—that is, current money stocks would be reduced, but the flow would continue unabated. While there is surely a benefit in treating symptoms, particularly when the patient is in great distress, the risks are that the costs will be onerous or that temporary relief will mask the need for drastic treatment.

The chair of the USSR State Committee on Statistics, Vadim Kirichenko, has stated that unsatisfied consumer demand reached 165 billion rubles (other estimates go as high as 500 billion rubles) in 1989,[37] and the deputy chair of the Supreme Soviet Commission on Economic Reform, Pavel Bunich, has estimated that there are five rubles in the hands of Soviet citizens for every one ruble's worth of retail goods.[38] This disparity exists despite an increase in 1989 of 4.8 percent in the gross output of consumer goods— one of the very few positive elements in that year's economic performance— and the purchase of hundreds of millions of dollars of foreign consumer goods and inputs.[39] Referring to the rate of increase in monetary income of the population and enterprises during the first eleven months of 1989, Deputy Minister Leonid Abalkin warned that "no increase in the output of consumer goods or growth in services can cover [such growth]—not in a year or any other period."[40] In conjunction with the enormous monetary overhang, the continued excessive growth of wages suggests that even massive imports of Western goods would quickly disappear from store shelves and would more likely lead to bitter recriminations over who received the goods and who did not than to any measure of long-term consumer satisfaction.

A related consideration would be that the foreign hard currency debt that financed imports would add to an already burgeoning problem for the Soviet Union: its net debt has been estimated to have risen from $15.7 billion in 1985 to $35.7 billion in 1989.[41] Anticipated reductions in the sale of oil (the Soviet Union's principal hard currency earner) over at least the first half of the 1990s, as well as other negative factors, make large-scale financed consumer imports a risky proposition in terms of credit rating and debt service, and also make direct purchases for hard currency a painful alternative in terms of foregone investment in machinery and other desirable industrial imports.[42]

These realities do not mean, however, that Western economic cooperation must play an insignificant role in keeping the Soviet Union moving toward a stable market economy. The key is to identify ways in which Western involvement can be leveraged. The best mechanism in this regard is private investment by Western firms founded on a supportive structure of intergovernmental cooperation. There are two approaches in particular by which this partnership can be especially effective.

Encourage trade and investment in key areas. Rather than diffusing the impact of Western imports, encouragement of commerce in particular areas can produce results for Soviet society out of proportion to the initial investment.[43] For example, a combination of intergovernmental cooperation and private initiative has resulted in a clearinghouse for information about the food processing industry that is likely to stimulate trade and investment in that area without governmental expenditures, subsidies, or special credits.[44] The leverage is twofold: First, modest efforts to help U.S. suppliers and Soviet buyers find each other should significantly reduce the substantial overhead in time, money, and risk that individual companies have experienced in attempting to conclude agreements in the area of food processing.[45] Second, food processing equipment sold to Soviet enterprises and farms may not only result in higher quality goods but also, in some cases, will prevent or retard the spoilage rampant in Soviet agricultural production and distribution. To the extent that such extra production (or, rather, lower spoilage) is realized, the hard currency expense of the initial procurement can be offset by sales of the food products for hard currency—the commonly used "buy-back" variant of countertrade. The director of the Institute for the USA and Canada of the USSR Academy of Sciences, Georgiy Arbatov, has documented in some detail the efficiencies that could be introduced in such areas as grain and other foodstuffs were diverted into investment in joint ventures.[46]

There are a number of other areas—for example, dock loading and unloading equipment, packaging, building materials, construction equipment, communication equipment, computer networks to facilitate banking functions, and commercialization of Soviet scientific and technological developments—in which initial investments can be expected to be repaid many fold. Moreover, many of these areas do not involve high technologies of concern with respect to export control.

It must be recognized, however, that there are systemic limits to the impact of Western investment, even when key sectors are carefully identified for their leverage potential. One such limit is the inconvertibility of the ruble. (The other principal limits are the lack of wholesale, retail, and capital markets.) While the achievement of full ruble convertibility ultimately depends on restructuring the Soviet economy so that it is capable of producing competitive goods in the world market, the Soviet Union, even in the short term, does have the means to supercharge the process of Western investment and accelerate its impact by instituting limited forms of convertibility. What is required is for the Soviets to make available for repatriation by Western firms a portion of the billions of dollars of natural resources in the Soviet Union that are currently underutilized because of technological or other shortcomings in the Soviet economy.

Both Western and Soviet analysts have recognized, for example, the role that the oil resources in the Caspian Sea fields and other areas could play in elevating Western investment to a qualitatively new level. In particular, John Hardt cogently argues that an intergovernmental direct investment agreement, together of course with the backing of Soviet officials and industry personnel, could provide additional incentives for U.S. companies to make the kind of very large, long-term investments needed to modernize the Soviet petroleum chain from exploration to refining.[47]

Hardt roughly estimates the increased value of production to the Soviet partner from Western investment in major Soviet oil fields—a margin that would not be attainable by the Soviets alone—at tens of billions of dollars over a decade. The Soviet government could make a portion of this sum available for the financing of other joint ventures either by underwriting repatriation guarantees or by means of the consortium model, in which hard currency earned by one member of the consortium is pooled for the benefit of other members. In effect, the Soviet partner (or the Western partner if it so agreed) in the oil venture would generate hard currency to allow repatriation of profits by other ventures in the consortium that generate ruble, but not hard currency, profits.

The only obstacle to releasing these petrodollars for the purpose of priming joint ventures is political, not economic, in nature. In fact, since the petrodollars would not be readily or soon available to the Soviets without Western investment, economics alone would counsel rapid exploitation of this resource. However, the Soviets have been extremely sensitive to the idea of foreign exploitation, in the negative sense, of their natural resources—a notion that is now being hotly debated.[48] It appears that the pressing economic need is winning over the political resistance, if one can judge from the signing in June 1990 of a letter of intent between the Chevron Corporation and the USSR Ministry of the Oil and Gas Complex for studying the feasibility of joint development of the giant Tengiz field on the northeast shore of the Caspian Sea, as well as the nearby Korolev field. According to President Gorbachev, the project would ultimately result in an investment of about 10 billion rubles in the Soviet Union. Soviet experts say that the Tengiz field has potential petroleum reserves of over 25 billion barrels. This proposed project follows the signing in May 1990 of another major oil exploration and production agreement with the French oil company Société Nationale Elf Aquitaine.[49] Developing new oil resources with Western help seems highly preferable to alternatives such as relying on Western credits and depleting existing gold and oil reserves, as has been proposed by Stanislav Shatalin, a member of the USSR Presidential Council.[50]

Oil is not the only natural resource that the Soviet Union could release for the generation of hard currency and the encouragement of Western investment. Another major, and currently underutilized, resource is timber and timber products. One Soviet economist and business person, noting that the Soviet Union possesses one-fourth of the world's timber reserves, refers to this resource as the Soviet Union's trump card on the world market. Yet another possibility, raised by Hardt, is for the Soviets to provide long-term leases to U.S. agribusiness for the development of prime arable land in the Ukraine and other areas.[51] Political and social resistance to this idea could be expected to be particularly strong, but there are undoubtedly ways to address Soviet concerns if the benefits to Soviet citizens are clear enough.

Encourage joint ventures. Aside from their merits as one means of directing investment into key areas of the Soviet economy, joint ventures generally merit support because of their intrinsic leveraging capabilities. There are several aspects to this leverage: First, they are cost effective for the Soviet side since the Western partner provides substantial investments of capital as well as technological and managerial know-how. The Soviet side often provides land, buildings, a work force, and other assets that are relatively unproductive in the Soviet economy. Second, joint ventures introduce, again at low cost, an essential element of competition at world market standards into the domestic Soviet economy. The alternative means of introducing such competition—by importing foreign products—requires either the immediate or deferred expenditure of hard currency (or convertible goods) by Soviet authorities or enterprises.

Third, joint ventures often produce their own ripple effect. For example, the McDonald's restaurant joint venture in Moscow initially relied on imports of Western furniture and equipment, but the Western partner hopes to encourage the creation of joint ventures in the Soviet Union to provide these and other supplies.[52] This ripple effect need not even be the result of planned expansion. As the experience in China demonstrates, the example of utilizing new technology and management systems set by a joint venture can spread to state enterprises with which it comes into contact.[53] Fourth, joint ventures can be a useful conduit for bringing Western expertise in "middlemen" activities into the Soviet Union. The Soviet consumer might benefit more from a few well-placed and well-motivated food collection and distribution ventures than from a large investment in new farm machinery. As already noted, however, many Soviet officials do not look with favor on such contributions. However, these attitudes may change as the need for market mechanisms, and the attendant need for intermediary functions, become clearer.

The major portion of the responsibility for making investments in the Soviet Union attractive for foreign firms rests with the Soviet government. However, it is important for Western governments to encourage this process by both removing obstacles and taking positive steps where possible. Since late 1989, the U.S. government has been searching its way toward a new policy of support for economic restructuring in the Soviet Union.[54] A milestone was President Bush's decision to sign a trade agreement with the Soviet Union at the June 1990 summit meeting with President Gorbachev in Washington. This action was taken despite substantial opposition in the U.S. Congress to any economic support until the economic blockade of Lithuania had been lifted and other aspects of the Baltic republics' separatist movements had been addressed. Bush's action thus demonstrated an awareness of the importance to U.S.-Soviet relations and U.S. interests of maintaining a momentum in economic cooperation, and it was a gesture that was no doubt appreciated by President Gorbachev in a time of great economic and political stress at home.[55]

Among the tangible benefits of the trade agreement and related measures ultimately could be the granting of most-favored-nation (lowest tariff) status to the Soviet Union, resolution of the lend-lease debt of the Soviet Union leading to a lifting of barriers to Soviet borrowing in the U.S. bond market, access to credits from the U.S. Export-Import Bank, and eligibility for insurance from the U.S. Overseas Private Insurance Corporation. Also of future potential significance was the decision of the United States to reverse its initial opposition to participation by the Soviet Union in the European Bank for Reconstruction and Development, which was established by a treaty among forty nations in May 1990. This is the first international market-oriented financial institution to which the Soviet Union has become a member, and it may lead in the future to the accelerated development of entrepreneurialism and a private sector in the Soviet Union.[56]

Yet another contribution to closer East-West economic cooperation was the decision of COCOM in June 1990 to remove controls on 30 of 116 restricted categories of exports to Warsaw Pact countries, with another 8 categories under consideration for removal from control lists within a few months. A U.S. official estimated that this action would eliminate barriers to the export of $45 billion worth of U.S. exports and would reduce the licensing caseload of COCOM by 50 percent. Among the commodities decontrolled are certain types of machine tools, computers, and telecommunications equipment—areas that account for a majority of COCOM licensing applications.[57]

These and future actions—such as an investment agreement under negotiation between the United States and the Soviet Union—constitute important signals to Western businesses that they will not be undercut and may expect some support in their efforts to break into the Soviet market. These efforts are difficult enough in the current Soviet economic climate. Intergovernmental cooperation can supply the crucial extra incentive for a Western firm to make the effort to overcome the difficulties and establish a profitable business in the Soviet Union.

NOTES

The author thanks Heidi Kroll and Mark Garrison for their helpful comments on this chapter.

1. See, for example, Nikolai Ryzhkov, "Following the Course of Scientific and Technical Progress," *Izvestiya* (18 December 1985): 1.

2. The questions of whether Western economic cooperation can make an impact on perestroika, and how long a period will be required for any such effects to be felt, are discussed in the last section of this chapter.

3. See Alan Sherr, *The Other Side of Arms Control: Soviet Objectives in the Gorbachev Era* (Boston: Unwin Hyman, 1988), 1–48, 137–72.

4. There may be a tendency for bad news to multiply, as evidenced by an opinion poll that showed that 82 percent of the sampled Moscow population thought that economic conditions in general were deteriorating, although only 33 percent said that their own position had worsened. See "The Policy is Correct but Change Should Be Faster," *Moscow News* 2 (1990). Flight from the ruble reached acute proportions by 1990, and recurrent rumors of internal currency devaluations have rattled the citizenry, feeding a growing crisis in confidence between the population and the state. See A. Kamanov, "Loading Up Train Cars with Money?" *Komsomolskaya pravda* (23 February 1990): 1.

5. For an early exposition of the merits of economic pressure, see Henry Rowen, "Living with a Sick Bear," *National Interest* (Winter 1986): 14. Aspects of this philosophy might explain the eagerness of some U.S. political figures to use U.S.-Soviet trade relations to influence Soviet behavior. See, for example, Richard L. Berke, "Nine G.O.P. Senators Attack Bush on Lithuania," *New York Times* (28 April 1990): 4.

6. When Gorbachev assumed the post of executive president in March 1990, he said that the preceding years of disappointment and upheaval had been necessary to convince Soviet society of the need for radical change. Within a month—having assessed the dangers of strikes by oil and coal workers, the rising militancy and conservatism of some trade unions, and the antipathy of the general population to price increases and other burdens of reform—he had become convinced that crucial elements of his much-heralded radical reform package would have to be delayed because the proper basis had still not been laid. See "Excerpts from Gorbachev Speech on Presidency," *New York Times* (16 March 1990): A6; Francis X. Clines, "A Free-Market Plunge? Gorbachev's Not Ready," *New York Times* (26 April 1990): A12. Gorbachev also appeared to be paying a heavy price for his decision to assume the presidency without a general election in that there was no basis for claiming a mandate from the people as he campaigned for their support for radical reform.

7. See, for example, S. Rodin, "Several Axioms about Ownership," *Sovetskaya rossiya* (17 January 1990): 3; V. Medvedev, "Discussing the Draft CPSU Central Committee Platform...The Question of Transforming Ownership Relations," *Pravda* (18 February 1990): 2.

8. Although confidence in the Communist party is extremely low and communist ideology has all but disappeared as a force in daily life, opinion polls confirm that many socialist values retain a strong influence in Soviet society. See *Moscow News* 15 (1990): 60 percent of a sample thought that the CPSU had led the country astray and 90 percent said the party had arrested the country's development; *Moscow News* 2 (1990): only 37 percent had a positive reaction to the word "communism" while 67 percent responded positively to "socialism." This ambivalence is manifest in the implementation of key legislation and economic programs. For example,

progress toward decentralization in 1988 (including the law on cooperatives and transfer in principle to full *khozraschet*) was offset in 1989 by retrograde measures restricting cooperative activities, export of goods, foreign commercial contact, expansion of wholesale trade, and "middlemen" activities. See John Tedstrom, "The Soviet Economy: A Preliminary Glance," *Radio Liberty Research* 574/89 (16 December 1989); Philip Hanson, "Prospects for Reform: Three Key Issues in 1990," *Radio Liberty Research* 36/90 (19 January 1990); Peter Gumbel, "Wholesale Trade in USSR Remains Negligible after Five Years of Perestroika," *Wall Street Journal* (20 November 1989): A14.

9. Fyodr Burlatsky was on the cutting edge or beyond when he ventured that "it was probably wrong to have rejected the ideas of the great revolutionary democrats of the past [led by Lenin] on the separation of the legislature, the executive, and the judiciary." Fyodr Burlatsky, "On the Soviet Parliamentarianism," *Literaturnaya gazeta* (15 June 1988).

10. Indeed, the executive branch had a stake in seeing that the legislature assumed a more visible role in decision making on economic policy in order to obtain a broader mandate and spread the risk of controversial new economic policies. Thus, Deputy Minister Leonid Abalkin virtually begged the Congress of People's Deputies to "take on [the executive branch's] behalf a decision on the choice of one of three (or four) options" for radical economic reform and warned that avoiding this responsibility meant "placing the functions of the legislature into the hands of the executive." Speech by L. I. Abalkin, *Izvestiya* (14 December 1989): 9–10.

11. Among numerous possible examples is the unpublished 1989 ruling of the Ministry of Justice prohibiting joint ventures from themselves becoming partners in joint ventures, thus creating unnecessary obstacles to broadening business and developing means for repatriating profits in hard currency. The failure to publish the ruling is a common Soviet administrative practice intended to strengthen the hand of the agency and frustrate recourse.

12. This influence extends to fundamental propositions, such as the importance of legislative control over the state budget and the means for effective implementation of such control. See, for example, discussions by Soviet legislators and academics described in Elizabeth Teague, "Executive Presidency Approved," *Radio Liberty Research* 114/90 (9 March 1990): 14–16.

13. See Hanson, "Prospects for Reform." Despite ambiguities and uncertainties about how it will be implemented, and limitations on the scope of activities it effects, the law on citizens' property passed by the Supreme Soviet in March 1990 (effective July 1990) could contribute significantly to the expansion of the private sector.

14. For example, a number of industrial enterprises associated with all-Union ministries were to be shifted in 1989 and 1990 to the control of the Moscow city government rather than being leased directly to organizations of workers or transferred to cooperatives. Also, part of the thrust of regional economic (and political) autonomy is to provide republics with greater control over economic units within their jurisdiction and not necessarily to extend the sought-after independence to the work place.

15. A survey of Moscow residents disclosed that 74 percent had a positive reaction to the word *competition* with only 10 percent registering a negative feeling. See "The Policy is Correct."

16. Another opinion poll showed that 39 percent of those asked would not want

to start their own business, 23 percent had no opinion, and slightly more than 33 percent said they would be interested. As reported in Laurie Hays, "Soviet Legislators Vote to Permit Some Private Property Ownership," *Wall Street Journal* (7 March 1990): A14.

17. One of the most useful contributions that joint ventures could provide in the Soviet Union would be to develop intermediary and expediting services—for example, in the area of bringing perishable goods to market in a timely way, or helping enterprises to develop marketing and distribution strategies. Unfortunately, such "middlemen" activities are still viewed through ideological glasses in the Soviet Union, where their practitioners are more likely to be labeled as parasites or speculators than as legitimate economic contributors. Decree 203 of the USSR Council of Ministers, promulgated in March 1989, effectively barred joint ventures from intermediary activities without the prior approval of the Ministry for Foreign Economic Relations.

18. Admittedly, the mechanism is not perfect. Few joint ventures can afford to support more than a handful of Western workers (some have none at all). Western managers are often preoccupied with mundane problems and with the pressure of achieving short-term results, and the longer-term benefits of investing in training programs are neglected. Nonetheless, partners on both sides of a joint venture are inevitably subjected to an intense learning experience, and their ability to understand each other's perspective is crucial to survival and success.

19. COCOM, the Coordinating Committee on Multilateral Export Controls, is made up of the NATO countries except Iceland and including Japan and Australia.

20. For a discussion of these technology transfer issues, see Christine Westbrook and Alan B. Sherr, *Briefing Paper #3:* "U.S.-Soviet Joint Ventures and Export Control Policy" (Providence, R.I.: Center for Foreign Policy Development, Brown University, 1990).

21. See William H. Kincade and T. Keith Thomson, "Economic Conversion in the USSR: Its Role in Perestroika," *Problems of Communism* (January-February 1990): 83.

22. Assumptions about the economic merits of Soviet defense conversion are open to question, as the mechanisms that have purportedly allowed higher quality on the military side may not be transferable to the civilian sector. It is also not clear that the conversion process, as it is being implemented, will have a significant impact on the degree of competition in the Soviet Union. For an extensive analysis of this latter question, see Heidi Kroll, *Briefing Paper #4*: "Reform and Monopoly in the Soviet Economy" (Providence, R.I.: Center for Foreign Policy Development, Brown University, 1990).

23. In a bizarre confrontation that pitched several leading Soviet economists against the U.S. Central Intelligence Agency, the Soviets insisted that the agency had chronically and grossly underestimated the burden of defense on the Soviet economy both by understating the size of the defense budget and overstating the size of the economy in general. Endorsing the views of a conservative Western analyst and drawing support from a committee of the Soviet legislature, Oleg Bogomolov put Soviet military spending at close to 200 billion rubles in 1990—20 to 25 percent of GNP. See Robert Pear, "Soviet Experts Say Their Economy Is Worse Than U.S. Has Estimated," *New York Times* (24 April 1990): A14. See also Georgiy Arbatov, "And If Without Cunning?" *Ogonek* 17 (April 1990): 8.

24. One U.S.-Soviet joint venture in this category is that between Polaroid Corporation and what was formerly the Ministry of Medium Machine Building (now merged into the USSR Ministry of Atomic Energy and Industry). The joint venture assembles cameras from imported components and also works on printed circuit boards that are sold to the U.S. partner. The assembled cameras (as well as film and individual pictures) are sold for rubles through a retail outlet.

25. Interview with Alexander Gromov, deputy director, Moscow City Fund of Science and Technology (January 1990).

26. See John Tedstrom, "Managing the Conversion of the Defense Industries," *Radio Liberty Research* 75/90 (1 February 1990).

27. The U.S. Department of Defense, long a bulwark against liberalization of export control policy and practice, is adapting to the changing picture in Europe. In March 1990 it announced a new policy of leaving to the judgment of the Department of Commerce decisions on the export of certain computers and other high-tech equipment from the United States to Eastern Europe and the Soviet Union. The action was explained as "intended to assist our exporting community and improve the competitive position of U.S. industry in international trade." Reported in *International Trade Reporter* 7 (4 April 1990): 464. Similarly, the U.S. National Security Council approved a plan in October 1990 to relax COCOM controls on export of certain high-tech equipment (including mini- and supermini computers, graphic work stations, software, and some telecommunications equipment) to the Soviet Union and Eastern Europe. See Michael S. Lelyveld, "U.S. Clears New Easing of Exports to Soviets," *Journal of Commerce* (25 October 1990): 1.

28. For comments by Western analysts and officials supporting these hypotheses, see, for example, Thomas L. Friedman, "Soviet Unrest Is Seen as Peril To Arms Talks," *New York Times* (6 May 1990): 20.

29. It is evident from the outset of the "two-plus-four" talks on German reunification that one of the Soviet Union's principal objectives was to ensure that a reunited Germany would honor East Germany's trade agreements with the Soviet Union, and, furthermore, that the two countries would build on what, from the Soviet viewpoint, is a very important trade relationship. West German Foreign Minister Hans-Dietrich Genscher confirmed that his country too saw the relationship as "of primary importance." See Serge Schmemann, "Moscow Opposing a United Germany in Western Orbit," *New York Times* (6 May 1990): 1. In view of Germany's inclination toward strong economic relations with Eastern Europe and the Soviet Union, the United States and the other developed capitalist states would risk a rift with Germany and encourage neutrality if they pursued an obstructionist, or even a significantly less enthusiastic, policy. All initial indications are, however, that such a divergence of policies will not develop.

30. See Thomas L. Friedman, "Havel's 'Paradoxical' Plea: Help Soviets," *New York Times* (22 February 1990): A1.

31. Increasing hard currency receipts from energy sales to Eastern Europe is one of the few options available to the Soviet Union to forestall a credit squeeze resulting from a growing hard currency debt. See Keith Bush, "Credit Rating of Soviet Union Slips," *Radio Liberty Research* 124/90 (4 March 1990): 8–11.

32. For a useful Soviet analysis of the "alarming" trends in Eastern Europe, see Aleksey Pushkov, "In Proud Isolation? Only after Creating a Full-Blown Market Will We Be Able to Enter the 'Common European Home,' " *Izvestiya* (26 April

1990): 5. It is also noteworthy that Western firms responded enthusiastically to the 1989 revolutions in Eastern Europe, sometimes at the apparent expense of pursuing opportunities in the Soviet Union. See, for example, Craig Forman, "U.S. Firms Plunk Down Cash in East Bloc," *Wall Street Journal* (1 June 1990): A12.

33. One provision of the trade agreement signed by the Soviet Union and Germany in June 1989 appears to be supportive in this regard, but is actually counterproductive. The agreement appears to guarantee that German joint venture partners will be able to repatriate their profit, including ruble profit, in Deutschemarks. The Soviet government can only keep this promise if it is rarely invoked, otherwise it will eventually open a floodgate in which low-value rubles are exchanged for freely convertible currency. Possible defenses include setting an unrealistic exchange rate or limiting the kind of German joint ventures only to those clearly able to earn their own hard currency. Neither reaction is desirable from the German perspective. Worse still would be a Soviet renunciation of its agreement. In addition, since trade agreements with other Western countries guarantee that their citizens will get equal treatment, the conversion guarantee applicable to German firms will arguably have to be extended to all foreign joint venture participants. For a biting critique of the conversion guarantee, see Alla Glebova, "Who's To Foot the Bill?" *Moscow News* 17 (1990): 10.

34. Interviews in West Germany in May 1989, confidential by agreement.

35. The decision in May 1990 by the Bush administration to reverse the U.S. policy against Soviet observer status at the General Agreement on Tariffs and Trade (GATT) was a clear signal that the ending of the Cold War had provided the Soviet Union with a major dividend and that its participation in the world economy need only be limited by the pace of its domestic reforms.

36. Imported goods would have some salutary effect on the budget deficit because "turnover" taxes on these goods could be substantial, particularly since foreign goods can be sold at high ruble prices. However, to the extent that these ruble revenues from imported goods are financed from the national treasury by the expenditure of hard currency or the incurring of hard currency debt, this deficit reduction mechanism cannot be considered ideal.

37. See *Pravitselstvennyi vestnik* (January 1990).

38. See *Radio Free Europe/Radio Liberty Daily Report* 235 (December 1989).

39. See *PlanEcon Report* 6 (7–8) (21 February 1990); N. Dorofeyev, "You Cannot Hide Shortages behind a Plan," *Moscow Trud* (24 January 1990): 2.

40. Speech by L. I. Abalkin, *Izvestiya* (17 December 1989): 9. According to the U.S. Central Intelligence Agency and the Defense Intelligence Agency, personal money income in the Soviet Union grew by about 13 percent in 1989. See CIA and DIA, "The Soviet Economy Stumbles Badly in 1989," paper presented to the Technology and National Security Subcommittee of the Joint Economic Committee of the U.S. Congress (20 April 1990), Figure 1. Moreover, initial descriptions of the government's new economic program, unveiled May 1990, indicate that wages may be at least partially pegged to price increases, thereby addressing the political problem of containing the population's anger over price increases but perpetuating the wage spiral.

41. See Bush, "Credit Rating of Soviet Union Slips," 8–11.

42. The Soviet Union found it necessary in June 1990 to deposit large amounts of gold with Western banks as collateral for loans to respond to creditors' concerns

about hundreds of millions of dollars in late payments. See Neil Behrmann, "Soviets Deposit Gold in Western Banks as Collateral for Easing Cash Squeeze," *Wall Street Journal* (4 June 1990): A3.

43. A study of the role of direct foreign investment in China has shown that it has played a significant positive role in economic development in large part because of its concentration both sectorally and geographically. See Shen Xiaofang, "A Decade of Direct Foreign Investment in China," *Problems of Communism* (March–April 1990): 61, 65–66.

44. The food processing industry was one of five priority areas identified by the U.S. and Soviet governments in 1988 as worthy of special attention by intergovernmental working groups. See Clyde H. Farnsworth, "Cabinet Approves Effort To Widen Trade with Soviets in Five Categories," *New York Times* (7 April 1988): A1. Subsequently, the Food Industries International Trade Council was formed by U.S. business people and trade associations to respond to the need for better information about Soviet needs and U.S. food processing companies positioned to do business in the Soviet Union. The council, together with the State Commission for Food and Procurement of the USSR Council of Ministers, RSFSR State Agro-Industrial Committee (Gosagroprom), the U.S. Department of Commerce, U.S. Department of Agriculture, and others sponsored a conference in Washington in June 1990 to advance U.S. investment and trade in the Soviet food processing sector.

45. At an initial meeting, attended by this author, of the precursor to the Food Industries International Trade Council in May 1989 in McLean, Virginia, even companies that had been operating in the Soviet Union for decades complained that lack of information about current needs and difficulties in finding appropriate partners in the Soviet Union effectively prevented the development of otherwise attractive business opportunities.

46. See Interview with G. Arbatov, *Moscow Trud* (25 April 1990): 3.

47. See John P. Hardt, "Soviet Economy on the Eve of the 13th Five-Year Plan, 1991–1995," paper submitted to NATO Economic Colloquium 1990, Brussels, Belgium (4–6 April 1990), 16. For similar views from a Soviet analyst, see Igor K. Lavrovsky, "Convertible Ruble from a Petrodollar," *Socialisticheskaya industria* (8 October 1989): 2.

48. See, for example, Lavrovsky, "Convertible Ruble from a Petrodollar," 2.

49. See David J. Jefferson, "Chevron, Soviets Sign Study Pact for Oil Venture," *Wall Street Journal* (4 June 1990): A3; Robert Pear, "Chevron and Soviets To Work toward Oil Venture," *New York Times* (3 June 1990): 13.

50. See interview with Stanislav Shatalin by Francoise Lazare, *Le Monde* (14 April 1990): 21, as reported in *Foreign Broadcast Information Service, Soviet Union* (FBIS-SU) (20 April 1990): 54. Prime Minister Nikolai Ryzhkov has also indicated his support for credits as a means of avoiding a shock therapy approach and bridging the Soviet economy to a more modern stage. See Moscow World Service (28 April 1990), as reported in FBIS-SU, "Ryzhkov Rules Out 'Shock Treatment' for Economy," (30 April 1990): 67.

51. See Interview with V. Lisichkin, "Business Relations with the West: Everything Is Up for Sale, but Not Everything Is Being Bought," *Pravda* (8 May 1990): 3. See also Hardt, "Soviet Economy."

52. Interview by author with Marc A. Winer, vice-president, McDonald's Restaurants of Canada, in Moscow (January 1990).

53. This process can also be stymied, however, by the many obstacles to innovation presented by the command economy system. See Shen, "Foreign Investment in China," 63.

54. The turning point in declared policy was a speech by Secretary of State James Baker in October 1989 in which he stated that "we want perestroika to succeed" and offered to provide the Soviet Union with experts who could offer "advice and technical assistance." See Thomas L. Friedman, "U.S. Offers to Aid Gorbachev's Plan To Revamp System," *New York Times* (17 October 1989): A1.

55. Soviet Foreign Minister Eduard Shevardnadze reportedly emphasized to U.S. officials the symbolic importance to the Soviet leadership of returning from the summit with a signed trade agreement. See Walter S. Mossberg and Gerald F. Seib, "Bush, Gorbachev Fail to Settle Differences over Germany on the First Day of Summit," *Wall Street Journal* (1 June 1990): A16.

56. The bank's charter states as its purpose to "promote private and entrepreneurial initiative" in Eastern Europe, and at least 60 percent of its loans must go to the private sector. However, because of its current lack of a market economy and political considerations, the ability of the Soviet Union to obtain such loans was limited during the first three years to the amount of its capital contributions. See Steven Greenhouse, "A New Bank Plans East European Aid," *New York Times* (30 May 1990): A14.

57. See Alan Riding, "U.S. To Relax Standards on High-Tech Exports," *New York Times* (8 June 1990): A6.

Appendix

List of U.S.-Soviet Joint Ventures

Compiled from the Center for Foreign Policy Development's computerized database of joint ventures, the list contains all U.S.-Soviet joint ventures registered with the USSR Ministry of Finance as of 1 June 1990. The list is arranged chronologically by the joint venture's date of registration and includes the following information: registration number, name of the joint venture, date of registration, location of the joint venture (city and republic), initial capitalization, foreign partners and their percentage share of the initial capitalization, Soviet partners and their percentage share of the initial capitalization, and the joint venture's sphere of activity.

LIST OF ABBREVIATIONS AND TERMS

Admin.—Administration
AG—Aktien Gesellschaft (Stock Company)
Agroprombank—Agro-Industrial Bank
APK—Agro-Industrial Complex
ArSSR—Armenia
Assn.—Association
AzSSR—Azerbaijan
BMMT—Sputnik Bureau of International Youth Tourism
BSSR—Belorussia
Co.—Company
Coop.—Cooperative
Corp.—Corporation
ESSR—Estonia
EVM—Electronic Computational Machine (computer)
FTO—Foreign Trade Organization
Gosagroprom—State Committee on Agriculture Industry
Goskino—State Committee on Cinema
Goskomizdat—State Committee on Publishing
Goskomizobretenie—State Committee on Inventions and Discoveries

Goskomnefteproduct—State Committee on the Supply of Petroleum Products
Gosplan—State Committee on Planning
Gossnab—State Committee on Scientific Technical Supply
Gosstandart—State Committee on Standards
Gosstroi—State Committee on Construction
GSSR—Georgia
GUM—State Department Store
IKI—Space Research Institute
IMEMO—Institute for International Relations and World Economy
Inc.—Incorporated
Internat.—International
IPK—Institute for the Improvement of Professional Qualifications
ISKAN—Institute for the USA and Canada
Ispolkom—Executive Committee
JV—Joint Venture
KaSSR—Kazakhstan
KB—Construction Bureau
KiSSR—Kirghizia
Kolkhoz—Collective Farm
LaSSR—Latvia
LiSSR—Lithuania
Ltd.—Limited
Min.—Ministry
MISI—V. V. Kuybisheva Engineering and Construction Institute of the "Order of
    the Red Banner of Labor" in Moscow
MSSR—Moldavia
MZhK—Youth Housing Construction Cooperative
n/a—information not available
NII—Scientific Research Institute
NPO—Research-Production Association
NTTM—Scientific Technical Creative Work of Youth
OKB—Experimental Construction Bureau
PO—Production Association
Promstroibank—Industrial Construction Bank
RPO—Regional Production Association
RSFSR—Russia
SA—Societe Anonyme (Incorporated)
SFMT—San Francisco Moscow Teleport
Sovkhoz—State Farm
TaSSR—Tajikstan
TPO—Technical Production Association
TsEMI—Central Economics-Mathematics Institute
TsUM—Central Department Store
TuSSR—Turkmenia
UkSSR—Ukraine
UzSSR—Uzbekistan
VASKhNIL—All-Union "Order of Lenin" Academy of Agricultural Sciences
VDNKh—Exhibition of National Economic Achievement

VEO—All-Union Electro-technical Association
VLKSM—All-Union Lenin Communist Union of Youth
VNIIPAS—All-Union Research Institute for Applied Automated Systems
VNII—All-Union Scientific Research Institute
VNPO—All-Union Research Production Association
V/O—Foreign Trade Association
VZIPP—All-Union Correspondence Institute of the Food Industry
Zhilsotsbank—Bank for Housing, Communal Economy, and Social Development

---

| 13 | PRIS | 11/26/87 |

Location: Moscow (RSFSR)
Initial Capital: 9,950,000 rubles
Foreign Partners and %Share: (1) Asea Brown Boveri (49%)
Soviet Partners and %Share: (1) Neftekhimavtomatika NPO (51%)
Activity: Automatic control systems for petrochemical and chemical industries

---

| 21 | DIALOG | 12/29/87 |

Location: Moscow (RSFSR)
Initial Capital: 15,800,000 rubles
Foreign Partners and %Share: (1) Management Partnerships Internat. (21.8%)
Soviet Partners and %Share: (1) Kamaz PO (32.6%); (2) IKI (72%); (3) TsEMI
   (13%); (4) GDIVTs, VDNKh (2.6%); (5) Vneshtekhnika V/O (9.8%)
Activity: Computer hard- and software; distribution services

| 37 | SOVELAN AROMA | 04/12/88 |

Location: Moscow (RSFSR)
Initial Capital: 300,000 rubles
Foreign Partners and %Share: (1) Elan Internat. (20%)
Soviet Partners and %Share: (1) VNII for Sea Fisheries and Oceanography (80%)
Activity: Chemical flavors

| 46 | STERKH-AVTOMATIZATSIYA | 05/13/88 |

Location: Moscow (RSFSR)
Initial Capital: 950,000 rubles
Foreign Partners and %Share: (total share 49%) (1) Honeywell, Inc.; (2) Honeywell
   GmbH (Austria)
Soviet Partners and %Share: (1) Orgminudobreniya Trust (31%); (2) OKB Mineral
   (20%)
Activity: Control systems design; software for improved efficiency

---

| 56 | PERESTROIKA | 06/16/88 |

Location: Moscow (RSFSR)
Initial Capital: 7,500,000 rubles
Foreign Partners and %Share: (%share n/a) (1) The Worsham Group
Soviet Partners and %Share: (1) Main Admin. for Construction of Engineering
   Structures, Moscow City Council; (2) Admin. of High-Rise Buildings and Hotels,
   Moscow City Council; (3) Main Admin. for Urban Architecture and Construction,
   Moscow City Council; (4) Dialog JV
Activity: Construction and renovation of buildings

---

65   LAIKS   07/06/88

Location: Riga (LaSSR)
Initial Capital: 100,000 rubles
Foreign Partners and %Share: (1) Ralex Internat.
Soviet Partners and %Share: (1) Institute of Electronics and Computer Technology,
  LaSSR Academy of Sciences (50%); (2) Inter-Latvia V/O, LaSSR Council of
  Ministers (25%)
Activity: Scientific research; experimental engineering for computer systems

---

104   SOVAMINKO   09/21/88

Location: Moscow (RSFSR)
Initial Capital: 2,000,000 rubles
Foreign Partners and %Share: (1) Unicorn Seminars, Inc. (49%)
Soviet Partners and %Share: (1) Mir Publishing (21%); (2) Rekord Assn. (20%);
  (3) Sintez Coop. (10%)
Activity: Publishing and printing; audio-visual materials; exhibitions

---

108   INTERMEDBIO-IMB   10/10/88

Location: Moscow (RSFSR)
Initial Capital: 4,000,000 rubles
Foreign Partners and %Share: (1) Interconcepts, Inc. (49%)
Soviet Partners and %Share: (1) Oktyabr Production Trust for Chemical
  Pharmaceuticals of Leningrad (21%); (2) Universervis Coop. (30%)
Activity: Export of goods and services; computer hard- and software

---

116   INFORMPRAVO   11/01/88

Location: Moscow (RSFSR)
Initial Capital: 125,000 rubles
Foreign Partners and %Share: (total share 49%) (1) Robert A. Weaver; (2) Jakko
  Leito (Finland); (3) Simeno Finance SA (Italy)
Soviet Partners and %Share: (1) Moscow City Bar (kollegia advokatov) (26%);
  (2) Union of Scientific and Engineering Societies (25%)
Activity: Consulting; legal services

---

147   DRESSER SOVIET ENGINEERING   12/02/88

Location: Moscow (RSFSR)
Initial Capital: 375,000 rubles
Foreign Partners and %Share: (1) Dresser Industries, Inc. (40%)
Soviet Partners and %Share: (total share 60%) (1) Kazankompressormash NPO;
  (2) Bolshevik NPO; (3) StankoImport V/O; (4) Soyuzkhimexport V/O
Activity: Consulting and engineering services

---

172   SOVINTERINVEST   12/26/88

Location: Moscow (RSFSR)
Initial Capital: 4,060,000 rubles
Foreign Partners and %Share: (1) USCO Investment Enterprise (12.3%)
Soviet Partners and %Share: (total share 87.7%) (1) Primorrybprom PO; (2) Photon
  PO USSR, USSR Min. of Instrumentation Industry; (3) IMEMO, USSR Academy
  of Sciences; (4) Azot PO, Min. of Manure Production; (5) Orbita-Sevis PO, USSR
  Min. of Instrumentation Industry; (6)VZIPP, GKUzobretenie; (7) Tsentralnoe
  Agrofirm, VASKhNIL; (8) Rosagroprominform RPO, VASKhNIL;
  (9) Uzbektekstil'mash Assn., USSR Min. of Machinery; (10) Central Studio for
  Documentary Films, Goskino; (11) All-Union Center MZhK
Activity: Intermediary services

---

179   HI TECH   12/28/88

Location: Groznyi (RSFSR)
Initial Capital: 700,000 rubles
Foreign Partners and %Share: (1) Foster Wheeler Intercontinental (45%)
Soviet Partners and %Share: (1) Grozneftekhim NPO, USSR Min. for Oil-Refining
  and Petrochemichal Industry (55%)
Activity: Engineering and management services for oil-processing enterprises

---

183   INTERSKRAP   12/28/88

Location: Moscow (RSFSR)
Initial Capital: 63,000 rubles
Foreign Partners and %Share: (1) American General Resources, Inc. (49%)
Soviet Partners and %Share: (total share 51%) (1) Primorskoe PO of the Fishing
  Industry; (2) Murmansk Shipyard PO; (3) Sovrybflot V/O
Activity: Operation of ship scrapyard; sale of used engines and equipment

---

203   TISSA-OGILVY AND MATHER   01/12/89

Location: Moscow (RSFSR)
Initial Capital: 430,000 rubles
Foreign Partners and %Share: (1) Ogilvy and Mather Worldwide (35%)
Soviet Partners and %Share: (1) Tissa JV (65%)
Activity: Advertising and marketing services

---

223   ISKUSSTVO I ELEKTRONIKA   01/24/89

Location: Moscow (RSFSR)
Initial Capital: 750,000 rubles
Foreign Partners and %Share: (1) Mobil Fidelity Sound Lab (50%)

Soviet Partners and %Share: (1) Center of Musical Information, Union of Composers (18%); (2) SoyuzKoncert PO, USSR Min. of Culture (16%); (3) Elektronika Center of Commercial Advertising Assn., Min. of Electronic Industries (16%)
Activity: Organization of performances; advertising; computer centers

---

240   KOMED   02/07/89

Location: Moscow (RSFSR)
Initial Capital: 200,000 rubles
Foreign Partners and %Share: (1) Phoenix Radiology Internat., Inc. (50%)
Soviet Partners and %Share: (1) Ekran NPO (25%); (2) VNII Medpribor (25%)
Activity: Medical equipment and related software; advertising

---

274   PSTI (PARUS SIBIR TORG INTERNAT.)   02/27/89

Location: Tashkent (UzSSR)
Initial Capital: 100,000 rubles
Foreign Partners and %Share: (1) Sibir, Inc. (49%)
Soviet Partners and %Share: (1) Parus Coop. (51%)
Activity: Personal computer assembly; software development

---

281   TBILISOFT   03/01/89

Location: Tblisi (GSSR)
Initial Capital: 64,000 rubles
Foreign Partners and %Share: (1) Ergo Group, Inc. (25%)
Soviet Partners and %Share: (1) Lenin Polytechnic Institute in GSSR (75%)
Activity: Personal computer assembly; software development

---

282   SPINDULIS   03/01/89

Location: Kaunas (LiSSR)
Initial Capital: 11,980,000 rubles
Foreign Partners and %Share: (1) Global Technology Group (48%)
Soviet Partners and %Share: (1) Pozhely Publishing House, LiSSR Goskomizdat (52%)
Activity: Printing and publishing; color separated photo positives

---

284   INTERLIK   03/02/89

Location: Moscow (RSFSR)
Initial Capital: 506,000 rubles
Foreign Partners and %Share: (1) Berusa (49%)
Soviet Partners and %Share: (1) Treatment and Consultation Coop. (51%)
Activity: Medical services; production and sale of related goods

---

287   ASK   03/06/89

Location: Moscow (RSFSR)
Initial Capital: 50,000 rubles
Foreign Partners and %Share: (1) Brownstone Productions (51%)
Soviet Partners and %Share: (1) USSR Union of Cinematographers (51%)
Activity: Production, sale, trading of films and videotapes; exhibitions

301   RANTARIN   03/15/89

Location: Khabarovsk (RSFSR)
Initial Capital: 424,000 rubles
Foreign Partners and %Share: (1) Eugene Enterprises, Inc. (50%)
Soviet Partners and %Share: (1) Rantarin Scientific-Production System, RSFSR
   Gosagroprom (50%)
Activity: Storage, processing and distribution of horns of northern deer

310   SOVAMTEST   03/17/89

Location: Moscow (RSFSR)
Initial Capital: 20,000 rubles
Foreign Partners and %Share: (1) GJI, Inc. (49%)
Soviet Partners and %Share: (1) Interbranch Consulting and Diagnosis Scientific
   Production Center, Central Council of Inventor's Union (51%)
Activity: Testing, consulting, engineering, training, and design services

313   HERMITAGE   03/20/89

Location: Leningrad (RSFSR)
Initial Capital: 950,000 rubles
Foreign Partners and %Share: (1) Transatlantic Agency (55%)
Soviet Partners and %Share: (1) Hermitage State Museum (45%)
Activity: Art exhibitions; publishing

315   AKVATON   03/21/89

Location: Odessa (UkSSR)
Initial Capital: 100,000 rubles
Foreign Partners and %Share: (1) Thurston Sails, Inc. (49%)
Soviet Partners and %Share: (1) Aquamarine Coop. (51%)
Activity: Sails and related products for yachts

317   INTERMET ENGINEERING   03/21/89

Location: Moscow (RSFSR)
Initial Capital: 670,000 rubles

Foreign Partners and %Share: (1) Metvac (50%)
Soviet Partners and %Share: (total share 50%) (1) Moscow Institute of Steel and
  Alloys; (2) USSR State Committee on Public Education
Activity: Licensing and patenting service; research and development

---

335   KAMCHATKA PACIFIC CO.   03/24/89

Location: Vladivostok (RSFSR)
Initial Capital: 150,000 rubles
Foreign Partners and %Share: (1) Soviet-American Co. of Sea Resources (49%)
Soviet Partners and %Share: (1) Lenin Fishing Kolkhoz of the Union Fishing
  Kolkhoz Assn., USSR Min. of Fishing Industry (51%)
Activity: Seafood; shipbuilding and related services

---

339   TEMPO   03/27/89

Location: Minsk (BSSR)
Initial Capital: 300,000 rubles
Foreign Partners and %Share: (1) Hemisphere Publishing Corp. (50%)
Soviet Partners and %Share: (1) Lykava Institute of Heat and Mass Exchange, BSSR
  Academy of Sciences (50%)
Activity: Publishing; software development; research and development

---

346   MOSKOVSKAYA PIZZA   03/28/89

Location: Moscow (RSFSR)
Initial Capital: 1,770,000 rubles
Foreign Partners and %Share: (1) Pepsico Eurasia Ltd. (49%)
Soviet Partners and %Share: (1) Moscow Restaurant Service, Moscow City Ispolkom
  (51%)
Activity: Organization of Pizza Hut restaurants in Moscow

---

363   AMSOVINVEST   03/31/89

Location: Moscow (RSFSR)
Initial Capital: 1,200,000 rubles
Foreign Partners and %Share: (1) AmSovInvest, Inc. (25%)
Soviet Partners and %Share: (total share 75%) (1) Central Committee of VLKSM;
  (2) Uzinbank; (3) Sovremennik Manufacturing Coop.; (4) Variant JV
Activity: Management information systems; recycling wastes

---

387   ADAN   04/17/89

Location: Sumgait (AzSSR)
Initial Capital: 3,500,000 rubles
Foreign Partners and %Share: (1) Amex Import-Export, Inc. (60%)

Soviet Partners and %Share: (total share 40%) (1) Avtozapchast Plant; (2) Glance
   Coop. Assn.
Activity: Consumer goods; support; import-export operations

---

389   PGD   04/19/89

Location: Moscow (RSFSR)
Initial Capital: 12,000 rubles
Foreign Partners and %Share: (1) Ollsten Trading Delaware Corp. (50%)
Soviet Partners and %Share: (1) Russkaya Pchela Production Coop. (50%)
Activity: Software development; technical services

---

393   MONO-AL   04/20/89

Location: Riga (LaSSR)
Initial Capital: 2,135,000 rubles
Foreign Partners and %Share: (1) American Laboratories, Inc. (60%)
Soviet Partners and %Share: (1) Mono Multibrach Coop. Firm (40%)
Activity: Latex products and insulating materials produced from recycled waste

---

400   ROMOS   04/21/89

Location: Moscow (RSFSR)
Initial Capital: 2,450,000 rubles
Foreign Partners and %Share: (1) Rodel Ltd. (15%)
Soviet Partners and %Share: (total share 85%) (1) Padaugava Scientific-Technical
   Coop. Firm, Moscow City Ispolkom; (2) Scientific Center, Moscow City Ispolkom;
   (3) Moskva-Avto Transportation/Sightseeing Coop.
Activity: Organization of tourist and entertainment facilities and services

---

401   ESTBERUSA   04/21/89

Location: Tallinn (ESSR)
Initial Capital: 1,562,000 rubles
Foreign Partners and %Share: (1) Berusa Corp. (24%); (2) ZIG (West Germany
   24%)
Soviet Partners and %Share: (1) Estagrostroy Industrial Management Assn. (52%)
Activity: Production and distribution of chemical products and construction
   materials

---

411   INTERSIGNAL   04/27/89

Location: Moscow (RSFSR)
Initial Capital: 100,000 rubles
Foreign Partners and %Share: (1) Berusa (50%)

Soviet Partners and %Share: (1) NII Center of Technical Documentation, USSR
  Glavarkhiv (50%)
Activity: Personal computers

----

412   SAAEK   04/27/89

Location: Moscow (RSFSR)
Initial Capital: 353,000 rubles
Foreign Partners and %Share: (1) World Ethnic Art and Entertainment (49%)
Soviet Partners and %Share: (1) Tekhnoexport V/O (22.7%); (2) Soyuzteatre
  (28.3%)
Activity: Restaurants; retail trade

----

415   KVORUM   04/27/89

Location: Moscow (RSFSR)
Initial Capital: 8,200,000 rubles
Foreign Partners and %Share: (1) Global Technology Group (23.5%); (2) Tabaki
  Corp. (Pakistan 11.6%); (3) Ramadon Investments (Singapore 5.8%)
Soviet Partners and %Share: (1) Main Computer and Data Processing Center, USSR
  Gosplan (40.2%); (2) Sotrudnichestvo Coop. (13.1%); (3) Sechenov Medical
  Institute at Moscow
Activity: Personal computers

----

423   NOVOLUB   05/03/89

Location: Moscow (RSFSR)
Initial Capital: 6,000,000 rubles
Foreign Partners and %Share: (1) Considar Project Development Internat. (50%)
Soviet Partners and %Share: (1) Vtornefteprodukt PO, RSFSR
  Goskomneftoprodukt (50%)
Activity: Waste oil recycling

----

429   SPECTRUM   05/05/89

Location: Moscow (RSFSR)
Initial Capital: 250,000 rubles
Foreign Partners and %Share: (1) Spectrum Internat., Inc. (15%); (2) Spectrum Ltd.
  (Britain 35%)
Soviet Partners and %Share: (1) Kompideya Coop. (5%); (2) Neptune Soviet-
  Swedish JV (45%)
Activity: Personel computers

----

433   INTERDESIGN   05/10/89

Location: Moscow (RSFSR)
Initial Capital: 94,000 rubles

Foreign Partners and %Share: (1) Astra Consulting Internat., Inc. (33%); (2) Ite
  Tangra Co. (Italy 33%)
Soviet Partners and %Share: (1) EVM Soyuz Science-Research Complex (34%)
Activity: Personal computers

---

444   TREN-MOS   05/12/89

Location: Moscow (RSFSR)
Initial Capital: 1,446,000 rubles
Foreign Partners and %Share: (1) Zeiger Internat., Inc. (50%)
Soviet Partners and %Share: (1) Trust of Cafeterias of Moscow Leninsky Rayon
  (50%)
Activity: Restaurants

---

455   YOUNG AND RUBICAM   05/17/89

Location: Moscow (RSFSR)
Initial Capital: 741,200 rubles
Foreign Partners and %Share: (1) Young and Rubicam, Inc. (49%)
Soviet Partners and %Share: (1) Vneshtorgreklama V/O (51%)
Activity: Consulting and advertising services

---

456   AMERICANO-TADZHIKSKOE   05/17/89
                 MEKHANOVOE PO

Location: Dushanbe (TaSSR)
Initial Capital: 1,432,000 rubles
Foreign Partners and %Share: (1) Duf Fur Dressing, Inc. (50%)
Soviet Partners and %Share: (1) Dushanbe Leather-Shoe PO (50%)
Activity: Processing of furs, sheepskin and leather; clothing

---

474   MOST   05/24/89

Location: Moscow (RSFSR)
Initial Capital: 600,000 rubles
Foreign Partners and %Share: (1) APCO Associates (50%)
Soviet Partners and %Share: (1) Infeks Informational-Consulting Coop. (50%)
Activity: Consulting and intermediary services

---

478   LILEO-ARTS   05/24/89

Location: Tblisi (GSSR)
Initial Capital: 100,000 rubles
Foreign Partners and %Share: (1) East-West Arts and Entertainment Group, Inc.
  (50%)

Soviet Partners and %Share: (1) Limo Multibranch Commercial Foreign Trading
   Firm, Rustavelli Assn. (50%)
Activity: Musical entertainment services and products

---

483   DAGUINAKS   05/24/89

Location: Makhachkala (RSFSR)
Initial Capital: 3,600,000 rubles
Foreign Partners and %Share: (1) Winsome Food Technology, Inc. (25%)
Soviet Partners and %Share: (1) Dagvino Agro-Industrial PO, Daghestan
   Gosagroprom (75%)
Activity: Production and marketing of fruit juice; intermediary services

---

492   INFORMATION COMPUTER ENTERPRISE   05/26/89

Location: Moscow (RSFSR)
Initial Capital: 372,549 rubles
Foreign Partners and %Share: (1) IDG Communications (49%)
Soviet Partners and %Share: (1) Radio and Communications Publishing PO, USSR
   Goskomizdat (51%)
Activity: Economic services; computers; fairs and exhibitions

---

493   ELOIGEO   05/29/89

Location: Moscow (RSFSR)
Initial Capital: 700,000 rubles
Foreign Partners and %Share: (1) Eloilex Laboratories Private, Ltd. (49%)
Soviet Partners and %Share: (1) Center for Geological Expeditions (36%);
   (2) Elektronorgtekhnika All-Union Assn. (15%)
Activity: Computer hard- and software for oil drilling

---

497   START TVORCHESKOE OB'EDINENIE   05/29/89

Location: Moscow (RSFSR)
Initial Capital: 100,000 rubles
Foreign Partners and %Share: (1) Douglas Production Internat. (40%)
Soviet Partners and %Share: (1) Kinotsentr All-Union Creative Assn, USSR Union
   of Cinema Artists (10%); (2) Ekran Coop. Creative Assn. (40%); (3) Leningrad
   Enterprise of All-Union Creative Activity, Kinotsentr PO (10%)
Activity: Printing, publishing, advertising and consulting

---

508   ASTA   05/29/89

Location: Moscow (RSFSR)
Initial Capital: 2,040,000 rubles

Foreign Partners and %Share: (1) Perch Electronic, Inc. (50%)
Soviet Partners and %Share: (1) Vneshagropromeksport PO (50%)
Activity: Electrical and radio products

---

509   KROVTEKHS   05/29/89

Location: Moscow (RSFSR)
Initial Capital: 48,100,000 rubles
Foreign Partners and %Share: (1) Carlile Corp. (49%)
Soviet Partners and %Share: (1) Soyuzpromstroikomplekt PO (51%)
Activity: Insulation, glues, groutings; marketing and construction

---

514   MABINVEST   05/30/89

Location: Moscow (RSFSR)
Initial Capital: 100,000 rubles
Foreign Partners and %Share: (1) Hudson Street Internat. Corp. (40%)
Soviet Partners and %Share: (1) All-Union Center for Patenting Services, USSR
  Goskomizobretenie (35%); (2) Sintez Coop. (25%)
Activity: Legal and consulting services; advertising

---

519   BELKA INTERNAT.   05/31/89

Location: Moscow (RSFSR)
Initial Capital: 100,000 rubles
Foreign Partners and %Share: (1) V.V.S. Internat. Group (50%)
Soviet Partners and %Share: (1) Belka State Coop. (50%)
Activity: Consulting, intermediary services

---

529   INTERTEST   06/01/89

Location: Moscow (RSFSR)
Initial Capital: 100,000 rubles
Foreign Partners and %Share: (1) Krystaltech Internat., Inc. (50%)
Soviet Partners and %Share: (1) Mayak Scientific Center for Coordinated Research
  Mashpriborintorg V/O (20%); (2) Kontest Production Coop. (30%)
Activity: Computer services

---

531   AZSUM   06/01/89

Location: Novo-Aleksandrovka (RSFSR)
Initial Capital: 249,000 rubles
Foreign Partners and %Share: (1) Summit Ltd. (50%)
Soviet Partners and %Share: (1) Azov Agro-Industrial Plant (50%)
Activity: Corn, soy, and alfalfa seeds

| 538 | SAGOER | 06/01/89 |

Location: Moscow (RSFSR)
Initial Capital: 18,600 rubles
Foreign Partners and %Share: (1) Sheldon Trading Co. (50%)
Soviet Partners and %Share: (1) Zarubezhgaz V/O (50%)
Activity: Construction and maintenance of oil and gas facilities, waste recycling

---

| 542 | BISTRO | 06/02/89 |

Location: Leningrad (RSFSR)
Initial Capital: 48,000 rubles
Foreign Partners and %Share: (1) Neva Ltd. (40%)
Soviet Partners and %Share: (1) Public Dining Trust of Petrogradskii Rayon (60%)
Activity: Fast food facilities; import-export of unprocessed food

---

| 546 | SOVMESTNYI PUT' | 06/02/89 |

Location: Moscow (RSFSR)
Initial Capital: 1,200,000 rubles
Foreign Partners and %Share: (1) User Internat. (70%)
Soviet Partners and %Share: (1) Panirina Coop. (30%)
Activity: Computers; waste recycling and sales

| 562 | SOVFINAMTRANS | 06/05/89 |

Location: Moscow (RSFSR)
Initial Capital: 1,591,011 rubles
Foreign Partners and %Share: (1) Haka (Finland 15%); (2) Transisco Industries, Inc. (20%)
Soviet Partners and %Share: (1) Zheldoreksport V/O (40%); (2) Neftekhimeksport VEO (25%)
Activity: Leasing of railway cars, tank cars, hoppers

| 613 | MOSCOW PROJECT MANAGEMENT | 06/16/89 |

Location: Moscow (RSFSR)
Initial Capital: 100,000 rubles
Foreign Partners and %Share: (1) Kent Management Group, Inc. (75%)
Soviet Partners and %Share: (1) IPK of Management Personnel, MISI (25%)
Activity: Development of public enterprises; management training and consulting

---

| 614 | SPANTEK | 06/16/89 |

Location: Moscow (RSFSR)
Initial Capital: 82,000 rubles

Foreign Partners and %Share: (1) JVT (45%)
Soviet Partners and %Share: (1) Sputnik BMMT (45%); (2) IKT-System
  Scientific-Production Coop. (10%)
Activity: Advertising and souvenir materials

| 626 | STIM | 06/20/89 |

Location: Moscow (RSFSR)
Initial Capital: 270,000 rubles
Foreign Partners and %Share: (1) Cook Products Internat., Inc. (50%)
Soviet Partners and %Share: (1) GUM State Department Store (25%); (2) Detskii
  Mir Trade Firm (25%)
Activity: Commercial marketing services

| 627 | FALKON | 06/20/89 |

Location: Moscow (RSFSR)
Initial Capital: 340,000 rubles
Foreign Partners and %Share: (1) Economic Development Partners Corp. (70%)
Soviet Partners and %Share: (1) Chelek JV (30%)
Activity: Construction and operation of hotels, sports facilities, houses, shops,
  restaurants, cable television network

| 629 | FIKO | 06/20/89 |

Location: Saratov (RSFSR)
Initial Capital: 865,000 rubles
Foreign Partners and %Share: (1) Kaufman Equities Ltd. (17%)
Soviet Partners and %Share: (1) Fiton Coop., Soviet Peace Protection Committee
  (83%)
Activity: Processing of polymer and waste materials; scrap metal; consumer goods;
  medical equipment

| 632 | SOVET BROKER | 06/20/89 |

Location: Magadan (RSFSR)
Initial Capital: 60,000 rubles
Foreign Partners and %Share: (1) Slava Internat. (50%)
Soviet Partners and %Share: (1) Magadanoblmestprom TPO (50%);
  (2) Magadannerrud State Coop. Enterprise
Activity: Organization of joint ventures, tourism, technical reequipment

---

| 649 | KHAD-DON | 06/23/89 |

Location: Rostov on the Don (RSFSR)
Initial Capital: 8,500,000 rubles

Foreign Partners and %Share: (1) ITI Trading Internat., Inc. (58%)
Soviet Partners and %Share: (1) Novyi Byt, Union of Production Coop. (42%)
Activity: Building materials; clothing; personal computers; medical engineering
   equipment; agricultural processing

---

651   KING MANUFACTURE OKTYABR   06/23/89

Location: Kharkov (UkSSR)
Initial Capital: 150,000 rubles
Foreign Partners and %Share: (1) King Furniture Manufacturer, Inc. (70%)
Soviet Partners and %Share: (1) Oktyabr Coop. (30%)
Activity: Consumer goods

---

659   EKOENERGETIKA   06/27/89

Location: Moscow (RSFSR)
Initial Capital: 200,000 rubles
Foreign Partners and %Share: (1) Hemisphere Publishing Corp. (49%)
Soviet Partners and %Share: (1) Krizhizhanovskii Energy Institute (51%)
Activity: Printing and publishing of scientific articles and books

---

662   ITTM   06/27/89

Location: Moscow (RSFSR)
Initial Capital: 100,000 rubles
Foreign Partners and %Share: (1) W. Post-Wilfrid Post Rastfach (West Germany
   40%); (2) Belliville Group Ltd. (50%)
Soviet Partners and %Share: (1) Model-2 Creative Scientific Production Center
   (5%); (2) Moscow Innovation Commercial Bank (5%)
Activity: Electronics, including computers; chemical and petroleum equipment;
   agro-processing

---

675   SKK SPACE COMMERCE CORP.   06/28/89

Location: Moscow (RSFSR)
Initial Capital: 182,000 rubles
Foreign Partners and %Share: (1) Space Commerce Corp. (50%)
Soviet Partners and %Share: (1) Main Admin. for Creation and Use of Space
Technology for National Economy (50%)
Activity: Launching space vehicles with Soviet carrier rockets

---

677   PARAGRAPH   06/28/89

Location: Moscow (RSFSR)
Initial Capital: 600,000 rubles
Foreign Partners and %Share: (1) Paragraph Corp. (50%)

Soviet Partners and %Share: (1) Commission for Study of Productive Natural
  Resources, USSR Academy of Sciences (25%); (2) Central
  Economic-Mathematics Institute, USSR Academy of Sciences (25%)
Activity: Personal computers, software development; high-tech toys

---

691   LITERATURNAYA GAZETA INTERNAT.   07/05/89

Location: Moscow (RSFSR)
Initial Capital: 1,428,600 rubles
Foreign Partners and %Share: (1) Ansat (30%)
Soviet Partners and %Share: (1) Literaturnaya Gazeta Publishing and Production
  Assn. (70%)
Activity: Biweekly periodical in English

---

698   SIT   07/07/89

Location: Tbilisi (GSSR)
Initial Capital: 2,000,000 rubles
Foreign Partners and %Share: (1) Sabey Corp. (60%)
Soviet Partners and %Share: (1) GSSR Union of Journalists (40%)
Activity: Placing brand emblems on sportswear; consumer goods; printing

---

709   SOUVENIR TRADING   07/13/89

Location: Moscow (RSFSR)
Initial Capital: 20,000 rubles
Foreign Partners and %Share: (1) Citra Trading (50%)
Soviet Partners and %Share: (1) Shafran Coop. (50%)
Activity: Souvenirs

---

713   RUS-HOTEL   07/14/89

Location: Moscow (RSFSR)
Initial Capital: 2,560,000 rubles
Foreign Partners and %Share: (1) John English Associates, Inc. (49%)
Soviet Partners and %Share: (1) Director of Solnechnyi Hotel (51%)
Activity: Modernization and operation of Solnechnyi Hotel

---

714   AMEREST HOTELS   07/18/89

Location: Tallinn (ESSR)
Initial Capital: 12,750,000 rubles
Foreign Partners and %Share: (1) Condenheim Hotel Corp. (20%); (2) Skanska
  (Sweden)
Soviet Partners and %Share: (1) ESSR Gosstroi (26.7%); (2) Estimpeks FTO

(18.6%); (3) ESSR Min. of Health (8%); (4) Tallinn PO of Water Supply and
Sewage (26.7%)
Activity: Construction and operation of five-star hotel

---

735   SVETOZOR   07/28/89

Location: Moscow (RSFSR)
Initial Capital: 1,810,843 rubles
Foreign Partners and %Share: (1) Polaroid Internat. (50.01%)
Soviet Partners and %Share: (1) Baltiets PO (12.29%); (2) Signal Plant (12.29%);
   (3) N/O NII of Radiation Technology (25.41%)
Activity: Polaroid technology-based production of industrial goods and medicine

---

759   STANBET   08/02/89

Location: Moscow (RSFSR)
Initial Capital: 100,000 rubles
Foreign Partners and %Share: (1) Kramer Music Products, Inc. (50%)
Soviet Partners and %Share: (1) Stas Namin Music Center, USSR Fund for Social
   Inventions (50%)
Activity: Musical management services and instruments; festivals, concerts,
   competitions

---

760   OLYMPIA AMROS   08/02/89

Location: Moscow (RSFSR)
Initial Capital: 415,000 rubles
Foreign Partners and %Share: (1) Olympian Embroidery (60%)
Soviet Partners and %Share: (1) Moscow Glavrossportprom (20%);
   (2) Rosvneshtorg V/O (20%)
Activity: Production and sale of sporting goods

---

761   FLEKS INTERNAT. LTD.   08/02/89

Location: Kishinev (MSSR)
Initial Capital: 200,000 rubles
Foreign Partners and %Share: (1) Lotos Trade Internat. (50%)
Soviet Partners and %Share: (1) Kudesnik Repair and Restoration Coop. (50%)
Activity: Restoration of monuments; building materials; medical instruments; sports
   equipment; sports and health-improvement facilities

---

765   ALBA   08/04/89

Location: Leningrad (RSFSR)
Initial Capital: 2,930,000 rubles
Foreign Partners and %Share: (1) Alba, Inc. (30%)

Soviet Partners and %Share: (1) Skorokhod Shoe Production Assn. (70%)
Activity: Shoes

---

773   INTA-UNION   08/04/89

Location: Brotseny (LaSSR)
Initial Capital: 1,680,000 rubles
Foreign Partners and %Share: (1) Great Lakes Paper Co. (75%)
Soviet Partners and %Share: (1) Union Coop. (25%)
Activity: Lamps and lighting equipment; lampshades; paint; wallpaper

---

779   EKOPSI   08/04/89

Location: Moscow (RSFSR)
Initial Capital: 384,000 rubles
Foreign Partners and %Share: (1) Internat. JV Consultants, Inc. (50%)
Soviet Partners and %Share: (1) Contact NTTM Center (10%); (2) Interact Coop.
   (37%); (3) Moscow State University (3%)
Activity: Management and consulting services

---

788   IDEJA   08/08/89

Location: Donetsk (RSFSR)
Initial Capital: 250,000 rubles
Foreign Partners and %Share: (1) Pen Enterprises, Inc. (60%)
Soviet Partners and %Share: (1) Donbass Experimental Socio-Production Youth
   Assn. (40%)
Activity: Computer production; construction

---

793   STOMADENT   08/09/89

Location: Kharkov (UkSSR)
Initial Capital: 2,822,000 rubles
Foreign Partners and %Share: (1) Dentsply Internat., Inc. (33.2%)
Soviet Partners and %Share: (1) Stomatologiya VNPO (66.8%)
Activity: Stomatological products and licences

---

820   KRAFTS TECHNOLOGIES   08/15/89

Location: Moscow (RSFSR)
Initial Capital: 30,000,000 rubles
Foreign Partners and %Share: (1) World Krafts, Inc. (50%)
Soviet Partners and %Share: (1) Agrokoopkompleks Foreign Economic
   Self-Financing Assn. of the Perm region (50%)
Activity: Building materials; agricultural products

---

823   SOYUZ MARINE SERVICE   08/17/89

Location: Moscow (RSFSR)
Initial Capital: 60,200 rubles
Foreign Partners and %Share: (1) Internat. Maritime, Inc. (27.5%); (2) Intertorg, Inc. (19.25%); (3) Internat. Interest Group, Inc. (8.25%)
Soviet Partners and %Share: (1) Odessa Coop. (15%); (2) Intergeoid Coop. (15%); (3) Shirshov Institute of Oceanography, USSR Academy of Sciences (15%)
Activity: Underwater research; consulting

831   SOVAMTEKSIML   08/21/89

Location: Dedovsk (RSFSR)
Initial Capital: 2,000,000 rubles
Foreign Partners and %Share: (1) Alex Import-Export, Inc. (30%)
Soviet Partners and %Share: (1) Dedovskoe PO of Technical Textiles, RSFSR Min. of Textile Industry (70%)
Activity: Consumer products; consulting

839   TAIS SPORT   08/22/89

Location: Moscow (RSFSR)
Initial Capital: 80,000 rubles
Foreign Partners and %Share: (1) Atlantika (Italy 22.5%); (2) DG Electronic Contractor (2.5%)
Soviet Partners and %Share: (1) Rustal Production Coop. (75%)
Activity: Sporting goods and facilities

841   INTEKS   08/22/89

Location: Tallinn (ESSR)
Initial Capital: 100,000 rubles
Foreign Partners and %Share: (1) TIW Systems, Inc. (49%)
Soviet Partners and %Share: (1) Institute of Cybernetics, ESSR Academy of Sciences (51%)
Activity: Computer hard- and software; sales; research and other services

843   RCB PRODUCTS INTERNAT.   08/23/89

Location: Moscow (RSFSR)
Initial Capital: 200,000 rubles
Foreign Partners and %Share: (1) R&L Internat., Inc. (25%); (2) CC Food Products (26%)
Soviet Partners and %Share: (1) Bioprocess (49%)
Activity: Agricultural products

---

847   INTERPRIBOR   08/24/89

Location: Minsk (BSSR)
Initial Capital: 200,000 rubles
Foreign Partners and %Share: (1) F.D. Processing and Machinery, Inc. (10%)
Soviet Partners and %Share: (1) Admin. of Housing Industry, Minsk City Ispolkom
  (30%); (2) Minskkommunteploset Production Enterprise (20%); (3) Effekt
  Engineering Production Coop. (20%); (4) Republican Commercial Center of
  BSSR Gossnab (20%)
Activity: Design of control systems; heavy equipment

---

873   FORBESPROGRESS   08/31/89

Location: Moscow (RSFSR)
Initial Capital: 1,000,000 rubles
Foreign Partners and %Share: (1) Forbes and Co. (55%)
Soviet Partners and %Share: (1) Progress Production Coop. (45%)
Activity: Technological equipment; construction

---

878   SINERGIYA-INTERNAT.   09/01/89

Location: Moscow (RSFSR)
Initial Capital: 15,660,000 rubles
Foreign Partners and %Share: (1) Aricard, Inc. (51.44%)
Soviet Partners and %Share: (1) Moscow Institute of Physical-Technical Problems
  (48.56%)
Activity: Publishing, engineering, consulting, commercial and transport services

---

883   REPKO   09/01/89

Location: Tbilisi (GSSR)
Initial Capital: 500,000 rubles
Foreign Partners and %Share: (1) Phargo Information, Inc. (25%); (2) Phargo
  Management and Consulting Ltd. (Canada 25%)
Soviet Partners and %Share: (1) Admin. of Pharmaceuticals, GSSR Min. of Health
  (40%); (2) Kod Coop. (5%); (3) Term Coop. (5%)
Activity: Software development; training and consulting services

---

892   SOVIET BRAND   09/05/89

Location: Magadan (RSFSR)
Initial Capital: 100,000 rubles
Foreign Partners and %Share: (1) MG Import-Export Internat. (50%)
Soviet Partners and %Share: (1) Magadan Joint Stock Trade and Industrial Firm;
  (2) Magadannerud State Coop. Enterprise; (3) Magadanoblmestprom TPO
Activity: Medical services; trade and intermediary services

| 913 | RIONI | 09/11/89 |

Location: Tbilisi (GSSR)
Initial Capital: 1,000,000 rubles
Foreign Partners and %Share: (1) B&D Import (51%)
Soviet Partners and %Share: (1) Gruzimpeks GSSR FTO, GSSR Council of
  Ministers (1%); (2) 50 Letiya PO of Tbilisi, USSR Min. of Industrial
  Communication (48%)
Activity: Consumer goods; electrical engineering

| 920 | CINEBRIDGE | 09/12/89 |

Location: Moscow (RSFSR)
Initial Capital: 218,000 rubles
Foreign Partners and %Share: (1) Traitell Internat. (50%)
Soviet Partners and %Share: (1) Gorky Film Studio (50%)
Activity: Film and videotape products; film services

| 930 | INTERROLS | 09/19/89 |

Location: Moscow (RSFSR)
Initial Capital: 496,000 rubles
Foreign Partners and %Share: (1) Westminster Internat. Trading (50%)
Soviet Partners and %Share: (1) Mosreaktivsbyt Industry and Trade Admin. (50%)
Activity: Chemical reagents and sorbents; packages for reagents

| 938 | ARAGIL | 09/26/89 |

Location: Yerevan (ArSSR)
Initial Capital: 500,000 rubles
Foreign Partners and %Share: (1) Accent on Travel, Inc. (50%)
Soviet Partners and %Share: (1) ArSSR Admin. of USSR Civil Aviation (50%)
Activity: Travel and tourist services

| 945 | NAGAL | 10/04/89 |

Location: Chaibuka (RSFSR)
Initial Capital: 450,000 rubles
Foreign Partners and %Share: (1) Indian Valley Meats (11%)
Soviet Partners and %Share: (1) Karenskii Sovkhoz (89%)
Activity: Deer-breeding products

| 947 | SOVCOMPUTERTRADE | 10/04/89 |

Location: Moscow (RSFSR)
Initial Capital: 300,000 rubles

Foreign Partners and %Share: (1) Holographic Systems, Inc. (50%)
Soviet Partners and %Share: (total share 50%) (1) Radioeksport V/O; (2)
  Radiotekhnika Store #1 (50%)
Activity: Personal computers; software development

---

962   VITA-KOMERC YU.B.   10/06/89

Location: Moscow (RSFSR)
Initial Capital: 500,000 rubles
Foreign Partners and %Share: (1) B&D Import (20%); (2) Yubex (Belgium 30%)
Soviet Partners and %Share: (1) Vita Production Coop. (50%)
Activity: Starch, tomato paste, casein and caseinate natrium

---

972   D A B INTERNAT.   10/12/89

Location: Leningrad (RSFSR)
Initial Capital: 100,000 rubles
Foreign Partners and %Share: (1) D A Internat. (51%)
Soviet Partners and %Share: (1) Bolshevik Zavod PO (49%)
Activity: Medical equipment; heavy machinery; marketing

---

989   ROSSIYA   10/19/89

Location: Moscow (RSFSR)
Initial Capital: 100,000 rubles
Foreign Partners and %Share: (1) Folkon Ltd. (45%)
Soviet Partners and %Share: (1) Assn. of Assistance to Moscow Culture Fund (10%);
  (2) Commercial Innovation Bank for Scientific-Technical Progress (45%)
Activity: Furniture; clothing; videotapes; paintings; souvenirs for export

---

990   BASKIN-ROBBINS-MOSCOW   10/19/89

Location: Moscow (RSFSR)
Initial Capital: 512,000 rubles
Foreign Partners and %Share: (1) Baskin-Robbins Internat. (8.39%)
Soviet Partners and %Share: (1) Mosrestoranservis (91.61%)
Activity: Ice cream cafes, organized as "Baskin Robins Internat."

1013   VILMS   10/24/89

Location: Moscow (RSFSR)
Initial Capital: 200,000 rubles
Foreign Partners and %Share: (1) Twain Trading Group (50%)
Soviet Partners and %Share: (1) Debal Coop. (50%)
Activity: Marketing; engineering services; research and development

---

| 1203 | MIG | 12/12/89 |

Location: Moscow (RSFSR)
Initial Capital: 76,100 rubles
Foreign Partners and %Share: (1) Maccol Pattern (34%)
Soviet Partners and %Share: (1) Preiskurantizdat Publishing House (66%)
Activity: Publishing in Russian and foreign languages; advertising; marketing

| 1210 | AMSCORT INTERNAT. | 12/14/89 |

Location: Moscow (RSFSR)
Initial Capital: 300,000 rubles
Foreign Partners and %Share: (1) Meplo-Group (50%)
Soviet Partners and %Share: (1) USSR VDNKh (10%); (2) Inforkom Coop. Firm (30%); (3) All-Union Economics Society (10%)
Activity: Consulting; advertising; JV partner searches; seminars; marketing

| 1211 | NORD | 12/14/89 |

Location: Moscow (RSFSR)
Initial Capital: 200,000 rubles
Foreign Partners and %Share: (1) American Importex, Inc. (60%)
Soviet Partners and %Share: (1) Moscow Assn. of Arts (40%)
Activity: Soviet and foreign culture projects; publishing; exhibitions

| 1214 | SPARK | 12/14/89 |

Location: Magadan (RSFSR)
Initial Capital: 50,000 dollars
Foreign Partners and %Share: (1) Battery (or Batarya Ing) Enterprise (50%)
Soviet Partners and %Share: (1) Magadannerud State Coop. Enterprise (50%)
Activity: Batteries

| 1216 | ZARIA SWAY KARSON TIME TECHNOLOGIES INTERNAT. LTD. | 12/15/89 |

Location: Penza (RSFSR)
Initial Capital: 2,768,000 rubles
Foreign Partners and %Share: (1) Shamm IIP Co. Ltd. (40%); (2) A. A. Karson Internat., Inc. (10%)
Soviet Partners and %Share: (1) Zaria PO of Penza (50%)
Activity: Clocks, watches and parts

| 1225 | OLMEL | 12/15/89 |

Location: Moscow (RSFSR)
Initial Capital: 210,000 rubles

Foreign Partners and %Share: (1) Incorporation (3.82%)
Soviet Partners and %Share: (1) Soyuzuchpribor All-Union Specialized NPO, (4.76%); (2) 777 Coop. (91.42%)
Activity: Consumer goods; scientific research services

1238   INTERBALT   12/22/89

Location: Leningrad (RSFSR)
Initial Capital: 6,439,000 rubles
Foreign Partners and %Share: (1) Internat. Project Development (50%)
Soviet Partners and %Share: (1) Baltic Marine Navigation Admin. (50%)
Activity: Operation of motor ship "Kalinin"; tourist and intermediary services

---

1244   ANKOR   12/25/89

Location: Minsk (BSSR)
Initial Capital: 500,000 rubles
Foreign Partners and %Share: (1) Pshimezhe Trade-Production Enterprise (Poland 25%); (2) Sherida Enterprise (25%)
Soviet Partners and %Share: (1) MISO Diversified Engineering-Construction Assn. (40%); (2) Vida Engineering-Construction Coop. (10%)
Activity: Research and development; recycling of industrial and construction wastes; consulting; trade; leasing; transportation; engineering; marketing

---

1251   SPEIT-MOSKVA   12/26/89

Location: Moscow (RSFSR)
Initial Capital: 60,000 rubles
Foreign Partners and %Share: (1) Pan American Commercial Services, Inc. (50%)
Soviet Partners and %Share: (1) Internat. Commercial Admin., USSR Min. of Civil Aviation (50%)
Activity: Loans and tours for foreign citizens; hotel management; tourist services

---

1256   POLUS   12/26/89

Location: Moscow (RSFSR)
Initial Capital: 640,000 rubles
Foreign Partners and %Share: (1) Atlantic G&S Corp.
Soviet Partners and %Share: (1) Agenstvo-Cherko Small State Enterprise
Activity: Spectator events; musical equipment and services; tourist services; gifts and crafts; consulting; advertising

---

1257   CONNECT INTERNAT.   12/26/89

Location: Moscow (RSFSR)
Initial Capital: 100,000 rubles

Foreign Partners and %Share: (1) Le Monti, Inc.
Soviet Partners and %Share: (1) Sovinterkontakt-Agroservis
Activity: Symposia and seminars; economic, social and managerial research; centers
   for personnel training in management, marketing, and tourism

---

| 1258 | SVZAL | 12/26/89 |

Location: Magadan (RSFSR)
Initial Capital: 1,430,000 rubles
Foreign Partners and %Share: (1) Bering Straits Trading Co.
Soviet Partners and %Share: (1) Severovostokzoloto PO
Activity: Exploration and industrial operation of natural resource fields; leasing
   equipment; consulting

| 1262 | KLIKERS | 12/27/89 |

Location: Riga (LaSSR)
Initial Capital: 300,000 rubles
Foreign Partners and %Share: (1) Roltex (50%)
Soviet Partners and %Share: (1) Vilkis Production Assn., Min. of the Consumer
   Services (50%)
Activity: Dry cleaning; articles made from metal; furniture; clothing

---

| 1268 | UNIK BUSINESS CENTER | 12/28/89 |

Location: Khabarovsk (RSFSR)
Initial Capital: 172,000 rubles
Foreign Partners and %Share: (1) World Class Products Ltd. (70%)
Soviet Partners and %Share: (1) Khabarovsk City Institute of National Economy
   (30%)
Activity: Leasing of copy machines, computers, telexes, and facsimile and accounting
   equipment; marketing; licences; consulting; translations; postal services

---

| 1281 | AMSOVMED | 12/29/89 |

Location: Moscow (RSFSR)
Initial Capital: 340,000 rubles
Foreign Partners and %Share: (1) Amsovmed, Inc. (50%)
Soviet Partners and %Share: (1) Admin. of Business Affairs Central Committee of
   VLKSM (25%); (2) NII of Tuberculosis, RSFSR Min. of Public Health (25%)
Activity: Medical care for kidney disease; construction of medical equipment,
   hospitals and clinics

| 1285 | SOVAM TELEPORT | 01/02/90 |

Location: Moscow (RSFSR)
Initial Capital: 310,000 rubles

Foreign Partners and %Share: (1) San Francisco/Moscow Teleport (SFMT) (50%)
Soviet Partners and %Share: (1) Applied Automated Systems VNII (50%)
Activity: Operation of satellite data channels between the USSR and the U.S.

1295   AGROIMPEKS   01/06/90

Location: Moscow (RSFSR)
Initial Capital: 600,000 rubles
Foreign Partners and %Share: (1) Active Auto (France 16.67%); (2) Belorus'
   Machinery, Inc. (16.67%); (3) Konela Belorus' (Finland 16.66%)
Soviet Partners and %Share: (1) Traktoexport FTO (16.67%);
   (2) Bobruyskfermmash PO (16.67%); (3) Mekhinstrument NPO (16.66%)
Activity: Gardening equipment; agricultural technology; metalworking and welding
   equipment; metal dishes; spare parts

1297   LENBRIDNS   01/08/90

Location: Leningrad (RSFSR)
Initial Capital: 1,000,000 rubles
Foreign Partners and %Share: (1) The Pineapple Oxygen Co. (50%)
Soviet Partners and %Share: (1) Vilma Trade Commercial Center of Leningrad
   (50%)
Activity: Television sets; computers; medical and agricultural equipment; hotels;
   tourist services

1304   SOVIET-AMERICAN ADVERTISING CO.   01/09/90

Location: Moscow (RSFSR)
Initial Capital: 640,000 rubles
Foreign Partners and %Share: (1) Zigzag Art and Advertising Ltd. (49%)
Soviet Partners and %Share: (1) Inturreklama V/O (51%)
Activity: Distribution and sale of advertising in videofilms and in printed
   publications; advertising by mail; exhibitions; consulting

----

1308   VOSTOKINVEST   01/10/90

Location: Ufa (RSFSR)
Initial Capital: 390,000 rubles
Foreign Partners and %Share: (1) Fendelity Internat. Trade, Inc. (20%);
   (2) East-West Handelsagentur und Consulting GmbH (West Germany 20%)
Soviet Partners and %Share: (1) Institute of Superpliant Metals, USSR Academy of
   Sciences (20%); (2) Vostok Concern (20%); (3) Republican Admin. of
   Pommstroibank (20%)
Activity: Research and development; refining of raw materials, recycled goods, and
   waste products

1331   IMAKS SHOW INTERNAT.   01/19/90

Location: Moscow (RSFSR)
Initial Capital: 300,000 rubles
Foreign Partners and %Share: (1) Design Expo Internat. (30%)
Soviet Partners and %Share: (1) IMAKS Art Center Coop. (70%)
Activity: Shows, concerts and musical performances; exhibitions

1333   LEIBER   01/19/90

Location: Tbilisi (GSSR)
Initial Capital: 550,000 rubles
Foreign Partners and %Share: (1) Stan Kornelius, Inc. (70%)
Soviet Partners and %Share: (1) Tbilisi Recording Studio (30%)
Activity: Advertising and organization of auctions, presentations and festivals; audio
  and video cassettes; advertising materials; consumer goods; tourist services

1336   INTERMIN   01/19/90

Location: Shevchenko (RSFSR)
Initial Capital: 700,000 rubles
Foreign Partners and %Share: (1) Berusa Corp. (15%)
Soviet Partners and %Share: (1) Prikaspiiskii Mountain Metallurgical Coop. PO
  (85%)
Activity: Dicalcium phosphate and feed additives

1348   MANTIGO   01/23/90

Location: Moscow (RSFSR)
Initial Capital: 200,000 rubles
Foreign Partners and %Share: (1) Amtrade Group, Inc. (60%)
Soviet Partners and %Share: (1) Zodiak Coop. (40%)
Activity: Industrial waste processing; construction and operation of hotels and sports
  facilities

1357   GENESIS COMPOSITE RUSSIA   01/25/90

Location: Vyborg (RSFSR)
Initial Capital: 948,000 rubles
Foreign Partners and %Share: (1) Genesis Composite, Inc. (38%)
Soviet Partners and %Share: (1) Okean Assn. (62%)
Activity: Ecologically safe automation; light covers, sails for yachts; paneling

1369   SOVARO   01/29/90

Location: Moscow (RSFSR)
Initial Capital: 180,000 rubles

Foreign Partners and %Share: (1) WTL Production, Inc. (50%)
Soviet Partners and %Share: (1) Muzika Publishing House (50%)
Activity: Advertising; exhibitions; publishing; production and rental of musical
feature films for television; consulting

1380   INTERTES   01/30/90

Location: Moscow (RSFSR)
Initial Capital: 1,500,000 rubles
Foreign Partners and %Share: (1) Internat. Trade and Communications, Inc. (20%)
Soviet Partners and %Share: (1) Central Design Office NPO, USSR Min. of
Communications (48%); (2) Internat. Institute of Problems of World Socialist
Systems (8%); (3) Vneshekonomservis (8%); (4) Moscow Commercial Bank for
Industry and Construction (16%)
Activity: Computerized economic trade information system for collection and
dissemination of Soviet and foreign economic and scientific information

---

1381   BAI   01/30/90

Location: Moscow (RSFSR)
Initial Capital: 1,200,000 rubles
Foreign Partners and %Share: (1) A. Citron Trading Co. (50%)
Soviet Partners and %Share: (1) Elbi NPO (50%)
Activity: Construction and operation of a center for business contacts;
marketing, consulting, leasing, publishing and printing services; software
development

1382   AGAT-KREDIT   01/30/90

Location: Moscow (RSFSR)
Initial Capital: 200,000 rubles
Foreign Partners and %Share: (1) Eastern Credit Ltd., Inc. (60%)
Soviet Partners and %Share: (1) Agat-Kredit Consortium (40%)
Activity: Research and development; software development; repair services; scientific
publications

1412   ALKOR TECHNOLOGIES INC.   02/08/90

Location: Leningrad (RSFSR)
Initial Capital: 50,000 rubles
Foreign Partners and %Share: (1) North Shore Trade Enterprise, Inc. (50%)
Soviet Partners and %Share: (1) Orion Scientific Production Coop. (50%)
Activity: Development and production of optical-mechanical devices; apparatus and
parts for physics research; advertising, publishing and printing services

---

1413   YARBIN   02/08/90

Location: Yaroslavl (RSFSR)
Initial Capital: 500,000 rubles
Foreign Partners and %Share: (1) Alben (25%)
Soviet Partners and %Share: (1) Yaroslavl Industrial Sewing Assn. (65%);
   (2) Yaroslavets Coop. (10%)
Activity: Clothing; consumer goods; exhibitions

1414   INTEREKS   02/08/90

Location: Kiev (UkSSR)
Initial Capital: 200,000 rubles
Foreign Partners and %Share: (1) Network Systems Analysis (50%)
Soviet Partners and %Share: (1) Ukragroproektstroiindustriya Design and Research
   Institute (50%)
Activity: Software development; other scientific technological products

1430   KONKORD   02/16/90

Location: Moscow (RSFSR)
Initial Capital: 120,000 rubles
Foreign Partners and %Share: (1) Citra Trading Co. (50%)
Soviet Partners and %Share: (1) Sodruzhestvo Coop. (50%)
Activity: Consumer goods made from faience, porcelain, ceramics, crystal, wood and
   plastics; hotels; tourist services

1433   BELKOM   02/16/90

Location: Minsk (BSSR)
Initial Capital: 1,000,000 rubles
Foreign Partners and %Share: (1) Vector Technology Group (25%)
Soviet Partners and %Share: (1) Belorussian NPO of Computer Technology (40%)
Activity: Computer systems; software development; scientific research and design;
   marketing; advertising; waste processing

1436   INTERBYT KASHTAN   02/16/90

Location: Kiev (UkSSR)
Initial Capital: 485,000 rubles
Foreign Partners and %Share: (1) American Trade Co. (50%)
Soviet Partners and %Share: (1) Admin. of Hair Style Services, Admin. of Consumer
   Services of the Kiev City Ispolkom (50%)
Activity: Hair dressing salons; arts and crafts; cosmetics and hair pieces; hotels

1440   CENTER FOR SCIENTIFIC   02/19/90
             AND TECHNICAL EXCANGE

Location: Moscow (RSFSR)
Initial Capital: 200,000 rubles
Foreign Partners and %Share: (1) Maryland University (50%)
Soviet Partners and %Share: (1) Central Institute of Economics and Mathematics,
   Department of Economics, USSR Academy of Sciences (50%)
Activity: Publishing; advertising; exhibitions; lectures

1441   INNOVATION, INFORMATION,   02/19/90
             AND INTELLIGENCE

Location: Moscow (RSFSR)
Initial Capital: n/a
Foreign Partners and %Share: (1) Innovation Internat. (25%)
Soviet Partners and %Share: (1) VNIIPAS (50%)
Activity: Software development

1457   VICTORIA-HOTEL   03/06/90

Location: Leningrad (RSFSR)
Initial Capital: 5,600,000 rubles
Foreign Partners and %Share: (1) Tarm Engineering (50%)
Soviet Partners and %Share: (1) Committee of Physical Training and Sports,
   Leningrad City Ispolkom (50%)
Activity: Construction and operation of hotel and sports facilities; related services

1458   VISTA   03/06/90

Location: Moscow (RSFSR)
Initial Capital: 200,000 rubles
Foreign Partners and %Share: (1) Americom Internat. Corp. (50%)
Soviet Partners and %Share: (1) Soviet Foundation for Charity and Health (50%)
Activity: Spectator events; exhibitions; leisure centers; consulting; audio and video
   equipment; construction and operation of hotels for the handicapped

1460   TECH MARK   02/23/90

Location: Riga (LaSSR)
Initial Capital: 275,616 rubles
Foreign Partners and %Share: (1) Aristids Lambergs Construction Co., Inc. (50%);
   (2) Mark Computer Production Corp. (0%)
Soviet Partners and %Share: (1) Elfor Coop. Laboratory for Introduction of
   Scientific Research (50%); (2) Sadzine Coop. for Repairs and Construction

Activity: Computer devices for measuring and control of automated working places; synthesis and purification of high-tech reagents for chemistry

---

1471   AMGRYZFILM

Location: Tbilisi (GSSR)
Initial Capital: 200,000 rubles
Foreign Partners and %Share: (1) Soventure Group, Inc. (50%)
Soviet Partners and %Share: (1) Spektr Kinostudio Coop. (50%)
Activity: Feature films; publishing

1524   TEKOM   03/26/90

Location: Moscow (RSFSR)
Initial Capital: 500,000 rubles
Foreign Partners and %Share: (1) I S Counseling Engineer Corp. (50%)
Soviet Partners and %Share: (1) BioREL Scientific and Technical Center, Krasnopresnensky Rayon Ispolkom (50%)
Activity: Research in ecology, biomedecine, radioelectronics and metallurgy; construction; intermediary services

---

1525   SAB   03/26/90

Location: Kharkov (UkSSR)
Initial Capital: 300,000 rubles
Foreign Partners and %Share: (1) Perestroika, Inc. (50%)
Soviet Partners and %Share: (1) Kharkov Self-Financing Engineering Branch Information Center for Automated Managing Systems (50%)
Activity: Consumer goods; computers; agro-processing

1529   SOVLAKS   03/28/90

Location: Moscow (RSFSR)
Initial Capital: 10,217,000 rubles
Foreign Partners and %Share: (1) Energy Conversion Devices, Inc. (50%)
Soviet Partners and %Share: (1) Kvant NPO (50%)
Activity: Ecologically sound systems to recharge electric and photoelectric modules

---

1531   ARIADNA   03/29/90

Location: Odessa (UkSSR)
Initial Capital: 480,000 rubles
Foreign Partners and %Share: (1) Amex Import-Export, Inc. (72%)
Soviet Partners and %Share: (1) Indtrikotazh Factory of Odessa (28%)
Activity: Clothing; light industrial production

| 1540 | MEDREX INSTRUMENTS | 03/29/90 |

Location: Moscow (RSFSR)
Initial Capital: 100,000 rubles
Foreign Partners and %Share: (1) Sai Systems Laboratories, Inc. (50%)
Soviet Partners and %Share: (1) Medrex Coop. (50%)
Activity: Software development; medical equipment

| 1548 | LATKHAAG | 04/03/90 |

Location: Riga (LaSSR)
Initial Capital: 1,000,000 rubles
Foreign Partners and %Share: (1) Haag Industries (50%)
Soviet Partners and %Share: (1) Experimental Hydro-Metereological Equipment
  Plant of Riga (25%); (2) Etalon Experimental Plant of Riga (25%)
Activity: Electronic equipment; research and development; consulting

---

| 1555 | START | 04/04/90 |

Location: Moscow (RSFSR)
Initial Capital: 1,000,000 rubles
Foreign Partners and %Share: (1) K.R.S., Inc. (51%)
Soviet Partners and %Share: (1) Mosagropromspetzremstroi PO (49%)
Activity: Construction; software development; consulting; advertising

---

| 1564 | EKOESKO | 04/09/90 |

Location: Sochi (RSFSR)
Initial Capital: 2,000,000 rubles
Foreign Partners and %Share: (1) Exposita (50%)
Soviet Partners and %Share: (1) Yuzhtechmontazh Trust (25%); (2) Ekologiya
  Coop. (25%)
Activity: Sewage purification and other environmental protection operations;
  research and development; consulting; marketing

| 1573 | KLODIKS | 04/09/90 |

Location: Moscow (RSFSR)
Initial Capital: 300,000 rubles
Foreign Partners and %Share: (1) Shihna Power Plant Control Engineering Co. Ltd.
Soviet Partners and %Share: (1) Institute for Problems of Admin., USSR Min. of
  Electrical Engineering and Instrument Making
Activity: Personal computers; appliances; operation of Klodiks-system; machine
  engineering

| 1577 | MIKS | 04/11/90 |

Location: Moscow (RSFSR)
Initial Capital: 600,000 rubles
Foreign Partners and %Share: (1) Catlett, Inc. (25%); (2) Microcomputer Center, Inc. (25%)
Soviet Partners and %Share: (1) Marx Scientific-Design Center (1.7%); (2) Youth Commercial Bank (20%); (3) Ados Scientific-Production Coop. (20%); (4) Sovremenik Coop. (8.3%)
Activity: Electronic equipment

| 1585 | AB-AVRORA BOREALIS | 04/13/90 |

Location: Vorkuta (RSFSR)
Initial Capital: 250,000 rubles
Foreign Partners and %Share: (1) Internat. Exploration and Engineering (40%)
Soviet Partners and %Share: (1) Polyapnouralgeologiya Assn., USSR Min. of Geology (60%)
Activity: Consumer goods; development of geological survey methods

| 1588 | KILIKIYA INDUSTRIES INTERNAT. | 04/13/90 |

Location: Byuregavan (ArSSR)
Initial Capital: 11,200,000 rubles
Foreign Partners and %Share: (1) Tri-Star Industries (60%)
Soviet Partners and %Share: (1) Armsbeatkhim PO (40%)
Activity: Consumer goods from plastic and other materials

| 1603 | VAIBRANT LAIF | 04/18/90 |

Location: Moscow (RSFSR)
Initial Capital: 1,000,000 rubles
Foreign Partners and %Share: (1) Universal Center of the Seventh Day Adventists
Soviet Partners and %Share: (1) Department of Public Health, Baimansk Raion Ispolkom
Activity: Mining activities and equipment; stone products; marketing

| 1610 | ARIF | 04/20/90 |

Location: Moscow (RSFSR)
Initial Capital: 500,000 rubles
Foreign Partners and %Share: (1) RHA Group (50%)
Soviet Partners and %Share: (1) Main Computer Center, USSR Min. of Construction for the Transportation Industry (50%)
Activity: Personal computers and computerized game systems

1626   INTERPARTNER   04/25/90

Location: Moscow (RSFSR)
Initial Capital: 200,000 rubles
Foreign Partners and %Share: (1) V G Enterprises (50%)
Soviet Partners and %Share: (1) Kulbit Coop. (50%)
Activity: Consumer goods; advertising; education services

1637   RUSS-LAN   04/28/90

Location: Moscow (RSFSR)
Initial Capital: 400,000 rubles
Foreign Partners and %Share: (1) Gordon Mining Consulting Corp. (25%)
Soviet Partners and %Share: (1) Patrica Lumumbi University of Friendship Between
   Peoples (75%)
Activity: Educational and consulting services; teaching Russian to foreigners;
   teaching marketing to Soviet specialists

1643   SAIS   04/28/90

Location: Moscow (RSFSR)
Initial Capital: 200,000 rubles
Foreign Partners and %Share: (1) Eastern Credit Ltd., Inc. (85%)
Soviet Partners and %Share: (1) VNII for Normalization of Machine Building (15%)
Activity: Publishing; advertising; consulting; exhibitions

1644   INKOTEK   04/28/90

Location: Mytishchi (RSFSR)
Initial Capital: 120,000 rubles
Foreign Partners and %Share: (1) n/a (50%)
Soviet Partners and %Share: (1) Ekotsenter Moscow Branch of Self-Financing
   Center Scientific-Technical Services (50%)
Activity: Consulting on metallurgy, construction materials and marketing; medical
   equipment; research and development

1656   CHRISTMAS   05/04/90

Location: Moscow (RSFSR)
Initial Capital: 250,000 rubles
Foreign Partners and %Share: (1) Natco Trading Co. (60%)
Soviet Partners and %Share: (1) Soyuzmultfilm Film Studio (40%)
Activity: Films; video and advertising products; dubbing and other film services;
   marketing; consumer goods

| 1657 | KENTAVR | 05/07/90 |

Location: Minsk (BSSR)
Initial Capital: 200,000 rubles
Foreign Partners and %Share: (1) Fru Internat., Inc. (50%)
Soviet Partners and %Share: (1) Elektron Coop. (50%)
Activity: Research and development; conferences; consulting

| 1667 | TRANSMEDIS | 05/08/90 |

Location: Moscow (RSFSR)
Initial Capital: 2,000,000 rubles
Foreign Partners and %Share: (1) USA Internat. (50%)
Soviet Partners and %Share: (1) Mosgortrans Interbranch PO (50%)
Activity: Transportation services; medical equipment

| 1680 | UNISON | 05/11/90 |

Location: Moscow (RSFSR)
Initial Capital: 600,000 rubles
Foreign Partners and %Share: (1) Uniquad, Inc. (50%)
Soviet Partners and %Share: (1) Adminstration of Business Affairs of Central
  Committee of VLKSM (35%); (2) Higher Komsomol School, Central Committee
  of VLKSM (15%)
Activity: Educational programs; operation of hotels; publishing, consulting and
  advertising services; consumer goods

| 1692 | GLOBE RESOURCE | 05/16/90 |

Location: Leningrad (RSFSR)
Initial Capital: 200,000 rubles
Foreign Partners and %Share: (1) Globe Developers, Inc. (50%)
Soviet Partners and %Share: (1) Resursosberezhenie Inter-Branch Center, Leningrad
  Soviet Ispolkom (50%)
Activity: Design, construction and operation of factories; tourist services

| 1710 | PERIODICA TRADING SERVICE | 05/18/90 |

Location: n/a
Initial Capital: n/a
Foreign Partners and %Share: (1) Rodale Press, Inc.
Soviet Partners and %Share: (1) Vneshtorgizdat V/O; (2) 50-ya Velikovo Oktyabr
  Sovkhoz
Activity: Printing

1717   INFERKON GROUP   05/22/90

Location: Sverdlovsk (RSFSR)
Initial Capital: 5,362,900 rubles
Foreign Partners and %Share: (1) Yukom (Belgium 0.28%); (2) Diamat (Poland
  0.22%); (3) Perestroika, Inc. (7.49%)
Soviet Partners and %Share: (1) Sverdlovkiy Agro-Manufacturing Plant (18.65%);
  (2) Matrybprom PO (55.93%); (3) Sukhalonskaya Wood-Processing Factory
  (7.45%); (4) Dal'geologia Manufacturing Geological Assn. (4.65%); (5) TPO of
  Local Industry, Sverdlovsk Regional Ispolkom (3.73%); (6) VNII for Standards in
  Machine Building, USSR Gosstandart (.18%); (7) Ferrous Alloys Plant (.21%);
  (8) Tsentr Moda PO (.18%); (9) Plant for Food Concentrates (.36%);
  (10) Agroprombank (.18%); (11) Dom Department Store (.36%)
Activity: Wood and food processing; consumer goods; marketing and engineering
  services

1722   AMICO INTERNAT. LTD.   05/22/90

Location: Moscow (RSFSR)
Initial Capital: n/a
Foreign Partners and %Share: (1) Internat. Business Ventures, Inc.
Soviet Partners and %Share: (1) Amiko Coop.
Activity: Tourist services; concerts and exhibitions

1734   MEZHDUNARODNYE ADVOCATY   05/24/90

Location: Moscow (RSFSR)
Initial Capital: 366,000 rubles
Foreign Partners and %Share: (1) Chadbourne and Park; (2) Harry Hedman
  Advokatbira KB (Finland); (3) Christoph Raabe GmbH (Austria)
Soviet Partners and %Share: (1) Lawyer Foundation of the USSR
Activity: Legal services; educational services; publishing; advertising

---

1735   EXTER INTERNAT.   05/24/90

Location: Moscow (RSFSR)
Initial Capital: 148,300 rubles
Foreign Partners and %Share: (1) Cherny Techpolodgi GmbH (FRG 40%);
  (2) Victoria Internat. Development, Inc. (10%)
Soviet Partners and %Share: (1) Plekhanov Professional Committee MINH (14%);
  (2) Moskvoretsky Student Club NTKTs Coop. (26%); (3) Yarmarka Coop., TsUM
  (10%)
Activity: Software development; training and consulting services

---

1737   SAB-SKRAI INC.   06/06/90

Location: Moscow (RSFSR)
Initial Capital: 1,000,000 rubles
Foreign Partners and %Share: (1) RHA Trading, Inc.
Soviet Partners and %Share: (1) Stiks Scientific-Technical Production Coop. of Moscow; (2) Himmotolog Scientific Integration Coop. of Moscow
Activity: Computer systems; communication networks; consulting and training services

---

1740   SAIBER   05/25/90

Location: Yuzhno-Sakhalinsk (RSFSR)
Initial Capital: 500,000 rubles
Foreign Partners and %Share: (1) Jon B. Jolly, Inc. (49%)
Soviet Partners and %Share: (1) Special KB of Means of Automation of Marine Research, USSR Academy of Sciences (51%)
Activity: Personal computers; naval and marine research equipment; medical equipment

---

1779   ROBOR   06/04/90

Location: Kishinev (MSSR)
Initial Capital: 200,000 rubles
Foreign Partners and %Share: (1) Microprocessor Solution Co. (60%)
Soviet Partners and %Share: (1) Emergency Medical Aid Clinic (40%)
Activity: Medical services and equipment; pharmaceutical research

Index

Abalkin, Leonid, 129, 283
Activity, spheres of joint venture, 164-68, 178, 257
Aeroflot, 251
Afghanistan, trade restrictions in, 16
Agad, E., 239
All-Union Council of Trade Unions, 145
All-Union Scientific Research Institute for Foreign Economic Relations, 31, 175, 208
Angell, Wayne, 129
ANT State Cooperative, 126
Arbatov, Georgiy, 284
Archer Daniels Midland, 196
Armenia, 164
Arms control, 269, 277-79, 282
Asea Brown Boveri, 247
Association for Cooperation with Foreign Countries, 31
Asulin, Romania, 77
Austria, 237; joint ventures with Eastern Europe, 68, 74, 219; joint ventures with USSR, 74, 140, 164, 171, 208, 214, 229
Autarchy, 12
Avex, 218, 230-31
Azerbaijan, joint ventures in, 164

Baltic republics, 18, 78-79, 122, 159, 264, 287. See also Estonia; Latvia; Lithuania

Bank for Agroindustrial Complexes (Agroprombank), 247
Bank for Foreign Economic Affairs (BFEA). See Bank for Foreign Economic Relations
Bank for Foreign Economic Relations (Vneshekonombank), 211, 237-38, 246, 248-49, 252
Bank for Housing, Communal Economy, and Social Development (Zhilsotzbank), 247
Bank for Industrial Construction (Promstroibank), 237, 247
Bank of America, 243 n.4
Banka Commercial Italiana, 236-37, 243 n.4
Banking: East European, 72, 235-36; Far Eastern, 17, 83, 236-38; joint ventures in Soviet, 235-43; problems in Soviet, 190, 231; Soviet, 14, 106-7, 129, 239-42, 248; Soviet operations with joint ventures, 144, 203; Western, 17, 31, 236-37, 248. See also specific banks
Bankruptcy, 5, 12
Banks, joint stock, 32, 235-43. See also Banking; specific banks
Bar, Yugoslavia, 76
Barclais Bank PLC, 243 n.4
Barter agreements, 90, 94, 102, 245, 250-51

About the Editors and Contributors

TATYANA M. ARTEMOVA is Leading Research Fellow, All-Union Research Institute for Foreign Economic Relations of the State Foreign Economics Commission, and author of numerous works on joint ventures in the USSR.

WILLIAM E. BUTLER is Professor of Comparitive Law at the University of London and Director of the Centre for the Study of Socialist Legal Systems, University College, London. He also serves as Special Counsel, Commission for Economic Reform, USSR Council of Ministers, and is an international and comparative lawyer, with special reference to Soviet law and East–West trade law. Professor Butler has authored numerous books, articles, and reference services on Soviet law.

JULIAN COOPER is Professor of Economics at the Centre for Russian and East European Studies, University of Birmingham, England. He is the author of many books and articles on Soviet economics and technology transfer issues.

IGOR G. DORONIN is a Senior Research Fellow at the Institute for World Economy and International Relations, USSR Academy of Sciences, and author of numerous writings on the reconstruction of external economic relations of the USSR.

ZINOVIY M. EVENTOV is a Research Fellow at the All-Union Research Institute for Foreign Economic Relations of the State Foreign Economics Commission and author of numerous articles on joint ventures in the USSR.

IGOR P. FAMINSKY is the Director of the All-Union Research Institute for Foreign Economic Relations of the State Foreign Economics Commission. He is a professor of economics and author of numerous books and articles on the international division of labor and East-West economic relations.

NOAH E. GOTBAUM is a consultant specializing in East European trade and investments with the Central Europe Trust Company, Ltd. in London. He was a former associate at the International Institute for Applied Systems Analysis (IIASA) in Laxenburg, Austria, and during 1989–90 he was the Robert Bosch Foundation Fellow in West Germany, working with the East–West Trade Committee of the West German Federation of Industry.

PHILIP HANSON is Professor of Soviet Economics at the Centre for Russian and East European Studies, University of Birmingham, England. He is a specialist in Soviet economics and East–West trade, and he has authored numerous books and articles. Currently he is a consultant for PlanEcon, Radio Liberty.

JAN H. KALICKI is the Senior Advisor of the Center for Foreign Policy Development and Senior Vice-President of international investment banking at Shearson Lehman Hutton. She is an Adjunct Professor of political science at Brown University and was the former chief foreign policy advisor to Senator Edward Kennedy, as well as a member of the Policy Planning Staff in the U.S. Department of State under Secretary Henry Kissinger and Secretary Cyrus Vance.

LYUDMILA S. KHUDYAKOVA is a Senior Research Fellow at the Institute of World Economy and International Relations, USSR Academy of Sciences. An author and co-author of a number of books and articles on the international finance and East–West credit relations, her book *American Banks on the International Markets* (in Russian) received the USSR Young Communist League's award in 1979.

IVAN S. KOROLEV is Deputy Director of the Institute for World Economy and International Relations, USSR Academy of Sciences. He is a professor of economics, and the author of many books and articles on international finance relations.

VYACHESLAV O. MASLOV is a Leading Research Fellow at the All-Union Research Institute for Foreign Economic Relations of the State Foreign Economics Commission and author of numerous articles on the operation of joint ventures in the USSR.

JOHN MORTON is a partner in the Boston law firm Hale and Door. He

1015   SOVAMPEKS   10/24/89

Location: Moscow (RSFSR)
Initial Capital: 2,092,000 rubles
Foreign Partners and %Share: (1) Citizen Ambassador Hauser (9%); People to
  People (6%)
Soviet Partners and %Share: (1) Admin. of Mechanized Works, USSR Min. of
  Petroleum and Gas Construction (15%); (2) Technical-Commercial Center, BSSR
  Gosplan (76%)
Activity: Technological equipment; furniture and wood products; building materials

---

1030   ROSINTERTEATR   10/26/89

Location: Moscow (RSFSR)
Initial Capital: 1,370,000 rubles
Foreign Partners and %Share: (1) Amsocon (56%)
Soviet Partners and %Share: (1) Rosinterteatr (44%)
Activity: Sewing, haberdashery and other consumer goods

1034   DYUPON-KOOPTUR DYUKO   10/26/89

Location: Moscow (RSFSR)
Initial Capital: 325,000 rubles
Foreign Partners and %Share: (1) El Du Pont de Nemours and Co. Automotive
  Products (50%)
Soviet Partners and %Share: (1) Kooptur Coop. (50%)
Activity: Car repair and painting; related products and equipment

---

1036   INFORMPROGRESS   10/27/89

Location: Moscow (RSFSR)
Initial Capital: 75,000 rubles
Foreign Partners and %Share: (1) Internat. Delaware Corp. (20%)
Soviet Partners and %Share: (1) Assn. of Electronics and Design Organizations,
  Center of Scientific Technical Activities, USSR Academy of Sciences (80%)
Activity: Research; engineering services; construction

1038   EL'BA   10/27/89

Location: Moscow (RSFSR)
Initial Capital: 200,000 rubles
Foreign Partners and %Share: (1) Pacific Fidelity Co. (51%)
Soviet Partners and %Share: (1) Mega Coop. (49%)
Activity: Software development; consulting, advertising, publishing, and translating
  services

1051   SKRIN   10/30/89

Location: Moscow (RSFSR)
Initial Capital: 100,000 rubles
Foreign Partners and %Share: (1) Spec Ltd. (Britain 40%); (2) Spec Ltd. (USA)
Soviet Partners and %Share: (1) Mirazh (60%)
Activity: Film festivals, performances and concerts; advertising; videotape services;
   publishing; film studios and hotels

1082   EVRIKOM   11/13/89

Location: Moscow (RSFSR)
Initial Capital: 100,000 rubles
Foreign Partners and %Share: (1) Quality Import-Export (30%)
Soviet Partners and %Share: (1) Soyuz Creative Research Assn. (10%); (2) Evristika
   Coop. (60%)
Activity: Audio and video technology; consulting; rental of videotape, audio and
   computer equipment; leisure activities

1086   EKSPERTEK   11/15/89

Location: Moscow (RSFSR)
Initial Capital: 31,100 rubles
Foreign Partners and %Share: (1) Wavetech Geophysical, Inc. (50%)
Soviet Partners and %Share: (1) Institute of Economics and Forecasting of Scientific-
   Technical Progress, USSR Academy of Sciences (45%); (2) Nikon Coop. (5%)
Activity: Market analysis; consulting; publishing; database of business information

---

1105   SODIDMED   11/21/89

Location: Moscow (RSFSR)
Initial Capital: 250,000 rubles
Foreign Partners and %Share: (1) Sidvim USA, Inc.; (2) Sidvim AG (Switzerland)
Soviet Partners and %Share: (1) Institute of Management Problems, Min. of
   Instrumentation, RSFSR Academy of Sciences; (2) Medical Clinic #78
Activity: Medical diagnosis and care; medical consulting; personnel training

---

1106   MS-GROUP   11/21/89

Location: Moscow (RSFSR)
Initial Capital: 48,000 rubles
Foreign Partners and %Share: (1) SMV, Inc. (37.5%); (2) Sea Concert, Inc. (12.5%)
Soviet Partners and %Share: (1) Muzikalnyi Servis Coop. (50%)
Activity: Musical equipment and services; editing; rental of musical equipment and
   studios; concerts; computers and programming

1107   MD SEAS   11/21/89

Location: Moscow (RSFSR)
Initial Capital: 1,000,000 rubles
Foreign Partners and %Share: (1) Professional Geophysic, Inc. (50%)
Soviet Partners and %Share: (1) Central Geophysical Expedition (50%)
Activity: "4-D" and "5-D" seismic technology; related technical devices and software

---

1111   ASTIKO   11/22/89

Location: Moscow (RSFSR)
Initial Capital: 350,000 rubles
Foreign Partners and %Share: (1) Eugene O'Neill Theater Center (10%)
Soviet Partners and %Share: (1) Union of Theater Workers (90%)
Activity: Conferences for theater managers, producers, actors; academic exchanges

---

1127   RACAP   11/24/89

Location: Riga (LaSSR)
Initial Capital: 100,000 rubles
Foreign Partners and %Share: (1) Aaron Carrol Associates (50%)
Soviet Partners and %Share: (1) Radiotekhnika PO (50%)
Activity: Radio-electronic equipment; computers

1131   KADEX   11/24/89

Location: Kiev (UkSSR)
Initial Capital: 8,500,000 rubles
Foreign Partners and %Share: (1) Discount Club of America (38%)
Soviet Partners and %Share: (1) Research-Production Coop. (42%); (2) Mikrograf
    Soviet-British JV (10%); (3) Leninskaya Kuznitsa Central Design Office (10%)
Activity: Thermic coating

1144   SAKSESS   12/01/89

Location: Moscow (RSFSR)
Initial Capital: 107,000 rubles
Foreign Partners and %Share: (1) Standard Republic Internat. (45%)
Soviet Partners and %Share: (1) Zamoskvoeche Youth Assn. (55%)
Activity: Publishing; advertising; tourist and sports equipment; tourist services

---

1158   MEDICAL INTERNAT.   12/04/89

Location: Moscow (RSFSR)
Initial Capital: 12,000,000 rubles
Foreign Partners and %Share: (1) U.S. Imaging, Inc. (50%)

Soviet Partners and %Share: (1) Zdorovaya Sem'ya Coop. (50%)
Activity: Medical care services; marketing; consulting

1163   VIST   12/04/89

Location: Moscow (RSFSR)
Initial Capital: 50,000 rubles
Foreign Partners and %Share: (1) FZ, Inc. (50%)
Soviet Partners and %Share: (1) Elvis Coop. (50%)
Activity: Software; waste processing technology; videotape/film production

----

1182   FIDIMEDI   12/08/89

Location: Moscow (RSFSR)
Initial Capital: 1,285,000 rubles
Foreign Partners and %Share: (1) U.S. Imaging, Inc. (52.1%)
Soviet Partners and %Share: (1) Music Foundation, USSR Union of Composers
  (27.9%); (2) Nikitskie Vorota Coop. (20%)
Activity: Video games, with distribution in the USSR and abroad

----

1186   INTERSOFT   12/08/89

Location: Moscow (RSFSR)
Initial Capital: 300,000 rubles
Foreign Partners and %Share: (1) Software Products Internat. (60%)
Soviet Partners and %Share: (1) Institute of Informatics Problems, USSR Academy
  of Sciences of USSR (40%)
Activity: Software development; personnel training

1194   LGA   12/11/89

Location: Tbilisi (GSSR)
Initial Capital: 630,000 rubles
Foreign Partners and %Share: (1) B&D Import (50%)
Soviet Partners and %Share: (1) Sh. Rustaveli Society (1%); (2) Tsida Coop. (49%)
Activity: Construction; building materials; metallurgy

1200   KO-STAR   12/12/89

Location: Moscow (RSFSR)
Initial Capital: 200,000 rubles
Foreign Partners and %Share: (1) Soventure Group, Inc. (50%)
Soviet Partners and %Share: (1) Tsentrnauchfilm Studio (50%)
Activity: Production and rental of movies; photo services; advertising; exhibitions;
  publishing; construction of film studios, hotels and business clubs

----

is also a lecturer and author of numerous articles on Western investment in China and a consultant on investment in socialist countries.

NATALYA L. PLATONOVA is a Senior Research Fellow at the Institute for State and Law Studies, USSR Academy of Sciences. She is the author of a number of works on international joint enterprises.

VLADIMIR V. RANENKO is the Department Head of the All-Union Research Institute for Foreign Economic Relations of the State Foreign Economics Commission and author of numerous articles on joint ventures in the USSR.

LYUDMILA A. RODINA is a Senior Research Fellow at the Institute of the Economy of World Socialist System, USSR Academy of Sciences, and author of a number of books and articles on the East–West economic cooperation.

NATALYA G. SEMILUTINA is a teacher of law in the Moscow State Institute of International Relations.

ALAN B. SHERR is Associate Director of the Center for Foreign Policy Development and Director of its Project on Soviet Foreign Economic Policy and International Society. He is the author of a book on Soviet arms control policy under Gorbachev and of numerous articles on trade and investment in the USSR.

ERIC A. STUBBS is Assistant Professor at the State University of New York, Stony Brook. He is a specialist in Soviet economics and international management and co-author of *Star Wars: The Economic Fallout*.

EVGENIYA L. YAKOVLEVA is a Senior Research Fellow at the Institute for World Economy and International Relations, USSR Academy of Sciences. He is the author of a number of books and articles on the development of new forms of the East–West economic cooperation and, most recently, *Joint Ventures in CMEA Countries Practice* (in Russian).